Wordsworth's Hawkshead

Joseph Farington's *Hawkshead and Esthwaite Water*, engraving published 1816.

Wordsworth's Hawkshead

T. W. THOMPSON

Edited, with Introduction, Notes, and
Appendixes by

ROBERT WOOF

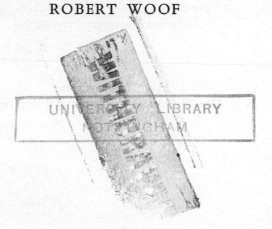

London
OXFORD UNIVERSITY PRESS
NEW YORK   TORONTO
1970

Oxford University Press, Ely House, London W. 1

GLASGOW NEW YORK TORONTO MELBOURNE WELLINGTON
CAPE TOWN SALISBURY IBADAN NAIROBI LUSAKA ADDIS ABABA
BOMBAY CALCUTTA MADRAS KARACHI LAHORE DACCA
KUALA LUMPUR HONG KONG TOKYO

SBN 19 212186 3

C

Printed in Great Britain by
The Camelot Press Ltd., London and Southampton

Contents

List of Plates

Acknowledgements

T. W. Thompson could not, of course, prepare his own list of acknowledgements. Some he has made within the text, and these remain; and some of the people that I list below I know that he also consulted. Let me here repeat my thanks to the Trustees of the Armitt Library, now the owners of the T. W. Thompson papers; and in particular, to the late Dr. Fothergill, Mr. Bruce Thompson and Mrs. Eileen Jay. My own contributions in both checking and supplementing derive from several years' work on Wordsworth matters and I cannot fully acknowledge all the long debts I owe to many friends and scholars; I name here only those generous people who have helped more immediately with the present task. For constant help I must record my deep indebtedness to the archivists and their staffs in the County Record Offices: Mr. Bruce Jones of Carlisle, Miss S. J. MacPherson of Kendal, and Mr. R. Sharpe France of Preston. Beyond searching in these great public repositories, I have been able to examine books in the Grammar School Library, Hawkshead; for this, and for the opportunity to check material from Ann Tyson's ledger, I am indebted to Mr. L. K. Brownson and the Governors of the Grammar School. From Mr. Brownson himself, as T. W. Thompson's executor, I have had many kindnesses. I am grateful to the Vicar of Hawkshead, Mr. R. Lindsay, for permission to examine parish documents in his keeping; and I would like also to thank here Mr. and Mrs. Leonard of Roger Ground, Hawkshead, who allowed me to interrupt their own work on the Parish Registers and provided a copy of their *Second Register Book . . . Hawkshead . . . 1705–1787* (Hawkshead, 1968). For permission to publish manuscript material I would like to thank my fellow Trustees of Dove Cottage Library, Grasmere.

Many people and institutions have given me help and advice and I am grateful to them: Mr. John Addy of Huddersfield; Mr. V. J. H. Coward of Wordsworth Lodge, Hawkshead; Miss Nesta Clutterbuck, Grasmere; Dr. S. Frost and through her, the Freshwater Biological Association, Windermere; Mr. S. Garnett, Morecambe; Mr.

Trevor Jones, Jesus College, Cambridge; Mr. C. Roy Hudleston; Mr. R. E. Latham; Rev. R. Lewis, Kendal; Mr. Edward Milligan, Friends' House Library, London; the National Trust; Dr. Geoffrey Nuttall, the University of London; Mr. George Pattinson, Windermere; Mr. Frank Robinson, Newcastle upon Tyne; Mr. D. P. Sewell; Mr. H. L. Short, Manchester College, Oxford; Mr. Kenneth Smith, Tullie House, Carlisle; Canon R. C. Tait, Grasmere; Mr. Peter Wallis, University of Newcastle upon Tyne.

For kind permission to reproduce the illustrations I am indebted to the following: for plate 2, Tullie House, Carlisle; for plates 4 and 9, the Trustees of Dove Cottage; for plates 6 and 7, the Freshwater Biological Association, Windermere; for plates 8 and 14, the Governors of Hawkshead Grammar School; for plate 15, Mr. G. P. Abraham; and for the endpaper map, to the Lancashire Record Office.

For many favours I must thank my colleagues in the University of Newcastle, not least in the Department of English and in the University Library. My primary thanks are to the Trustees of the Lord Adams Fellowship, the University of Newcastle upon Tyne, for the gift of time in which I have been able to edit and supplement the work of T. W. Thompson, a task fundamental for the edition of Wordsworth's early verse notebooks which I am preparing with Carol Landon for the Clarendon Press. I would also like to acknowledge that my research has benefited from the support of the Research Committee of the University of Newcastle upon Tyne, and of the British Academy.

Newcastle upon Tyne, May 1970.

Introduction

IT needs some sophistication to distinguish between Braithwaites, sometimes Brathwaites, in late eighteenth-century Hawkshead: and it was T. W. Thompson who first taught me to know the Rev. William (who was melancholy) from the Rev. Reginald (who was cheerful). It was his kindness that allowed me to use his typescript, *Wordsworth's Hawkshead*, for my own work on Wordsworth's verse notebooks. After his death I suggested to Mr. Thompson's executor, Mr. L. K. Brownson, that the work might be published. I knew that it was unorthodox, that references, for example, were by no means completely given; Mr. Thompson had told me that he had deliberately kept references to a minimum (though, in fact, a good many were incorporated into the text) because he had designed the book in the first place for the non-academic reader; he assured me that in his papers and notes there were full references and sources. This is a not unimportant point, in that his book contains unique material which has not been used before and is available no longer: the John Ireland manuscript, the Fletcher Raincock reminiscence as recorded by Miss Saul, the Swainson letters, the drawing of the carving in Wordsworth's room at Ann Tyson's Hawkshead cottage, the list of schoolboys who subscribed to the New School Library founded at Hawkshead in 1789; these are some of Thompson's sources for which one can no longer find the originals. One hopes indeed that this very publication will bring about the rediscovery of some of these unique documents. It is good meanwhile to know that all T. W. Thompson's notes are to be in the safe keeping of the Armitt Library, Ambleside, to whose Trustees he bequeathed all his papers, and by whose most generous permission his manuscript is now published. The sorting of this vast repository of notes has proved an onerous task and the papers will not be available until 1971.

It was not therefore possible for many of the notes to be consulted for the preparation of this volume, but as editor of Thompson's final manuscript, as far as it is possible, I have checked his readings against those many documents that are in public archives. And I have not hesitated to add, in footnotes, new material from these archives, sometimes supplementing, occasionally contradicting T.W.T.'s significant findings or questions. T. W. Thompson had not the advantage of the present-day County Record Offices, for he wrote this book in his old age, constantly confined by ill-health, using the notes that he had accumulated over sixty years. So simple errors of fact and minor misreadings of manuscripts I have corrected and have been in a position to remove many of such honest hesitations, as 'As far as I can tell from my notes . . .' or, 'I may not have copied correctly . . .' But as one reads, the dignity of the writer, a researcher and questor of a high order, is apparent, and one comes to delight in the very delight he takes in the tangible world of Wordsworth's Hawkshead. T.W.T. has written his book like a well-ordered con-versation, willing to digress, but always centring back to the village people living and acting together in their society. His personality— and he was clearly a natural teacher—is a quiet, presiding presence; and within his limits he was a writer of poise, even artistry. Thus, as he himself might say in his open manner as he introduces a new personage into his account of Hawkshead, I had better put down what I know about him.

T. W. Thompson was born on 17 February 1888 at Ratherheath, Burneside, near Kendal. His father was William, and his mother, T.W.T. tells us, was the granddaughter of John Wilson (1794–1880) of the Causey, Windermere, of a family originally coming from Coniston. Thompson went to Kendal Grammar School where he was one of the outstanding boys in the Sciences; but his contribu-tions to the school magazine, *The Kendalian*, make it clear that his interest in dialect and in Lake District customs had begun before he left for Jesus College, Cambridge, in 1906, on a £30 Exhibition from the College, and an £80 Exhibition from the School. The College records state: 'Father cannot keep his son beyond travelling expenses'. Thompson followed the arduous course of taking the Natural Science Tripos in two years, in Chemistry, Physics, Mineralogy, and Geology—though the examination in the last subject was delayed, through his ill-health, until Michaelmas 1908 and the corresponding practical examination early in 1909. It was during that Christmas vacation that Thompson became seriously interested in gipsy lore and language (his papers and books on these matters have gone to the Bodleian Library, Oxford). In Lent Term 1909 he took his B.A. with second class honours.

After one year at Faversham Grammar School, Kent, Thompson was for five years a master at the Queen Elizabeth Grammar School, Gainsborough. In 1918 he moved to the King Edward School, Sheffield, where, in his three years there, he established a new Science Sixth. Then to Repton where again he had a leading role in the reorganization of sixth-form work; for, until this time, only the Classical Sixth was available to boys on a normal basis; extra fees had to be paid for tuition in Modern Languages, History, and Science. Lord Fisher of Lambeth was Headmaster at the time, and in February of this year he generously sent this recollection:

T. W. Thompson was a master at Repton from 1920 to 1944; as a history of Repton has said, one of a group of masters of great teaching ability who maintained a steady flow of scholarship winners at Oxford and Cambridge. He came to serve under the Chief Chemistry Master, W. M. Hooton who had become a House Master. Hooton remained his Chief. But in his quiet way Thompson became in effect the mainspring of Chemistry teaching and I regarded him as such. (A. W. Barton, afterwards Headmaster of the City of London School was Head of the Physics Department. They worked splendidly together.) He was a very good and sound and *quiet* teacher. Nothing particularly exciting or stimulating about him to outward view. And that is what he was in ordinary life, too, quiet and unassuming, but always sound and as a person quietly efficient and composed. And then, as one came to find more and more, there were concealed *interests* in him which made him a very interesting and indeed on his own lines a very exciting person. We found that he was a real expert on the real gypsies. He knew them, had lived with them (I think) and could speak Romany. In that field he had a reputation with the experts. I did not know then of his passionate study of Wordsworth. I saw him once after he had retired in his beloved Hawkshead and saw then this other great and consuming and ennobling passion of his life. Always sound and efficient, always knowledgeable, he was also always quietly companionable and these hidden fires of interests out of the common did all the time ennoble him and made his friendship very valuable.

Thompson retired in 1944, and went, with his wife, to live in the cottage in Hawkshead he had owned already for some ten years,

Grandy Nook. Quietly he entered local life, became a Governor of Hawkshead Grammar School, and in 1950, the centenary of Wordsworth's death, his interest in the poet came into the open with a dialect play, to be performed mainly by schoolboys, called, like this book, *Wordsworth's Hawkshead*. In 1956 he emerged as an historian of the area with his *Hawkshead Church, Chapelry and Parish*, enlarged in 1959, and now reprinting. In the mid-1950s he and his wife left Hawkshead for Windermere, but his wife's illness and his own increasing disabilities were to make the last decade of his life trying and difficult. He died in March 1968.

It was during the last painful years that he wrote *Wordsworth's Hawkshead*, surely a considerable imaginative act, a portrayal of a society in action. The book's fascination is in its duality; the everyday persons of the small town come alive in their dealings with one another; and, at the same time, there is the extra dimension: one is constantly brought back to Wordsworth, what he must have known, or what he could have known. A great deal of the oral tradition about Wordsworth is recorded here, and it can never be done on the same scale again: that Thompson had no privileged access to private family documents—such as those now in Dove Cottage Library—forced him to try another way, to ask questions and to write down answers. Much of the material thus obtained gives clues rather than full answers, but his conversations and recordings of unique memories provided directions. And when he turns to documents, his readings are usually fuller and sometimes more correct than the readings of others; entries, for instance, in Ann Tyson's ledger for 1788 and 1789 have been misread, and though the ledger does not tell us everything we would like to know about the length of time Wordsworth spent in Hawkshead during his Cambridge vacations, Thompson's precise readings unostentatiously set matters right; and details in the accounts of Wordsworth's uncles who were administering John Wordsworth's estate, supplement his correction. It is all a jigsaw, each piece tiny, but satisfying when it fits.

The lame boy of *The Prelude* Thompson superbly identifies as Philip Braithwaite, and this in its turn becomes one of the means of his settling, surely once and for all, that Wordsworth did live in Hawkshead town as legend has always had it; but nicely enough, and to Thompson alone the credit belongs, he establishes that Wordsworth, after about four years in the middle of Hawkshead, moved with the Tysons to Colthouse. Ann Tyson, Wordsworth's Dame, and her joiner husband, Hugh, in Thompson's hands transcend their workaday ledger with its rough accounts and the brief facts of their marriage and deaths in the Parish Registers, and come through as people. And this is not because Thompson yields to any unconscious wish to impose a shape on to them or to turn them into fiction; it is because he is patient with the details of the facts, and because of the sheer accumulation of prices of cakes or mourning handkerchiefs or candles or wood-cutting or payments for the Wordsworth boys. As their environment is gradually built up, they emerge. And here the modern reader has to be himself patient with Thompson's rather old-fashioned and unhurried tone; while at the same time he must not let himself be oppressed by the detail. He will not be able to keep in the forefront of his consciousness all the dates, the ancestries, the infant deaths, the young wives who die, the names of houses and places around Hawkshead; but this will not matter; he can return to check, and meanwhile, with each fragment the whole composition is strengthened.

If Ann Tyson lives because we know about many things that surrounded her, it is worth remembering that she, in her turn, clearly fed Wordsworth's own sense of the abiding value of accounts of things as they really happened. T. W. Thompson does not explore this literary aspect of Ann, but it is worth saying in this historical context. The domestic tale is the kind of story Wordsworth makes use of in his poetry; not the impersonal ballad narrative, but the tale, often pathetic in its content, which was anchored to actuality by personal knowledge. The tale of the Jacobite and the Hanoverian Whig (*Excursion*, VI) is one of Ann's stories; so is the tale of Benoni and his deserted mother which not only forms the subject of Wordsworth's schoolboy ballad (see pp. 65–9), but was later to colour the narrative of *Peter Bell*. Another such story is that of the two shepherds, father and son, who lost their sheep, a tale which finally appeared in *The Prelude*, but was drafted originally as an episode in the story of 'Michael'.[1] Indeed the whole basis of the narrative of

[1] I have discussed this more completely in 'John Stoddart, "Michael", and *Lyrical Ballads*', *Ariel*, I, April 1970, pp. 7–22.

'Michael' appears to come from what Wordsworth heard in his youth; and now that we recognize that Ann spent a considerable time in Rydal as a young woman, it is a certainty that the Grasmere story of a statesman's family, oddly enough, living, Wordsworth believed, in Dove Cottage, was entirely linked with Ann Tyson. Wordsworth's tribute in the prologue to 'Michael' is an impressive testament to Ann's tales 'homely and rude':

> It was the first
> Of those domestic tales that spake to me
> Of Shepherds, dwellers in the valleys, men
> Whom I already loved . . .
> And hence this Tale, while I was yet a Boy
> Careless of books . . .

Dorothy later commented that Ann told tales 'half as long as an ancient romance'; in her boarder, Wordsworth, the longest staying of all her boys, she clearly had a willing listener.

The habit of listening persisted, and there are other poems based, in part or entirely, on Wordsworth's liking for having a tale told him. Of the 'Female Vagrant' he later wrote: 'All that relates to her sufferings as a sailor's wife in America, and her condition of mind during her voyage home, were faithfully taken from the report made to me of her own case by a friend who had been subjected to the same trials and affected in the same way.' Tom Poole told him the story of the murderer, Jack Walford, and this became the basis of the poem later known as 'The Somersetshire Tragedy'. A peasant 'whom we met near the spot' told Wordsworth and his sister the story of Hart-Leap Well 'so far as concerned the name of the well, and the hart, and [he] pointed out the stones.' Only to look for the origins of Wordsworth's tales in printed literature is to miss something of the poet's nature; his is the tale that a man might and often did tell to other men. He uses of course the artfulness of poetry, but the illusion he wishes to achieve is that of a person speaking a tale from the heart. Ann Tyson taught him to listen, and thereafter, although books often did give him important images, he was a poet who listened.

One of the virtues of this book, T. W. Thompson having conceived it and provided its structure, is that others can add and refine. It does not say everything of importance about Wordsworth's Hawkshead, and it is no substitute for *The Prelude*. The light it casts on the poetry is oblique, and as history it is far from comprehensive. It reminds one of Wordsworth's own apprehension of the difficulties standing in the way of the biographer and historian:

The obstacles which stand in the way of the fidelity of the Biographer and Historian, and of their consequent utility, are incalculably greater than those which are to be encountered by the Poet who comprehends the dignity of his art. The Poet writes under one restriction only, namely, the necessity of giving immediate pleasure to a human Being possessed of that information which may be expected from him, not as a lawyer, a physician, a mariner, an astronomer, or a natural philosopher, but as a Man. Except for this one restriction, there is no object standing between the Poet and the image of things; between this, and the Biographer and Historian, there are a thousand.

[*Preface to Lyrical Ballads*, 1802]

Thompson's dialogue about Hawkshead invites participation, and readers will find themselves bringing details from their own store. Some such elements I have been able to add in the Appendixes and in the Notes. The patterns shift, as they do in life, with the addition of another particle of knowledge. Mrs. Knott, for instance, whose death in 1785 has, as Thompson presents it, a tinge of pathos, takes on a slightly different character when we read in a letter from R. Dore to Sir Michael le Fleming, of Wednesday, 9 March 1785: 'In conformity to the line I dropt you Sunday on the departure of M^rs. Knott, whose loss the *kind* world condoles with in her having taken too freely from the Bottle . . .'.

It is thus from the people of Wordsworth's Hawkshead and its neighbourhood that Thompson writes; the basis is particularity. Without any sense of the importance for agriculture generally of the Enclosure Acts of the end of the eighteenth century, one will come away from this book knowing about the Claife Heights Enclosure—but only because Thompson wants to tell us something about William Braithwaite. He is not an economic historian, or one who uses detail to support a generality. One could, for instance, pull out of this book the sense of change that came over Wordsworth's

B

landscape, and the poet's resentment at it. The enclosure of Claife Heights, the fell on the west side of Windermere north of the Ferry, involved some 1,500 acres; the Act was in 1794, and it took five years to complete the change, and Wordsworth, when he returned in 1799 was disappointed, at least in part, at finding different that landscape which had nurtured his youth. The initiator of this reform, which of course made possible modern agriculture and afforestation, was John Christian Curwen, and Wordsworth, on aesthetic grounds fought a rearguard action against change. It informs his *Guide to the Lakes*, where it is not petty conservatism, but a sense of the sacredness of landscape that drove him to care for such niceties as the colour of houses (hating white) or the inappropriateness of larches.

Again, the book, without giving a specific history of iron foundries in the Lake District, makes us aware of the need those industries had for timber, and aware of the slate quarries that kept William Rigge rich, and the Kirkbys busy, so that the area, besides being the home of certain families, is also a place where working men live. We see Hawkshead so confident of its trade in 1790, so effectively linked with Kendal by the Ferry route, that it builds a new Market House. And this comes out of Thompson's wanting to tell us about, for instance, Hugh Tyson's work, or the Knott family, and their relation with Ann Tyson, and thus their certain place in Wordsworth's schoolboy world. In such incidental ways Thompson reveals to us a Lake District marvellously different from the leisure area, the National Park that we know now. But even that stage in the process of change was beginning, though Thompson—and it is his strength —never makes general issues central. Rich people were coming for relaxation. The Christian-Curwen family, about which Thompson is entirely illuminating, fall nearly into this category, in that John Christian owned Workington Hall as well as Belle Isle; but nevertheless that family is essentially local. It is rather Wilberforce, coming up for his summers to Rayrigg who is one of the moderns. Thompson does not mention him, but Wilberforce is so close that one wonders whether he had any contact with Wordsworth at this stage. He was, of course, a friend of Wordsworth's uncle, William Cookson and had stayed at Rayrigg intermittently from 1780 (see

notes p. 117). A new letter of his to Uncle William, who through
Wilberforce's influence was about to get the rich living of Forncett,
and with it, apparently, the promise of a stall at Windsor, does not
directly tell us anything about Wordsworth, but it does remind us of
the social class his relatives moved in, and tantalizingly shows us that
Wilberforce knew Hawkshead. Wilberforce wrote to Cookson on
12 April 1788: '. . . I rejoice too in the favourable account from
Windsor, & anticipate my poppings in on the little fat Canon. . . . I
am anxious ab^t. Rayrigg & beg you will press Barton to procure me
an answer immediately—Write me but a Line only write—I have
changed my mind ab^t. M^r. Braithwaite's House [Belmount, see
pp. 52–3] under the persuasion, on recollection, that the marsh I had
apprehended is by no means formidable, & I have desired Keene of
Hawkshead to procure me particulars.' Only two days later Wilberforce wrote again, with some urgency, to Cookson: 'I must have
either Rayrigg or Belmont & I beg you will let me hear from you
instantly ab^t. them.' (Record Office, Kendal.)

I have been bold enough to add four appendixes, which do, I
think, belong to *Wordsworth's Hawkshead*. The first is concerned
with a new manuscript of Hawkshead's other poet, Charles Farish,
known to Wordsworth at school and later. The work of Farish's
brother, John, hitherto unpublished, was a topic of conversation
between the two young poets, and had some influence on *Salisbury
Plain*. The second appendix deals with a vexed problem, and since
the documents involved admit of ambiguity, I have tried to present
fully what is to be known about nonconformity in Hawkshead from
somewhat earlier than Wordsworth's time there to somewhat later
than his comments of the 1840s. It is all part of the society in which
he grew up. The third appendix is a series of letters largely from
Eleanor Braithwaite of Hawkshead to the grandmother of three boys
who lodged with her and who were pupils at the Grammar School.
These letters show: the difficulty of travel to and from Hawkshead;
the uncertainty of holiday dates; a glimpse of the Wordsworth boys
not knowing where they would spend their first holiday after their
father's death; the grandmother's anxiety about scholarly standards;
the fact that local families, like the le Flemings, entertained the children of their friends; that usually both rooms and beds were shared in

the small Hawkshead houses; and a rare glimpse of the headmaster William Taylor, hearing the younger boys read, and in dispute with a man of influence, John Christian. The fourth appendix focuses on the Grammar School, its teachers and pupils. Registers have not survived, but library books have, and these are a primary source, not only for the history of taste, but for the identity of many of the boys who were pupils, a great number of them known to Wordsworth and his brothers. The biographical notes appended to some of these names reveal, among other things, some connections with Wordsworth's later life.

Now that so much primary source material about Wordsworth—his letters and his manuscripts—is available, there is much to be said for considering what an oblique light can reveal about the poet: and T. W. Thompson has discovered more than many would have believed possible about Wordsworth's Hawkshead.

PART ONE

Hugh and Ann Tyson and their Boarders

Hugh and Ann Tyson and their Boarders

James Braithwaite and Hawkshead parish obligations—marriage of Ann's sister, Dorothy—marriage of Hugh and Ann—ancestry of Hugh—Widow Caddy—Hugh Tyson's account book—his joinery work—Matthew Hodgson—Hugh's debtors

IT is inevitable that Ann Tyson should have a prominent place in any study of Wordsworth's Hawkshead. She was his Household Dame, as he phrased it, throughout the eight and a quarter years he was at Hawkshead Grammar School; and during his first two long vacations from Cambridge he stayed with her for about five months in all. Moreover, he assures us in *The Prelude* of their fondness for each other; a regard that fell little short of motherly love on her side and filial affection on his, deepened, it may be, by her being childless, and him, motherless at first, and then an orphan.

By birth, Ann Tyson was a Braithwaite, and there is no doubt at all that she is the 'Ann Braithw^t Daught^r of James Shoomak^r of Town' who was baptized at Hawkshead on 2 June 1713. She had younger sisters Dorothy and Eleanor ('Hellin^r') whose christenings took place on 22 March 1715, and 11 September 1717, respectively; but it is not likely that the 'Willm Son Jam^s Braithw^t of Hawksh^d Shopkeep^r', baptized on 27 April 1720, was a brother of theirs. Ann's father appears to have been the younger of two sons of a William Braithwaite, hatter, of Sawrey Infra, otherwise Near Sawrey. If so, he was christened on 19 December 1686, two years later than his brother Thomas, who also became a shoemaker. There were a great many Braithwaites at the two Sawreys in the seventeenth and eighteenth centuries, more particularly at Far Sawrey.

Tenure in the manor of Hawkshead was customary, and not at the will of the lord or lords of the manor. In earlier times each customary tenement had to supply and furnish a man-at-arms in the event of invasion or incursion by the Scots; but in the eighteenth century the only obligation—and it did not apply to the newer holdings—was to provide in turn a churchwarden, Overseer of the Poor, or Surveyor of the Highways for that Quarter of the parish in which the tenement was situated, the office to be filled for one year only at a time. Though one cannot be sure, it rather looks as if this obligation lay on James Braithwaite's house in Hawkshead Town, as in 1722 James Braithwaite of Hawkshead was Surveyor of the Highways for the Hawkshead Quarter, which included Hawkshead Field and Hawkshead Fieldhead, whilst in 1731 'Thomas Braithw^t of Sawrey for James Braithw^t house in Hawks^d' was Overseer of the Poor of the Hawkshead Quarter. That Thomas was acting in respect of this house could mean either that James Braithwaite was dead and it was occupied by his widow, or that, though still living, he was unable for some reason to 'serve his turn'. Substitutes were allowed with the approval of the Twenty Four, the elected body of Sidesmen, six from each Quarter, who were responsible for the proper ordering of parish affairs. Records of the burials at Hawkshead of 'James Braithwaite of Town' in 1727, and of 'James Braithwaite Household^r' in 1735 do not solve the problem of just when Ann's father died; but evidently he was not a long liver. Nor was Thomas Braithwaite, the Sawrey shoemaker, for he died in 1736.

In the following year, on 3 October, Ann's sister Dorothy was married by licence to John Nevinson, a barber who had come to Hawkshead from the parish of Barton in north Westmorland. His certificate of Legal Settlement, which is dated 16 April 1737, is still preserved at Hawkshead. Addressed to the Churchwardens and Overseers of the Poor of 'the parish Township or Division of Hawkshead in the County of Lancaster', it reads: 'Wee whose Hands and Seals are hereunto Subscribed and putt, being Churchwardens and Overseers of the poor of the parish of Barton in the County of Westmerland, do hereby Certifie own and acknowledge, That John Nevinson, Barber, is an Inhabitant Legally Settled in our said parish of Barton, who for better Convenience of Business is desireous to Inhabit in your said parish or Township of Hawkshead, If therefore the said John Nevinson hereafter become Chargeable to your said parish or Township, Wee do hereby promise for Ourselves and Successors to receive take back or otherwise provide for him as the

Law directs . . .' By his wife Dorothy, this stranger to Hawkshead had two daughters, Eleanor and Margaret, who were baptized on 25 July 1738, and 5 May 1741, respectively; and of him and them I shall have more to say presently. But of Dorothy all I can add is that she died at the age of twenty-nine, and was buried in Hawkshead churchyard on 19 September 1744.

Hugh Tyson and Ann Braithwaite, 'Town', were married at Hawkshead 'By Banns' on 23 May 1749. Ann, who was then thirty-six, had been in domestic service, no doubt in Hawkshead parish at first, but later at Rydal with a Mr. and Mrs. Michael Knott who married in or about 1739. Her husband, a master joiner in Hawkshead Town, was a year younger, judging from the age ascribed to him when he died. He was a native of the parish, and in her old age Ann was fond of saying that he had been at the Grammar School as a Sandys Charity boy, which may well be true, as he could read and write and keep accounts. But there is some uncertainty as to his parentage and early upbringing.

It arises in the first place from the absence of any satisfactory record of his baptism at Hawkshead, for the only entry in the registers that could refer to it reads: 'A bastard of Issabell Tysons of foulyeat [Foldgate]', baptized 25 August 1714. The mother, I may add, was neither baptized nor married at Hawkshead; nor was there any later insertion of the child's name, or any indication that it died in infancy. As the date and surname are right, the probability is that the child was Hugh.[1]

The next mention of Hugh in public records is in 1748, the year before his marriage to Ann. He was then either the principal or a principal witness in an appeal against a 'Magistrates Order' that Mrs. Caddy, a widow, should be granted poor-law relief by the Hawkshead Division.[2] The Overseer of the Poor for the Division in 1748

[1] T.W.T. has not noticed that on 29 September 1726 the Hawkshead Parish Register records a burial: 'Issa: Tyson from Graithwt fieldhead Spinster'. Hugh would be twelve on his mother's death, and, having no home of his own, would become at this time the Sandys Charity boy that his wife always said he was.

[2] Something of the unfortunate Mrs. Caddy is recorded in the Order Book, Quarter Sessions, Kendal, 1738–50 (Westmorland County Archives), signed, incidentally, by Wordsworth's grandfather as Clerk of the Peace. The Haverbrack magistrates (in Beetham Parish) had ordered Jane Caddy to be removed from there to Hawkshead, but at Michaelmas 1748 this order was quashed at the Quarter Sessions,

was John Hodgson of Hawkshead Town acting in lieu of John
Waterson of Waterson Ground, and in his account is this entry: 'To
Hugh Tyson & my self & Horses going to Haverbrock [Haverbrack,
near Milnthorpe, in south Westmorland] to give Notice of Appeal
& Expences', eight shillings. Other entries show that the Overseer
also went to obtain evidence, and perhaps another witness, to Bolton
and to Seathwaite. I am not sure which Bolton is meant, but the
Seathwaite he visited was the hamlet and chapelry of that name in
the Duddon valley on the Furness side of the river. Tysons were
numerous there; and so they were at Broughton-in-Furness, which
Hugh visited at much the same time, but at his own expense it
seems, though as he booked it in his ledger he may have intended to
recover the cost of the journey. The appeal was heard at Kendal,
where John Hodgson and his two supporters, who were Hugh Tyson
and Daniel Tyson, had to spend three days. Board and lodging for
the three men came to about £1; and Hugh was paid 1s. 6d. as com-
pensation for loss of earnings, and 1s. in respect of his horse. The
appeal seems to have succeeded, presumably by proving that the
Hawkshead Division neither was nor should be Mrs. Caddy's 'place
of Legal Settlement'.

The presence of Hugh and Daniel Tyson as witnesses suggests that
Widow Caddy was a Tyson by birth, whilst disagreement as to
where she was entitled to receive poor-law relief may indicate that
before her marriage, which seems to have taken her to Bolton, she
had lived both at Hawkshead and at Seathwaite in Dunnerdale,
where in his early days Hugh Tyson almost certainly also lived. For
to Ann's claim that he was at Hawkshead Grammar School as a
Sandys Charity boy must be added a statement attributed to Wordsworth that, as a small boy boarding with the Tysons, he particularly
wanted to go to the Duddon valley because Mr. Tyson, who had
lived there for a time when young, had often talked to him about it.
Wordsworth made this statement, I learnt, to his cousin Richard's

'. . . upon examination of Witnesses & hearing Counsel on both sides'. At Christmas
it was insisted that Haverbrack took responsibility: Jane, the widow of William
Caddy, was 'very poor & entirely unable by her own Endeavours to support herself
& her young Child, & that she has frequently applied to the Churchwardens of
Haverbrack aforesaid for relief'. The latter were ordered to pay costs and one shilling
per week. It is not clear why Hugh was brought in as a witness.

daughter Dorothy, then or afterwards Mrs. Benson Harrison, when telling her of his first visit, and how on that occasion he had to be carried part of the way back to Hawkshead. I owe this information to the late Arthur Paul Brydson, whose wife Catherine was a granddaughter of Benson and Dorothy Harrison, and who noted it from Mrs. Harrison herself.

Though the evidence I have cited can scarcely be regarded as conclusive, it affords strong support for the view that Hugh Tyson was the illegitimate son of an Isabel Tyson who later became Mrs. Caddy. But if he was, she does not seem to have had him with her when he was elected a Sandys Charity scholar of Hawkshead Grammar School, for more than once in her old age Ann Tyson told Braithwaite Hodgson of Briers, then a schoolboy of thirteen to fifteen, that he was chosen because he had no home of his own. And there, from lack of further evidence, I must leave the matter.[1]

Hugh Tyson's account book, which Ann used for a time after his death, has survived, and is now in the keeping of the Governors of the Hawkshead Grammar School Foundation. It is a substantial volume whose pages, a few of which have crumbled, measure $16\frac{3}{8}''$ by $6\frac{3}{8}''$.[2] The entries, which begin in 1743, show that before his

[1] Of course T.W.T.'s suggestion is not tenable, but in the process of reaching it he has brought out what seems to be a connection between Hugh Tyson and the widow Caddy, and this is of interest itself and needs further explanation.

[2] Mrs. Heelis ('Beatrix Potter') gave an account in a letter of 16 January 1920 to Gordon Wordsworth of her discovery of the ledger:

> In 1913 I bought some farm property in Sawrey from a family, whose ancestor had been a master of the grammar school. A good many books seem to have 'gone a-missing'. I recovered a number from the peat house. I burnt some. If they had had any connection with Wordsworth, there was nothing to show it—The fly leaves were torn out. I still have a volume of that very dry work Rapin's History, with Dr Bowman's autograph.
>
> The ledger was in a sad state. I dried it in slabs and gradually worked apart & mended the leaves. (MS. in Dove Cottage Library.)

Thomas Bowman was headmaster of Hawkshead School, 1786–1829. From the deeds of the Sawrey property, now owned by the National Trust, it appears that the peat house was on land purchased from the Baines family: H. T. Baines had been headmaster of Hawkshead School, 1861–81. The ledger may have been left at School after the making up of the last schoolboy bill in 1790, or may have come there through Thomas Bowman, Ann's executor (see pp. 145–6).

The book itself, repaired and rebound in 1968, has some 114 numbered leaves. The accounts are not ordered chronologically, but the following main groups emerge:

marriage he had built up a joinery business large enough to warrant his employing three men in 1747, when he also had temporary help from Leonard Tyson of Gallowbarrow. In 1750, when he had two men working for him, which was the usual number about that date, he had temporary assistance from Leonard's man; and on a rather later occasion Leonard's son Nicholas, then a journeyman, gave him a helping hand. Leonard, who was married in 1728 and died in 1771, may have been a kinsman of his.

In the 1740s and 1750s Hugh's work sometimes took him to distant parts of the parish such as Skelwith, Monk Coniston, Grizedale, Satterthwaite, and Graythwaite, and even beyond its bounds, to Elterwater, Church Coniston, and Bowness, for example, and to Rusland, Parkamoor, and Bouth, all of which were then in the parish of Colton. In 1749, when he and John Grainger were working at Bowness, they 'lay at Boat', otherwise the Ferry Inn, where the charge was 1d. a night for the two of them. And when in the same year they were working at Coniston, Hugh for four days and John for five, they 'Lay Down at Thomas Hodgons' at a total cost of 3d. John Grainger, who had been apprenticed to Hugh, was a journeyman in 1749, his age being either twenty-two or twenty-three. The charge for his work was 8d. a day with meat, whereas for Hugh's, it was 10d. If no meat was provided, the charges were generally 6d. a day more, but exceptionally only 4d. or as much as 8d. a day. In the course of this work at Bowness and Coniston Hugh used sprigs[1] of three sizes costing 1½d., 2d., and 3d. a 100; little flooring nails at 2d. a 100, and very large ones at four times that price; lath nails at 3d. a 100; and large spikings and double spikes at 8d. a 100. At Bowness he supplied a lock and a snap, charging 10d. each for them.

2–22: Hugh's joinery accounts, 1743–63
22ᵛ–29ᵛ: shop and joinery accounts of particular persons, 1773–9
30ᵛ–46ᵛ: schoolboys' accounts, 1784–9
54ᵛ–58, 103ᵛ–107: Ann's expenses with five butchers, 1788–9
107ᵛ–113: shop accounts, 1759–77, with the book used upside-down
113ᵛ–114: fragmentary accounts
The rest of the leaves are blank, with 105–6 missing, and 111 omitted accidentally in the numbering. The new binding is larger than the original (16¾″ × 6½″), and on the spine is 'Ann Tyson's Ledger'.

[1] sprig—a small slender nail, either wedge-shaped and headless, or square-bodied with a light head on one side.

Round about the middle of the century, and particularly in the late 1740s, Hugh made a variety of articles for his customers. Tables are often mentioned in his accounts, the most expensive being 'a Large Dining Table' priced at £1. 6s. od., which he made for Mrs. Thomas Parke of Bouth. For large snap tables[1] he charged John Suart of Town £1 and Robert Knipe of Tarn Hows 18s.; whilst for the latter he made a small oak snap table for 9s. Chairs rarely appear, but for William Keen of Satterthwaite he made '9 Black Chears at 16 pence pr. Chear.' For a corner cupboard he charged 10s., and for clock-cases 12s. and 21s., the costlier being for Robert Green of Great Boat. He made a pair of bed-stocks for as little as 1s. 6d. On the other hand, when he made a four-poster for John Sawrey of Town the bed-stocks cost 8s. 6d., the tester 3s.,[2] a cornice 2s., and the headboard 1s. For a dressing-table his charge was 12s., for a large looking-glass 16s., and for a 'Chist of Drors' £2. On the eve of his own wedding, it may be noticed, he 'Bout a pair Chist of Drors' for £3. 3s. od. from Mrs. Thomas Braithwaite of Castle, Near Sawrey, and credited her husband's account with the amount. At the same time he framed two maps for her for 2s., and let her have '½ lb. Tee', the cost of which he entered as 3s. but subsequently altered to 2s. 8d. There is no record of his having sold either of the chests of drawers again.

In the eighteenth century the carts used in the Lake District usually had solid wheels known as clog wheels fixed to the axletree. For making a cart or a pair of clog wheels Hugh's charge was from 8s. to 9s. His early joinery accounts also show that he charged 5s. 6d. for an entrance gate he supplied to the Braithwaites of Briers, Far Sawrey; 2s. each for a door and door cheeks; 2s. 6d. and 3s. 6d. for window shutters, and 1s. 4d. for a window frame; 3s. 8d. for two 'Dials'— wooden troughs for carrying off water—and 2s. for a 'Phat', otherwise a vat, for Richard Harrison of Coniston Waterhead; 1s. each for

---

[1] snap table—Mary Moorman ('Ann Tyson's Ledger', *Cumberland and Westmorland Antiquarian and Archaeological Society's Transactions*, L, 1951, pp. 152–63) suggests 'a folding table that fastened with a snap or clasp, for we have another example of this in the entry:

for making Snap table with clasp   5s. od.
for a brass snap   8d.'

[2] tester—the wooden canopy of a four-poster.

'Swag Joystes', that is joists that would swag or give a bit; 1s. 1d. a
100 for 'Sap Lets' or 'Lats', in modern English laths (though in
Middle English lattes); 2s. for '12 foot of Thick ocke Board'; 8d. and
10d. a pair for hinges, 4d. to 6d. each for snecks, 4d. each for tool
handles, and 3d. each for drawer knobs; 8d. for a 'Jack and Knife
Box' for John Sawrey, butcher; 4d. for 'Setting up a Steel mill' to
grind bones to powder; 4d. for making a 'haster', a stand or screen
for concentrating the heat of the fire on to a joint of meat; 4d. each, to
the Braithwaites of Briers, Far Sawrey, for boarding charpots,[1] but
6d. each to another customer; 4d. each as a rule for framing pictures;
3d. for turning a pillar; and finally 8d. for cutting down a fir tree at
Coniston.

Entries in Hugh's ledger made in 1750 under the heading 'Worke
for Doctor Hodgon' have an added interest. Hugh himself was
employed on it for three days, his man for one, and Leonard Tyson's
man for one, the charges for their time being 4s., 1s. 4d., and 1s. 2d.
respectively. In addition, there are charges of 6s. 6d. for 'Shilving
Shop' and finding wood and nails, £1. 8s. 0d. for a 'Nest of
Drowers', 10s. 6d. for a table, 3s. for a sink, 1s. for a 'fraim for Still',
and 8d. for a corn kist or chest. Then follows this item: 'for Shop
Rent 13 weeke @ 6d. pr. [week]', 6s. 6d.; which shows that a shop
was in the Tysons' house, or somewhere on their premises.

The 'Doctor Hodgon' who rented this was Matthew Hodgson,
apothecary and surgeon; a man well known in the town and parish
of Hawkshead for over seventy years. A son of Robert Hodgson of
Kellet, some five or six miles from Lancaster, he was born in 1729,
and must therefore have gone to Hawkshead as soon as he had
finished his training, evidently at the age of twenty-one. As a
bachelor he boarded with the Tysons (according to his great-grand-
daughter, Miss Mary Hodgson of Greenend, Colthouse, from whom
I had this information in 1911), though there is no evidence of this in
Hugh's accounts, or that he rented the shop for longer than three
months; but if he paid cash there would be no need for entries, and

---

[1] Boarding charpots—making the wooden packing cases for the pots of char, the
small trout-like fish found in a few of the lakes and at that time preserved in spices.
For a full discussion of this delicacy see M. L. Armitt, *Rydal* (Kendal, 1916), pp. 286–
301.

very probably he did so. He is first mentioned in the Hawkshead Parish Registers in 1756, when his eldest child was christened Anna-Bella. His first wife, Ann, daughter of Thomas Dixon of Ings, near Windermere, bore him seven children before her death in 1771; and he had ten more by his second, Fanny, daughter of Samuel Irton of Irton Hall, Cumberland, whom he married in 1778, when she was already living at Hawkshead, as we shall see later. Matthew was ninety-two when he died at Colthouse on 19 March 1822, and Fanny was ninety-seven when she died, also at Colthouse, on 20 August 1853. These ages and dates are inscribed on a large altar tomb in Hawkshead churchyard which also commemorates eight of Matthew's children. It is probable that he boarded with the Tysons and had his apothecary's shop there from 1750 to 1755.

Purchases by the Tysons are scarcely ever recorded in the accounts during Hugh's lifetime, presumably because they were in the habit of paying for them at once. In the exception already cited, that of a pair of chests of drawers, no money changed hands. And I suspect it was the same in 1755 when on 6 November Hugh, making provision for the winter, 'bout cheses of John Sorrow 70 pound at 2¾d.', and beef, doubtless for salting, '60 pound at 2¼d.'. The vendor, John Sawrey, for whom he had done other work, besides making a four-poster bed in 1752, is likely to have owed him money as he was a notoriously bad payer, in later life at any rate. The churchwardens paid their bills for work Hugh did for them when their year of office was almost over, 17s. 10d. in 1745, 19s. 2½d. in 1749, and £1. 5s. 0d. in 1751, to take three examples when the sums he received were appreciable. But several of his customers were in no hurry to settle their accounts, the slowest being the Braithwaites of Briers, for whom he boarded a great many charpots over the years, and did a good deal of varied work from 1743 onwards. They could well afford to pay; but when he opened a new set of accounts in January, 1759, the first thing he noted was that Mr. Braithwaite of Briers owed him £1. 15s. 1d.

In addition to allowing long credit, Hugh was prepared to lend cash, or 'cas' as he called it, being used, it seems, to the original pronunciation of this French loan-word; and to lend it not only to Leonard Tyson and his wife, but also to some of his customers, including John Suart, a Hawkshead currier, and John Sawrey's father, Peter, who was first a mercer and then a grocer. The sums lent were relatively small, the largest being 12s. to 'John Biby wife', and of this he 'receved of her back' 3s. The second largest was 8s. to Leonard Tyson's wife.

Ann Tyson's grocery trade—John Nevinson—Ann's drapery trade—dressmaking—pins stockings funerals—Hugh's work in 1774—debts and loans—disposal of charcoal—the Backbarrow Co.

During the first ten years of his married life Hugh Tyson's joinery business declined to such an extent that by 1759 he could cope single-handed with all the work that came his way; and never after, it seems, did it rise above this level. That may be one reason why Ann went into business as well, a thing she could easily manage, as they had no children, and fairly often Hugh would be away in the day-time. What she did was to set up shop, very likely in the room that Matthew Hodgson had used. When she first did so is uncertain; but the accounts begun in January 1759 show that in a small way she was then both a grocer and a draper. And these she continued to be for the next twenty years or so. The new accounts, which are entirely in Hugh's handwriting, are for the most part a mixture of his and Ann's. For the first few years, though, he now and again entered joinery items in his old accounts, in which, I may say, there is a second mention of tea.

Ann's grocery trade was mainly in the choicer and less bulky commodities, many of them imported; and of these tea seems to have been the chief, judging from the amount she sold and the fact that she stocked so many different qualities, her prices for which ranged from 8s., through 6s. 8d., 6s. 4d., 6s., 4s. 6d. and 4s. 4d., to 3s. 4d. and 3s. 2d. a pound. The most popular with her customers was that at 4s. 4d., for which in 1774 she supplied 'Bohea tea'. At the beginning of the eighteenth century Bohea tea meant a black tea from China of the finest quality, but later it came to mean just the opposite so far as quality was concerned, and evidently by 1774 the change in meaning was far advanced. Green tea is rarely mentioned in Ann's accounts, but in 1774 her brother-in-law John Nevinson bought from her an ounce for 6*d*., as well as half a pound of black tea for 2*s*. 2*d*. She often sold half a pound of black tea at a time, but sometimes the amount was only two ounces, and exceptionally it was as much as a pound.

Sugar came after tea in order of importance. Her usual prices for it were 6*d*. a pound for brown sugar, evidently the kind that at a later date was sometimes called 'moist', and 10*d*. and 10½*d*. for 'Lofe Shuger', which was fully refined white sugar moulded into conical, but not sharply pointed, lumps. John Nevinson got brown sugar from Ann by the quarter-stone, for which he paid 1*s*. 6½*d*.; but most of her customers were content to buy their sugar, whether brown or white, by the pound. She also stocked 'Candy', a crystallized sugar prepared by slow evaporation, her charge for it being 1*s*. a pound. This is first mentioned in her accounts in 1762, which is seven years previous to the earliest example cited in the *Shorter Oxford English Dictionary* of the presence of this French loan-word in English. In 1759 she also sold 'Candit Lemon', presumably peel, at 2½*d*. for two ounces.

For 'Corrants' she charged 7*d*. a pound in 1767, and in 1765 and 1772 she supplied a pound each of currants and 'Resons' at 1*s*. 1*d*. for the two. Rice was 3½*d*. a pound in 1764. She also stocked the condiment variously known as Jamaica pepper, pimento, and allspice, which is said to combine the flavours of cinnamon, nutmeg, and cloves. In 1774 she supplied John Nevinson with an ounce of 'Jamakey pepper' for 1½*d*., and another customer with 'Jamack pepper' at 2*d*. for two ounces.

The rest of the groceries in which she dealt are of less interest. But it is worth mentioning that she sold hops for home brewing at 1*s*. a pound; and that for laundering she supplied starch as well as soap, both at 7*d*. a pound, and 'Stone Blue', which was made from indigo (another import), and either starch or powdered chalk, at 2*d*. an ounce. And though she did not deal regularly in bacon, she let her niece Eleanor Nevinson have a pound and a half for 1*s*. in 1776.

In the spring of this year Ann's brother-in-law, John Nevinson, a widower since 1744, finally left Hawkshead; the last entry in his apparently unsettled account with the Tysons is dated 29 April. His daughters stayed behind, and Eleanor's first purchase on credit from her aunt was made on 8 May. John Nevinson's account shows that in

c

1772 Hugh made a table for him for 6s., three 'Wigg Boxes'[1] at 8d. each, and an 'astrug' or ashbox for 10d. He also lent him 10s. 6d. on 28 April, and a further 7s. 6d. on 22 May. Then comes a charge of 1s. 6d. 'for shifting', which means, I take it, that Hugh put in a day's work ('without meat') helping Nevinson remove, either to another house in Hawkshead or to somewhere else. It is not clear just what happened, but around this time his daughters Eleanor and Margaret boarded with the Tysons from Christmas Day until the following 10 August, when there was 'Left [unpaid] from Board of Nel & pegg' the sum of £10.[2] John Nevinson was back in Hawkshead in 1774, when, as we have seen, he was getting groceries from Ann, on credit. At the same time he was being debited for a little drapery, probably supplied to Eleanor. Where he went in the spring of 1776 is not known, the most likely guess being that he went back to Barton in north Westmorland, where he could get poor relief if need arose. It should be noted that this Nevinson is not the John Nevinson of Stang End and later of Oxenfell who was having children baptized at Hawkshead from 1770 onwards. This John, like his contemporaries, Daniel and William Nevinson, of Hodge Close, was a 'slate getter'.

In considering Ann's drapery trade I will begin with materials, and first of all with 'cloth', which undoubtedly means woollen cloth suitable for wearing. Ann stocked many different qualities, ranging in price from $8\frac{1}{2}d.$ to 2s. and even 2s. 6d. a yard These figures, and there are other prices later, relate to the year 1773, when about a dozen of Ann's customers, several of whom lived at a distance from Hawkshead Town, had running accounts with her. Among these was 'Betty Peney', who can be identified as the Mrs. Elizabeth Penny of Grizedale whose husband, William Penny, died on 16 January 1773. It was she, evidently a lover of good materials, who paid 2s and 2s. 6d. a yard for cloth; but she also bought some at 1s. 2d. The wealthy Mr. and Mrs. George Knott of Coniston Waterhead, buying largely for the clothing of their servants, with Henry, their man, usually doing the shopping for them, paid anything from

---

[1] Probably boxes for wigs, small wedge-shaped buns or cakes.

[2] I read: 'August 10 Came to board [blot] may Day': it is not clear whether May to August or August to May is meant; the latter is more likely in view of the price.

8½d. up to 1s. 10d. a yard. And Matthew Coward, a Sawrey tailor who was penurious when he died in 1776, bought cloth in 1774 at 1s., 1s. 1½d., 1s. 3d.,. 1s. 4d., and 1s. 6d. a yard, his purchases including 'A yard Cloth for Caps' at 1s. 6d.

In the previous year this tailor or perhaps his wife had 'a quarter Stript Cloth' from Ann at a cost of 3d., and in 1774 a Mrs. Stevenson, wife of a Hawkshead tallow-chandler, had a yard and a half of it at 1s. 3d. a yard. Check is more often mentioned in the accounts, and Mrs. John Gibson, wife of a Hawkshead attorney, and a descendant of the Quaker Sandys of Roger Ground, had four and a half yards of it at 1s. 3d. a yard, in 1774, and then a further five yards at 1s. 1½d. a yard. In 1773 she had bought '3 Nails Muslin' for 9d. (a nail being one-sixteenth of a yard, two and a quarter inches), a trifling expenditure compared with Widow Penny's, who, in 1774 had 'half a yard and half a quarter' of muslin at 4s. 6d. a yard, which comes to 2s. 10d.; and again in 1775 she had a yard and a quarter at 8s. 6d. a yard, and was charged 10s. 7½d.

When it came to buying lawn, Betty Penny was nearly as extravagant, for in 1774 she purchased from Ann half a yard at 6s. a yard, and 'half a yard and half-quarter' at 8s. a yard. Mrs. Alexander of Keen Ground, who was also a widow but older, bought lawn in 1777 and again in 1778: she had only a quarter of a yard each time of the cheaper quality. In 1759 Ann charged 6d. for '3 Nails of Cambrick', and in the following year 1s. for '3 quarters Glais^d Linn', which means these two linens cost 2s. 8d. and 1s. 4d. a yard respectively. The cheapest she stocked was huckaback, which appears in the accounts as 'hugaeback'. Of this she sold nine and a quarter yards to the Knotts in 1773 at 10½d. a yard.

Entries in the accounts for 1773–5 show that Ann made men's shirts. She charged Mr. John Gibson 9½d. and Matthew Coward 10d. for 'Making a Shirt', thread and buttons. Oddly enough the word 'making' is not used in any of the entries I have noted that refer to women's gowns; but the sums she charged are proof in themselves that they were for the making only. Here are some of them: John Hodgon, for his wife Agnes, 'A gown Linen', 1s. 2d.; Matthew Coward, doubtless for his wife, 'A gown Linen', 10½d.; Mr. George Knott, probably for a maid, 'A gown Linen & tape', 11d.; and Mrs.

Stevenson, perhaps for herself, 'A gown Linen by Elinor Nevenson',
1s. 0½d. And to these may be added from Mr. Gibson's account:
25 November 1775, 'Nely Nevenson a quarter Cottan Gow[n]',
apparently a sleeveless garment stopping just below the waist, 3½d.
The last two entries suggest that Ann sometimes employed her niece
to make things for her customers. There is another entry in which
Nell is mentioned. It is in Mrs. Stevenson's account, and reads: 'by
Elinor Nevinson' a yard 'Cottan thred tape', 1s. 4d. Eleanor's part in
this transaction would hardly have been worth recording if she had
merely delivered the goods for Ann. So it may be that she supplied
them from her own stocks at Ann's request. Indeed it is quite possible
that Eleanor Nevinson did sewing for people on her own account;
but if so, I have no other proof of it than that she bought lawn,
muslin, and pins from Ann.

Besides shirts and gowns, Ann occasionally made other things for
her customers. In 1775 she charged Mrs. Alexander 3d. for 'Making a
wascoat', and Mrs. Stevenson 3d., also for 'Making a Wescoat'. The
two ladies, who were mother and daughter, each had a yard and a
quarter of flannel from Ann for this purpose, Mrs. Alexander paying
1s. 2d. a yard for it, and her daughter a penny more. Both had need
of extra warmth, Mrs. Alexander because she was old, and Mrs.
Stevenson because she was mortally ill. Shortly before her death she
also had from Ann 'A pair of Black Mitts' at a cost of 1s. and as Ann
does not seem to have dealt regularly in these, it is possible that she
made the 'Black Mitts' specially for Mrs. Stevenson. This may be
said, too, of the check apron she let Mrs. Alexander have for 2s. 5d.
in the following year, a price which obviously includes both material
and cost of making. And perhaps I should add to this list of things
she may have made, since they do not appear to have been part of
her regular stock-in-trade, the tablecloth at 4s. 4d. entered in Mr.
Knott's account in 1774, and the hood at 2s. 6d. in Matthew Coward's
for the same year.

In the latter's account there is a very unusual entry for 1774: 'To 8
rows of Necklaces', 4d. The word *necklace* must here be used in the
sense of a lace or ribbon for the neck, a sense stated in the *Oxford
English Dictionary* to have become obsolete by 1740, though evidently not in Hawkshead. Clearly a charge as low as 4d. must be for

making only, and not for the materials as well. But of what were these necklaces made? Fortunately the accounts provide the answer: 'To Lawn and Cambrick and thred', 1s. 3d. It does not follow that all Hawkshead necklaces of the 1770s were made of these two fine linens. Muslin is a not unlikely substitute, and ribbon a possibility. This last Ann was selling at 8d. a yard in 1774, whilst her charge for ribbons for men and boys was round about 9d. each.

And here let me say something about pins, seeing that they figure more prominently than one would expect in Mr. Knott's account for 1774, the year, I may add, during which his wife Catherine reached the age of twenty-one and bore him a second son. First, she had no less than half a pound of pins, costing 1s. 7d. (as against Eleanor Nevinson's two ounces for 5d.). Next she got 'by Henery a Sheet Menikin pins', and then, again by Henry, a further 'Sheet Menikin pins'. For these Ann charged 5d. each, as she did for two more sheets of pins, not specified as menikin, which she supplied to Mrs. Knott in the following year. The word Menikin, which I have failed to find in any dictionary or word-list I have been able to consult, is not the Furness dialect form of manikin; but it could, I suppose, be a parallel formation from men instead of man. Anyhow, I imagine that Menikin pins were very small ones, such as might be required in making necklaces, say, or baby clothes. It looks as if Mrs. Knott, who also bought buttons from Ann, had a sewing maid or visiting seamstress whom she kept busy. But pins were more expendable then than now as the heads were apt to come off. According to the 1895 edition of *Chamber's Encyclopaedia*, the type of pin used in the eighteenth century, and in fact up to about 1840, 'had a globular head of fine twisted wire made separately and secured to the shank by compression from a falling block and die. These old pins had the disadvantage of frequently losing their heads.'

To return to the question of the major aspects of Ann's stock-in-trade, there are things of some importance still to be noticed, such as stockings and handkerchiefs. Though most people in and around Hawkshead then wore woollen stockings knitted at home, she still sold a good many pairs, judging by the 1773-5 accounts. In Mr. Knott's, for instance, there are charges of 9s. for '4 pair Stockings for Henery at 2s 3ᵈ', and of 8s. 8d. for '2 pair Stockings for Jo at 4s 4ᵈ'.

These prices for men's stockings are her lowest and highest. Others I have noted are 3s. 4d. in the Stevensons' account at the time of Mrs. Stevenson's death, and 3s. in Dr. Matthew Hodgson's account. For stockings for herself Mrs. Gibson was charged 2s., 2s. 8d., and 3s. a pair; and for women's stockings generally Ann's price-range was from 2s. to 3s. a pair. Two pairs of black stockings supplied as part of the mourning order when Mrs. Stevenson died are each priced at 2s.; and Agnes Hodgson had a black pair at 2s. 3d.; whilst Betty Penney and a Mrs. Benson of Elterwater were each charged 3s., the one for a pair of 'thred Stockings', the other for a pair of cotton ones. Earlier, Ann had sold a pair of girl's stockings for 1s. 10d. As for 'handcorchifs', Ann sold them from 4d. to 5s. each. The Gibsons had them from her at 4d., 7d., 1s. 5d., and 2s. 8d. each; Mrs. Alexander at 2s. 8d.; and either Mr. or Mrs. Knott at 5s. For a black handkerchief Mr. Gibson was charged 2s. 8d., and Mrs. Alexander and Betty Penny each 5s.

From mourning handkerchiefs I pass to funerals There were three for which Hugh Tyson was undertaker during the period 1759–79: those of 'Martha Taylor of Hawkshead Aged 87', on 5 April 1767; 'Ann Wife of William Stephenson Town', aged thirty-nine, on 19 May 1775; and 'Elizabeth Widow of Robert Alexander of Keen-g^{d}', aged seventy, on 4 March 1779, the burial in this instance being in the church. For the coffins, including furniture, that is to say, handles and perhaps plates, Hugh's charges were 14s., 14s. 6d., and 10s. respectively. Ann's price for fine crape for the shrouds was a uniform 1s. 6d. a yard, but the length required varied from nine and three-quarter yards to seven and a half. For making the shrouds and dressing the corpse she charged 2s., and 2s. 6d. When Mrs. Stevenson died she also supplied two crape hatbands at 2s. 4d. each, as well as the stockings already mentioned.

There is little else that is new in Hugh's joinery accounts for the later period. He continued to board charpots for the Braithwaites of Briers, and did a good deal of repair and other work for them at the rate of 1s. a day—evidently with meat, as his charge without it had by then risen, with the rising cost of living, to 1s. 8d. a day. In 1774 he supplied the Braithwaites with a '14 foot Inch and half fir plank' at 3d. a foot, '14 foot of Deal Boerd for Wash Box' at 2d. a foot, and

'6 foot of Ash Board for Cobert' also at 2*d*. a foot, making a total of 6*s*. 10*d*.

Mr. Stevenson's account for the same year includes the following items: 'to 18 foot of Square wood at 1½ for Cowhous Doar Cheeks', 2*s*. 3*d*.; 'Making of Doar Cheeks', 1*s*. 2*d*.; 'Making 2 Doars 2 Days Worke', 3*s*. 4*d*.; 'A Doar Cheeke for Great Doar', 1*s*. 6*d*.; and 'Making and hanging Doar Mending the other', 2*s* 2*d*. In the following year he charged Mrs. Alexander, then living in Hawkshead it seems, 4*s*. 6*d*. for making a door and hanging it, and Betty Penny 1*s*. for 'Mending Beds', 5*d*. for a 'Drower Lock for Richard Chest' [Richard being her son], and 5*d*. for a 'Snap and Screws'. Compared with the work he had done earlier this is joinering in a minor key. There were about this time four joiners in Hawkshead and three more just outside, two at Gallowbarrow and one at Hannakin; and there was not enough work to go round. This probably explains why Hugh did other jobs occasionally, such as (from Mr. Stevenson's account for 1774) 'Wone Day at Hay', 1*s*.; 'Won Day Shearing', 1*s*.; 'Won Day Leading Corn', 1*s*.; 'Won Day Graveing Peats', 1*s*.; 'Won Day Making Thoˢ Nouble peat hows', 1*s*. 8*d*. William Stevenson, or Stephenson as the Parish Registers have it, must have been a farmer as well as a tallow-chandler, in a small way at any rate.

In 1775 the Tysons tried to collect the money then owing to them. The Braithwaites of Briers, who had been running an account with Hugh since 1743 and had paid little or nothing since 1759, owed him £24. 13*s*. 2*d*. During 1775 they paid on account sums of £2. 2*s*. 0*d*., £4. 5*s*. 0*d*., and £2. 0*s*. 0*d*.; but there is no note in the Tysons' ledger of any further payments. Ann's debts were less serious, as none of them went back further than 1773. In some cases she, too, had to be content for the time with part payment. Mr. John Gibson, the attorney, paid £1. 1*s*. 0*d*. out of the £1. 19*s*. 8*d*. he owed; poor Matthew Coward, who had bought nothing from Ann since May 1774, found £1. 11*s*. 6*d*. towards discharging his debt of £2. 14*s*. 3*d*.; and Mrs. Benson of Elterwater, a widow, who owed £1. 6*s*. 4½*d*., paid £1 on account. A worse case was that of Mr. James Alexander of Keen Ground. On 29 January 1776, he owed £1. 9*s*. 1½*d*., and on 6 March he paid 5*s*. 2*d*.; and yet he had a maid and a boy to shop for him. After 1775 the Tysons rarely allowed credit; but they did to old

Mrs. Alexander, Mr. James's mother, and even, in the closing weeks of her life, they lent her 'cas'—3s. on 12 January, another 3s. on 23 January, 2s. on 16 February, and then 3s. again on 1 March, which was the day before she died, of 'a Cough' it says in the Parish Registers.

Some explanation of these and earlier loans by the Tysons seems to be called for, especially as most of them were made to people as well or better off than they were. An entry in Mrs. Stevenson's account for 1774 gives a hint, for it reads: 'Lent Cas for Chaing', 3s. During a large part of the eighteenth century there was not enough cash in circulation in the district, despite the fact that Hawkshead's weekly market was the principal market in the southern Lakeland for woollen yarn, leather, and provisions. This chronic shortage of ready money, which led to delays in paying for goods and services, lasted until the Kendal banks of Messrs. Wakefield & Co., and Messrs. Maude, Wilson, and Crewdson opened, simultaneously, on 1 January 1788. It is not so clear why the Tysons always seem to have had cash to lend. There is no mention of interest in their ledger, from which it would appear that the loans were kindnesses. Hugh, it may be added, subscribed 3s. in 1765 towards the cost of providing a ring of six new bells for Hawkshead Church, whereas Leonard and Nicholas Tyson, after promising 2s. 6d., failed to find the money. Hugh also very often contributed a penny or two to Briefs—parochial collections authorized by Royal Warrant or Letters Patent for building or rebuilding churches, or repairing damage due to fire, flood, or other disasters, or to ransoming the captives of Barbary corsairs.

Hugh was never called upon to fill any office in the parish. But in 1777–8 Mr. Stephen Green of Hill Top, Near Sawrey, who was away in London, gave him the responsible and unfamiliar job of seeing to some coppice wood that was due for cutting, which happened every fourteen to sixteen years. It was to be cut, barked, and made into charcoal, the bark to be sold for tanning and the charcoal for smelting iron ore. The first indication of this in Hugh's account, which runs from 24 April 1777 to 9 February 1778, is a note saying: 'Mr Green Barke In Hackshead flat & Copes Sould in the year 1777 May 28 to Mr Willson Kendal 28 quarter & half at 10s 6d pr [quarter]', £14. 19s. 3d. On 2 October Hugh 'Recd for Bark of Mr Willson' £14. 19s. 0d. Of this he set aside 7s. 'for present eus', and

sent £4. 0s. 0d. to Mr. Green. Having money in hand, he then paid
Edward Braithwaite £5. 11s. 9d. for 'Cotting wood and peeling
Barke', and William Braithwaite £2. 18s. 4d. for 'Coling the same
wood'. In addition, he spent a shilling with the 'bark peeler' and
another with the 'colyer' when paying them; an expense which was
allowable on all such occasions. It occurs only once in the account he
kept of his petty expenditure, which amounted in all to 7s. 4d., and
consisted largely of postal payments for letters he had received from
Mr. Green.

The disposal of the charcoal is the subject of two major entries in
Hugh's accounts. The first tells us that he 'Lay out for Leading Coal
to Willm Atckinson Whaithcad thc Sum of £3. 2s. 9d.', and the
second that on 9 February 1778 he 'Rec^d of the Backbarrow Company for the O^cs of Mr Stephen Green for Coals for 13^Doz [and] 10
Sacks the Sum of £27. 13s. 4d.' Charcoal sacks, as then used,
measured two yards by one, and when filled and tied up they had to
stand five feet high. As there were 166 of them to be taken to
Thwaite Head, a good four miles away by road, and as the carts then
in use were very small, a great many journeys must have been
necessary; hence the high cost of delivering the charcoal. Its ultimate
destination is uncertain, as the Backbarrow Co., which was founded
in 1711 and dissolved in 1818 after selling its properties and leases to
the rival Newland Co., had a number of iron-works in operation in
1778, all of them in High Furness, except one which was in Cartmel.
When the company was reconstructed in 1749, the Machells, who
had previously held one half of the share capital of £16,000, first of
all acquired the whole of it; and then they allotted £1,000 of it to
each of nine principal owners of coppice woods in High Furness and
nearby parts of South Westmorland, in exchange for a new furnace
which they, the wood-owners, had combined to build at Penny
Bridge. This deal, the main purpose of which was to ensure that the
Backbarrow Co. would have adequate supplies of charcoal in the
years ahead, had a minor sequel in 1772, when a number of smaller
owners of coppice woods, including Mr. Stephen Green of Near
Sawrey, were each invited to invest not less than £100 in the company. As it had rebuilt its Backbarrow furnace in 1770, and was for
this and other reasons in a very strong competitive position, he is

likely to have accepted the invitation. If he did, the Backbarrow Co. would almost certainly be given the first chance to buy the charcoal he had for sale in 1777.

But was the charcoal his? And if so, why did Hugh Tyson state that the money he received for it was for the occupiers 'of Mr Stephen Green', in other words for the tenants of Hill Top? No answer to these questions can be found in Hugh's ledger; nor any to the further questions of who repaid the £1. 7s. 7d. of his own money which he seems to have laid out on Mr. Green's behalf whilst acting as his agent, or how much he got for the time he spent and the work he did in this capacity. Stephen Green, whose wife Ann died in 1761 after bearing him two daughters, eventually returned to Near Sawrey, but probably not to Hill Top. At any rate in the Hawkshead Parish Registers among the burials in 1787 is that of 'Stephen Green of Near Sawrey Boarder Died May 6 Buried 8 in Church Aged 61'.

Ann Tyson and the Knotts—Richard Ford and Co.—Bonaw—William Ford—George Knott—Ann Tyson and Bonaw

Meanwhile Ann, too, had a job, of which I first heard in 1906 from Miss Mary Hodgson of Greenend, Colthouse, whose source of information was a Philip Braithwaite who boarded with Hugh and Ann Tyson in 1781, as I shall show later.[1] I later noticed that Dorothy Wordsworth refers to this job in her *Recollections of a Tour made in Scotland A.D. 1803.*[2] Speaking of 1 September, she says: 'We were now among familiar fireside names. We could see the town of Bunawe, a place of which the old woman with whom William lodged ten years at Hawkshead used to tell tales half as long as an ancient romance. It is a small village or port on the same side of Loch Etive on which we stood, and at a little distance is a house built by a Mr Knott of Coniston Water-head, in the service of whose family the old woman had spent her youth. It was an ugly yellow-daubed building, staring this way and that, but William looked at it with pleasure for poor Ann Tyson's sake'. According to Philip Braithwaite, Ann went to Scotland with Mr. and Mrs. George Knott on

[1] See below, pp. 37–46.
[2] See Sharp's edition (1874), pp. 144–5, or *The Journals of Dorothy Wordsworth* ed. de Selincourt (1941), p. 309.

several occasions; and he remembered her saying that the journey there and back was mostly by sea, which was apt to make her sick.

If I am to explain properly about Mr. and Mrs. George Knott and their connection with Bonaw I must dip again into the history of the Furness iron industry, starting this time with Richard Ford, a native of Middlewich, Cheshire, born in 1697, who became manager of the iron-works at Cunsey in 1722. Three years later he married Elizabeth, daughter of the Rev. William Bordley, Vicar of Hawkshead; and by her he had ten children, including a son William who was baptized at Hawkshead on 17 January 1728. He left Cunsey in 1735, and built a furnace at Nibthwaite, on land leased from Thomas Rigg, a landowner in the Crake valley, who assisted him financially but took no part in the management of the business. At the same time he diverted a 'little of the water out of the River Crake for the benefit of the furnace, but without doing any damage', it was argued, 'to the river or any fishery therein'. But there was trouble from the start; the validity of the lease he had been granted was disputed, and in particular Thomas Rigg's assumption that he was the owner of the river-bed in the neighbourhood of the furnace. These differences were a hindrance to Ford, and led to a costly law-suit in 1746. In the end matters were adjusted, with the result that in 1750 Richard Ford & Co. were granted a lease for 100 years.

Meanwhile they had built a bigger furnace some six miles further south, at Newland, near Ulverston. In 1735 Ford had agreed not to acquire another site for iron-works within ten miles of Nibthwaite, but that difficulty had been overcome by arranging with his sister-in-law, Agnes Bordley, that the lease of the land at Newland should be in her name. The furnace there was built in 1747 by the newly formed company, in which half the share capital was held by Richard Ford, and a quarter by his twenty-year-old son William, then of Grizedale. The remaining quarter was equally divided between Michael Knott of Rydal and James Backhouse of Finsthwaite, two coppice wood owners with no working knowledge of the iron industry. They were content to leave the management of the company to the Fords, one or other of whom later acquired James Backhouse's share in it. For the rest of his life Richard Ford lived at Newland, and William at first there, and then in Ulverston for a time.

The reorganization of the Backbarrow Co. in 1749,[1] and the grip it then got on future supplies of charcoal, left the Newland Co., as it was often called, with little scope for further development in High Furness. A refinery and a forge were added at Nibthwaite in 1751, but for the site of a new furnace the Fords looked elsewhere, and in 1752 they decided on Bonaw in Argyleshire, on the river Awe just before it enters Loch Etive. The fact that an earlier venture at Invergarry in the Scottish Highlands, a venture whose promoters were mainly Furness and Lonsdale men, had ended in 1736 in complete disaster, did not deter them, and before the end of 1752 they had obtained, not only long-term wood-leases, but also a lease running for 110 years of no less than thirty-four square miles of land on the south side of Loch Etive. In the following year they built a furnace, known as the Lorn Furnace, and a number of storehouses, at Bonaw; and they constructed a quay on Loch Etive, for whenever it was possible transport was to be by water. In addition, they began building good stone houses for the skilled workmen they were bringing from Furness, and one for the 'housekeeper' they were installing. They built some cheap houses, too, for low-paid labourers recruited locally, and several farm houses, a church, a school, and eventually (but not till about 1785) an inn at Taynuilt. And there for the moment I must leave Bonaw, and return to Furness.

Richard Ford died in 1757 at the age of sixty, and was buried at Ulverston. Though he had several other children still living, he seems to have left everything he possessed to his son William, who certainly came into the Grizedale Hall estate, and into his father's share of the Newland Co. With his own and the Backhouse share, he thus owned seven-eighths of the share-capital of what on his succession to the managership became known as William Ford & Co. He was then thirty, and already he had done most of the detailed work in connection with the development of the Bonaw estate. This he continued to do until it was completed; but it is not possible to follow the progress of the work as all Bonaw records prior to 1780 have been destroyed or lost.

In or about 1751 William Ford married Catherine, the youngest daughter of Richard Harrison of Coniston Waterhead. He and his

[1] See above, p. 21.

bride first lived at Ulverston, where their eldest child, a daughter Catherine, was born in 1752 or 1753. They then moved to Coniston Waterhead, where in the years 1754 to 1762 they had five more children. Two of them were sons, both christened Richard, but the first died in infancy, and the second as a boy. Two daughters also died in infancy, and that left only Catherine and Agnes, the latter of whom was baptized at Hawkshead on 5 December 1761. Just before that, on 7 October in the same year, 'Mr Richard Harrison an Householder Coniston Waterhead' was buried at Hawkshead. Born in 1676, he was the last male Harrison to live at Coniston Waterhead, an estate, the largest in Monk Coniston, his grandfather had bought at the end of the Civil Wars. Now, if not earlier, it passed into the hands of William Ford; but after losing his wife at the age of forty-six in 1765, he himself died in 1769, aged only forty-one, or possibly forty-two. She was buried at Hawkshead, he at Ulverston.

I have not seen William Ford's will, but it seems to be quite certain that he bequeathed all, or almost all, he had to his two surviving daughters, in trust presumably as both were minors, Catherine being sixteen and Agnes seven. To his elder daughter he left Coniston Waterhead, and to his younger the Grizedale Hall estate, including the residence on it known as Ford Lodge which his father had built, the Hall having become a farmhouse. His holding in the Newland Co., amounting to seven-eighths of the total share capital, he divided between his daughters nearly but not quite equally, Catherine getting one-fourteenth more of it than Agnes did. The remaining one-eighth of the company's capital was still held by Michael Knott of Rydal. He had never taken an active part in the management of the company, and it is unlikely that he did so after the death of William Ford, whose trustees were probably saddled with the job of directing the company themselves, with or without the aid of a manager.[1]

---

[1] Michael was agent for the le Flemings of Rydal. He also was allowed—perhaps through his marriage to Susannah le Fleming—to use the timber on his customary holdings in the Rydal estate for the making of charcoal for his own profit. When he enlarged his house (the one now known as Rydal Mount) about the middle of the century by adding the large west wing to the original statesman's house (or toftstead), he is said to have used the timber of more than sixty trees from other tenants' land and thus saved his own for the lucrative charcoal-burning. It must have been especially galling to his neighbours that with some of the hewn wood he built a coaling-house. See M. L. Armitt, *Rydal*, p. 34. Michael, like Wordsworth, was a Distributor of Stamps.

Whatever the arrangement, it did not last long, for in 1772 George Knott, Michael's son and heir, then a man of twenty-nine, married young Miss Catherine Ford, and so acquired Coniston Waterhead, and nearly half the share capital of the Newland Co. His holding was increased to over a half—to nineteen thirty-seconds to be exact —by the death of his father in the same year. He then decided to move from Rydal[1] to Coniston Waterhead, and to take over the management of the Newland Co., whose official title then became George Knott & Co. He seems to have been a lively, energetic man, with good intentions, but no previous experience of the iron industry or any other. His mother, Susannah, was a member of a high-ranking local family, the Flemings of Coniston and Rydal, her father being Major Michael Fleming of Rydal, a younger son of Sir Daniel, and at one time M.P. for Cockermouth. She had an uncle George, afterwards Sir George, who became Bishop of Carlisle, and a brother William who eventually succeeded both to the Fleming baronetcy and to the Rydal estate. It was with her, George Knott's mother, that Ann Tyson was in service for some years before her marriage in 1749. Miss Mary Hodgson had this information from Philip Braithwaite, who recalled a story bearing on the point which Mrs. Tyson used to tell when he boarded with her. It appears that as a small boy George Knott did not care for oatmeal porridge, and that neither his nurse nor his mother had much success in their efforts to induce him to eat it. So with Mrs. Knott's approval Ann took a hand in the matter. Knowing something of the boy's likes and dislikes, she made the porridge very thick, and then spread honey over it. And that proved to be the solution. Ann left soon afterwards, apparently to be married, and thought little more about the incident until she first went to Bonaw with Mr. and Mrs. George Knott and their children, when she found to her astonishment that he still had

[1] George does not seem to have used his house in Rydal. He leased it for three years in December 1783 to a Mr. Daulby (from near Ipswich, but a friend of William Roscoe of Liverpool), who retained it until his own death in 1798 when it was sold by George's eldest son, Michael, to Ford North from Liverpool for £2,500. In 1812, after disputes with the le Flemings, Ford North sold the house to them, and thus Rydal Mount was available for rent in 1813 when Wordsworth took it. Coniston Waterhead, meanwhile, was virtually rebuilt by Michael Knott and became known as Monk Coniston, a rebuilding 'in the finest style of modern Gothic', in the words of the *Lonsdale Magazine*, III, 31 May 1822.

his porridge made and served in the same fashion. Whether Ann Tyson had been in service at Rydal with one of the Knotts before Mrs. Michael Knott engaged her is an open question, as Dorothy Wordsworth might easily have used the words 'spent her youth' rather loosely.

Though their married life extended to less than twelve years, George and Catherine Knott had eight children. They were all christened at Hawkshead, George in 1773, Michael in 1774, Catherine in 1776, Susannah in 1777, Dorothy in 1778, Agnes Ford in 1780, William in 1782, and Edward Richard in 1783; and three of them, Susannah, Dorothy, and Edward Richard, were buried there as infants. During their first year or two at Coniston Waterhead, a house which had been rather neglected for some years previously, the Knotts spent freely in having it repaired, redecorated, and to a large extent refurnished. George Knott then turned his attention to the estate, which he extended and greatly improved. The number of trees he planted on it has been overstated owing to confusion with Miss Agnes Ford's plantings at Grizedale, but it certainly ran into thousands. He also decided to build a holiday house at Bonaw where he and his family could stay during their summer visits to the Highlands; and this he did, but it is not known when it was ready for their occupation. In 1773 and 1774 he seems to have gone to Bonaw alone, and to have stayed, as William Ford did, with the company's housekeeper there. The 'large mansion', as Alfred Fell calls it in his *Early Iron Industry of Furness and District*[1] could have been ready by 1775 I believe; on the other hand it might not have been occupied by the Knotts until a year or two years later. According to Alfred Fell, it was vacated after George Knott's death, which occurred on 4 January 1784, at the age of forty, and the contents sold. The goods, he says, 'were rouped after being called at 5 different churches and advertised at all public places in this part'. A young boy from Inverary conducted the sale, acting both as auctioneer and as clerk. He was handicapped by not knowing the names of some of the

[1] Published Ulverston 1908 and reprinted, Cass library of industrial classics (No. 2), 1968. T.W.T.'s discussion of Bonaw here and below draws upon Fell's book (pp. 390–414), from which T.W.T. quotes several letters. I have been unable to trace the MS. originals.

things he was selling. Mrs. Knott, I may add, died on 6 March 1785, at the age of thirty-two. Like her husband she was buried in the chancel of Hawkshead Church, where there are two memorials to them and to their children who died in infancy. One is an engraved flag on the floor, the other a mural tablet which bears George Knott's arms.

Ann Tyson's visits to Bonaw with the Knotts cannot, then, have taken place earlier than 1775 or later than 1783; and if, as Philip Braithwaite said, she went to Scotland on several occasions with them, it is likely that she went both before and after she and Hugh first had Grammar School boys as boarders, which was in 1779. When she had the shop, she could get her niece, Nell Nevinson, to look after it whilst she was away. When she had Grammar School boys as boarders, she could go during their summer holidays, which began about 20 June, and lasted six weeks. So far as I know, there is no record of her duties when she was away with the Knotts; but on one of her visits, it is said, she acted as the company's housekeeper for a month or so, presumably in an emergency. Miss Mary Hodgson learnt this from Philip Braithwaite, and he from a Mrs. Ashburner whose husband was a furnaceman at Bonaw at the time. He and his wife were living at Sawrey when Ann Tyson died, but went back later to where he belonged, which was somewhere in the Ulverston district. Mrs. Ashburner had a story about Ann when she was acting as housekeeper at Bonaw. One of the workmen's wives, it seems, lost no time in sending word to her to say she was ill, and to ask if she could have some wine. Ann did not go at once, and when she did, she found the woman up and about, but left her some wine all the same. About a fortnight later Ann had the same message and request from the same woman. This time she went round promptly and found her in bed. The poor woman spoke feelingly of her ailments and of the way they recurred; and finally, as there was little response from Ann, of how the wine always did her good. 'I didn't think to bring any,' Ann told her, 'not after last time.' 'After last time?' the woman asked. 'What do you mean?' 'I mean,' said Ann, 'that getting up and buckling to soon had you right last time, and likely it will again when you give it a chance. So I won't hinder you. I'll bid you good day and be gone.'

The company provided wine for the sick, of whom there were many at Bonaw, and one of the duties of the housekeeper was to dispense it. This is implied in a letter of Mrs. Knott's written in the early 1780s. Mrs. Park, then housekeeper at Bonaw, had inquired about wine, but had not said, Mrs. Knott points out, whether it was for giving to gentlemen who called or to the poor when sick, therefore she could say nothing until she knew. Rum and water would do for most of the gentlemen, she added: it was what they gave themselves. Being hospitable to visitors was, then, another of the housekeeper's duties; and though the Knotts were in residence, Ann may have had to do a little entertaining. But there was no lavish hospitality at Bonaw as there had been at Invergarry. Speaking of the neighbouring landed proprietors, George Knott says in one letter that 'they are Hawks and Birds of Prey', and in another he doubts whether an honest man can be found among them. They were not easy to deal with, but on the whole the Newland Co. handled them with fair success. One of them, who was constantly calling on the housekeeper in the hope of getting a free drink or two, was eventually offered only a dish of tea on his visits; but I am not sure whether this was in George Knott's time, or a little later when Matthew Harrison was in charge. He began as 'Mr Knot Clark' or 'Mr Knot Steward', to quote from the Hawkshead Parish Registers for 1781 and 1782, and eventually he dominated the Furness iron industry.

The skilled workers at Bonaw, mostly Furness men who rarely settled in their new surroundings, were paid at the same rate as at Newland, namely 6s. a week with meat; and there can be little doubt that the most onerous of Ann's duties as acting housekeeper would be seeing to the provision of meals for the furnacemen whilst they were on the job, for there was then no innkeeper in the neighbourhood to undertake this service on behalf of the company. It is not unlikely that some of the Highland labourers were also partly paid in kind, but on this point I have no precise information. The furnace workers at Bonaw, as elsewhere, expected drinks to be supplied by the owners as well as meat; and George Knott & Co. were generous in their provision of barrels of ale, kegs of whisky, and an occasional bladder of snuff. But that was a matter for the chief agent or steward and not for the housekeeper.

D

Two other things which the company supplied at Bonaw were wool and oatmeal. Speaking of the workmen's wives and widows in one of his letters, George Knott says that it would be a pity to let them want wool for spinning 'in these dear times', as it is a great means of keeping them out of debt. In point of fact they took up to fifty stones a week. Most of the yarn they spun was taken to Furness for disposal, the greater part of it being sold in Hawkshead market to Kendal woollen manufacturers, handloom weavers, and merchants. Oatmeal, from which two staple articles of diet were made—porridge and oatcake or haverbread—was then of paramount importance in the Highlands, as it was in Cumberland, Westmorland, and Furness. The company purchased vast quantities of it, and that bought at Carlisle was considered much better than any to be got from Inverness or from Ireland. They allowed their workmen to have it at rather less than the current retail price, charging them sometimes as little as 1s. 6d. a stone for it, and rarely more than 2s. 6d. They also sold it to others in the neighbourhood, as is evident from two letters cited by Alfred Fell. In the summer of 1782, when there was a great scarcity of oatmeal, Matthew Harrison wrote to the agent at Bonaw: 'I observe you have got a supply of oatmeal which, by your distributing so freely, I fear will soon be gone, if this should be the case you may sew up all your mouths as I do not think a ton could be procured in the whole country. It is now 26s. per cwt at Hawkshead . . .; if the workmen can afford to pay a better price than 20s. they should pay it, but by no means let it go out otherwise than to workmen.' And George Knott writing to the agent in 1783 says: 'I thought you had received ready-money for Sir James Riddell's meal, but can clearly see the principle he has gone on and have nothing but law or to sit down with the loss.' The housekeeper seems to have had nothing to do with the distribution of oatmeal, unless it was to supply it to those in distress, for it was her duty to care in some measure for them as well as for the sick.

Distress arising from one cause or another was common among the Highland labourers and their families. The men's wages were low, and drink a temptation to many. In any case there were the aged and the maimed, the widows and orphans, and families with too many mouths to fill, or in which either husband or wife was feeble, feckless, or hopelessly improvident. Some of these poor folk Ann Tyson must have had to relieve during her term as acting housekeeper at Bonaw. In addition to encouraging the women to spin woollen yarn, the company allowed each householder to keep a cow, and provided 'grass' for it at a cost of 12s. a year. This provision took the form of a common grazing ground or pasture, which inevitably led to a certain amount of trouble. In 1782 George Knott wrote to the agent about the number of useless people, such as tailors and weavers, on the company's estate at Bonaw, pointing out that it was 'these sort whose cattle crowd the grass'. And on 1 September 1783, on his return from what proved to be his last visit to Bonaw, he wrote: 'I think you have far too many people on the lands'. And it rather looks as if the schoolmaster had too many cows on the company's 'grass'. Anyhow, the agent, writing in 1782 or thereabouts, reports that 'Collin McIllerah ye Schoolmaster has at last lowsed his 4 head of cattle from the Pinfold, for which I received 30s. for 15 days at 6d. per head each in the 24 hours.' Some disturbance followed, probably because he put them all back on the common pasture, from which they seem to have been impounded, the contention being, I fancy, that he had no right to graze so many on it.

More serious abuses at Bonaw form the subject of a strongly worded letter by George Knott. Writing to the agent in 1781, he charges him with drinking too frequently with captains of ships, retailing whisky, trading on his own account, and chattering unwisely; and he mentions that the quay is being used by smugglers. 'Put a stop, if possible', the letter continues, 'to that confounded drinking in general, and by your shewing the example it may be more easily done, for I believe there is not such another drunken hole in the Kingdom.' The reformation George Knott desired did not materialize; so a fresh agent was appointed, and some improvement followed. Smuggling continued, however, and a year or two later the new agent writes: 'We had a great seizure here last week, 34 casks of brandy covered overhead in ye bark in ye Barkhouse, but none concerned about the Furnace except John Muncaster who had the key.'

Such, in brief outline, was the Bonaw that Ann Tyson came to know well during her summer visits there with the Knotts. There were no raids by Highlanders resulting in the wrecking of buildings and the murder of workmen as there had been at Invergarry; but she had plenty to tell never the less. And evidently she had an eager, even avid, listener in William Wordsworth during his early years at Hawkshead School.

Richard and William Wordsworth become pupils at Hawkshead School—John Gibson, attorney, and his connection with John Words-worth—identification of Ann Tyson's house in Hawkshead—Isaac Postlethwaite—Philip Braithwaite

John Wordsworth of Cockermouth, attorney-at-law, and law agent to Sir James Lowther, afterwards first Earl of Lonsdale, notes in his private memorandum book that his sons Richard and William went to Hawkshead School at Whitsuntide 1779, Mr. Cookson paying the entrance fee;[1] and that in December 1779, he himself paid Hugh Tyson £10. 10s. 0d. for 'half a Year's Board from Entry', and a further 10s. 6d. for half a year's washing, these payments being for the two boys. Their ages when they entered the school were eleven and nine, Richard having been born on 19 May 1768 and William on 7 April 1770. The Mr. Cookson who paid the entrance fee was their maternal grandfather William Cookson, a Penrith mercer whose wife Dorothy was a Crackenthorpe of Newbiggin Hall, and whose daughter Ann had married John Wordsworth at Penrith on 5 February 1766, and had been buried there on 11 March 1778, aged thirty. On her death, if not before, her five children—Richard, William, Dorothy, John, and Christopher—went to live with their Cookson grandparents at Penrith; and it seems to have been from

---

[1] See photograph, Plate 4. Mark Reed (*Wordsworth: the Chronology of the Early Years, 1770–1779*, p. 47) suggests that John Wordsworth throughout his account book is using 'Whitsuntide' to refer to the Scottish term day, 15 May. John Wordsworth's book is most properly described by his own title: 'Rental of Lands & Schedule of real & Personal Securities belonging to Mr Wordsworth', but it does include accounts of payments for his children's education.

Following other scholars T.W.T. has read 'M^ts Cookson' as 'Mr Cookson', but the illustration shows that 'M^ts' is unequivocally 'Mistress': on the opposite page is a note: 'Gave M^ts Tyson for her Additional Trouble and Attendce upon Richard. 1. 1. 0' [one guinea].

there that the two eldest first went to Hawkshead School in the summer of 1779, a year for which William Cookson presented his son-in-law with a very big bill.

In Book V of *The Prelude* William Wordsworth tells of an experience he had during his first week at Hawkshead. It was late in the day and wandering alone he chanced to cross

> One of those open fields, which, shaped like ears,
> Make green peninsulas on Esthwaite's Lake
>
> (V.457–8)

and from there, though it was twilight, he saw distinctly on the opposite shore a pile of clothes, left, as he supposed, by a bather. He watched until it grew dark, but no one claimed them. Evidently he had gone as far south as Strickland Ees, the big ear-shaped peninsula on the western side of Esthwaite Water; and by the time he got back to the Tysons it must have been about midnight. When it was light again, the unclaimed garments on the eastern side, where, opposite Strickland Ees, the road from Windermere ferry to Hawkshead approaches and then skirts the lake shore, inevitably told their sad tale; and a party of men in a boat, with the aid of grappling irons and long poles, tried to recover the body. William Wordsworth cannot have been far away, for he continues:

> At length, the dead Man, 'mid that beauteous scene
> Of trees, and hills and water, bolt upright
> Rose with his ghastly face; a spectre shape
> Of terror even! and yet no vulgar fear,
> Young as I was, a Child not nine years old,
> Possess'd me; for my inner eye had seen
> Such sights before, among the shining streams
> Of Fairy Land, the Forests of Romance.
>
> (V.470–7)

The Hawkshead Parish Registers for the year 1779 complete the story in these words: 'James Jackson School-Master of Sawrey was Drowned in Esthead-water in Bathing June ye 18th Buried June ye 20th in C^h Yard Aged 21 Years'.

Here, then, is further proof that William Wordsworth first

entered Hawkshead School in June 1779,[1] only a week or two before the end of the Spring Half. And here, in his statement that he was 'not nine years old', is the reason for the assumption generally accepted at one time that he first went there in 1778, for the error appears in the 1850 text of *The Prelude*, as well as in the much more recently printed 1805 text from which I have been quoting. In this text there is another and worse underestimate of his age; in Book I, in the passage which begins:

> Well I call to mind
> ('Twas at an early age, ere I had seen
> Nine summers) when upon the mountain slope
> The frost and breath of frosty wind had snapp'd
> The last autumnal crocus, 'twas my joy
> To wander half the night among the Cliffs
> And the smooth Hollows, where the woodcocks ran
> Along the open turf.   (I.309-16)

It goes on to tell of woodcock-snaring on moonlit nights, apparently on Keen Ground High and Charity High, two grassy hills of morainic origin which lie between Hawkshead and Hawkshead Moor; of his 'shoulder all with springes hung' as he made his way there; of his anxious scudding from snare to snare after they had been set; and of how

> Sometimes it befel
> In these night-wanderings, that a strong desire
> O'erpower'd my better reason, and the bird
> Which was the captive of another's toils
> Became my prey; and when the deed was done
> I heard among the solitary hills
> Low breathings coming after me, and sounds
> Of undistinguishable motion, steps
> Almost as silent as the turf they trod.   (I.324-32)

[1] Only if one takes literally (as surely one should not) Wordsworth's assertion that the episode of the drowning was in 'the very week/When I was first entrusted to the care/Of that sweet valley' (*Prelude*, V.450-2) need one question that Wordsworth first went to Hawkshead at Whitsuntide 1779. T.W.T.'s argument is implicitly directed against Gordon Wordsworth's statement that ' "At Whitsuntide" appears to mean after the summer holidays' ('The Boyhood of Wordsworth', *Cornhill Magazine*, CXXI, 1920, 415), and against those who held that Wordsworth began at Hawkshead in 1778.

This was in his first Autumn Half at Hawkshead School, as the 1850 text makes plain; and although only nine years old, he had in fact already seen ten summers. What the Tysons, then in their middle sixties, felt and did about these nocturnal ventures we shall never know, I fear; nor even whether they were in the habit of locking or bolting their outside door before they went to bed.

About a fortnight after Richard and William Wordsworth were first sent to Hawkshead their father seems to have been there on business in his capacity of Coroner of the Seigniory of Millom, a large tract of territory in south-west Cumberland, bounded by the sea and the rivers Esk and Duddon, which Sir James Lowther had purchased in 1774.[1] At any rate, in 1932 the late William Heelis, a solicitor with offices at Hawkshead and Ambleside, noticed on the back of an old conveyance executed in the summer of 1779 a pencil note dated 25 June (or just possibly 28 June) which read: 'Customary Tenements in the Lordship of Millom', and underneath 'Received of John Wordsworth when he left me the Sum of Two Guineas for information and advices tendered instanter and for copies of the Writings to be sent him by Daniell Satterthwaite the week after next.' That is the note as William Heelis gave it to me, but he explained that in the original a number of the words were abbreviated. He said the handwriting in both note and conveyance was that of John Gibson, a Hawkshead attorney. At the time I thought it strange that he should have been consulted about customary holdings in the lordship of Millom, but discovered later that he had connections with the parish of Millom, and may well have come from there to Hawkshead, of which he was not a native. I noticed, too, when examining the Hawkshead Registers that his son George Graham Gibson died of a fever on 26 June 1779, at the age of twelve, and was

---

[1] John Wordsworth took into his keeping most of the estates Sir James Lowther purchased for his election purposes. The Millom estates of Sir Hedworth Williamson were bought in 1774 after the latter's financial failure, but matters were still not settled five years afterwards. John Wordsworth explained to Sir James on 10 December 1779 that Edmund Gibson, Sir Hedworth's solicitor, refused to finalize the transaction until he himself was paid (The Records, The Castle, Carlisle). It was perhaps about this difficult situation that John Gibson had advice to give. For more about John Gibson see below pp. 181–90. Edmund Gibson, solicitor, lived at Whicham, near Millom. The Parish Registers there have no mention of Edmund or of John Gibson.

buried in the churchyard two days later. In the following years William Wordsworth became well acquainted with John Gibson, whose quips and pranks delighted many generations of Hawkshead schoolboys. Daniel Satterthwaite, by whom he was to send 'copies of the Writings', was a Cockermouth saddler with whom John Wordsworth had dealings. He came frequently, perhaps regularly, to Hawkshead Market, and contributed 10s. 6d. towards the cost of rebuilding the Market House in 1790.

After their fortnight (or less) at Hawkshead School in June 1779, Richard and William Wordsworth were on holiday until the beginning of August, when they returned to the Tysons for the start of the Autumn Half. The question of where Hugh and Ann were then living, whether it was in Hawkshead Town or at Colthouse, a hamlet on the other side of the valley and therefore in the Claife Quarter of the parish, is answered in a document I found in the church safe in 1951. It is a detailed account, running to six pages, of the sums received in the course of a 'Parish Collection in August 1779, on His Majesty's Letter, for the use of the Society for the Propagation of the Gospel in Foreign Parts'. The first three pages record the sums subscribed by householders in the Hawkshead Quarter or Division of the parish, that is in Hawkshead Town, Hawkshead Field, and Hawkshead Fieldhead; and among others, by Hugh Tyson, who contributed 6d., and the Misses 'Nevison', who gave a like amount. His name occurs on page 1, and theirs on page 2; pages on which most of the other names are known to be those of inhabitants of Hawkshead Town, since they are so recorded in the Parish Registers. Hugh Tyson's name appears immediately after that of Myles Robinson, a house-carpenter who lived at the foot of 'the highway from Hawkshead Town to Walker-ground', or Vicarage Lane as it is now called, his house being on the south side of the road. I know this because I once owned it, and had title-deeds for it going back to 1744. Its side is exactly opposite the front of the house which has been known since the latter part of the nineteenth century as Ann Tyson's Cottage, and alternatively as Wordsworth's Lodge, which in local speech means the place where he lodged or boarded. Its proximity to Myles Robinson's suggests, even if it does not prove, that this house on the north side of Vicarage Lane, just after it has passed through Grandy Nook, was Hugh and Ann Tyson's home in 1779.

Ann Tyson's Cottage stands a few yards back from the road, on the farther side of what was once a small open square but is now an enclosed garden. Built somewhere about 1700, in a style whose not uncomely plainness is relieved only by a porch and a drip-course,[1] it has two ground-floor windows, one on each side of the porch, and two above, of which that on the right as one faces the house is not as tall as its fellow. This shorter upstairs window lights the room identified as Wordsworth's by reason of his name being carved on the window-seat in it.[2] Little was thought of this until a keen Wordsworthian, believed to have been Professor Knight, got to know about it in the 1870s. On making inquiries in 1906, I learnt that the window-seat in Wordsworth's room, being badly decayed, had been replaced by a new one some twenty years earlier, but that the joiner who did the work, John Brockbank of Hannakin, had made and kept a copy of the names carved on the old seat. When I visited him, he told me that he had in fact made two copies, the first for 'an off-come gentleman who set great store by them', and the second for himself, 'just in case as you might say'. He still had his copy, I found; and later in the day he showed it to me. It read:

PHIL^P BRAITHWAITE

1781

WM WORDSWORTH

He was sure that the date had been carved by Philip Braithwaite, who was a 'better hand at the job', he said, 'than what Wordsworth was'. Aged eighty-two when he died in 1915, John Brockbank could just remember an old Philip Braithwaite, a lame man who

---

[1] Mr. V. J. H. Coward, the present owner, tells me that the original large stone slabs of the roof had to be replaced in his father's time—about 1900; and that the stone sides of the porch, much weathered, broke about 1955 and have been replaced by wood.

[2] Wordsworth also carved his name on a desk in Hawkshead Grammar School, and later, he, Coleridge, and Dorothy carved their initials on the Rock of Names, fragments of which survived the blasting when Thirlmere was turned into a reservoir. The poem 'To Joanna' turns somewhat humorously on an incident in which the poet is upbraided for such chiselling.

lived at Far Sawrey, and had, he thought, been schoolmaster there. But before telling what I know of him, I must return for a moment to Ann Tyson's Cottage to notice that in recent times, when layers of old paint were cleaned off the sole of a small window-opening at the stair-head, the initials R. W. came to light. Deeply scratched, not carved, they could have been the work of Richard Wordsworth, as the sole is an old one I believe.

I had better glance, too, at the house on Church Hill latterly known as Wordsworth's Cottage. Two houses at some time in its history, it stands a little way back from the road, between the pillared house at the top and a ginnel or narrow passage leading to the Town Spout or Spout House. It was occupied during the latter years of the nineteenth century by Isaac Hodgson, postman, and his wife Hannah, both of whom died there, he in January 1907, aged seventy-eight, and she in August 1912, aged eighty-two. The claim that Wordsworth once boarded there originated with Isaac; or so I was told in the summer of 1907 by John Brockbank, and also by Isaac Postlethwaite, a shoemaker then aged sixty-four. Both were old friends of his, and both were with him when he first advanced it waggishly, ostensibly to help a gentleman who seems to have been puzzled, as well he might be, by Wordsworth's reference to the 'famous brook . . . boxed Within our garden'.[1] 'You'll have heard speak of the Town Spout', Isaac remarked to him; 'but happen you didn't know, sir, as it runs under my garden'. They were in the Queen's Head, and the gentleman called for another round of drinks. 'Yes,' said Isaac, 'from what you've been saying, sir, it's beginning to look as if it was our house where Wordsworth lodged as a lad.' Greatly interested, the unwary stranger plied him with questions; and then, after a time, they went off together to consider the matter further on the spot. None of Isaac's companions thought for a moment that he was serious; nor was he, it seems. But as time passed he began to claim with growing conviction that his house on Church Hill had been 'Wordsworth's first lodge' at Hawkshead, and even pointed out the window of the upstairs room that had been his; a window shown in the reproduction in Eric Robertson's *Wordsworthshire* of a drawing by Arthur Tucker of the Hodgsons' house as

[1] *Prelude*, IV.40–1.

seen from the garden at the rear.[1] But according to Mrs. Hodgson, the identification of this room as Wordsworth's was based neither on local tradition nor on any discovery that she or her husband had ever made, but solely on the word of a stranger whom she had shown over the house, presumably the gentleman Isaac had first met in the Queen's Head. I trust I have not been unfair to either of them.[2]

For information about Philip Braithwaite of Far Sawrey I was referred to Miss Mary Hodgson of Greenend, Colthouse, who in her young days, I was told, had known both him and William Wordsworth, and would have much to say about them if she was in the mood. This little old lady, who died in April 1915 at the age of ninety-two, though reputedly rather difficult, proved to be the best helper I had during my early researches into Wordsworth's Hawkshead. She was the last survivor of the children of Braithwaite and Martha Hodgson of Greenend; her father, who died there in 1861, was a son of Thomas Hodgson of Briers, Far Sawrey, where he was born in 1781; whilst her mother, whose life-span was from 1793 to 1875, was a daughter of Henry Forrest of Fieldhead. Miss Mary was acquainted with Philip Braithwaite during the last twenty to twenty-five years of his life, when despite his lameness he was a not infrequent visitor to Greenend. He owed a good deal to her grandfather and father, and during her childhood he nearly always brought her some little present. Wordsworth she first met when she was eighteen, and had gone with her mother to call on Mrs. Benson Harrison, a daughter of Wordsworth's cousin Richard, at Green Bank, Ambleside.[3] Self-conscious, and all the more so because of her diminutive stature, she was standing all alone in the room, when Wordsworth noticed, and came across to talk to her. This kindness meant much to her; and from then onwards she took a great interest in him, and especially in his school-days at Hawkshead, of which he spoke on that occasion. But my present concern is with Philip Braithwaite; and of him she had a tale to tell that is worth repeating, and supplementing from documentary and other sources.

[1] Published 1911, p. 102.

[2] The unwary stranger of this anecdote appears to have been Canon Rawnsley whose cheerful speculations about the Church Hill house are contained in letters to William Knight (see *Poetical Works of Wordsworth*, ed. Knight, 1883, III, pp. 410–13).

[3] See Additional Note for p. 165, Appendix V.

This Philip Braithwaite—for I shall have to mention two others—came to Far Sawrey from London as a small boy. His father, who had gone there from Hawkshead, was a hatter; and, though Miss Hodgson did not remember his Christian name, it is almost safe to identify him as the Philip Braithwaite, hatter, who married Alice Taylor at Hawkshead on 27 August 1759, for he, like his bride, was 'of this parish', and there is no later mention of him in the registers. Anyhow, young Philip's father did not do very well for himself in London, neither as a journeyman, when he had a very mean master, nor when he set up in business on his own account. Then, at an early age, both he and his wife died of a sickness that was raging, leaving two or three young children, who became a charge on the parish. Philip, who was born in 1764, if the age assigned to him when he died on 12 October 1849, is correct, seems to have been their only son. Later he was adopted by Philip Braithwaite, a blacksmith at Far Sawrey who had no children of his own; his uncle, Miss Hodgson said, or great-uncle. The latter appears to be correct, for there is no doubt that he is the Philip Braithwaite of Far Sawrey, Smith, who died on 28 April 1782, aged seventy-six. A son of John Braithwaite of Peppers, Far Sawrey, he was baptized at Hawkshead on 21 August 1705, and married there on 26 October 1730, to Eleanor Maber. He and his wife, who died in September 1772, had no children baptized there.

When he first came to Far Sawrey, young Philip was weakly and lame, but he grew into a strong lad, with one leg, however, either slightly deformed or a bit shorter than the other. He went for a while to the little school at Far Sawrey that had been built and endowed by William Braithwaite of Fold in 1766; and for a while he helped his great-uncle, by now a widower, in the smithy. Then at the age of twelve he was apprenticed to a farmer, that being what he wanted, and had always wanted he used to say. He did well as a farmer's boy; but after a few years, four to five it would seem, he had an accident whilst at work and, as it made him a good deal lamer than he was before, his master asked to be relieved of him. It was considered to be a reasonable request and was granted. I have a lingering doubt as to the boy's lameness before the accident, but no evidence to the contrary. Its sequel, the ending of his apprenticeship, upset him; and for some reason he never forgave the doctor who attended him. That was why, Miss Mary thought, he would never have a doctor when he was schoolmaster at Sawrey and in his old age; a fact that grew into the legend that 'He never, during his long life, had occasion for the services of a doctor', to quote from an obituary notice of him in the *Westmorland Gazette* of 20 October 1849. A second upset followed, for his great-uncle, whose health was beginning to fail and earnings diminish, declared that he could not maintain the boy; and that, if he could not support himself, he would have to go back to London, to the parish from which he had come to Far Sawrey.

From this fate he was saved by Miss Mary's grandfather, Thomas Hodgson of Briers, who was only a young man at the time. He boarded Philip and clothed him, and whenever he could found work for him to do. But the boy's usefulness to him was very limited, and he decided that if possible he must have more schooling, and that in any event his place of Legal Settlement must be determined and certified in case he ever had to seek parish relief. Thomas Hodgson's first move was to get him admitted to Hawkshead School as a member of the Writing Master's Class, and to arrange for him to board with Hugh and Ann Tyson. The date can be fixed, as Philip Braithwaite told Miss Hodgson that the Master of the School was then Edward Christian; and his tenure of the office was limited to the Spring Half of 1781.[1] Philip, who can have seen little of him, spoke of him as a kind man; and certainly it was considerate of him to allow the boy, who was then sixteen, to join the Writing Master's Class, which was intended for much younger local boys whose requirements did not extend beyond reading, writing, and arithmetic. At first Philip hated this going back to school, but he stayed long enough to reach the top of the class, and to be taught mensuration and surveying, and how to keep accounts. He was still with the Tysons when John Wordsworth first came to board with them in January 1782, but left them very soon after. His schooling had been interrupted, however, by a visit to London for the purpose of getting his place of Legal Settlement certified; a visit which was not at all to his liking, and from which he returned as quickly as possible. According

---

[1] In fact, Christian was Master from July 1781 to July 1782, see p. 342. *The Cumberland Pacquet* noted his appointment 5 June 1781. See also p. 127.

to Miss Hodgson, he told his inquisitors that, when he could leave school and start earning, he would never need maintenance or monetary help from anyone. He never wanted to see London again, and never did.

There is no doubt whatever that he is the Philip Braithwaite who carved his name and the date 1781 on the window-seat in Ann Tyson's Cottage. And there is little doubt that he is the Hawkshead schoolboy referred to by Wordsworth when he is telling in Book VII of *The Prelude* of the visions he had as a child of the many splendours and wonders to be seen in London. After wondering

> Whether the bolt of childhood's Fancy Shot
> For me beyond its ordinary mark
>   (VII.88–9 (1850))

he continues:

>   but in our flock of boys
> Was One, a cripple from his birth, whom chance
> Summoned from school to London; fortunate
> And envied traveller! When the Boy returned,
> After short absence, curiously I scanned
> His mien and person, nor was free, in sooth,
> From disappointment, not to find some change
> In look and air, from that new region brought,
> As if from Fairy-land. Much I questioned him;
> And every word he uttered, on my ears
> Fell flatter than a cagéd parrot's note,
> That answers unexpectedly awry,
> And mocks the prompter's listening.
>   (VII.90–102 (1850))

Surely the boy was Philip Braithwaite. But was he in fact a cripple from birth, or could it be that, by never telling of his accident, or in some other way, he led his young fellow boarder at the Tysons to suppose that he had been born lame? All I can usefully add is that he is unlikely to have told him either of his accident or the purpose of his visit to London, two subjects on which he was very touchy, and sometimes a bit 'queer', to use Miss Mary Hodgson's word when speaking of the mood that came over him when either was mentioned in his presence. It should be remembered, too, that William

Wordsworth was only eleven when Philip Braithwaite, then seventeen, left the Tysons, and virtually passed out of his life.

Miss Hodgson had gathered a little information from each about the other. Wordsworth told her that Philip Braithwaite, though too lame to take an active part in their games, could walk up to twenty miles with the aid of a stick, and instanced long expeditions on foot which they had made together. The longest was when they crossed Lake Windermere at the ferry, and then went on to explore the Winster valley, which was new ground to both of them. On another occasion they went to Dale Park, where they found a recently abandoned charcoal-burner's hut, and decided to spend the night in it, but changed their minds in the end. And in the autumn they made their way to Graythwaite woods in search of nuts, an expedition then popular with Hawkshead schoolboys, it seems. Wordsworth has a poem on the subject, 'Nutting', but in it there is no mention of a companion. Philip Braithwaite told Miss Hodgson that when he boarded with the Tysons he never had much conversation with Richard Wordsworth, but that William talked to him quite a lot, and was always asking him questions about one thing or another, anything in fact that he, Philip, happened to know something about because of his greater age and wider experience. He saw very little of John, but thought that perhaps he was the nicest of the Wordsworth boys he had known.

On leaving the Tysons early in 1782 Philip Braithwaite returned to Far Sawrey and remained there. How he subsisted for the next fifteen years or so is something of a mystery. There is nothing in print about this period of his life, and Miss Hodgson did not know much more than that her grandfather Thomas Hodgson and others employed him periodically to do clerical work, or cast up accounts, or maybe a bit of surveying. To this I can add that in a deed executed in 1792, in which he witnessed the signature of one of the Sawrey Braithwaites, he described himself as a 'Scrivener', which means, I take it, that he was a professional penman and copyist. I was told about this deed by the late W. H. Baines of Near Sawrey. A temporary job which Philip claimed to have had was referred to by Miss Hodgson as 'helping Clarke in his surveys'. I did not understand at the time, but discovered later that she meant James Clarke, land-surveyor and landlord of the Swan Inn, Penrith, who in 1787 published *A Survey of the Lakes of Cumberland, Westmorland, and Lancashire, together with an Account, Historical, Topographical and Descriptive of the Adjacent Country*, a second edition of which appeared in 1789.

It was not until the end of the eighteenth century that Philip Braithwaite was appointed Master of Sawrey School. In a short history of the school by Alexander Craig Gibson, 'using nearly the words of a communication respecting it, made to a local newspaper in 1853', it is stated that 'his recommendations to the charge . . . [were] that he was a sober young man, and had not been thirteen weeks to school in his life.' Sober he certainly was, unlike his immediate predecessor during his later years as Master; but he was not very young; and the canard, for such it was, about the extreme brevity of his own schooling, ought not to have been given the semblance of fact by A. C. Gibson, whose history of the school was included in a paper on 'Hawkshead Parish' read before the Historic Society of Lancashire and Cheshire, and published in its *Transactions* in 1866.[1]

The stipend of the Sawrey schoolmaster was small. He was allowed to have the interest on the £300 with which the school was endowed by its founder, and on the £40 bequeathed to it by Thomas Braithwaite in 1795; but the quarterly charge was limited to 1s. per pupil, and even that was not payable for six poor children nominated by the trustees. If the attendance was thirty—and Philip Braithwaite raised it to that—the reward for his labours would be about £22 a year, which was less than the earnings of a skilled manual worker such as a joiner or a waller. And this was at a time when there is mention in a Hawkshead Vestry minute, dated 26 December 1800, of 'the High price of every necessary Article of Life'. Eventually something was done to improve the master's pay. In a Charity Commissioners' Report dated January 1820, it is stated that the 'interest of £300 and of £40, amounting annually to £16 16s., is paid regularly to Philip Braithwaite, the present schoolmaster'; after which come the words: 'On account of the insufficiency of the master's income, the quarterage was raised a few years since by the trustees, with the approbation of the inhabitants, from 1s. which was prescribed by the trust deed, to 3s. for reading, and an additional shilling for writing and arith-

[1] Pp. 153–74; for his remarks on Philip Braithwaite see pp. 165–6.

1. From an undated water-colour of Wordsworth's Lodge, Hawkshead. After being used for Nonconformist meetings in the mid-nineteenth century (up to 1862), the room up the steps was for some years a tramps' lodging. Artist unknown.

2. Belmount, built in 1774 by Reginald Brathwaite, Vicar of Hawkshead.

metic respectively.' There were 'between 20 and 30 scholars', including four paupers' children educated free of charge; so Philip may have been receiving somewhere about £40 a year in all. (In 1826 Miss Ann Braithwaite left £100, the interest on which was to be paid to the Master of Sawrey School.) At all times attentive to his duties, and diligent in their performance, he won the regard of his pupils, we are told, and the esteem of their parents; 'while his simple-minded integrity', says Gibson, 'gained him the respect of the villagers'.

The school, a little whitewashed building with a tiny belfry, was situated at Far Sawrey, on a rocky knoll which had previously been part of 'the waste'. Soon after its erection it was licensed for public worship, and for a time religious services were held there; but long before Philip Braithwaite became Master of the school these had been allowed to lapse. With the approval of the three school trustees, two of whom were Thomas Hodgson and William Taylor of Briers, he revived the services, and for many years read Evening Prayer on Sunday afternoons in the schoolroom. Another thing he did was to form and train a choir, which he himself conducted. It met in the schoolroom, and from time to time gave concerts there. It was much appreciated, and after a time attracted members from Hawkshead, Miss Mary Hodgson told me. Philip, who never married or employed a housekeeper, was then living at Spout House, Far Sawrey; and there he remained for the rest of his life.

When their schoolmaster had passed the age of seventy, and there were still no signs of his retiring, some Sawrey ratepayers began to say that it was time he made way for a younger and better qualified man. Their main argument was that he was a bad speller, and therefore unfit to teach others to spell. They also stressed his limited education, and probably exaggerated the shortness of his schooling as a boy, for the canard that he 'had not been thirteen weeks to school in his life' seems to have originated at this time. On the other hand, there were those, and among others Braithwaite Hodgson, for long a trustee of the school, who did not want a change of master, and could see no need for it. During the next two controversial years, however, many of his supporters must have been converted to the view that there must be a change, for at a specially convened ratepayers meeting at the end of this period there was a very large

E

majority in favour of it. As a result, the trustees asked Philip Braithwaite to tender his resignation. This he refused to do, on the ground that it would not be in the best interests of the school. So they had no option but to dismiss him. That was in the summer of 1837, after he had served the school for a period of years variously estimated as forty, nearly forty, and upwards of forty.

Following his dismissal at the age of seventy-three, Philip Braithwaite lived for another twelve years, during which he neither sought nor received any financial assistance. He may have earned a trifle now and then, but for the most part he was dependent on his savings. How he could have saved much of his meagre, and for a long time inadequate, income, it is hard to see; nevertheless he had, and during the remainder of his long life he had enough to live on. There was wonder at this; and more wonder when it was learnt after his death in October 1849, that in his will he had bequeathed the sum of £300, less legacy duty, in trust for the benefit of the master *bona fide* teaching the school at Far Sawrey.[1] One last thing about him: having heard something of his story from Braithwaite Hodgson, in or about the year 1845, his one-time fellow boarder, William Wordsworth, looked in to see him, and was given a glass of elderberry wine, the only strong drink he ever allowed himself to taste, and that but rarely.

Gilbert Crackenthorp, Kendal schoolmaster—the Rev. Reginald Brathwaite—Wordsworth's visits to Belmount—book club

And now I must return to Hawkshead in the year 1781. Entries for this year in John Wordsworth's Memorandum Book show that his

---

[1] When the will of 'Philip Braithwaite . . . Yeoman' was proved on 27 October 1849 his estate was declared to be 'under the Value of Six Hundred Pounds'. The will, made in 1848, in his eighty-fourth year, is handsomely penned and suggests that Philip, when a scrivener, had had experience in a law office. The legacy had a proviso —a proud gesture—forcing the Sawrey community to recognize that Philip's wish was to serve the school: 'and it is my will and mind that for the purpose of perpetuating the remembrance of the aforesaid gift or Legacy of three hundred pounds in favour of the said School at Sawrey aforesaid I do hereby order and direct that a full extract of all the words in this my will respecting the same shall be recorded in the Townships Books of Sawrey aforesaid and further that a stone Tablet shall be fixed up in the School house there with an appropriate inscription briefly setting forth the amount and object of the said Legacy or Bequest under this my Will.' (Lancashire Record Office.)

eldest son was seriously ill in the summer. They record that he gave Mrs. Tyson a guinea 'for her Additional Trouble & Attend[an]ce upon Richard'; that Dr. Atkinson's fee 'for Journey to attend Richard' was a guinea and a half; and that a Mr. Crackenthorp, who paid it, had been repaid in full in the autumn. This Mr. Crackenthorp was a Kendal man with Hawkshead connections, as I will show in a moment, and not one of the Crackenthorpes of Newbiggin Hall from whom John Wordsworth was descended on his mother's side; and that being so, it can safely be assumed that the Dr. Atkinson he called in was the John Atkinson, M.D., of Kendal who died there in 1788. For minor ailments the Wordsworth boys were attended by Charles Robinson of Hawkshead, whose qualifications did not include a degree in medicine; but they hardly ever required his services.

During the first two and a half years his sons were at Hawkshead School, John Wordsworth made a good deal of use of the 'Revd Mr Crackenthorp', as he styles him. At the beginning of the year 1780 he owed him £1. 13s. 8d. 'for sundry Disbursm[en]ts' during the previous half year, and sent him this sum by the boys when they returned to Hawkshead on 10 January. For the Spring Half 1780, which ended on 13 June, Mr. Crackenthorp's bill, which John Wordsworth paid on that day, must have included Cockpennies,[1] for it came to £5. 6s. 10d. Some entries lack detail: thus for the Spring Half 1781, all that is noted is the total, £17. 2s. 4d., for all bills delivered at Whitsuntide, and that the money to meet them in full was sent to Hawkshead by Mr. Cookson's man. But an entry, dated 24 January 1782, reads: 'Paid Hugh Tyson in full of his, Mr Crackenthorp's William Mackereth's and Jos: Wilson's [bills] £15. 14s. 1d.'. So for two and half years at least the Rev. Mr. Crackenthorp was in touch with Richard and William Wordsworth at Hawkshead; which is a sufficient reason, I think, for saying briefly who, and what manner of man, he was.

Said to have been born at Kendal in 1715, he was baptized there on 17 June 1717 in the name of Gilbert; he was the younger son of Richard Crackenthorp, an attorney descended from the Crackenthorps of Little Strickland in north Westmorland. They were a

[1] See below, p. 90.

junior branch of the Newbiggin Hall family, their progenitor being a John Crackenthorp who died at Little Strickland in 1594. As a boy, Gilbert Crackenthorp attended Kendal Grammar School, from which he was admitted to St. John's College, Cambridge, as a sizar on 29 May 1734, at the age of eighteen. Six years later he was ordained deacon, and licensed to the curacy of Astwood, Buckinghamshire. Then on 7 June 1743, on the nomination of the Mayor, Aldermen, and Burgesses of the Borough of Kirkby Kendal, he was licensed by the Bishop of Chester to be Master of the Grammar School in his native town. The next we hear of him is in 1745, when the rebel army, six thousand strong, commanded by Prince Charles Edward Stuart, the Young Pretender, reached Kendal on its southward march on the evening of 22 November, and halted there over the 24th, which was a Sunday. On the morning of that day 'the principal officers, with three ladies one of whom was the lady Ogylvie, attended divine service in the church. The service was performed by Mr. Crackenthorp, master of the grammar school; Dr. Symonds, the vicar, having quitted the town through fear.'[1]

On 10 April 1760, 'Gilbert Crackenthorp of the Parish of Kirkby Kendal in the County of Westmorland Clerk and Ann Ridgeway of this Parish Spinster' were married at Hawkshead by licence. He was then forty-four, and his bride only four or five years younger. She was a daughter of Robert and Jane Ridgeway, and probably a niece of the Samuel Ridgeway who was 'Steward of the Furnace' at Cunsey from 1712 until his death at an early age in 1722. There is evidence that Gilbert Crackenthorp knew Hawkshead long before 1760, but no hint as to why he should have done so, nor any information as to when Robert Ridgeway, who was not a native of the parish, first came to live there. His daughter Ann had rather less than ten years of married life, for she died on 17 January 1770. There is a memorial to her on the floor of the Bellingham Chapel in Kendal Parish Church: it is in Latin, and contains the loving words 'Charissimæ conjugis'. Next to it is a memorial inscription in English to her successor. It reads: 'Here lie the Remains of Elizabeth Wife of Mr Gilbt. Crackenthorp, Master of the Grammar School in Kendal,

[1] See C. Nicholson, *The Annals of Kendal*, p. 136; also Additional Notes, Appendix V.

Daughter of Robt. & Elizabeth Wilson of the Coffee House in Highgate, who died the 2ᵈ of January 1774 aged 53'.

Robert Wilson, stuff weaver, father of Gilbert Crackenthorp's second wife, bought the White Hart Inn, Butchers' Row, Highgate, in 1711 for £248, and went to live there as landlord, but continued to be a weaver as well.[1] During his lifetime the inn became known as Robbin's (i.e. Robert's) Coffee House, and later as the Coffee House. In the second half of the eighteenth century, when his daughter Elizabeth may have been landlady for a time before her marriage, it was the favourite meeting place of the more sociable of Kendal's leading citizens, especially those who liked to hear and discuss the latest news. A newsroom, believed to be the first in the town, was established there in 1779; and in the 1780s, when coaches were a novelty, the Coffee House was their stopping place and booking office in Kendal. The newsroom was frequented by the Rev. Thomas Symonds, Vicar of Kendal from 1745 to 1789, who had become a Doctor of Divinity in 1773; the Rev. Caleb Rotherham, the Younger, minister of the Presbyterian, later Unitarian, chapel in the Market Place from 1756 to 1796; and the Rev. Gilbert Crackenthorp. In his unpublished *Memoir of My Own Life*, John Ireland (1735–1808), who began as a handloom weaver and became a woollen manufacturer, mentions that once at the Coffee House he heard the Rev. Gilbert Crackenthorp and the Rev. Caleb Rotherham having a great argument, 'the one a match for the other', about the war in America, which was of special interest in Kendal as it stopped for the time being the export of its frieze—light woollen cloths known as Kendal Cottons—to Virginia and Maryland. This mention of Gilbert Crackenthorp is prefaced by the statement that he had a reputation in the town as a knowledgeable and witty talker, skilled in argument.

John Ireland's main reference to him is as Master of the Grammar School, to which he, John, had sent his son John. The boy did well enough at first, but later his father was dissatisfied with his progress, and thought of sending him to Hawkshead Grammar School

---

[1] See *Local Chronology: Kendal* (Kendal and London, 1865); and for the rest of this discussion of Crackenthorp, see John F. Curwen, *Kirkbie Kendall* (1900), especially pp. 60 and 171.

instead. John Ireland was born and bred at Hawkshead: he kept close contact with it, as he went to the market there nearly every week to buy yarn: he knew that under the Rev. James Peake its school had grown rapidly in numbers and repute; and almost next door to it he had a sister, Mary, with whom his son could board. But he did not relish having to tell Mr. Crackenthorp, who had known him since he was a boy, and who was always very affable when they met. Then the Master's second wife died; and before long it was said that he was retiring. On hearing this, John Ireland lost little time in calling at his house in Kirkland to let him know that he thought of 'sending young John to Hawkshead Grammar School for his last two or three years schooling. Mr Crackenthorpe approved of this. "It's the best thing you can do, John", he said. He always called me John. "There's no better School hereabouts, and no better School-master than James Peake. As a man, I hope I can hold my own with him. As an instructor, prompter, & admonisher of Youth, despite my years I am but a Journeyman, while he is a Master of the Craft, Mystery, or call it what you will, even a Profession if you like". Those were his words as near as makes no matter. The bit about the Journeyman and the Master caught my fancy, and I set them down as soon as I got home.' For that we may be grateful, I think.

It was announced in the *Cumberland Pacquet* for 28 May 1774, that the 'free Grammar School of Kendal being vacant by the Resignation of the Rev. Mr. Gilbert Crackenthorpe, the Trustees give Notice that they intend to choose a Master on Monday, the 2nd day of July next. . . . The salary is £35 per Annum, with a neat and commodious Dwelling House, and from the situation, Trade, and Populousness of the Place and adjacent Country, the supposed other Emoluments to a diligent man would be very considerable; together with a fair and promising Prospect of a well endowed Chapel on the first Vacancy being annexed.' The supposed other emoluments were, I take it, the voluntary payments to the Master at entrance and annually at Shrovetide, the latter being known as Cockpennies. These gifts, which were customary, except in respect of very poor scholars, could treble or even quadruple a master's salary, provided he kept the number of boys in the school at a high level. This should not have been difficult at Kendal; but Gilbert Crackenthorp may not have been unfailingly diligent in this respect, as John Ireland, speaking of him as Master of the Grammar School, says the trouble with him was that he lacked ambition. In the parish of Kendal as it then existed there were fourteen chapelries in the country adjacent to the town; but at no time does he seem to have been curate of any of them. Nor did he seek a curacy when he retired at the age of fifty-eight or fifty-nine from the mastership of the Grammar School. Evidently he had enough to live on, including a £600 mortgage on the White Hart Inn or Coffee House which he may have had from his second wife.

After his retirement in 1774, Gilbert Crackenthorp seems to have spent a good deal of time at Hawkshead. I have noted that he signed the Marriage Registers as a witness on 21 November 1775, and as officiating minister on 10 April 1776. That he was in Hawkshead at times in 1779, 1780, and 1781 there is ample proof in John Wordsworth's Memorandum Book. And in his *Memoir*, John Ireland speaks of meeting him there on several occasions, one of which was in 1782, and another in 1785. But I have no later information about him, except that he made his will in 1787, and, according to the Parish Register at Kendal, was buried there on 26 May 1793, at the age of seventy-seven or seventy-eight, and not seventy-three as is stated on his tombstone. He had no son, and the two daughters his first wife bore him are said to have predeceased him.

According to John Ireland, 'Mr Crackenthorp stopped with two or three different people at Hawkshead, but more often than not it was with Mr Braithwaite at Belmont, the two being very good friends.' His host at Belmount was the Rev. Reginald Brathwaite, who was Vicar of Hawkshead, or more correctly its Stipendiary Minister, from 11 March 1762, to his death on 6 October 1809. A son of Gawen of Brathay, who was descended from the Brathwaites of Ambleside Hall, he was christened at Hawkshead on 9 March 1737/8, and educated under the Rev. Isaac Knipe at Ambleside, and then at St. John's College, Cambridge, where he graduated as thirteenth Wrangler in 1759, and two years later was elected a Fellow of the college. By then he had been ordained deacon, and at the beginning of 1762 King George III nominated him to be incumbent at Hawkshead, his institution taking place just four days after he was ordained priest. From 1764 to 1788 he was also Rector of Astwick and Vicar of Arlesey, Bedfordshire. In 1770, owing to his marriage, he had to relinquish his fellowship, and the college presented to him the Rectory of Brinkley, Cambridgeshire, which he retained for the rest of his life. But throughout his ministry he resided in the parish of Hawkshead, and served his other cures by proxy. From 1765 he was Domestic Chaplain to the Duke of Roxburgh; and from 1791 to 1802 he was Prebendary of St. Cross with Morgan in Llandaff Cathedral. This preferment he owed to Dr. Richard Watson, Bishop of Llandaff, who lived at Calgarth on the shores of Windermere, and rarely visited his diocese.

In 1770 Reginald Brathwaite married Frances, widow of Samuel Irton of Irton Hall, Cumberland, he being thirty-two at the time, and she six or seven years older. Only daughter and heiress of Robert Tubman, a Cockermouth mercer whose wife Martha was a Christian of Ewanrigg, she had married Samuel Irton (1714–66) in 1752. He had a business in London, and for most of their married life he and Frances lived in Crown Court, Old Soho, for he did not succeed to the Irton Hall property until 1762. During the four years he enjoyed it, he spent freely on it; which he could well afford to do, for as a merchant he grew wealthy at a relatively early age. In the parish of Hawkshead he bought the Hawkshead Hall and Grizedale Hall estates, amounting together to upwards of 1,000 acres, including 200 acres of valuable woodland. By him Frances had nine children, but among them were twins who died on the day they were born; and a daughter who lived for only a week. Of the remaining six she brought all, except her eldest son George, to Hawkshead when she married Reginald Brathwaite. By him she had two more sons: Reginald Tubman, baptized on 3 September 1772, and Gawen, baptized on 1 December 1774, the latter as 'Son of the Worshipful and Revd Mr Brathwaite, Minister of Hawkshead', for by then he had become a Justice of the Peace for the County of Lancaster. And in 1774, the vicarage at Walker Ground being too small for their needs, he built Belmount, a square mansion house in the Georgian style, situated on rising ground between Hawkshead Hall and Out-gate, at a little distance from the road, and with a fine view of Esth-waite Water to the south.[1]

It was here, a good half-mile from Hawkshead Town, that Gilbert Crackenthorp stayed with the Brathwaites; and here, too, that William Wordsworth seems to have been a not infrequent visitor, at any rate during his earlier years at Hawkshead School. He himself told Braithwaite Hodgson that as a schoolboy he had known the Rev. Reginald Brathwaite; and Canon Samuel Taylor, a great-great-grandson of Martha Irton, one of Frances's children, found among her letters and papers a statement that as a girl she had seen William Wordsworth 'on several occasions as he used to come to Belmount'. Her description of him as 'an eager young boy' makes it plain that he was then in his early years at Hawkshead School. Why he went to Belmount is not very obvious: Martha's brothers Edmund and Samuel Irton had left Hawkshead School by 1780, and gone, one to Trinity College, Cambridge, and the other into the East India Company's service; whilst her half-brothers Reginald and Gawen Brathwaite were as yet too young to go to the Grammar School. Was the attraction, then, the master of the house, who is known to have been kind and jovial, or the Rev. Gilbert Cracken-thorp when he was staying there; or could it have been Mrs. Brath-waite, who had previously lived first at Cockermouth and then in London? Martha Irton's use of the word 'eager' in describing him suggests that he asked a good many questions. I have no evidence of his visiting Belmount during his later years at school; but one of his friends, John Spedding of Armathwaite, certainly did so in 1785–6. This is revealed in letters written in those years to Martha Irton by

[1] Reginald did not die until 1809 but he appears to have left or to have been pre-pared to leave Belmount in 1806; Dorothy Wordsworth wrote to Catherine Clarkson on 6 November 1806 about attempts to find a house suitable for themselves and for Coleridge: 'We would have gone back to Grasmere, or taken a house near Hawks-head (Belmont), but this he [Coleridge] was against.' In the event the Wordsworths took Allan Bank at Grasmere. The view from Belmount, now the property of the National Trust, is still a remarkably fine one. It was the subject of a plate in *Select Views in Cumberland, Westmoreland and Lancashire* by Joseph Wilkinson (1810) for which Wordsworth wrote an introduction (later to develop into his own *Guide to the Lakes*). See Plate 5; and Introduction, p. xix.

his sister Mary, and published by Samuel Taylor under the title 'A Lakeland Young Lady's Letters'.[1] Taylor does not disclose the identity of the writer, but there is no doubt about it. In his paper on 'The Irtons of Irton Hall' he says that Martha Irton was born at Irton Hall on 3 May 1766, about three weeks after her father's death in London, and that on 3 January 1787, she married William Fell of Scathwaite and Ulverston.

Hawkshead was fortunate in having Reginald Brathwaite as incumbent at a time when the ministration of the clergy was at its lowest ebb, and in having him permanently resident in the parish. An energetic, purposeful man, he was conscientious in the discharge of his ministerial duties, and indeed zealous in some respects, as witness the number of adult baptisms during the earlier half of his incumbency of from forty-seven to forty-eight years. Moreover, he knew his parishioners intimately, and where there was need of his help he seems to have given it readily. One instance must suffice. George Robinson of Great Boat, otherwise Ferry Inn, had lost an eye in his youth 'from a potatoe wantonly thrown at him'. In his old age he lost the other as a result of an accident when following his trade, which was that of a wood-turner. The sequel to this accident, which happened about 1795, is related by Joseph Budworth in a footnote to his poem 'Windermere' (1798). 'Through the humane perseverance of the Rev. Mr. Brathwaite, of Belmount', he writes, 'in February he procured for him the ten-pound pension; and, I remember, on a stormy day, rode to inform him of it.' From Belmount to the Ferry is four and a half miles. In Hawkshead Church there is a memorial to the Rev. Reginald Brathwaite: 'His friends have caused this stone to be erected as a testimony of their respect to his memory.' He is said to have disliked such memorials; which may explain why there are none to his wife Frances, who died at Belmount on 18 July 1801, aged seventy, and was buried in Hawkshead Church, and to their elder son Reginald Tubman, who died on 29 July 1789, aged sixteen, and was buried at Hawkshead.

There are two further entries in John Wordsworth's Hawkshead accounts that are worth mentioning. The first, dated 1781, is 'Gave

[1] *Transactions of the Cumberland and Westmorland Antiquarian and Archaeological Society*, XLIII (1943), pp. 96–116.

Subscription to Books', 10s., that is 5s. each in respect of Richard and William. This was to enable them to become members of the Boys' Book Club, and to borrow books from its small but ever growing library of modern works in relatively inexpensive editions.[1] My impression is that boys tended to abuse Book Club volumes by writing their names in them. Thus in No. 47, which is the second volume of a four-volume *Naval History of Great Britain* (London, 1758), Gawen Brathwaite has got as far as 'Gawen Brat' on the front fly-leaf, and at the back of the book John Danson has completed his signature. The remaining thing worth noting from John Words-worth's Hawkshead accounts is that when he had three sons in the school, that is in 1782 and 1783, he paid five guineas in Cockpennies, whereas the usual amount at Hawkshead at this date was one and a half guineas per boy. In 1782 he appears to have sent the five guineas by Daniel Satterthwaite, the Cockermouth saddler.[2]

Removal of Tysons to Colthouse, autumn 1783—Joseph Bowman—Old Beckside—Ann Tyson in Greenend Cottage—Wordsworth's brief stay with the Rigges of Greenend—evidence from the Prelude *for Greenend Cottage*

Were Hugh and Ann Tyson still living in Hawkshead Town in 1782? In his short poem 'There was a Boy', first published in 1800, and later incorporated in *The Prelude*, Wordsworth tells of a grave in Hawkshead churchyard; the grave of a boy born and bred in the vale who was 'taken from his mates and died . . . ere he was full twelve years old', twelve being a correction of the ten he first wrote. The churchyard, he adds—and here I follow the 1805 text of *The Prelude* —hangs

> Upon a Slope above the Village School,
> And there, along that bank, when I have pass'd

[1] Thomas Bowman himself explains the distinction to be made between this early Book Club and the New Library which he founded in 1789; see his Proposals (number I) in Appendix IV, where I discuss the books and subscription lists of the New Library.

[2] Son of James, saddler; grandson of Daniel Fearon, shoemaker, whose heir he was; he would be a Lowther man since his property was bought for the Lowthers in 1761 by the agent John Robinson, and allowed him back for a peppercorn rent in return for his vote.

>   At evening, I believe that oftentimes
>   A full half-hour together I have stood
>   Mute—looking at the Grave in which he lies.
>   (V.418–22)

The 1850 text has:

>   And through that churchyard when my way has led
>   On summer evenings . . .
>
>   (V.394–5)

These lines do not fall far short of proof that Wordsworth was then living in Hawkshead, and not across the valley at Colthouse, nearly half a mile away. It is worth while, then, trying to date the burial; and that, as it happens, is easily done. In 1782 'John Vickars a Charity Boy from Cragg Died July ye 28th Buried ye 30th in C^hyard'; and again in 1782 'John son of Willm Tyson Gallabarrow Taylor Died Aug. ye 25th Buried ye 27th in C^hyard Aged 12'. For our present purpose there is no need to decide which of the two it was. But Wordsworth told his cousin Dorothy afterwards Mrs. Benson Harrison, that the grave was that of a Hawkshead boy named Tyson, a pupil at the Grammar School who had been a playmate of his. This information I had from Arthur P. Brydson, whose wife Catherine, as I have said, was a granddaughter of Mrs. Benson Harrison. In the earlier and longer part of 'There was a Boy' Wordsworth is of course speaking, not of John Tyson, but of a boy compounded of himself and, in lesser degree, of his friend William Raincock who, he tells us in a prose note, excelled in the art of blowing 'mimic hootings to the silent owls'.

The removal of Hugh and Ann Tyson and their boarders, Richard, William, and John Wordsworth, from Hawkshead Town to Colthouse apparently took place in the autumn of 1783. At any rate, Miss Mary Hodgson quoted Philip Braithwaite as saying that Mr. Tyson died of an 'inflammation of the chest' after they had been there only a few months, and the Hawkshead Parish Registers record that in 1784 'Hugh Tyson of Colthouse Joiner Died March ye 1st . . . Aged 70', and was buried in the churchyard two days later. He had previously suffered from asthma, Philip said, and, since the move, the only joinery he had done was to make a few things for the house, and for a young Mr. Bowman, a newcomer to Colthouse who was then living at Beckside, but who did not stay there for long. He was very good to the Tysons, and saw to it that Hugh had the best medical attention when he was seriously ill.

This Mr. Bowman is mentioned in 1784 in an entry in the Hawkshead Parish Registers that reads: 'Joseph Hodgson The Son [of] Mr Joseph Bowman of Colthouse was born June ye 10th 1783 Publicly Baptized June ye 10th 1784 Private Baptism was given to the above Child last year June ye 17th by the name of Joseph only & given into Court so'. This private baptism was recorded in the Registers at the time; but after 1784 Mr. Joseph Bowman's name does not appear there. Clearly he is the 'Joseph Bowman of Bampton, Gentleman', who married 'Elizabeth Law, Spinster, of Ulverston', by licence at Ulverston on 10 June 1782; and this couple are the 'Joseph Bowman and his wife Elizabeth, maiden name Law', who had a daughter, Elizabeth, baptized at Penrith in 1793, and buried there in 1794. Bowman was then near his old home, for Bampton, Westmorland, is only about nine miles from Penrith.

His sojourn at Colthouse must have been at Beckside, for Green-end, the only other residence there, did not become vacant in 1782–3 whilst Beckside, which had been the home of one branch of the Satterthwaite family for at least four or five generations is known to have passed out of their hands in 1782. This happened following the death in the previous year on 15 May of a 'Mr John Satterthwaite of Beckside', a widower, aged fifty-five, who was survived by two sons, William, born in 1757, and Joseph, who was two years younger. From Hawkshead School both had gone to St. John's College, Cambridge, where Joseph still was when his father died, and when Beckside was sold; but William, who presumably inherited it, was back in Hawkshead, for after graduating as a B.A. in 1780 he returned there as Assistant Master at the Grammar School, a post he held till some time in 1782, in which year, on 14 July, he was ordained deacon by the Bishop of Winchester. Joseph's early record is similar: after taking his B.A. in 1783, he was ordained by the Bishop of Chester on 28 September in that year, and taught at Hawkshead School in 1783–4 and again in 1786.

I do not know whether Joseph Bowman bought the Beckside estate in 1782 or merely rented the residence from the buyer. And I have been unable to find out what else this customary holding comprised. Mr. John Satterthwaite's will, which might have answered the question, is not in the Lancashire Record Office at Preston; nor are those of two other Beckside Satterthwaites who died in his lifetime. But certain entries in the Hawkshead Parish Registers, notably one that records the death in 1743 of a William Satterthwaite, suggest that the holding may well have included a second and smaller dwelling-house, for he is stated to have been of Old Beckside. Indeed, it looks as if Old Beckside still existed in 1784, as Philip Braithwaite mentioned both Beckside and it when telling Miss Mary Hodgson about young Mr. Bowman and Hugh Tyson, and spoke of it as the old farmhouse, and as if the Tysons were living there when Hugh was critically ill.[1] But she herself, though born in 1823 or 1824 at Greenend in the same bit of Colthouse as Beckside, could not remember Old Beckside; and recently, in answer to my inquiry, Mrs. Raymond Jay of Croft Foot, Colthouse, has been good enough to tell me that it is not shown on the very large scale Ordnance map of Colthouse and district engraved in 1851. Its site, size, and the views it afforded, must therefore be regarded as unknown; and that being so, it would be profitless to say more about it.

As will appear in detail later, Ann Tyson continued to board Grammar School boys until December 1789, and at one period had as many as eight at once,[2] and yet could let two of them each have a 'room extraordinary', presumably a bedroom or sitting room to himself. Her house, then, must have been much bigger than the typical rural cottage. That alone makes it highly probable that it was the humbler, though not the smaller, of the two houses, one on either side of the entrance to Scarhouse Lane, at Greenend in the largest and most northerly of the three tiny groups of houses which, with the Friends' Meeting House and Burial Ground, constitute the scattered hamlet of Colthouse. It is a house that still exists, and for many years has been spoken of as Greenend Cottage, but is not so distinguished from its superior neighbour in the eighteenth-century

---

[1] Probably they were not, as will appear later. T.W.T.
[2] See below, p. 75.

registers.[1] Miss Mary Hodgson told me that after Ann Tyson retired

[1] T.W.T.'s discussion here is the most exhaustive yet in the effort to solve the problem of the identification of Ann Tyson's dwelling in Colthouse. He was able to obtain no help from wills, maps, or deeds and had to rely heavily upon *The Prelude* itself and Miss Mary Hodgson, then over ninety. It is clear from an earlier draft of T.W.T.'s manuscript that he had first argued that one of the Beckside dwellings must have been Ann Tyson's house. In this he was following Mrs. Heelis and Oliver de Selincourt (who first published a note on Mrs. Heelis' realization that passages in *The Prelude* indicated a Colthouse dwelling and that the Parish Register entry of Hugh Tyson's death in Colthouse supported this). Then both Mary Moorman and Isabel Ross (see bibliography) proposed Greenend Cottage; and T.W.T., the first to realize that Wordsworth lived in both Hawkshead Town *and* Colthouse, also finally accepted Greenend Cottage as the probable Colthouse dwelling. Impressive though it is, the case for Greenend Cottage still lacks decisive documentary evidence.

The Land Tax Bills for the Division of Claife in the parish of Hawkshead (Lancashire County Records) show a single assessment for Greenend—3s. 8½d. This amount, presumably for both dwellings, was paid annually by William Rigge until his death in 1786, and then, until her death in 1790, by his widow. The property then went (by sale?) to William Taylor who left it in 1819 to his nephew Braithwaite Hodgson, Mary Hodgson's father. After Mary Hodgson's death, and then that of her niece, Miss Peacock, the property came, in 1944, to the National Trust; and they, alas, have no deeds. The term, 'Greenend', is thus confusingly applied to both houses, and all that can be established is that Ann Tyson, if she was in one of them—as seems likely—was a tenant of first the Rigges and then William Taylor who lived in the other. The present names, Cottage and House, are too recent to be useful. As the following reminiscence of Mr. William Knipe indicates, Greenend Cottage used to be Greenend Farm. Mr. Knipe was born there in 1882, the year after his father had taken over the running of the farm from the Hodgsons. He writes:

In 1888 My Father also took over Colthouse Farm which was being farmed by Wm Satterthwaite being much better land and more productive—In 1890 He gave up the land belonging to Greenend Farm, but retained some of the Farm Buildings. *Also* by Agreement with M^iss Hodgson the Farmhouse—as long as Required. My Father Died in 1900. Now this is when the name Cottage was given to the Farmhouse. The Land or Lands belonging to Greenend Farm had been split up or sold previously. It had ceased to be a Farm. I well remember M^iss Grace Peacock and M^iss Hodgson Calling it Greenend Cottage. That was the end of *the Farm.* (Letter of 25 June 1959 in the possession of Mr. V. J. H. Coward, Hawkshead.)

In Mr. Knipe's family there was no tradition that Ann Tyson had ever lived in Greenend Farm/Cottage. It must be borne in mind that *The Prelude* was almost unknown until after 1850 when Wordsworth and men like Philip Braithwaite were dead. Its impact was slow, and T.W.T. as a young man talking before the First World War to the very old Miss Mary Hodgson, would not have sharply in focus the need to know exactly where Ann Tyson lived in Colthouse. The arguments based on *The Prelude* could, with some persuasiveness, be applied as well to Greenend House as to Greenend Cottage: nineteenth-century additions to the House make it hard to visualize what it looked like in Wordsworth's time. This remains, therefore, something of an open question.

she lived there with a niece, whom she did not name; and that she had had this information both from her father and from Philip Braithwaite. Her father, though only a schoolboy at the time, had reason to know where Ann Tyson was then living, as I will show,[1] and Philip Braithwaite, who very rarely visited her, it seems, whilst she had schoolboy boarders, later made a point of dropping in to see her now and again; it was from him that Miss Mary got several of the particulars I owe to her about Ann Tyson's last few years.

That Ann moved into a house as large as the second at Greenend (i.e. the present Greenend Cottage) only after her retirement at the age of seventy-six is most unlikely. On the other hand, had she been living there before, her reluctance to seek a new home so late in life would be natural, as evidently she could still afford the rent. So I shall take it for granted that she was living in what is now called Greenend Cottage whilst she still boarded Grammar School boys, and then show that she may not have lived anywhere else at Colthouse.

Study of the Hawkshead Parish Registers shows that the occupier of one of the residences at Greenend from about 1750 or just after until his death there on 30 June 1786, at the age of eighty-three, was Mr. William Rigge; and that during part of this time Mr. John Gibson, the Hawkshead attorney, and his wife Elizabeth, by birth a Sandys of Roger Ground, lived in the other house. They were there as late as 1774, but sometime between then and 1779 they moved to Roger Ground. I did not discover who followed them at Greenend, but the property was let in the autumn of 1782 to James Bell, a tanner. He is the James Bell of Penrith who on 8 October in that year was married by licence at Hawkshead to Agnes, daughter of Samuel Holme, a Colthouse tanner who occupied one of the three farms, now merged into one, at Townend. At the time of her marriage Agnes was an 'Infant', in other words a minor. She bore her husband a son Edward, but he died on 29 April 1783, and she at the age of seventeen on 13 August in the same year. As a result it is virtually certain that James Bell, who probably came to Colthouse as a journeyman tanner, gave up his Greenend tenancy in the autumn of 1783. And that is when Hugh and Ann Tyson moved to Colthouse, assuming that Philip Braithwaite was not mistaken about

[1] See below, p. 146.

3. Greenend House on the left, Greenend Cottage on the right: the 'boxed' stream (*Prelude* IV, l. 40), flowing from the garden of the Cottage to that of the House, goes under the entrance to Scarhouse Lane, shown here.

4. Two pages from the account book of John Wordsworth, the poet's father, showing payments for his sons at Hawkshead, 1779–83.

Hawkeshead School at White's 1779. —

N:B: Mrs Cookson pd the fee to the Master &c
on Entrance. —

	£	/	©
1 Decr 1779 Paid Hugh Tyson pr rect —	12	11	3
Jny 1780 Sent Mr Crackenthorp pd Boys	1	13	8
19 June pd Hugh Tyson —	11	0	6
pd Mr Crackenthorp in full —	5	6	10
Jany 17d Paid Hugh Tyson in full —	11	13	7
July 1 Hawks head by Ed Cookson's Bro — in full to White's 1781	17	12	4
Sepr 1781 — pd at Hawkshead as on the other Side —	1	11	0
At same time pd Ed Crackenthorp what he pd do —	1	11	6
Janny Paid Hugh Tyson, in full of his, Mr Crackenthorp's, Wm Mackereth's & pr Wilson's	15	4	1
pd him for the 3 Boys in full to White —	24	10	5
1783 Jan 14 pd Tyson pr rect —	25	8	4½
March pd Mr Danl Satterthwaite —	5	5	0

5. *Esthwaite Water from below Belmount*, from *Select Views in Cumberland, Westmorland and Lancashire* by Joseph Wilkinson (1810), a book of engravings with an anonymous essay by

Hugh's death only a few months later. This coincidence suggests that it was to the second Greenend house in which the Bells had lived that the Tysons went when they left Hawkshead Town.

From Wordsworth himself Miss Mary Hodgson heard only one thing about Ann Tyson and Colthouse, and that was on the occasion when he had noticed her standing alone at Mrs. Benson Harrison's and had come over to speak to her. He asked her about her home, and on hearing that it was Greenend, Colthouse, he told her that he and two of his brothers during their schooldays at Hawkshead had once spent two or three weeks there with a Mr. and Mrs. Rigge. It was at a time when Mrs. Tyson, with whom they boarded nearby, could not do with them; or so Mrs. Rigge thought, and came and fetched them away. She intended to have them for only a day or so until she could find somewhere else for them to board until they could go back to Mrs. Tyson; but in this she failed, and let them stay on with her in spite of her husband's protests that he could not tolerate boys in the house. She was very good to them, and he, finding them quieter than he had expected, sometimes had a few words with them; but on the whole, Wordsworth said, they were glad when they could return to Mrs. Tyson. As the only boarders she had in Mr. William Rigge's lifetime were Richard, William, and John Wordsworth, it must have been they of whom Mrs. Rigge relieved her. Most likely it was during Hugh Tyson's fatal illness and till after the funeral. There is no certainty though that it was.

The Parish Registers record that 'Mrs Anne Rigge Relict of Mr Wm Rigge of Colthouse Gent' died on 26 January 1790, aged seventy-seven, and that she, like her husband, was buried in Hawkshead Church, though there is no memorial to either of them there. They are the 'Wm. Rigge, of Sawrey, Hauxhead, yeo. & Ann Sawrey, Beckside, Wiccham' [Whicham in south-west Cumberland], who were married by licence at Broughton-in-Furness on 2 August 1730. For the next twenty years or thereabouts they lived at Near Sawrey, where seven of their eight known children, of whom three were sons, were born: their youngest child was born at Colthouse in 1752. The only one who concerns us here is Mary, who was baptized at Hawkshead on 3 January 1738/9. As the owner of ancient customary estates at both Near and Far Sawrey, and later as the occupier of Greenend, William Rigge served as Churchwarden for the Claife Division of Hawkshead parish in 1758, 1761, and 1782; as Overseer of the Poor for the same Quarter in 1749 and 1769; and as Surveyor of the Highways for the High End of Claife in 1767. In addition, he was a member of the Twenty Four for a number of years. By his will, which is dated 21 April 1783, and was proved on 18 July 1786, he left to his wife his property at Near and Far Sawrey, his sheep (presumably heaf-going or hefted),[1] several closes of land, and his personal property. His other bequests were monetary, and amounted to £2,000 for the benefit of three of his daughters, and £700 to David Benoni, son of his deceased daughter Mary Rigge. Of her and Benoni I shall have more to say shortly; but first let me finish about Ann Tyson's 'rural dwelling'.

When in Book IV of *The Prelude* Wordsworth tells of his return to her during his first long vacation, that is in the summer and early autumn of 1788, he says, to quote the 1805 text:

> Great joy was mine to see thee once again,
> Thee and thy dwelling; and a throng of things
> About its narrow precincts all belov'd,
> And many of them seeming yet my own. . . .
>
> The rooms, the court, the garden were not left
> Long unsaluted, and the spreading Pine
> And broad stone Table underneath its boughs,
> Our summer seat in many a festive hour;
> And that unruly Child of mountain birth,
> The froward Brook, which soon as he was box'd
> Within our Garden, found himself at once,
> As if by trick insidious and unkind,
> Stripp'd of his voice, and left to dimple down
> Without an effort and without a will,
> A Channel paved by the hand of man.
>
> (IV.29–45)

In the 1850 text he refers to 'the sunny seat/Round the stone table under the dark pine', as 'Friendly to studious or to festive hours' (IV.47–9). Otherwise there is no factual difference between the two texts.

[1] See below, p. 278.

Of the old houses still existing at Colthouse the one to which these lines seem best to apply is the second at Greenend, now known as Greenend Cottage. Very long and uniformly narrow are two of the characteristics of the cottage: hence the phrase 'its narrow precincts'. It is large, with five rooms on the ground floor and five or six upstairs; and at the back of the house, in other words the end farthest along Scarhouse (locally Scarrus) Lane, which bounds it on its long south-south-western side, there is a yard (doubtless Wordsworth's 'Court') and some outbuildings. The narrow front of the house faces east-south-east, and on this side, the sunniest available, is an orchard replacing the garden of Wordsworth's schooldays. Longer than it is wide, it extends as far to the south-east as the road from Hawkshead through Colthouse to Wray. Gone, of course, are the pine tree and the stone table; but through the orchard, in 'A channel paved by man's officious care' (IV.56 (1850)), and seemingly an old one, flows Spring Wood Ghyll, Colthouse's only beck (unless one counts a tributary coming from further north that joins it opposite Beckside). The main stream, though scarcely 'of mountain birth', for it rises at no great height, descends obliquely yet abruptly to Colthouse, and on arrival there may justly be described as unruly and vociferous.

To complete Wordsworth's evidence as to where he boarded at Colthouse, here is another quotation from the 1805 text of *The Prelude*, this time from Book VIII.

> There was a Copse
> An upright bank of wood and woody rock
> That opposite our rural Dwelling stood,
> In which a sparkling patch of diamond light
> Was in bright weather duly to be seen
> On summer afternoons, within the wood
> At the same place. 'Twas doubtless nothing more
> Than a black rock, which, wet with constant springs
> Glister'd far seen from out its lurking-place
> As soon as ever the declining sun
> Had smitten it. Beside our Cottage hearth,
> Sitting with open door, a hundred times
> Upon this lustre have I gaz'd . . .
>
> (VIII.559-71)

For months he persisted in fancying it was now a burnished shield suspended over a knight's tomb, now an entrance to some magic cave or palace for a fairy of the rock; but he would not go and see, and never did, his wilful fancies mattering more to him than the unromantic truth.

'The scene cannot be identified', says de Selincourt in a note on this passage; and that was true enough when he wrote.[1] Now it can be stated with little fear of contradiction that the 'upright bank of wood and woody rock' to which Wordsworth refers was the northern half of Spring Wood on the very steep and somewhat rocky lower slopes of Colthouse Heights; a wood that faces westwards, and in which there are at least one or two springs. That it was directly opposite what Wordsworth calls 'our rural Dwelling' is strictly true if by the latter he meant the house at Greenend to which attention has been called. As already stated, its narrow front faces east-south-east; and the northern half of Spring Wood, of which it has an uninterrupted view, is east-south-east of the house, and at a distance from it ranging from barely 300 yards to about 400 I should say. Had the house faced in a quite different direction, it would have been far less likely that Wordsworth, sitting by the hearth with the door open, could have seen the sparkling patch of diamond light that appeared in Spring Wood on bright summer afternoons or evenings when the sun was declining. As it was, he may not at first have been in just the right place to notice it, but having once seen it he seems to have made sure that he could do so again and again. He gives no indication of the date or his age at the time; but it may well have been in the summer of 1784, his first at Colthouse, when he was a little over fourteen.

[1] De Selincourt's edition of *The Prelude* was published in 1926 at a time when Wordsworth was thought to have lodged with Ann Tyson only in Hawkshead. For an account of the discovery over the years that Wordsworth lived at Colthouse see Mary Moorman's *William Wordsworth: The Early Years* (1956), pp. 84–5. The realization that Wordsworth lodged with the Tysons first at Hawkshead, then at Colthouse, is T.W.T.'s. He suggested it, though without producing the evidence cited above, in a programme note for the Wordsworth Centenary Celebration at Hawkshead, 1950 (cited by Mark Reed: *Wordsworth: the Chronology of the Early Years*, 1967, p. 56).

Mary Rigge and David Benoni—David Kirkby

My reason for returning to the Rigges of Greenend in the persons of Miss Mary and her son Benoni is that Wordsworth mentions both, but without disclosing their identities. This happens in a rather cryptic prose note on a couple of verses in his poem 'Peter Bell'. The verses are:

> A mother's hope is here;—but soon
> She drooped and pined like one forlorn;
> From Scripture she a name did borrow;
> Benoni, or the child of sorrow,
> She called her babe unborn.
>
> For she had learned how Peter lived,
> And took it in most grievous part;
> She to the very bone was worn,
> And, ere that little child was born,
> Died of a broken heart.
>
> (906–15)

This is related of the last of Peter Bell's dozen wedded wives, a young Scottish girl, who had been as light and beauteous as a squirrel, and as wild, but who every Sunday had twice gone two miles to kirk no matter what the weather; as imaginary a character as Peter Bell was. The prose note, which conceals as much as it reveals, reads as follows:

Benoni, or the child of sorrow, I knew when I was a school-boy. His mother had been deserted by a gentleman in the neighbourhood, she herself being a gentlewoman by birth. The circumstances of her story were told me by my dear old dame, Ann Tyson, who was her confidante. The lady died broken-hearted.

In no uncertain fashion the Hawkshead Parish Registers make it plain who he was talking about by recording the baptism on 17 June 1759, of 'David Benoni Bastard Child of Ms Mary Rigge of Colthouse David Kirkby the Supposed Father of Conistone'; and the burial on 16 May 1760, of 'Ms Mary Rigge Daught of Willm [of] Colthouse'. She was then twenty-one.

David Kirkby, who was eight years older than Mary Rigge, was a son of 'Mr' William Kirkby of Thwaite at the head of Coniston Water, a property that included Kirkby Quay. In 1727 he, William, had married Agnes, daughter of Hugh Addison, farmer and weaver, then or later of Colthouse. David's choice of a wife, when he finally made it, fell on his sixteen-year-old neighbour Agatha Sawrey, daughter of Anthony of Townson Ground, Coniston Waterhead, another farmer and weaver. They were married at Hawkshead on 13 April 1762, and had ten children christened there between 1763 and 1784. William Kirkby was one of the Twenty Four from 1736 until his death in 1769, and David, who succeeded him at Thwaite, was straightway elected in his stead as a member of this body, the overriding authority in the conduct of parish business; and he remained a member of it until his death in 1814 at the age of eighty-four. He was Overseer of the Poor for the Monk Coniston and Skelwith Quarter in 1781, and Churchwarden in 1782; and when in 1789 it was decided to rebuild the Market Shambles at Hawkshead and to include in the new building both a yarn market and an assembly room, he was elected a trustee, but contributed only one guinea towards the cost. I will say no more about him here, except that he is commonly styled 'Mr.' in parochial records, and that in his day Kirkby Quay was a busy place owing to the growth and continuing prosperity of the trade in Coniston slates.

Among the juvenilia Ernest de Selincourt has printed from Wordsworth manuscripts is a feeble ballad dated 23 and 24 March 1787.[1] Written during his last year at school, it is clear that it had its origin in what Ann Tyson told him about Mary Rigge's unhappy end; and for that reason it is repeated here.

A BALLAD

'And will you leave me thus alone
And dare you break your vow?
Be sure her Ghost will haunt thy bed
When Mary shall lie low.'

---

[1] See *Wordsworth's Poetical Works*, I, pp. 265–7. The title, 'A Ballad', is added by de Selincourt.

So spoke in tears—but all in vain
The fairest maid of Esthwaite's vale,
To love's soft glance his eye was shut
His ear to Pity's tale.

And oft at Eve he sought the bridge
That near her window lay;
And gayly laughed with other maids
Or sung the hour away.

She saw—and wept—her father frown'd,
Her heart began to break;
And oft the live-long day she sat
And word would never speak.

Oft has she seen sweet Esthwaite's lake
Reflect the morning sheen;
When lo! the sullen clouds arise
And dim the smiling scene.

Reflected once in Mary's face
The village saw a mind more fair;
Now every charm was all o'erhung
By woe and black despair.

And oft she roam'd at dark midnight
Among the silent graves;
Or sat on steep Winander's rock
To hear the weltering waves.

Her father saw and he grew kind,
And soon Religion shed
Hope's chearing ray to light her to
Her dark, her wormy bed.

For now her hour of Death was nigh,
And oft her waft was seen
With wan light standing at a door,
Or shooting o'er the green.

She saw—she cried—"'tis all in vain
For broken is my heart,
And well I know my hour is nigh,
I know that we must part.

Heaven told me once—but I was blind—
My head would soon lie low;[1]
A Rose within our Garden blew
Amid December's snow.

That Rose my William saw—and pluck'd,
He pluck'd and gave it me;
Heaven warn'd me then—ah blind was I—
That he my death would be.

And soon these eyes shall cease to weep
And cease to sob my breath;
Feel—what can warm this clay-cold hand?'
—Her hand was cold as Death.

To warm her hand a glove they brought,
The glove her William gave;
She saw, she wept, she sighed the sigh
That sent her to her grave.

The knell was rung—the Virgins came
And kissed her in her shroud;
The children touch'd—'twas all they durst
They touched and wept aloud.

The next day to the grave they went,
All flocked around her bier;
Nor hand without a flower was there
Nor eye without a tear.

Such was Wordsworth's imaginative rendering of Ann Tyson's story of Mary Rigge. The poem strikes me as a first draft that calls for drastic revision of the earlier verses, and a general bracing up; but after he was seventeen the author seems to have given it no more thought. The bridge that lay near Miss Mary's window was Pool Bridge on the road across the Esthwaite valley from Hawkshead to Colthouse: it could be seen to the south-west from the front windows of her home, which faced slightly to the west of south.[2] On the other hand, one cannot be sure of the identity of 'steep Winander's rock' on which she sat to hear the 'weltering waves': it is too near to

[1] 'My head will soon lie low': words attributed to William Taylor on his deathbed, June 1786 (*Prelude* x. 502).
[2] It was refronted and enlarged in 1830–1. T.W.T.

being a generality; but somewhere in the neighbourhood of the Ferry is suggested by the wording, and as she was given to wandering about alone she may have gone as far. That Ann Tyson, then living in Hawkshead Town, should have been her confidante would seem strange but for the fact that by 1759 Ann was selling draperies as well as groceries. True, there is no mention in the Tysons' ledger of the Rigges of Greenend buying either, but if they did and paid ready money for their purchases, they would not be set down there.

Evidently Ann Tyson had a goodly stock of tales to tell Wordsworth when he boarded with her.[1] There were the long narrations of doings at Bonaw, and the story of Miss Mary Rigge's desertion and death; and Wordsworth vouches for three more that he heard from her. The first is the tale of 'A Shepherd and his Son', and their search for a missing sheep; a tale he retells in Book VIII of *The Prelude* (in the 1805 version ll.221–311). It was 'recorded by my Household Dame', he says; and once he interrupts his own narrative to quote her.

> 'For take note',
> Said here my grey-hair'd Dame, 'that tho' the storm
> Drive one of these poor Creatures miles and miles,
> If he can crawl he will return again
> To his own hills, the spots where, when a Lamb,
> He learn'd to pasture at his Mother's side.'
> (VIII.252–7)

The other two stories Wordsworth heard from Ann are referred to in his prose note on *The Excursion*.

From this point the conversation leads to the mention of two Individuals who, by their several fortunes, were, at different times, driven to take refuge at the small and obscure town of Hawkshead on the skirt of these mountains. Their stories I had from the dear old Dame with whom, as a schoolboy and afterwards, I lodged for nearly the space of ten years. The elder, the Jacobite, was named Drummond, and was of a high family in Scotland; the Hanoverian Whig bore the name of [Sir George] Vandepat, and might perhaps be a descendant of some Dutchman who had come over in the train of King William.[2]

---

[1] See Introduction, pp. xv–xvi.   [2] See *Wordsworth's Poetical Works*, V, pp. 458–9.

Ann Tyson's spelling—other boarders with the Tysons—the Maudes
—Robert Greenwood—Rowland Bowstead—Robinson Wordsworth
—William Knott—Christopher Wordsworth

After her husband's death, Ann Tyson began to keep accounts in the ledger he had used. Gordon Wordsworth speaks of them as incoherent, and in many respects incomplete; of the spelling as fantastic, and the arithmetic as inaccurate. There are many entries, in the later years especially, in hands other than Ann's. But in those she herself made, was her spelling so very fantastic? Certainly it was not based on memory of the written or printed word, though Wordsworth assures us that she read her Bible on Sunday afternoons until she dropped asleep, using it as a pillow for her head. It was rather an untutored attempt to set down the sounds of the spoken word as she knew it. Spellings based on dialect pronunciations are not much in evidence, the only obvious examples being *canls* and *canles* for candles; the abbreviation *shoud* for shoulder; *Houdm* for the surname Oldham; and the odd-looking Christian name *Rechet* for a dialect form of Richard. Her *Mackret* for Mackreth, though I have never heard it, should perhaps be included, as it reflects a dialect tendency to replace *th* by *t*. Like Hugh she wrote *cas* for cash, that being, as we saw earlier, the original form of a sixteenth-century French loan word. Though they may not be survivals, her *botens* for buttons and *vel* for veal are of interest, as the word button is derived from Old French *boton*, and veal from Anglo-French *vel*.

Her omission of a vowel before *l*, *m*, and *n* when they follow another consonant, as in *canls*, *candls*, *botl*, *Houdm*, and *mutn* is phonetically correct; but she does not always do it, in proof of which *apels*, *botens*, *riben*, and *resins* may be cited, in addition to *moutton*, which occurs only once. Understandably, but in this instance not quite correctly, she omits the obscure or indeterminate vowel in unstressed final syllables, and writes, for example, *gartrs*, *letrs*, *kwartr*, *shugr*, and *velvt*; but *garters* and *shuger* also occur in her handwriting. She is consistent in writing *her* for hair, *ped* for paid, *keks*, *cekes*, and *ceks* for cakes, *peper* for paper, *resins* for raisins, and *Swenson* for Swainson—in brief, in writing *e* for the long *e* heard in these words.

But she errs phonetically in writing *pets* for peats, *bef* for beef, and probably *vel* for veal, as here she is using *e* to represent a different sound, namely long *i*. Of her other spellings, considered as attempts to record the spoken word, *shugr* and *shuger* are preferable to sugar; *kwartr* and *kweir* to quarter and quire; *huni* and *hune* (with *hounie* doubtful) to honey; *careg* to carriage; *Hodgen* to Hodgson; *Mey* to May; and *cok*, *egs*, *glovs*, *hors*, *lam*, *ouns*, *nek*, and *tee* to the accepted spellings of these words. Nor, from the same viewpoint, is *cole* inferior to coal, *lof* to loaf, *mor* to more, *cofe* to coffee, *foul* to fowl, *genes* to guineas, and *penes* or *penys* to pennies.

Apart from spellings of people's names, the only others I have noted but not yet mentioned are *boks* as well as box, *bok* as well as book, *lege* and *legg* as well as leg, *hupe* for hoop, *lon* for loin, and *recved* for received. Her *Wilm* and *Willm* should be pronounced as bisyllables, I take it, as she also has *Willam* and *Willom*, as well as William, and the abbreviation *Wm*. Christopher she reduced to *Cerst*, or something very near it. John, Robert, Peter, and Dick are spelt in the usual way; and so are surnames like Sawrey with which she had long been familiar. But Wallace, a relatively new one to her, she writes as *Walis* and *Wals*, using the letter *s* in the second of these spellings as a syllable; whilst when she first met with Maude as a surname she spelt it *Mode*. And with that I will leave the question of Ann's spelling, having shown, I hope, that it was not fantastic, but a creditable attempt to spell by ear; indeed very creditable, considering that she was over seventy, and can have had very little schooling as a child, or much need to write whilst her husband was alive.

The accounts, including some that are wholly in handwriting other than Ann's, extend from August 1784, to December 1789, when she retired. They cover all the half-years in between; and are a satisfactory record, except for the year 1786, of who boarded with her and when. Up to June 1785, her only boarders were the three Wordsworth boys who moved with the Tysons to Colthouse— Richard and William, who had been with them since Whitsuntide 1779, and John who first came to them in January 1782. On 1 August 1785, they were joined by their brother Christopher, then aged eleven; but Ann had all four of John Wordsworth's sons at one and the same time for one Half only, as Richard, when he was seventeen and a half, left in December 1785 and was articled to his cousin Richard, an attorney at Whitehaven.[1] In January 1786, Ann had a new boarder 'Mr Greenwood', that is, Robert Hodgson Greenwood, son of David Greenwood, yeoman, of Ingleton, who in 1764 had married Jane Hodgson of Thornton-in-Lonsdale. Their son Robert was baptized at Ingleton on 21 February 1768, and was therefore about eighteen when he first boarded with Ann. He had previously been at Heversham Grammar School.

According to the account book, Ann had another new boarder in January 1786, making five in all. But he is not named; and his account occurs immediately after a Maude account for the Half beginning 23 July 1786, and between it and another Maude account which is undated. The chances are that it, too, is a Maude account, and that it should have been dated 23 January 1787, not 1786. Judging from the Wordsworth and the other accounts, the Spring Half began on 23 January in 1787, but on 19 January in 1786; whilst the fact that the 'little weekly stipend' was only 2d. is consistent with its being a Maude account. I shall assume that it is, and that both it and the undated account relate to the Spring Half, 1787.

After the summer holidays in 1786, the three Wordsworths and Greenwood returned to Ann on 24 July, which was rather early for the start of an Autumn Half. On the previous day two 'Mr Modes' had come to board with her, for the first time, I feel sure. They were

---

[1] In an exchange of letters between Richard and his uncle, Christopher Cookson, we get a glimpse of Richard, now away from school, but still conscious of it; and a muted reference to the death of the headmaster, William Taylor, to whom Wordsworth paid such fine tribute in *The Prelude* (X.487-515). Christopher Cookson wrote on 7 June 1786:

> Your Grandmother desires you would send an old shirt over here, that fitts you in the hands & Neck, as she is now making you a fresh sett, against you come over to meet your Bros. at the summer vacation. I had the pleasure of hearing of them Yesterday & am happy to inform you they are all well, they give little hopes of Mr Taylors recovery . . .

(William Taylor died on 12 June 1786 aged thirty-two.) Richard, living at the house of his other guardian, his uncle, Richard Wordsworth, replied:

> Honoured Uncle/I received your Letter at Whitehaven not having any old shirts that fit me My Aunt & I thought it best to send one of the new ones which fits me very well in ye hands & neck but is rather too short. . . . I suppose My Bros will be breaking up some time at ye latter end of this Month.

sons of Joseph Maude of Kendal, a wealthy merchant who became senior partner in the bank opened in Kendal on 1 January 1788 by Messrs. Maude, Wilson, and Crewdson. He is the Joseph Maude of Sunderland in County Durham who early in 1768 married Sarah Holme of Kendal. He and his wife lived at Sunderland until 1775, when they moved to Kendal, where he died in 1803, and she in 1831. In addition to three daughters, they are said to have had nine sons, all of whom outlived their mother. I can name only eight, of whom Thomas Holme, Frederick, and William were born at Sunderland, and Joseph, Warren, Edwin, Charles, and John Barnabas at Kendal. According to John Ireland, all Joseph Maude's sons were sent to Hawkshead Grammar School, 'a tribute to the School as no man in the town [Kendal] was keener on getting value for the money he expended'. All the eight sons I have named were there;[1] but it is virtually certain that some of them were at other schools as well.

One of the two Maude boys who boarded with Ann Tyson during the Autumn Half 1786, was William, who is named straight away in an entry which reads 'Mr Willam a bok 2s. 8d.' He was Joseph Maude's third son, and was born 28 August 1772. His brother is not named in the Maude accounts, which are few in number and brief. I thought at one time that it was Thomas, the eldest of the family, born on 4 May 1770, who in addition to William had boarded with Ann; but that was because of my imperfect recollection of a story about him I heard in 1906 from Joseph Swainson, a Kendal wool merchant I have to thank for introducing me to *The Prelude*. The pith of the story, as I remembered it, was in Thomas Maude's reply to a rather gushing lady, a great admirer of Wordsworth. Having heard that they were at school together, and had lived for a time under the same roof, she wanted Mr. Maude to tell her what had impressed him most about Wordsworth as a boy. Tom Maude was neither enthusiastic nor very informative; but she persisted, and at last got an admission from him that there was one thing about Wordsworth he would never forget. 'I knew there must be something,' she cried triumphantly. 'Do tell me; quick; what was it?' 'Only this,' said Tom. 'He was the uneasiest bedfellow I've ever

[1] Seven donated money to the New Library, and Thomas shared in giving a book; see Appendix IV.

had.' That was the story as I remembered it. But when, after some searching, I unearthed the record I'd made of it in 1906, I found that in answer to the question 'Did you live with him [Wordsworth as a schoolboy] for a long time?' Thomas Maude had replied: 'Inside a week, ma'am.' And that, if it is true, rules out the possibility of his having been Ann Tyson's second boarder of the name of Maude; in which case it must have been Frederick, Joseph Maude's second son, born 19 July 1771, who came with William to board with her in July, 1786. Neither of the Maudes who lived with her stayed for more than a year, whereas Thomas, who seems to have been at Kendal Grammar School first, remained at Hawkshead School until 1788, when he went to St. John's College, Cambridge. It must be assumed that his stay with Ann Tyson was for a few days only.[1]

In July 1786, Ann received yet two more new boarders, Gawthrop on the 20th and Losh on the 25th. The former, whose initials are given as T. H. in a later entry, was Thomas Holden Gawthrop, born on 5 June 1768, a son of the Rev. William Gawthrop, Vicar of Sedbergh from 1766 to 1798. Before coming to Hawkshead at the age of eighteen, Thomas Gawthrop was at Sedbergh School. In November 1786 he was admitted to St. John's College, Cambridge, but did not go there until the following October. Losh can safely be identified as the William Losh of Woodside, near Carlisle, who contributed a guinea in 1790 towards the cost of books bought for the New Library, founded in the previous year, at Hawkshead School. Born in 1770, he appears to have been the youngest of the seven sons of John Losh, sometimes known as the 'Big Black Squire', who,

[1] Whether or not Thomas was the second Maude brother to lodge with Ann Tyson for the Autumn Half, 1786, he certainly had many years of contact with Wordsworth. 'Toss Maude' is scribbled and repeated over half a page in Wordsworth's early notebook devoted to the *Vale of Esthwaite*, Verse MS. 3., and, of course, Thomas (1770–1849) was at St. John's College, Cambridge, though a year later than Wordsworth. He was Mayor of Kendal in 1800, and Wordsworth's early acquaintance with him must explain a kind action which Dorothy records in her Journal for 9 June 1800: 'poor Girl called to beg, who had no work at home, and was going in search of it to Kendal. She slept in Mr. Benson's [?], and went off after Breakfast in the morning with 7d. and a letter to the Mayor of Kendal.' Often referred to as Colonel Maude, in 1803, during the invasion crisis, he became Lieutenant-Colonel Commandant of the Kendal Volunteers. He retired from banking in 1812 (see below, p. 249).

after his marriage to a Miss Liddell, lived for a few years in New-castle upon Tyne before settling at Woodside. His younger sons George and William were educated at Newcastle 'for commercial life', and then went abroad to complete their studies, William to Hamburg, where he became a friend of Alexander von Humbolt. In Dr. Henry Lonsdale's *Worthies of Cumberland* there is no mention of his having been first at Hawkshead School, but there is no doubt that he was, though only for the Autumn Half 1786, so far as is known.[1] The reputation the school then had for mathematical teaching may well have been the reason his father wanted him to be there before going to Hamburg. Earlier the squire had sent his elder sons, John and James, to the mathematical tutor, John Dawson of Sedbergh, between their leaving Wreay School and going to Trinity College, Cambridge.[2] William Losh, a good linguist, lived for a time in Sweden, and later became consular representative at Newcastle of both Sweden and Prussia. A Tyneside industrialist, interested in alkali manufacture, iron works, and engineering, he collaborated with George Stephenson in the development of the locomotive.

Throughout the Autumn Half 1786, Ann Tyson had eight boys boarding with her, two of whom were 18, two 16, and the other four between 12 and 14, or possibly 15. Thomas Gawthrop and William Losh each had a 'room extraordinary', for which the charge was an additional 10s. 6d. for the half-year. The entries in their accounts which give this information are in an educated handwriting,

[1] But from a letter of 2 June 1786 from Eleanor Braithwaite to Mrs. Senhouse (for whom see Appendix III), it is clear that Losh was already at Hawkshead in the Spring Half of 1786: 'please madam to lett your Servant return ye ticking Bags by mr Losh as ye are Usefull . . .'

[2] We know from James Losh's diary (Tullie House, Carlisle) that after Wreay (schoolmaster, Mr. Gaskin) he attended a school in Penrith whose Master was, according to the Trinity College Admissions Register, a Mr. Moreby: 'I was there one year', wrote Losh, 'under the care of a man no way calculated to acquire an ascendancy over my mind, or lead me on to improvement in my studies.' Since Losh went up to Cambridge in 1782, he probably was tutored by John Dawson in Cambridge vacations, a common practice. Dawson (1736–1820) lived at Sedbergh, though he was not attached to Sedbergh School. He was a largely self-taught mathematician and a successful tutor; eleven of his pupils became Senior Wranglers and many were highly placed. Three of Wordsworth's contemporaries were among these—Godfrey Sykes, Thomas Jack, and Thomas Harrison; for their subsequent careers, see Alphabetical List in Appendix IV.

probably that of an Assistant at the Grammar School. Had they been in Ann's they might have specified whether it was a bedroom or a sitting-room. It is more than likely that she also had a maidservant living in the house. She could well afford one, as a girl's wage, assuming board and lodging were provided, would not be more than about £4 a year. And she needed more help than her niece Eleanor Nevinson, still living in Hawkshead Town with her sister Margaret, could give her. She was seventy-three, and in addition to housework there must have been a great deal of cooking and baking, washing and ironing, and sewing and darning to be got through. By agreement she had to do the boys' washing; and even bread, mostly oat, or haver as it was called locally, had to be baked at home, for there was no baker or confectioner in Hawkshead in those days.

Ann began the Spring Half 1787 with seven boarders, only William Losh having left. But after eleven more weeks with her, Thomas Gawthrop also departed, to return to Sedbergh School it appears, perhaps to make doubly sure that he was eligible for a Lupton Scholarship, confined to former pupils of that school, when he went into residence at St. John's College, Cambridge in the following October. In due course he was elected to one, but not until three years later. Though his academic record was undistinguished, Thomas Gawthrop became a Lupton Fellow in 1793, and was a Senior Fellow from 1810 to 1817. He served as Steward from 1812 to 1815, and was then presented by the College to the Rectory of Marston Morteyne in Bedfordshire. He died 2 November 1836, leaving three children by a second marriage.

One of the Maudes left her at the same time as Gawthrop did, and the other at the end of the Spring Half 1787. To complete their education, both boys were sent to the Manchester Academy, which was established in 1786 to carry on the traditions of the older nonconformist academies of Richard Frankland and Caleb Rotherham the Elder, and the Warrington Academy, at each of which an education of university standard had been provided for Dissenters, whether intended for the ministry, a profession, or for commerce. Richard Frankland's Academy, 1670–98, was at Natland, near Kendal, from 1674 to 1683, though it ought not to have been allowed within five miles of an incorporated borough; whilst Dr. Caleb

6. From a photograph of the Ferry Inn, Windermere, taken sometime before 1870. The wide arched cote-house of 1790 is to the right, and Curwen's later three-storey addition to the left. The other buildings are the old stables, cowhouses and brewhouses. These were all pulled down in 1879, and replaced by a hotel, now Ferry House, used by the Freshwater Biological Association.

7. Carriage and horse in the ferry. This boat was replaced by a steam ferry in spring 1870.

Rotherham, whose academy lasted from 1733 until his death in 1752, and in which the prime subjects taught, apart from divinity, were mathematics and natural philosophy, was Minister of the Presbyterian chapel in the Market Place at Kendal from 1716 to 1752. The newly established Manchester Academy was strongly advocated by his son Caleb, then Minister of this chapel, with the result that a number of Kendal boys went there. The first three, all admitted in 1787, were Edward Holme, Edward Wakefield, and Frederick Maude. They were followed by William Maude in 1788, Charles Morland in 1790, Warren Maude in 1792, and Edwin Maude in 1795. Edward Holme, the only one of these students whose father was a Dissenter, and the only one not 'intending to follow commerce',[1] was seventeen when admitted, and the others either fifteen or sixteen. Except Edward Wakefield, they had all been at Hawkshead School, for a time at any rate. Edward Holme, who had the greater part of his schooling at Sedbergh, left the Manchester Academy and then studied medicine at the universities of Edinburgh, Göttingen, and Leyden, the last of which conferred an M.D. on him. His interests were very wide, his memory prodigious; and it has been said that when he spoke, 'Parr, and Herschell, and Faraday, and Dalton, and Gough, and Wordsworth in turns were silent'.

There is little I can add about Frederick and William Maude. In 1793 they attended a dinner in Kendal 'to mark Tho[s] Harrison's success'.[2] Harrison was a Kendal boy, a Quaker, educated at Hawkshead School, and coached by John Dawson, before going to Queens' College, Cambridge, in 1789; whilst his success was that of being Senior Wrangler and First Smith's Prizeman. At the dinner Thomas Bowman, then Master of the school, received a few subscriptions to the New Library Fund, and among them were half a guinea each from Frederick and William Maude. All Joseph Maude's sons eventually gave something; but none of them who were at school after the New Library was founded in 1789 either subscribed

---

[1] See Francis Nicholson and Ernest Axon, *The Older Nonconformity in Kendal* (1915), p. 353; on p. 376 it is mistakenly supposed that the Mayor of Kendal in 1800, and again in 1814, was the father of the four boys, and not Thomas, Wordsworth's contemporary.

[2] See list of former schoolboys, Appendix IV.

G

to it as schoolboys, or presented a book to it on leaving. This applies to the five youngest sons, two of whom, Joseph and Barnabas, went to Queen's College, Oxford, and were afterwards ordained; and two, as we have seen, went to the Manchester Academy. Barnabas is said to have been fourteen when he matriculated at Oxford on 15 January 1795, but in point of fact he was only a little over twelve, the date of his birth being 1 November 1782.

When the 1787 Autumn Half began on 5 August, Ann Tyson had four Wordsworths boarding with her, William, John, and Christopher being joined by a young Richard Wordsworth from Whitehaven. Born in 1777, he was a son of their cousin Richard (1752–1816), the attorney to whom their brother Richard was articled, and a grandson of their uncle and guardian Richard Wordsworth (1733–94), Collector of Customs at Whitehaven. He was the youngest boy Ann had boarded for some time. Robert Greenwood, who during the previous Half had been admitted to Trinity College, Cambridge, also returned to her, but not until 16 August. In July, William Wordsworth had been admitted to St. John's College, Cambridge, and both he and Greenwood were due to go into residence in October. They left Ann during the second week in that month, Greenwood being charged for seven weeks' board, and Wordsworth for nine. William Wordsworth, then seventeen and a half, had been with Ann Tyson eight and a quarter years. At the end of that 1787 Autumn Half there was another wrench, for John Wordsworth, who had reached the age of fifteen, and had boarded with her since he was nine, also left the school. He entered the service of the East India Company, and lost his life when the East Indiaman he commanded, *The Earl of Abergavenny*, was wrecked off Weymouth on 5 February 1805. In 1792 he sent by Christopher a half-guinea subscription to the New Library at Hawkshead School.

In Book II of *The Prelude* Wordsworth tells of a day, evidently in June 1786 or 1787, when he and some of his school-fellows, having hired a boat at the Ferry, rowed across the lake to Bowness. On landing they went to the White Lion Inn, and up through the garden to a small bowling green which surmounted it. Having more money than might have been expected so near the end of one of their half-yearly terms, they refreshed themselves with 'strawberries and mellow cream'; after which they played on the smooth green through half the afternoon, their shouts making 'all the mountains ring'. But ere night fell, Wordsworth says, they returned

> Over the dusky Lake, and to the beach
> Of some small Island steer'd our course with one,
> The Minstrel of our troop, and left him there,
> And row'd off gently, while he blew his flute
> Alone upon the rock.
>
> (II.172–6 (1805))

The flautist was Robert Greenwood. In a letter to William Mathews, written on 3 August 1791, Wordsworth gives us a further glimpse of him. 'I heard from Greenwood', he says, 'for the first time the very day I received your last. He is in Yorkshire with his father, and writes in high spirits, his letter altogether irregular and fanciful. He seems to me to have much of Yorick in his disposition; at least Yorick, if I am not mistaken, had a deal of the male mad-cap in him, but G. out-madcaps him quite'.

Greenwood was 16th Wrangler in 1791, and was elected a Fellow of Trinity in 1792. For some years after graduating he was tutor to the sons of Lord Stamford, 'who in recognition of his admirable conduct while under his roof', says George Pryme, 'afterwards gave him a living tenable with his Fellowship.' When his tutoring was over, Greenwood returned to Cambridge, and spent the rest of his life there (except perhaps the closing year) as a Senior Fellow of Trinity, for he never married; and though he was Vicar of Chesham, Buckinghamshire, from 1822 until his death in 1839, he never resided there. He held various college offices, and according to Pryme his judgement was so esteemed by the other Fellows that they 'often appealed to him for his opinion'. He was, says the same writer, 'a man of great humour and good sense. . . . He said things drily himself and left others to laugh.'[1]

He died at Ingleton, possessed of the farm there that had been his

---

[1] See George Pryme, *Autobiographic Recollections* (Cambridge, 1870), pp. 87–8. Wordsworth must have seen something of Greenwood on his visits to his brother, Christopher, Master of Trinity from 1820. We find Christopher's son, John, giving Wordsworth news of Greenwood as late as 22 April 1839. John wrote:

Poor Greenwood still continues much in the same state, and may remain so for

father's, and almost certainly in the house in which he had been born. After his father's death in 1799 he let the farm, but on the understanding that the tenant reserved two rooms for his use whenever he wanted to go there, which he did very frequently, especially during the long vacation. In his younger days he enjoyed helping a bit on the farm. And thereby hangs a tale, which I heard from Gordon Wordsworth in 1907; a tale first told by Christopher Wordsworth, and one that was a favourite with William. A Trinity don, whom Greenwood did not like very much, being on a northern tour decided to call on him at his Ingleton retreat. 'His reverence is out', the farmer's wife told him, 'helping my husband with the hay: they're leading, and there's no time to loss as it's blowing like rain. But maybe you'll call again', she suggested, 'a bit later on.' The visitor said he would, and in the early evening made a second call. This time he was luckier. 'I'll go and tell his reverence you're here, sir,' the farmer's wife said. 'They've finished in the fields, and he's in the cow'us now helping with the milking astead o' me.' 'If I may, I'll come with you,' said the visitor. 'I'd like to see his reverence milking a cow.' After greetings, he watched for a few moments, and then exclaimed: 'Why, Greenwood, you look as if you'd been doing this all your life.' 'And, as you know, I haven't,' said Greenwood. 'But, my father being a statesman, I was born and bred to it.' His fellow don was puzzled. 'What exactly do you mean?' he asked. 'Exactly what I said,' Greenwood assured him, 'no statement could be plainer. But if you don't understand, we must leave it at that.' And he changed the subject by asking his caller if he would care to stay to a farmhouse supper. Greenwood was, of course, using the word statesman in its

months or even years. His legs have entirely failed him, and though not actually bed-ridden, he cannot rise from his chair without assistance. The lower part of his body in short seems to be totally disabled, but the upper retains its energies, his intellect is perfectly clear, he is glad to receive a visit from a friend, and he can read even the smallest print without spectacles. (MS. in Dove Cottage Library.)

It is interesting to find that Greenwood was associated with Wordsworth's earliest poetic endeavours, for Mary Wordsworth wrote to her nephew, Christopher, on 14 August [1854]: 'Your Uncle used to speak of a Sonnet which, coupled with one from his Schoolfellow Greenwood, he once sent t[o] the Gent^s. Magazine from Hawkshead.' (MS. in Dove Cottage Library.) The inscription on his tombstone in Ingleton churchyard adds the detail that he was the son of David and Jane Greenwood and died on 3 December 1839, aged seventy-two.

northern sense of estatesman, the owner, or more usually the customary tenant, of a small landed estate which he farmed himself. Christopher Wordsworth later acted as interpreter.

The only schoolboy boarders Ann Tyson had in 1788 were Christopher and Richard Wordsworth, but throughout the year, and for the Spring Half 1789, a Mr. Bowstead boarded with her as well. He is easily identified as the Mr. Rowland Bowstead, 'Writing Master in the School', who on the foundation of the New Library in 1789 presented to it a copy of the Abbé Grosier's *General History of China . . . Translated from the French*, a two-volume work published in the previous year. He joined the school staff in January 1788 in place of Joseph Varty, who left Hawkshead early that year, but returned some five to six years later, and became Writing Master again. Thus it fell to Bowstead to write the inscriptions in from two-thirds to three-quarters of the books presented to the New Library by the Master and his Assistants, by boys on leaving the school, and by former pupils, more especially those who were at Cambridge. When examining some crumbling sheets and scraps of paper in the School Library I came across one which showed that Rowland Bowstead as a boy had been at Bampton Grammar School in north Westmorland, the school at which the founder of the New Library, the Rev. Thomas Bowman, had been educated under the Rev. John Bowstead, a native of Great Salkeld, who was Master of Bampton School from 1776 to 1832, and who claimed that during those fifty-six years he had educated two hundred priests. Rowland Bowstead, who may have been a near contemporary of Thomas Bowman, must have been educated by the Rev. John as well, but I failed to discover how they were related, if at all, or even where Rowland was born.

Near the end of his third half-year with Ann Tyson, on 2 June 1789, 'Rowland Bowstead Gentleman' married Agnes, the twenty-year-old daughter of John Sawrey, the butcher who supplied Ann with meat. Their child was born three months afterwards. His bride had a sister Emma or Emmy, ten years older than herself; and on 25 October 1788 she had married Thomas Garnett, a non-graduate Assistant at the Grammar School. He took the Red Lion Inn,[1] and

---

[1] In the Alehouse Recognizances he appears as landlord there from 1790 to 1795 (Lancashire Record Office).

later ceased to be a schoolmaster. Rowland Bowstead was of Hawkshead Town when his daughter Margaret, born on 14 November 1789, was baptized on 15 January 1790; and still 'of Town' when his daughter Ann, born 2 September 1791, was baptized on 15 January 1792. On both occasions he is described as 'Writing Master'. But when his son Thomas was born and privately baptized on 6 January 1794, the entry in the register refers to him as 'Master of the Mathematics'; which suggests that Joseph Varty had returned and been reinstalled as Writing Master. The infant Thomas survived, and was publicly baptized on 24 July 1794 at Lancaster. Rowland Bowstead had become, or was about to become, an assistant at Lancaster Grammar School.

In the Tysons' ledger there is a short sale account which reads:

24th April 1788	
Cash Rec^d by Mrs Tyson from Jno.	£ .. s .. d
Borwick on the Sale Acc^t.	3 .. 6 .. 8¾
Recved [*in Ann's handwriting*]	3 .. 3 .. 0
3rd Nov^{br} 1788 Gave Mrs Tyson in Cash	0 .. 10 .. 0

The auctioneer was the 'John Borwick of Borwick Ground Gent', who died on 5 October 1892, aged forty-seven. The Parish Registers also disclose the reason for the sale by recording the death of Margaret Nevinson of Town on 1 February 1788, also at the age of forty-seven. The house which she and her elder sister Eleanor had occupied since the Tysons boarded them in the early 1770s had been given up, and the whole or a good part of the furniture sold. There is little doubt that Nell then went to live with Ann, to help her at first, and later to care for her. Miss Mary Hodgson had heard from Philip Braithwaite and from her father that Ann had a niece who lived with her in her old age; and, though she could not name her, I can find no alternative to Eleanor Nevinson.

Throughout her final year as 'Household Dame' Ann Tyson had at least four boarders, including yet another Wordsworth, making six in all during her ten and a half years. He was Robinson Wordsworth, youngest son of Richard, Collector of Customs at Whitehaven, and therefore first cousin to Christopher, and uncle of the young Richard who had been with her since August 1787. Robinson was fourteen when he first came to her on 25 January 1789. He joined the Book Club straight away, and when the New Library was opened in August 1789 he subscribed to it, the charge in each case being 5s. a year. But when Ann retired at the end of the year he left the School, as is shown by the inscription in the book he then presented to the New Library. It is a copy of the second edition of Dr. Middleton's *Life of Cicero* in three volumes, published in 1741.[1]

On 7 March 1789 Ann Tyson was due to receive another new boarder, who is entered in her book as 'Wm Knot'; but very probably he did not come then, as underneath the original heading, which is not in her handwriting, she has written '24 July', and the account is for one half-year only. For the Autumn Half, 1789, Richard and Robinson Wordsworth returned on 27 July but Christopher not until a week later. The new boy was George Knott's third son, William, now seven years old, and an orphan. His presence must often have turned Ann's thoughts back to her years of service with his grandparents at Rydal, and to her summer visits to Bonaw with his parents; and, old as she was, it would be strange indeed if her feelings towards him differed from those which led Wordsworth to describe her as 'so motherly and good'. He alone of her boarders was still at school when she died in 1796; and, though Miss Mary Hodgson's recollection of his name was hazy, it can only have been to him that Philip Braithwaite was referring when he told her of a pupil at Hawkshead School who as a new boy had boarded with Ann, and with whom she had kept in touch during her retirement. Until she was nearing her end, it pleased her, he said, to have this boy, and perhaps a friend, to tea or supper two or three times every half-year;

---

[1] Robinson Wordsworth (1775–1856), after one year at Hawkshead School, went to Yarmouth Customs House (I owe this detail to D. B. Sewell) and five years later, probably through the influence of John Robinson, a powerful patron of nearly all his Wordsworth relatives, young Robinson became Collector of Customs at Harwich. On his marriage in 1797, his mother being still alive and his late father's money therefore tied up in securities, he was forced to ask Wordsworth to repay £250 of the money he owed the family for his education—Wordsworth's inheritance not yet having been paid by the Lowthers; see *Wordsworth Letters: Early Years*, pp. 184–8. There, Dorothy quotes Losh's news 'that it was universally reported in Cumberland that he [William] had used his Uncle's children very ill. All these things are very unpleasant, besides their claims are so just that it is absolutely necessary that something must be done.'

and rarely did he go away, it appears, without some little present she or her niece had baked for him.

Proof that William Knott was still at school when Ann Tyson died is contained in the lists of boys, at one time as high as thirty-seven, who subscribed to the New Library from August 1789 to the end of 1797. His name occurs in the last three lists, 12th out of 12 in 1796₂, 11th out of 11 in 1797₁, and finally 8th out of 9 in 1797₂.¹ By the end of 1797 he had been eight and a half years in the school, but as he was still under sixteen he may have stayed on longer. He did not present a book to the New Library on leaving; so it is impossible to say just when his schooldays ended.

The next youngest of the boarders Ann Tyson had when she retired was Richard Wordsworth of Whitehaven, who was then twelve.² He appears to have stayed on at the school until he was fourteen or fifteen. But there is no mention of him in the New Library records, and the only tangible proof that he was in Hawkshead after 1789 is that he carved or scratched his name on a stone inside the building erected in 1790 to serve as a Market House, with a Court or Assembly Room above. That building is now the Town Hall, and it was in its Lower Hall that the carved or scratched signature was uncovered about 1930 when some plaster on one of the walls had to be renewed. In the Market House as originally built this particular room housed the butchers' stands, and apart from the ceiling the interior does not seem to have been plastered.

Christopher Wordsworth, who had been with Ann Tyson for nine Halves when she retired, remained at Hawkshead School for a further two and three-quarter years, during which he boarded, still at Colthouse, with a young farmer named John Rainforth and his wife. A member of the Book Club in 1787, but seemingly not in 1788, he subscribed to the New Library from its opening; and when he left the school in October 1792 he presented to it a copy of Dr. William Robertson's *Historical Disquisition concerning the knowledge which the Ancients had of India*, a work published in the previous year.

---

¹ From this point onwards T.W.T. frequently refers to the Spring and Autumn Halves by an under-written 1 or 2: e.g. 1796₂ means Autumn Half, 1796.

² D. B. Sewell tells me that Richard was baptized at St. Nicholas Church, Whitehaven, on 10 February 1777 and died, unmarried, at St. Helena on 30 May 1796.

In the lists of library subscribers he is placed 5th in August 1789, and 1st from August 1790 until he left. This means, I should think, that he was top of the highest class in the school for more than two years; a class which included 'all the Boys in Greek', to use Thomas Bowman's words. Dorothy Wordsworth, writing to Jane Pollard on 26 June 1791, says of Christopher that 'his abilities though not so great perhaps as his brothers', meaning William's, 'may be of more use to him as he has not fixed his mind upon any particular species of reading or conceived an aversion to any. He is not fond of Mathematics, but has resolution sufficient to study them because it will be impossible for him to obtain a fellowship without a knowledge of them.'

Going up to Trinity College, Cambridge, in October 1792, Christopher Wordsworth was 10th Wrangler in 1796, and was elected to a Fellowship in 1798, but had to relinquish it when he married in 1804. His wife died in 1815; from 1804–20 he was successively Rector of Ashby-with-Oby and Thirne in Norfolk, Dean of Bocking in Essex, Rector of St. Mary's, Lambeth, in Surrey, and of Sundridge in Kent. The last two of these livings, which he held in plurality, he exchanged in 1820 for the rectory of Buxted-with-Uckfield in Sussex. When at Bocking he served for a time as Chaplain to the Archbishop of Canterbury, and later he was Chaplain for a while to the House of Commons. In 1820 he returned to Cambridge as Master of Trinity College, an office he held until 1841, when he retired to Buxted, where he died in 1846. He was Vice-Chancellor of Cambridge University in 1820–1, and again in 1826–7. His chief publications were *Ecclesiastical Biography* in 1809–10, a fine collection of selected and annotated lives which ran to six volumes; *Christian Institutes* in 1836, a selection filling four volumes from the writings of the great English divines; and his learned, though scarcely conclusive, attempts in 1824–8 to prove that King Charles I was the author of *Eikon Basiliké*.

Ann Tyson's charges for boarding and extras—cockpennies—book costs—Mr. Mingay—Wordsworth boys' journeys to and from school—pocket money—Ann Tyson's baking and cooking—food, skates and shoes—tailoring and hats—stationery, postage charges—settlement of accounts

Ann Tyson's charge for boarding Hawkshead schoolboys during the period August 1784 to December 1789 was at first 6 guineas and then 6½ for each half-yearly term of about twenty-one weeks, or slightly less now and again. Newcomers had to pay 6½ guineas from the beginning of the Spring Half 1786, but for John Wordsworth's sons the charges does not seem to have been put up until August 1787. It was the same for Robert Greenwood when he was nineteen as for William Knott at the age of seven. For periods shorter than a half-year Ann's charge was from 6s. 3d. to 6s. 5d. a week, as in all such cases she would have received 6½ guineas had the half-year been completed. The charge included washing. Mr. Bowstead had to pay seven guineas a half-year for board and lodging, and an additional 16s. for washing. The advances in less than a decade in the half-yearly charge for boarding boys from 5 guineas, with washing extra, to 6 and then 6½ guineas, including washing, were due in the main to the general rise in prices in the 1780s; a rise which was causing concern in Hawkshead. The highest fee, 6½ guineas, was by no means excessive. At the Friends' School, Kendal, boarders were received by Jonathan and John Dalton from 1787 onwards at £14 per annum exclusive of washing; and even as far back as 1722 the terms for boarding there were cited as '£14 per Ann (Washing and Tea excluded)'.

In Ann Tyson's accounts fuel and light are treated as extras. The entries in the earliest of them, which is for Richard, William, and John Wordsworth, 1784$_2$, include 6s. 4d. for a cart of coals on 25 October, 1s. 6d. for a cart of peats soon after, 7½d. for a pound of candles on 7 August, subsequently 7½d. for a further pound, then 8d. each for three more pounds. Here let me say that the carts then in use were rather small, and that so far as Hawkshead was concerned coals then meant charcoal. Its price in Ann's accounts is never less than 6s. a cart, and never more than 6s. 6d. For peats, which are mentioned less frequently, and scarcely at all in the later accounts, the charge is always 1s. 6d. a cart, except in 1786₁, when it is 2s. By then candles cost 8½d. a pound. For some reason peats had suddenly become much dearer, as is well illustrated in the accounts for the Poor House at Sand Ground in the Hawkshead Quarter of the parish. For 'Peats geting & Leading'[1] the price paid was 6d. a cart in 1778, but in the 1790s the usual charge was first 1s. and then 1s. 6d. a cart. Sand Ground at that date might well have had a peat-moss of its own, as, of course, would Greenend. Title deeds show that the house opposite Ann Tyson's cottage in Hawkshead Town then had a peat-moss at Hawkshead Fieldhead and two 'at the Tarns', otherwise Tarn Hows, as well as a bracken-garth at Brathay, the Customary or Lords' Rent for each of them being ½d. a year.

No doubt Wordsworth was thinking of his early years at Hawks-head School when he wrote in *The Prelude*

> Eager and never weary we pursued
> Our home amusements by the warm peat-fire
> At evening
>   (I.534–6)

for he goes on to tell of their battles at noughts-and-crosses 'with pencil and with slate', and of their combats at Loo or Whist with an assemblage of cards, 'husbanded through many a long campaign' which constituted a pack only because the face-values of not a few of them had been altered to that end. At Colthouse, judging from Ann's accounts, he and his brothers were neither extravagant nor particu-larly careful in the matter of fuel and light. In 1786₂, and again in 1787₁, they had two carts of coals, which is as much as Mr. Bowstead ever allowed himself in one half-year. With regard to candles, there is some doubt. I have noted that in 1785₂ they were charged for only three pounds; that candles at 8½d. a pound appear in both the 1786 accounts; and that an Assistant at the school included in 1787₂ an item which reads 'Wᵐ Stevenson Candles . . . o. 10. 9¾'. This is obviously a bill for candles supplied during two Halves, and some either not charged for, or charged, but not paid for, earlier than that. For downright extravagance it is necessary to turn to Thomas

---

[1] Dorothy Wordsworth, on a walk 'to Brathay by Little Langdale and Collath and Skelleth', found this a pleasing sight; she wrote in her Journal for 16 June 1800: 'Collath was wild and interesting, from the Peat carts and peat gatherers . . .'.

Gawthrop's accounts.[1] In 1786₂ he had three carts of coals at 6s. each, a cart of peats at 1s. 6d., and 13 pounds of candles at 8½. a pound. That makes £1. 8s. 8½d.; but he must have had a fourth cart of coals, as the Grammar School Assistant finally responsible for his bill charged him £1. 14s. 9d. for 'share of Candles Fire &c'. During the eleven weeks he boarded with Ann in 1787₁ he had a further three carts of coals. True, he had a 'Room Extraordinary'; but so did William Losh, and his share of 'Fire & Candles' in 1786₂ came to 14s. 3d. Greenwood's share of 'Coals Candles &c' for the same half-year was 6s. 7d., and Robinson Wordsworth's for 1789₁ 5s. 4½d.

The boys are also charged in Ann Tyson's accounts for 'Share of School Coals' or 'School Fire'; but though I noted every Wordsworth entry of this type, save one perhaps, all I have are the following: Richard, William, and John, 3s. 9d. in 1784₂; William, John, and Christopher, 5s. in 1786₁; Christopher, 2s. in 1788₂, 6d. in 1789₁, and again in 1789₂; Richard of Whitehaven, 1s. 6d. in 1788₁, and 1s. in 1788₂; Robinson, 6d. in 1789₁, and the same in 1789₂. As there was only one fire, and there were just over a hundred boys in the School, the charge of 6d. per boy for a half-year was about right I should say. It would bring in enough to buy eight carts of coals, sufficient fuel to maintain a good fire during the weeks when one was needed. The other charges should be interpreted, it seems, on this 6d. basis. Richard Wordsworth of Whitehaven was with Ann Tyson for five Halves before she retired, and the 2s. 6d. he was charged for 'School coals' is in accord with this, even if the putting of 1s. 6d. on his 1788₁ bill and 1s. on his 1788₂ account is odd.[2]

---

[1] But Gawthrop was 18½ and in his last year at school, as was Wordsworth, and it is not surprising that boys preparing for university should need more light and fuel, in that they read more.

[2] It is less odd than T.W.T. surmises. The neat and finished Senhouse accounts (see Appendix III) make more clear than Ann Tyson's rough ledger that payment for school coals was at irregular intervals—when and as coal was needed. On 17 February 1783 the two Senhouse boys paid William Taylor 1s. 6d. each, on 29 November 1784 1s. 3d. each, and on 17 February 1786 again 1s. 3d. each, for school coals. Significantly the amounts in the Senhouse accounts, and the Halves when they were charged, correspond exactly to those in the Wordsworth accounts. Thus the Wordsworths' 5s. paid in 1786₁ was for four boys, not three as T.W.T. interprets it; it must include Richard, although by then he had left school, since there had been no charge for school coals since 1784.

Although Hawkshead School was Free from its Elizabethan foundation, there were charges, little more than nominal, made for tuition in writing, which was not considered a grammar school subject. Up to 1789 it was 1s. a half-year, payable to the Writing-Master in cash, or entered in the bill as for the Writing-Master. During his lifetime John Wordsworth paid it in respect of his sons; but in Ann Tyson's accounts there is no mention of the Writing-Master until 1788, when in Christopher's account 'Writing Master . . . o. 1. o' is entered. But I fancy some of the shillings borrowed from Ann by his elder brothers were to pay the Writing-Master. In their 1785₁ account, for instance, three entries in Ann's own hand-writing read: 'Lent mr Rechet '1s.; 'Lent fcr '3s.; 'Lent Willoin '1s. Two are crossed out, and the second entry is left unfinished. John Wordsworth seems to have had tuition in writing almost to the end of his school-days: at any rate 'John Cop[y] Book . . . o. 1. o' occurs in the 1787₁ account. His father wrote beautifully; and there is no doubt that at least a few boys went on having handwriting lessons until they were fourteen or fifteen. Christopher and Robinson Wordsworth both did, as their 1789 accounts show. Christopher's for 1789₁, and Robinson's for both 1789₁, and 1789₂, contain 'Writing Master . . . . o. 1. o' twice over in each, which proves, I think, that Thomas Bowman had decided to make 1s. a quarter the official charge for tuition in handwriting, though perhaps only so far as older boys were concerned, for in William Knott's account for 1789₂ there is only one entry reading 'Writing Master . . . . o. 1. o'. There are no such entries in young Richard Wordsworth's accounts.[1]

---

[1] T.W.T.'s inference that younger boys paid less than older for the Writing-Master's attentions is not borne out by other schoolboys' accounts. On 18 January 1787 Henry and Charles Morland paid Joseph Varty, the Writing-Master, 'To four Quarters Writing & Accts. £1. o. o' (Record Office, Kendal). James and William Senhouse were also paying 2s. 6d. a quarter for the Spring Half of 1784; in October 1784 they paid 10s. 6d. each, and in 1785 12s. each for two quarters of writing— which, in James's case, at least, included 'counting'. These four boys were aged between ten and twelve. The variation in amount charged demonstrates clearly that tuition from the Writing-Master was at the option of parents. The Wordsworth boys had more attention from the Writing-Master than Ann Tyson's ledger indicates. In 1784₂, for instance, Ann has nothing about the Writing-Master, but Christopher Cookson paid him £1. os. 8d.

In lieu of fees, the Master of Hawkshead School received Cock-pennies, at any rate in respect of boys who did not reside in the parish. This voluntary but customary payment, due at Shrovetide, appears regularly in the Spring Half accounts for the Wordsworth boys. Clearly it was $1\frac{1}{2}$ guineas each irrespective of age. The only puzzling entry is that for 1786_1, when the sum due for John Wordsworth's sons is given as £6. 10s. 6d. On the same line as this figure, and just in front of it, an intermediate total is entered: it is £5. 15s. 6d. No explanation is offered, the only word used being 'Cockpenys'. The circumstances were that Christopher had entered the school at the beginning of 1785_2, and Richard had left at the end, and during that one Half, all four of John Wordsworth's sons were at the school. The intermediate total, $5\frac{1}{2}$ guineas, must have included Cockpennies for William, John, and Christopher amounting to $4\frac{1}{2}$ guineas, and a 1-guinea charge for something else, which I take to be the entrance fee for Christopher, payment of which had been deferred.[1] In 1786_1, Robert Greenwood evidently paid his Cockpenny in cash, which he borrowed from Ann Tyson; but 'Cock penes . . . 1. 11. 6' occurs in her 1787_1 account for him. They were not discontinued until 1829, though both cock-fighting and attendance at cock-fights were prohibited in a set of 'Hawkshead School Rules' drawn up by James Peake and printed in 1772.

William and Christopher certainly, and Richard Wordsworth probably, were pupils 'in Greek' at Hawkshead School. Judging from Ann Tyson's ledger William reached the highest class in January 1785, when he was still under fifteen, as the 1785_1 account for the three Wordsworths then at the school includes a Euclid at 4s. 6d. and a Greek Exercises at the same price, both early purchases. During the previous half-year William had written to his guardians for some books. What is noted in their accounts is the payment on 20 Septem-

[1] The 'Cockpenys' ledger entry is perhaps more confusedly written than T.W.T. indicates; it must, as he says, have included three $1\frac{1}{2}$-guinea cockpennies, but the remainder is not explained. Christopher's entrance fee was not part of it; Christopher Cookson, as administrator of John Wordsworth's estate, indicates in his accounts that the normal $1\frac{1}{2}$-guinea entrance fee was paid for his nephew Christopher on 10 December 1785. The account for Master Samson Senhouse, who entered Hawkshead at the same time as Christopher, shows that this fee went to 'Mr Taylor & y^e Usher', probably a guinea to one and half a guinea to the other.

ber 1784 of 8*d.* postage on a letter from 'Master William Wordsworth at Keswick' asking for these books.[1] The guardians' accounts
also show that in 1786 Wordsworth had a 'Hedricks Lexicon' costing
£1, a Demosthenes at 4*s.*, and two other books for 7*s*;[2] whilst in
Ann Tyson's Wordsworth account for 1786₂ two entries read
'Books .... 1. 1. 0' and 'Book .... 1. 1. 0'. In her Robert Greenwood
account for 1786₁ an entry 'Paid for Anabasis .... 0. 7. 0' is crossed
through, presumably when the 7*s.* was repaid. The Hawkshead
bookseller in the 1780s was William Todhunter, who was also a
hatter.[3] About 1793 he moved to Kendal, where from 1796 to 1832
his museum, a 'remarkable collection' in J. F. Curwen's opinion, was
a feature of the town. It was a small museum, not open to the public,
in a room behind his shop at Hawkshead, and some of the schoolboys
there used to call in the evening to ask about his specimens.

Speaking of his boyhood, in a prose note on his 'Ode to Lycoris',
Wordsworth says: 'Before I read Virgil I was so strongly attached to
Ovid, whose *Metamorphoses* I read at school, that I was quite in a
passion whenever I found him, in books of criticism, placed below
Virgil. As to Homer, I was never weary of travelling over the scenes
through which he led me. Classical literature affected me by its own

---

[1] T.W.T.'s source here is Gordon Wordsworth's article, 'The Boyhood of
Wordsworth' (1920): unfortunately, this item is not in the surviving guardians'
accounts that I have examined. T.W.T. thought that Keswick might be a mistake
for Hawkshead.

[2] Again from Gordon Wordsworth; these items do survive in the accounts and I
quote them separately below, together with an entry for an earlier book purchase:
'Febry 23 [1784] Cash paid for 2 Vol Homer & 1 Vol Lucian for my Nephews' ... 8*s*.9*d.*;
26 January 1786, 'my Nephew W^m. for two Books' ... 7*s.* (both these are from
the accounts of Uncle Richard Wordsworth of Whitehaven); 13 March 1786, 'To
Cash paid Ant^y. Soulby for a Hedricks Lexicon for W^m ...' £1; and on 8 August
1786, 'Anthony Soulby a Demosthenes for William ...' 4*s.* (these last two items are
from the accounts of Christopher Cookson). Anthony Soulby was a Penrith bookseller. 'Hedricks Lexicon' was Benjamin Hederick's *Lexicon Manuale Graecum*, a
Greek-Latin/Latin-Greek word-book which went through several editions in the
eighteenth century.

[3] William Todhunter of Hawkshead may have been a hatter as well as a bookseller,
but according to Christopher Cookson's accounts, it was Mrs. Sarah Todhunter who
was paid in February 1787, £1. 8*s.* 5½*d.* 'for hats', while in August 1788 £1. 2*s.* 0*d.*
was paid to William Todhunter, presumably for books—in the same accounts in
1791 he is specifically called 'bookseller'.

beauty.' Nor does Wordsworth leave us in any doubt of his appreciation of geometry as presented in Euclid's *Elements*, of which, in common with other boys in the highest class at Hawkshead, he studied the first four books and the sixth. Twice in *The Prelude* (V.64 ff. and VI. 178 ff. in the 1805 text) he writes of its appeal to him.

> Mighty is the charm
> Of those abstractions to a mind beset
> With images, and haunted by itself;
> And specially delightful unto me
> Was that clear Synthesis built up aloft
> So gracefully. . .
>
> (VI.178–83 (1805))

John Wordsworth's trustees and the guardians of his children record the payment on 10 December 1785 of £5. 4s. 0d. to Mr. Mingay for 'teaching R W^m. John & Christ^r to dance';[1] and in 1789, Robinson Wordsworth borrowed 10s. 4d. from Ann Tyson to pay Mr. Mingay. The dancing master who taught fencing and some French, is best remembered for the Military Academy in connection with Hawkshead School which he opened on 12 January 1789.[2]

---

[1] The Senhouse account for the same date shows that each boy was charged one guinea for the quarter beginning 1 September; 5s. for ball money; and, in the case of Master Samson, a new boy, an extra 5s. entrance fee. This explains exactly the Wordsworths' £5. 4s. 0d.—one guinea per quarter each plus 5s. each. This last sum was probably entrance fee, but possibly ball money.

[2] The full extent and nature of W. T. Mingay's activities can best be learnt from a series of advertisements that appeared from 1781 onwards in the *Cumberland Pacquet*. On 24 July of that year it was reported:

> Mr. Mingay's ball at Cockermouth, on Friday last, exceeded any thing of the kind ever seen there, in point of dress and elegance, and the performances of his pupils were highly applauded by a very polite and numerous company.

Two years later on 22 July 1783 the first advertisement connected with Hawkshead School made its appearance:

DANCING

MR. MINGAY begs Leave to acquaint the Parents of Young Gentlemen, at Hawkshead School, that he proposes attending there on the 11th of August; to teach Dancing and the French Language. Mr. Mingay takes this Opportunity of returning Thanks to those Ladies and Gentlemen who have already honoured him with their Commands, and hopes by exerting his utmost Abilities to merit a Continuance of their Favours.

Terms 1l. 1s. per Quarter, Entrance 5s. to those who have not been under his Tuition.

By the time the Wordsworth boys were having dancing (and probably French) lessons in 1785, Mr. Mingay had obviously been for at least two years established as an itinerant teacher of those subjects in Hawkshead. Clearly he had much to draw him to Hawkshead as his wife was from that district. At the same time he had connections with a school in Carlisle, as a notice in the *Cumberland Pacquet* for 23 December 1783 indicates:

DANCING

M R. MINGAY most respectfully informs the Ladies and Gentlemen of CARLISLE and its Environs, That he is engaged at Miss BIRD's BOARDING SCHOOL, and that he purposes opening a Public SCHOOL, on the 19th of January, 1784, for teaching the most fashionable Dances, now in Use at Court and the first Assemblies in Great Britain. He flatters himself, from the utmost Exertion of his Abilities, to give Satisfaction to those Parents who mean to honour him with the Care of their Children.

Mr. MINGAY begs Leave to acquaint the Ladies and Gentlemen, who have already favoured him with their Commands, that he is now in LONDON, under the most eminent Masters, for the Purpose of acquiring the newest Taste, and making every improvement suitable to his Determination of omitting Nothing in his Power, to merit a Continuance of their Favours.

N. B.   Gentlemen also taught the SMALL SWORD.—Particulars may be known by applying to Mr. MINGAY.

Similar announcements appear in the Januarys of 1785 and 1786; an addition in the latter notice runs:

☞ Mr. MINGAY purposes teaching in LANCASTER early in *May*, of which due Notice will be given.

The next notice about the Carlisle school and Assembly Room classes was printed in the newspaper for 10 September 1788, and is indeed dated from Lancaster. It looks as though Mr. Mingay was gradually moving south. Then comes the announcement of the proposed Military Academy at Hawkshead; it appears in the *Cumberland Pacquet* for 15 October 1788:

MILITARY ACADEMY,
HAWKSHEAD, LANCASHIRE.
Mr. MINGAY

B EGS Leave to inform his Friends and the Public, That he is fitting up, and intends opening, on MONDAY the 12th of January, 1789, a genteel and commodious House, in a pleasant and airy Situation, adjoining *Hawkshead School*, for the Reception of Young Gentlemen, as Boarders, where such Youths as are committed to his Care will be prepared

H

Mr. Mingay's Military Academy did not attract many pupils, and lasted only a short time. In a circular announcing its closure he gave as the reason his decision to join the Army himself. He did so, and is said to have become a bandmaster, and to have been killed by a 'stray or misdirected shot' when his band was 'playing the regiment on to the field of battle. Leastways that is what Mrs. Mingay was told.' I

either for the *Army, Navy, University,* or *Counting-House,* at Twenty-five Pounds a Year, and Three Guineas Entrance.

The Languages and Sciences taught in this Academy, on the above Terms, are, English, Latin, Greek, and French; Writing in all Hands; Arithmetic, Merchants Accounts, Navigation, Geography, and the Use of the Globes; Dancing, Fencing, and Music.

The Young Gentlemen will have the Advantage of receiving the Classical and Mathematical Parts of their Education, at Hawkshead School; the Head Master of which is the Rev. T. BOWMAN, A. M. and Fellow of Trinity College; the First Assistant CHARLES FARISH, A. B. of Queen's College, *Cambridge.* The other Branches will be taught by Mr. MINGAY, and Able Assistants.

Mr. MINGAY assures his Friends, That Nothing will be wanting to render the Situation of his Pupils pleasant and agreeable; their Morals, Manners, and Address, will be particularly attended to; and their Constitutions, Tempers, and Genius, judiciously consulted.

$*_*^*$ Any of the Young Gentlemen of Mr. BOWMAN's School may be taught French, Dancing, Music, or Fencing, by the Quarter, on the usual Terms.

ACADEMY, HAWKSHEAD, *October* 12, 1788.

There are one or two details here extra to those found in the printed circular which was discovered among the Rawlinson papers (see *Hawkshead,* Henry Swainson Cowper, 1899, pp. 500–1), most important being the inclusion of the name of the First Assistant at Hawkshead School, Charles Farish. Farish, who had left Hawkshead for Cambridge in 1784, is best known for his poem, *The Minstrels of Winandermere.* See below, pp. 134–5 and Appendix I. Dancing had a real importance for Wordsworth from the time he was fourteen years old (see below, pp. 125–7), and Mr. Mingay must have promoted this enthusiasm. It has not been noticed that he was also responsible for Wordsworth's earliest knowledge of French. The American, Charles Sumner, writing from Keswick on 8 September 1838, reports a conversation he had with Wordsworth at Rydal Mount:

I amused him not a little by telling him that a Frenchman recommended himself to me, on my arrival in Paris, as a teacher of French, by saying that he had taught the great English poet, Wordsworth. The latter assured me that he had not had a French instructor since his dancing-master! (*Memoir and Letters of Charles Sumner,* ed. E. L. Pierce, U.S.A., 1878, p. 356.)

Mingay was in Hawkshead in 1791 when Daniel Gardner paid him the usual guinea a quarter to teach his son, George, French. (For Gardner see Alphabetical List, Appendix IV.)

am quoting from a note made in 1885 by the Rev. John Allen, then Vicar of Hawkshead; a note almost certainly based on information supplied to him by Thomas Bowman of Roger Ground, only son of the Rev. Thomas Bowman. Mrs. Mingay is the Elizabeth Mingay of Barkhouse-Bank, in the neighbouring parish of Colton, who was buried at Hawkshead on 23 January 1825, aged seventy-one. And Mr. Mingay's only known son William, who was at Hawkshead School with Braithwaite Hodgson, and who died as a young man, is undoubtedly the 'William Adolphus Mingay of Walkerground Surgeon' who died there on 2 March 1807, aged twenty-two, and was buried in Hawkshead churchyard on the 5th.

In the 1805 text of *The Prelude* Wordsworth tells us that

> One Christmas-time,
> The day before the Holidays began,
> Feverish, and tired, and restless, I went forth
> Into the fields, impatient for the sight
> Of those two Horses which should bear us home;
> My Brothers and myself.
>
> (XI.345–50)

And later he says:

> Ere I to School return'd
> That dreary time, ere I had been ten days
> A dweller in my Father's House, he died,
> And I and my two Brothers, Orphans then,
> Followed his Body to the Grave.
>
> (XI.364–8)

The year therefore was 1783, when the Wordsworths at Hawkshead School were Richard, William, and John. They made the journey to and from school on horseback, for as yet there was no feasible alternative. But did they ride two on one horse, as the mention of only two horses suggests; or were there two led horses, one each for Richard and William, in addition to the horse ridden by the man who brought them over, on which he could mount John, just turned eleven, in front of him for the journey from Hawkshead to Cockermouth? The latter is the more likely, as in the 1850 text of *The Prelude* the reference is not to 'two Horses' but to 'led palfreys'.

Though it matters little, I am interested nevertheless, because there was a school rule at the time forbidding boys to ride two on one horse; a rule made in 1781 by the Rev. Edward Christian during his brief Mastership, following an accident attributed to the practice, or aggravated by it. I heard of it from Miss Mary Hodgson, who said that Wordsworth mentioned it when talking to her father at Green-end about their schooldays. Braithwaite Hodgson, who was at Hawkshead School in the 1790s, told him that the rule was still in force then, and that it was generally observed in the vicinity of Hawkshead, but not further afield. He then spoke of two former pupils of the school, John Gunson and Ned Tyson, contemporaries of Wordsworth, who fairly often came over from Ulpha-in-Dunnerdale to borrow books from the New Library, to which they subscribed. Usually they rode two on one horse, but when they neared Hawkshead one or other of them dismounted, and walked by the side of his companion for the rest of the way. They deceived nobody, Braithwaite Hodgson added; but 'Tommy', in other words the Rev. Thomas Bowman, appreciated the gesture. John Gunson (1769–1828), was of Kirk House, Ulpha, where he succeeded his father Joseph Gunson, yeoman, in 1792. The Rev. Edward Tyson (1771–1854), son of Thomas Tyson, farmer, of Borrowdale Place, Eskdale, was curate of Ulpha from 1797 to 1800, and incumbent of Seathwaite-in-Dunnerdale, in succession to 'Wonderful Walker', from 1802 to 1854.

After their father's death, John Wordsworth's sons probably spent the summer holidays at Penrith in the Cooksons' house under the guardianship of their maternal uncle Christopher Cookson, and the winter holidays at Whitehaven with their other guardian, John Wordsworth's brother Richard. In the summer of 1784 'horse hire', 5s., is entered in their guardians' accounts, presumably the cost of bringing Richard, William, and John from Hawkshead to Penrith, although it appears to be inadequate for that purpose. In January 1785 the phrase 'chaise hire' appears for the first time, and it had cost £2. 18s. 8d. just before that Christmas to bring four boys from Hawkshead to Whitehaven; whilst in 1789 the cost for Christopher was 8s. 6d. Travelling to and from school by chaise had its draw-backs: costs were high, and at that time many of the roads were not at all good. It is hardly surprising, then, that there were reversions to journeying on horseback. One such was in the summer of 1787, as a letter from Penrith by Dorothy Wordsworth to Jane Pollard makes plain:

I was for a whole week kept in expectation of my Brothers, who staid at school all that time after the vacation begun owing to the ill-nature of my Uncle who would not send horses for them because when they wrote they did not happen to mention them, and only said when they should break up which was always before sufficient. . . . At last however they were sent for, but not till my Brother Wm had hired a horse for himself and came over because he thought someone must be ill. . . .[1]

In Ann Tyson's Wordsworth account for 1787$_1$ the charge for boarding William, John, and Christopher is entered first as £19. 11s. 6d. and then as £20. 9s. 6d. because of their late departure. Ann's ledger affords a second example of reversion to travelling on horseback. It is in her Christopher Wordsworth account for the half-year beginning 22 January 1788, and reads 'Jan. 22 Paid Horse hire for 2 Horses . . . . 0. 12. 0'. The handwriting is not hers. Nor is it clear why she should have paid the cost, unless it was that a Hawkshead man had gone to Whitehaven to bring Christopher to school, or had taken him there at the beginning of the Christmas holidays and not been paid.[2]

Payments by Ann to Robert Wallace for 'careg' are common in the Wordsworth accounts up to the end of 1787. They occur, too, in Thomas Gawthrop's account for 1787$_1$, and in Robinson Wordsworth's for 1789$_2$. In respect of John Wordsworth's sons there are as many as three payments in 1785$_2$, and again in 1787$_1$. They varied in amount from 2s. to 3s., and obviously were for luggage, a box being specified on two occasions. There is no indication as to where Robert Wallace picked up this luggage. He lived at Colthouse, and is described in the Hawkshead Parish Registers as a carrier in 1783 and a farmer in 1787; and a few years later he was supplying meat to the Poor House at Sand Ground. When he married Margaret Askew at Torver in 1770 he was said to be 'of Ulverstone'; and it is very likely that as a carrier he went there and to Kendal regularly.

In Book II of *The Prelude* Wordsworth tells us that, except for a

[1] See *Wordsworth Letters: Early Years*, pp. 3–4, letter dated late July 1784.
[2] See Additional Notes, Appendix V.

'little weekly stipend', he and his school-fellows lived for three-quarters of the time in 'pennyless poverty'. When Ann Tyson's accounts begin in 1784₂ she was dealing out 14*d*. a week to Richard, William, and John Wordsworth, but she does not say how this not ungenerous allowance was divided between them. The total remained at 1*s*. 2*d*. a week after Christopher had joined his brothers in August 1785, but again there is no indication as to how it was shared. In 1787₂ it was 6*d*. for William, and until she retired, Christopher had 3*d*. a week. So did Robinson Wordsworth in 1789, Ann Tyson's last year as a 'Household Dame'. For the Maudes, Richard Wordsworth of Whitehaven, and William Knott, it was 2*d*. a week each. That is all I have noted, except that Greenwood, Gawthrop, and Losh did not have pocket-money doled out to them weekly by Ann.

After referring to their poverty through 'three divisions of the quarter'd year', Wordsworth goes on to say that from the half-yearly holidays they returned to school 'with purses more profusely fill'd', and to tell of the more costly repasts, the excursions, and the picnics they could then afford for a while, and of their husbanding a little money so that later 'in the long length of those half-years' they could enjoy an outing or two. Just how much money John Wordsworth's sons had on their return to school we do not know, for as Gordon Wordsworth has pointed out their guardians' accounts throw only a fitful light on how well their purses were then filled. Sums varying from 5*s*. 3*d*. to 1 guinea are entered, he says, at the end of some vacations, but not regularly, William on the whole faring better than his brothers.[1] Of course they did not pay cash at Hawkshead for anything that could be put on the bill. On the other hand, they did not often borrow cash from Ann Tyson, unless it was to pay the postage on letters they received, or to meet some school charge. In 1786₁ William seems to have had a guinea from Ann, but probably it was to pay for a book or books. In Christopher Wordsworth's 1788₁ account there is an entry I fail to understand. It reads: 'ped Cash from Dick . . . . 0. 4. 4'.[2] Of Ann's other schoolboy boarders,

---

[1] T.W.T. never saw the guardians' accounts, which are helpful here: see Additional Notes, Appendix V.

[2] Possibly this represents Ann's repayment of a loan of 4*s*. which Christopher had borrowed from his fellow boarder, Richard Wordsworth of Whitehaven.

Robert Greenwood borrowed £2. 2s. 0d. and £1. 1s. 0d. from her soon after his arrival in January 1786, and a further 10s. 6d., subsequently crossed out, later in 1786₁; whilst in 1786₂ she twice lent him 10s. 6d. No reason is given for any of these borrowings, but it is reasonable to assume that Greenwood required all or most of the money to pay his Cockpenny and to buy books. In William Losh's account for 1786₂, his only Half with Ann Tyson, 6s. is entered as 'Cash lent him'; and in Richard Wordsworth of Whitehaven's bill for 1787₂ the first item I have noted is 'To cash lent for a Book .... 0. 5. 0'.

The passage in Book II of *The Prelude* from which I have been quoting begins with these words:

> No delicate viands sapp'd our bodily strength;
> More than we wish'd we knew the blessing then
> Of vigorous hunger, for our daily meals
> Were frugal, Sabine fare!

(II.79–82 (1805))

Before considering what the staples of their meals are likely to have been, it may be as well to say something about Ann Tyson's facilities and equipment for cooking and baking. It is certain that she would have a bakestone (pronounced bakstn) for making haver-bread, but not an oven; and that all her cooking, and most of her other baking, would be done over an open fire made, not in a grate, but on a raised or unraised hearth, the only fuels at her disposal being wood, peat, and charcoal. Her pans would be hung over the fire on a crook adjustable as to height by means of a rack; consequently they would have to have fixed or movable bools for handles, like a kettle or a bucket has, but preferably with a fixed ring at the highest point. There were two ways of supporting the rack and crook. In the older, they were fastened to a beam known as the 'rannle bawk' or 'balk' which was fixed across the chimney before it narrowed to a flue, but at a good height above the hearth, or to the iron balk if there happened to be one instead of the usual beam. The newer way, which may not have been generally adopted at Hawkshead by the 1780s, was to incorporate them in a fireside crane, which consisted of a fixed vertical axle, and a horizontal arm high up that could be rotated into or out of the chimney opening, and to which the rack and crook were rigidly attached. Sometimes the 'rannle bawk', or the horizontal arm of the fireside crane, had a chain and crook fixed to it as well. They were 'for a kettle or boiler to supply hot or warm water at the same time as something was being cooked', says one writer, but surely that was not the full extent of their usefulness.

The bakestone, which before the end of the eighteenth century generally had a large rectangular iron plate instead of the original stone, was supplemented by the girdle, a circular iron plate with a detachable bool so that it could be hung over the fire or stood over it on an iron brandreth (tripod) of suitable height. Haver-bread, a thin oat-cake, was made on the bakestone in big batches, and kept either in ceiling-racks attached to the beams, or more often in wooden chests with lids known as bread-arks or bread-kists. In Ann Tyson's day, home-made white bread was a rarity in the district. It was baked, if at all, on the hearth in bread pans, which stood on four legs, and had lids that were put on and covered with glowing embers when it was time to brown the top crusts.

Though Ann Tyson is unlikely to have made white bread, it is almost certain that she would use wheat flour when making pasties, fatty cakes, and suet dumplings and puddings, all of which were customary fare in the district during her later years. Fruit pasties, a great standby in the nineteenth century, were becoming popular in the last quarter of the eighteenth in High Furness; or so it would appear from a manuscript 'Household Book' in which an Elizabeth Wilson of Coniston made a variety of entries, and among them some accounts for the years 1778 to 1781, and a number of recipes. The latter included instructions for making what she called 'Apple Cake', 'Corant Cake', and 'Raisen Cake', each of which consisted of a thin layer of fruit between two pastry crusts that were to be cut out with the aid of an upturned plate. In short they were pasties, to give them the name used locally for such confections from the beginning of the nineteenth century or thereabouts. Elizabeth Wilson's recipes, despite their early date, do not suggest lack of experience in making them but rather the reverse. She specified, for instance, that if possible the apples should cook quickly enough for the slices to be put in raw; failing which they should be partly cooked beforehand with little or no water, as otherwise they would make the bottom crust too wet and soft. She stated, too, that before use the currants should be washed, soaked for a while to swell and soften them, and then dried on a cloth; and that a little brown sugar should be put in with them, and a 'sufficiency of Butter'. The 'cakes' were to be baked on the girdle, a little hole being made in the top crust to let out the steam if there was likely to be any.

Pasties retained their popularity with country folk throughout the nineteenth century: indeed they were baked in greater variety during the latter part of the century than ever before or since; in the oven I need hardly say, for by then it had completely replaced the girdle in farmhouse and cottage alike. On the other hand, the once popular fatty-cakes of the district, which were pastry cakes baked in the frying-pan and usually served hot for dinner, were made less and less after 1850, and scarcely at all by the 1890s. Nevertheless I was able to sample them as a small boy as my mother still made them then. She had become familiar with them when, for eight or nine years before her marriage, she lived with her grandfather John Wilson (1794–1880) at the Causey, Windermere; and at her married home at Ratherheath, near Kendal, she had to use a frying-pan with a bool up to about 1900, as till then there was a fireside crane in the kitchen, and an iron 'rannle bawk' in the main living-room, and consequently a rack and crook in each. I mention this because it is roughly true to say that fatty cakes went out with the hanging frying-pan, which lent itself to making them, whereas its successor did not.

As I remember them, fatty cakes were getting on for half an inch thick, and were of three kinds. In all three the main ingredients were flour and lard, but in one of them the lard was partly replaced by dripping, and in making these a little salt was added. In the other two, which were slightly sweetened, the only fat used with the lard was a small amount of butter. They were either plain cakes, in which case they were eaten with syrup or jam, or they contained dried fruit, preferably chopped raisins, so far as I was concerned. All three varieties were made in the Windermere district when John Wilson was a boy. Moreover, and in this instance strictly relevant as to date, Elizabeth Wilson of Coniston included in her 'Household Book' recipes for making two thickish pastry cakes that were to be cooked in the frying-pan. The first consisted of ordinary pastry with currants in it, and a little finely chopped candied peel. The second contained fine oatmeal as well as flour in the proportion of one to three, and dripping in addition to lard. Beef dripping was generally used, but Elizabeth Wilson recommended bacon dripping when it was available, as it was so much easier to mix in, and the taste it gave to the cake was more to her liking. She specified that it should not be more than a quarter of the total fat and might well be a little less. Her 'Household Book', I may say, turned up at the Causey one day when my mother was helping her grandfather to look for a deed he wanted to consult. After his death it passed into the hands of his daughter-in-law Mrs. Sarah Wilson, afterwards Gibson, of Beckside, Windermere, who lent it to me whilst I was still at school, and was collecting information about the local way of life in earlier times. A Canadian descendant of John Wilson was allowed to take it back with him at the end of the 1914–18 war, in which he served. Elizabeth Wilson was John's great-aunt, possibly by birth but more probably by marriage.

For breakfast Ann is sure to have given her boys oatmeal porridge, served with brown sugar or syrup and milk. There would be haver-bread and butter to follow, and cheese for all who ate it. Those who did not, may have had a boiled egg now and again, or more often a bit of pasty. There would be milk to drink. Mid-day dinner, I should say, would be the only meal at which the boys got meat. Usually it would be butchers' meat, mutton more often than beef, boiled more often than roast, lamb when in season, veal and pork occasionally, salt beef in winter, and just possibly 'mutton-ham', i.e. leg of mutton cured by smoking. The main alternatives are likely to have been ham and bacon, the rarer ones poultry and rabbit. According to Elizabeth Wilson, small plain suet dumplings were eaten with boiled salt beef, and batter pudding with hot roast beef. She also mentioned mutton broth thickened with barley as an extra: there was no meat in it, the broth being made from the liquid left after mutton had been cooked by simmering with water. For the second course the usual provision at the relevant date seems to have been one of the following: suet dumplings of one kind or another, and dump-lings with thick suet crusts; rice or barley pudding made in an iron pan with a bool, and containing dried fruit; and fatty-cake, freshly made and eaten hot, or pasty, cold or warmed up. Elizabeth Wilson also mentioned custard and junket.

For late tea or very early supper young people commonly had a boiled egg, with pasty to finish the meal. As the local haver-bread was thin, Ann Tyson may well have supplemented it by making what Elizabeth Wilson called 'Thick Haver Cakes'. Her recipe for making them was to work wheat flour into cold, stiff oatmeal porridge left from breakfast until the mixture could be rolled out into a cake or cakes about three-quarters of an inch thick. After shaping and trimming, each cake was to be cut into from four to six portions according to its size; and they were to be baked on the girdle, split and buttered, and eaten hot. Obviously they would be improved by spreading syrup, jam, or honey on them. There would hardly be time for another full-scale meal before the boys had to go to bed, but possibly they had more milk and either a piece of ginger bread or a ginger snap. Elizabeth Wilson had recipes for both, and it is worth noting that they were made from oatmeal, and that she cut out her snaps with the aid of a small saucer.

These citations and guesses have been included as an indication of the daily meals Ann Tyson is likely to have provided for her schoolboy boarders, of the 'frugal, Sabine fare' that Wordsworth later regarded as a source of bodily strength. Though her boarding charges were low, it would be untypical of her kind if she did not give her boys a sufficiency of good homely food; but in regard to meat she might have been rather frugal, for that was usual in the district, even among the farmers. Fortunately her ledger furnishes evidence on the point in the form of entries of purchases she made from John Sawrey, the butcher, in 1788, when Eleanor Nevinson was living with her from April onwards if not earlier, and when her only boarders were Mr. Bowstead, Christopher Wordsworth, who was thirteen when the year began, and Richard Wordsworth, who was ten, or possibly eleven. A few examples of these entries are given below in normalized spelling, and with the price or price-range per pound added in square brackets where necessary so that weights can be calculated. The price-range for beef, and the prices for joints of mutton, lamb, and veal not stated in Ann Tyson's account with John Sawrey, are taken from Elizabeth Wilson's 'Household Book'. The assumptions made are that neck of mutton means the whole neck, leg of veal the whole leg, and quarter of lamb and mutton the forequarter.

		s.	d.
3 March	A shoulder of mutton [3½d.]	1	[tear in MS.]
10 ,,	A leg of mutton [4d.] . . .	2	6
17 ,,	Beef [2¾d. to 4½d.]	3	11
17 ,,	Loin of veal [4d.]	2	0
. . .	. . . .	.	.
5 May	A neck of mutton [3d.] . .	2	8
11 ,,	A leg of veal [3¼d.] . . .	2	8
18 ,,	A Pluck		11
. .	. . . .	.	.
17 August	A leg of mutton, 4 lb at 4d. .	1	4
1 September	A quarter of lamb [3½d.] . .	2	0
9 ,,	A quarter of mutton [3d.] . .	4	2

In all, between 3 December 1787 and 14 August 1788 Ann spent with John Sawrey a total of £3. 19s. 9d.; and yet during this period she had boarders for not more than twenty-five weeks; thus she was not particularly frugal in the provision of butchers' meat for them.[1]

When the school hours are taken into account Wordsworth's hunger is understandable. In 1588 it was laid down in the Founder's Statutes that in summer they should be from 6, or at the latest 6.30, to 11 in the morning, and from 1 to 5 in the afternoon; and that in winter, in other words from Michaelmas to Lady Day, the morning and afternoon sessions should be from 7, or at the latest 7.30, to 11

[1] The case for Ann's more plentiful provision is stronger even than T.W.T. allows; for, during approximately the same period, she also spent with two other butchers, £1 15s. 9d. with Michael Satterthwaite and £2 18s. 7d. with Edward Satterthwaite. In February 1789 she appears to have ceased doing business with John Sawrey and to have taken some of her custom to Isaac Sawrey and Henry Forest. The latter's final account, for 14s., was settled on 22 January 1790, and it is the last account to be recorded in the ledger. Ann had no more schoolboys, and must have taken the book into school to have the bills made up, and there, as we have seen, it may have remained.

and from 12.30 to 4. These hours were still being observed two hundred years later; which must not be regarded as unusual, as in 1789 the Governors of Cartmel Grammar School affirmed that in summer the hours there were from 6 a.m. to 12 noon, with an hour off for breakfast, and from 2 to 6 p.m.; and that in winter, when there was no school before breakfast, they were from 8 a.m. to 12 noon, and from 1 to 5 p.m. So far as I know, there was never a breakfast interval at Hawkshead School in the summer; but Miss Mary Hodgson reported her father as saying that in the 1790s, when he was there, morning school did not begin until 6.30, except in May and June, when it started at 6. During these months Ann Tyson's boarders must have had breakfast about 5.15, and, during the rest of the time when winter hours were in operation, about 5.45. From then until dinner was a long time, even if they got it as early as 11.30, which is not unlikely. Farmers, who were in the habit of keeping their clocks half an hour fast, often had dinner at '12 bi t'clock'; and they had usually had a mid-morning 'drinking', as the snack at 9.30 to 10 o'clock was called. That is what the boys needed, for even if they had had a jorum of oatmeal porridge for breakfast, and something to follow it, I expect they felt a bit empty long before morning school was over. There is sure to have been a break in the four-and-a-half or five-hour session; and on a boulder at the higher end of the Market Square an old lady had a stall on which there was something to eat. But if the boys were penniless, except for their 'small weekly stipend' (and what they were saving for an outing), they could spend only a halfpenny a day on the average, and some of them less than that. Besides, there was the afternoon to think about, for in summer school did not end till 5 o'clock, and it would be nearly half-past before they got their third meal of the day.

There was the possibility, of course, of getting extra things to eat and drink and having them put down on the bill; and one of Ann Tyson's boarders did this during his short stay with her to a far greater extent than any of the others. It was Thomas Gawthrop, son of the Vicar of Sedbergh. His account for 1786₂ includes 6 cakes, 4s. 10d.; 8½ pounds of sugar, mostly loaf at 10½d. a pound; 2½ hoops of apples, 2s. 9d.; 6 ounces of tea, 2s. 2d.; 2 fowls at 9d. each; a bottle of wine, 2s. 6d.; a pound of raisins, 7d.; and nutmegs, 8d. The capacity of the hoop, a circular dry measure, varied from place to place, and I cannot say how many pounds of apples he had, but about 30 is a reasonable guess as the average cost cannot have been much more than 1d. a pound in the autumn. After the Christmas holidays Gawthrop was not so free in his spending on credit, but during the ten or eleven weeks he was with Ann in 1787₁ he had 6 cakes at a total cost of 4s. 10d., and broke fresh ground by having eggs, 5d., and milk, 6d.

In the Wordsworth accounts cakes are mentioned, but rather irregularly, the entries being as follows: 1785₂, William, a cake 1s. 6d., and Dick, a cake, 2s.; 1786₁, William, cakes, 3s.; 1786₂, Christopher, 4 cakes, 2s.; 1787₁, William, John, and Christopher, 4 cakes at 8d. each, 2s. 8d.; 1787₂, Christopher, 4 cakes, 2s. 8d.; and 1788₁, Christopher, 6 cakes, 3s. In 1786₂ William, John, and Christopher matched Gawthrop's tea by having coffee, 3s. 9d., put down on their bill, and 6½ pounds of sugar, some at 7d. and the rest at 7½d. a pound. But it did not happen again, and the only other sugar entries in their accounts are 1 pound of loaf sugar, 10½d., in 1787₁, and 'to Ann Parker, sugar, 2s.', in 1787₂. During his final nine weeks at Hawkshead School in 1787₂ William not only increased his cash resources by borrowing 10s. from Ann Tyson, but boldly obtained on credit several pounds of honey, for first there is a composite entry 'Some hounie a hors', 3s., in his account, and then 'Willm huni', 1s. 9d. At the same time Richard of Whitehaven, then a new boy, had a pound of honey, 7d., and so did Robert Greenwood. There are no other references to honey in Ann's ledger, unless by any chance the very puzzling entry 'heter Bell', 3s. 2d., in the Wordsworth account for 1784₂ can be interpreted as heather honey.[1] In this account 'John Birthday', 1s. 6d., occurs in Ann's handwriting, and below it Richard's birthday, 1s. 6d., in another hand. It was the right half-year for John's, which was on 4 December, but not for Richard's, which was on 19 May. The second birthday entry, then, must have been made to repair an omission in the 1784₁ account. There are no more such entries, but in 1789₁ Christopher had a bottle

---

[1] Mrs. Heelis suggested to Gordon Wordsworth that this entry was 'Keten Bell'— Catherine Bell, 'perhaps a washerwoman', but this name does not appear in the Parish Registers. A straightforward reading would be 'Letter Bill'.

of wine at 2s. 4d. which may have been for his birthday on 9 June.

The nature of the cakes that William and his brothers had from Ann Tyson as extras is never specified. In the nineteenth century, a certain Mary Noble's 'Hawkshead Cakes' were currant pasties, and on the strength of this it has been suggested that Ann Tyson's cakes may have been the same. Mary Noble came to Hawkshead from Liverpool or thereabouts, and as a stranger selling currant pasties mainly to strangers (for the local people baked their own) she called them 'Hawkshead Cakes', and for trade reasons the name was retained by her successors. I have never heard natives speak of pasties as cakes, but it is as 'Corant Cake', 'Raisen Cake', and 'Apple Cake' that they appear, as we have seen, in Elizabeth Wilson's 'Household Book', and for that reason (and not because of Mary Noble's later trade usage) the possibility of Ann Tyson's cheaper cakes being currant and raisin pasties cannot be ruled out. On the other hand, the cakes for which she charged 1s. 6d. and 2s. were too costly to have been pasties. My guess is that they were fruit cakes with plenty of butter and eggs in them. Elizabeth Wilson has a recipe for such a cake as well as one for a Christmas cake. Incidentally, she sold butter in Hawkshead Market in the early 1780s at from 3d. to 4d. a pound, and eggs at from 5d. to 8d. a score.

William Wordsworth and his brothers had an account with Peter Sawrey, and included in Ann's bill for 1787$_2$ are the following entries in another hand:

To Peter Sawrey for last year	14	10$\frac{1}{2}$d.
To D^o for this $\frac{1}{2}$ year	9	4$\frac{1}{2}$d.
To Ann Parker, Sugar	2	0 d.
To Peter Sawrey this half year . . .	18	8$\frac{1}{2}$d.

Ann Parker's 2s. for sugar was allowed, but the rest were crossed through and left out of the corrected bill on the opposite page. Evidently Peter Sawrey's bill was going to be forwarded as a separate account to be paid directly to him: with bills of any size that seems to have been the practice.[1] In Christopher's account for 1788$_1$, however, the third entry is 'To Peter Sawrey . . . . 14s. 10$\frac{1}{2}$d', and apparently he got this sum in the following August by way of Ann

[1] For a fuller discussion of how the guardians paid the Hawkshead accounts see Additional Notes, Appendix V.

Tyson. The account appears to have been running for a long time; but there is nothing in Ann's ledger to show what it was for. The Parish Registers supply an answer though, for they record the death on 4 February 1793 of 'Peter Sawrey of Town Grocer . . . Aged 85'. Originally a mercer, he had changed his stock-in-trade to groceries a great many years earlier. He was the father of John Sawrey, the butcher, who was sixty-six when he died at Walker Ground on 8 April 1799. Ann Parker, who supplied the Wordsworths with coffee as well as sugar, was a daughter of Thomas Parker, a Hawkshead currier, and landlord of the Eagle and Child. She died unmarried on 7 November 1811, aged seventy-five.

On 9 February 1765 Ann Parker's sister Elizabeth had married 'George Park of the Parish of Penrith Saddler', a son of 'John Park of Nab in Rydal Husbandman'; and straightway, or very nearly so, he had established himself as a saddler in Hawkshead, where he remained until his death at the age of fifty-four on 25 July 1796. On another occasion I shall have a good deal more to say about him and his eldest son Tom; but here I will comment only on a bill of his for £1. 8s. 6d. which is entered, simply as 'Park's Bill', in the Wordsworths' account for 1786₁. It occurs almost at the beginning of this account, which suggests that it was presented at the end of 1785 for something which was supplied in that year. But what? Gordon Wordsworth, who refers to George Park as an ironmonger, which he was to a limited extent, asks in parenthesis if he sold skates. That, I think, is a pertinent question, for during the early spring of 1785 there was a very prolonged, severe frost: Esthwaite Water was frozen over with thick ice, and so were large areas of Windermere. It was, I feel sure, of this memorable frost that Wordsworth was thinking when he wrote the fine passage in Book I of *The Prelude* which tells of his experiences and pleasures when skating as a schoolboy at Hawkshead, and he referred a little later to 'Esthwaite's splitting fields of ice' from under which

> The pent-up air, struggling to free itself,
> Gave out to meadowgrounds and hills a loud
> Protracted yelling, like the noise of wolves
> Howling in troops along the Bothnic Main.
>   (I.540–3 (1850))

The type of skate then in use consisted of a steel blade fixed in a wooden bed, which was roughly shaped to fit the foot, and secured to it by means of leather straps. But I do not know whether any special leather footwear was necessary, and have little idea what a pair of such skates cost in the 1780s. The charge of £1. 8s. 6d. for the three Wordsworths at Hawkshead School in 1785₁ seems to be too high for skates alone. Anyhow, the great frost of 1785 must have caused a very big demand by Hawkshead schoolboys for skates; and of the local craftsmen and shopkeepers George Park is the most likely to have satisfied it. It is significant, too, that the only purchases John Wordsworth's sons are known to have made from him were almost certainly in the year 1785. And to this I may add that Tom Park, with whom Wordsworth was well acquainted, was an outstanding skater, and on 18 December 1796, at the age of twenty-eight, 'Thomas Park of Town Saddler was drowned in Esthwaite Water by falling through the Ice . . .'[1]

In his *Cornhill* article of 1920, Gordon Wordsworth refers to the Hawkshead shoemakers' bills, at first from Mackreth and then from Suart, which John Wordsworth and his executors had to meet. They were heavy, he says, and cites the payment to Suart of £6. 4s. 9d. in 1784 for the three Wordsworth boys—Richard, William, and John —then at Hawkshead School.[2] He gives the average price of a pair of new shoes as 5s. 6d., and the mean cost of mending a worn pair as 1s. 3d. Shoemakers' charges are rarely included in Ann Tyson's accounts, the only ones I have noted being 'Willm Mackret', 15s. 6d., in her 1787₁ bill for William, John, and Christopher Wordsworth; 'Paid John Suart the Shoemaker his Bill', 16s. 7d., in Richard Wordsworth of Whitehaven's account for 1789₂; and 'Wᵐ Suart', 1s. 5d., in Robert Greenwood's for his final seven weeks, part of 1787₂. John and William Suart, both of Hawkshead, were father and son. Born in 1727, John Suart was married in 1751 to Prudence, daughter of Hugh Cowperthwaite, then landlord of the Red Lion. William, the eldest of their three sons, was baptized on 30 January 1757, and married in 1780 to Ann Wilson, by whom he had a large family. In

---

[1] For more about George Park, see below, pp. 200f., and Additional Notes, Appendix V.

[2] Gordon Wordsworth is misleading here: see Additional Notes, Appendix V.

I

the Parish Registers he is always described as a shoemaker. But when his mother died in 1800 at the age of seventy-four she is entered there as 'Prudence Wife of John Suart of Town Currier'. From this entry, and from a much earlier description of him, it appears that John Suart, who died in 1808, was primarily a leather-dresser, and that with him the making and repair of shoes was a secondary occupation. William Mackreth, whose father Daniel was a shoe-maker, was born in 1743, and married in 1775 to Agnes Askew. In the Parish Registers he is then described as a shoemaker; but when he died in 1798 his death and burial are recorded as those of 'William Mackreth of Town Inn-keeper and Shoemaker'.

After John Wordsworth's death the making of suits for his sons is said by Gordon Wordsworth to have been entrusted mainly to Whitehaven tailors. At Hawkshead their tailor for all ordinary pur-poses was the William Tyson of Gallowbarrow whose son John's death in 1782 at the age of twelve was mentioned earlier. Payments to him occur in John Wordsworth's Memorandum Book, and occasionally his bills are added in at the end of Ann Tyson's accounts: 6s. in 1784₂, 14s. in 1785₁, and 17s. 6d. in 1787₁. The last mentioned sum may have been for more than one half-year; but the 14s. in 1785₁ cannot have been. If it was for repairs only, this particular bill seems to have been unduly big. Some idea of William Tyson's charges for his work can be got from the Poor Accounts, which show that in 1786–8 he was paid 2s. 6d. and 3s. for making new suits for paupers, and 1s. and 1s. 3d. for mending their old suits. His eldest son, William, who was well known to Grammar School boys interested in birds' eggs, was described as a tailor when he married Sarah Swainson at Hawkshead in 1784. I am not quite sure about the father, but my impression, based on a study of the registers, is that he was not baptized, married, or buried there.

Payments to two Hawkshead mercers appear in John Words-worth's Memorandum Book. One of them, David Moore, is described in the registers as a 'Scotchman', the local name for a pack-man, and as such he will be considered in a more appropriate place. The other was Joseph Wilson, who was referred to as a tailor in 1748, but who for many years before his death in 1792 at the age of sixty-seven was Hawkshead's leading or only mercer, a man of sufficient standing in 1779 to be styled 'Mr.'. The only mercer's bill, probably his, that was added in at the end of an account by Ann Tyson was one for 6s. 7½d. in 1785₁. There are mercery items entered by Ann in the Wordsworth's bills, including a handkerchief, 4s. 10d. in 1785₁, and ribbons, mainly for John, at 1s. 10d. and 6d. in 1786 and 1787. The handkerchief must have been to wear, but it is not stated who acquired it. And here, since Joseph Wilson might have supplied them, I may as well mention the garters at 3d. a pair purchased by the Wordsworth boys in 1784 and 1785; the gloves at 1s. 9d. for three pairs they had in 1784₂; and those Christopher and both the White-haven Wordsworths bought in 1788₂ and 1789₁ at from 1s. 4d. to 1s. 7d. a pair. The buttons for which Ann charged 8d. in 1784₂ may also be noticed in passing. Of more interest is her entry in 1785₁ which reads: 'mr Wilsen her dresen', 9d. The boys wore their hair long or semi-long, and 'Mr' Joseph Wilson's usual charge for dress-ing it was 3d. each. But shortly before he left school in 1787₂ William paid 6d. for what must have been a more elaborate treat-ment; and so too did John, who may perhaps have worn his hair beribboned.[1] In St. Mary's churchyard, Ulverston, there is a memorial with a Latin inscription to Joseph Wilson, the Hawkshead mercer; his wife Elizabeth (1728–1806), daughter of William Taylor, yeo-man, of Wellhouse, Osmotherley, in the parish of Ulverston; and to their son the Rev. William Wilson, M.A., B.D., who was baptized at Hawkshead on 28 March 1752, and died at Moreton, Essex, in 1822. Going to St. John's College, Cambridge, from Hawkshead School in 1770, he was successively Scholar, Fellow, Junior Dean, and Senior Fellow of the College, which in 1796 presented him to the Rectory of Moreton. He made bequests to Hawkshead School Library, St. John's College, Cambridge, and Broughton Beck School, Osmotherley, and to its Master.

There is little about buying hats in Ann Tyson's accounts: an unnamed hatter's bill for 1s., presumably for repairs, was added in

---

[1] In 1785₂ Ann Tyson records barber's charges of 6d., 1s., 9d.; as there were four boys at school that Half, these prices may not reflect special attention to hair; but during that autumn Mr. Mingay was giving dancing lessons, and at the end of November held a Ball. The three Senhouse boys paid a total of 2s. 3d. for 'hair cutting & Dressing for yᵉ Ball'.

1785_1, and payment of 2s. 3d. for a hat was entered in 1786_1, but that is all. And from other accounts the only gleanings are that one of the Maudes got a hat for 1s. 6d.; that Robert Greenwood during his first half-year at Hawkshead bought several at a total cost of 8s.; and that Richard Wordsworth of Whitehaven had one repaired for 2d. These hats were almost certainly of felt.

In William Wordsworth's account for his final nine weeks at Hawkshead in 1787_2 there are the following entries, indicating some interest in 'splendid clothes' even before he arrived at Cambridge:

Velvet sold by Mrs Tyson	4	$1\frac{1}{2}$d.
Velvet , „ „ „	1	$4\frac{1}{2}$d.
Paid Robert Dixon for Making	1	10d.
Ditto for Silk	4	9d.

The last is a simplification of an entry made in Ann's ledger which reads: 'Wordsworth to R^t Dixon for Stocks œ Silk', 4s. 9d. This entry, probably by Robert Dixon himself, is crossed through. John Wordsworth, who was nearly three years younger than William, had velvet priced at 3s. 3d. from Ann Tyson before he left school at the end of 1787_2; and in Christopher's account for 1788_1 a charge of 2s. $3\frac{1}{2}$d. for 'John Stocks' occurs. Robert Greenwood, who left at the same time as William Wordsworth, also had velvet from Ann, the cost, together with 'making & Co', being 5s.; and Thomas Gawthrop's bill when he left during 1787_1 included 'velvet', 1s. $4\frac{1}{2}$d. Finally, Christopher Wordsworth's account for 1789_2, which was Ann Tyson's last half-year as a 'Household Dame', ends with the entries 'Velvet', 2s. 9d., and 'Making', 1s. 9d. He did not leave school until October 1792.

It is clear that Ann supplied the velvet, and that the boys who bought it from her wanted it mainly so that they could have jackets made of it. William Wordsworth appears to have had a waistcoat as well, and Gawthrop a waistcoat only. The stocks, probably two each, made for William and John Wordsworth would be some kind of stiff, close-fitting neckcloths such as were generally worn by men at that date. But I am in doubt as to what is implied by the phrase 'Stocks & Silk'. Its reduction to 'Silk', if not due to laziness, rather suggests that this costly fabric may have been used in making William's stocks. On the other hand, he may have had stocks like John's but rather larger, and a small piece of silk as well. There is nothing in the rest of the account to prove that he did, though 'Mˢ Jane Swenson', 3s., might conceivably be relevant. The Wordsworth boys had writing paper from Mrs. Swainson regularly, but the cost, so far as my notes show, was never more than 1s. 6d. in any half-year. From the Churchwardens' Accounts it appears that she was a seamstress as well as a shopkeeper: at any rate in 1772 she was paid £1. 16s. 0d. in 1759, 'for cloth & making a new surpice'. So it is just possible that she made some little bit of finery for William Words-worth when his schooldays were ending. In the list of contributors to the Parish Collection for the S.P.G. in 1779 the first name after the Minister's is 'Mrs Jane Swainson'. She gave 1s., and Robert Dixon, who was also of Hawkshead Town, contributed 6d.

Though John Wordsworth's sons bought writing paper regularly, they were sparing in the amount of it they had.[1] It was dear if, as the dictionary says, a quire consisted of only twenty-four or twenty-five sheets, for one of the Maudes paid 1s. for 'a kweir of peper', and Thomas Gawthrop 1s. 4d. twice for what seems to have been a quire each time. He got his paper from George Oldham, who was described as a linen draper in 1783, but as a grocer when he died in December 1787. Other Wordsworth entries which bear on letter-writing are 'Ink and Quils', 6d., in 1785₁; 'A Penknife', 1s., in 1785₂; and 'Sealing Wax', 6d., in 1786₁. Quills or quill-pens were made from the large wing feathers of the goose, turkey, or swan, the goose in particular. The barrel or quill of the feather was prepared by removing the outer membrane and the pith, after which it was hardened, and then pointed and split with a penknife, whose original functions was to make and repair quill-pens. Formerly it was a small, unjointed knife, provided with a sheath for carrying in the pocket. Quills held the field until 1840, when pens with steel nibs began to displace them, rapidly but not completely for a long time. In 1890,

[1] An item at the bottom of the 1785₂ account in a more formal hand than Ann's indicates a rather greater consumption of stationery, presumably for school-work: 'Quills & Paper', 1s. 0d., paper, 2s., ink, 6d. This account comes at the end of the one half-year when the four brothers were at school together.

for example, the Stationery Office issued 4,000 gross of quill-pens to the various Government departments as against between nine and ten times that number of steel pens. There is no mention in Ann Tyson's accounts of lead pencils, though at that time, and in fact over a very long period, they were all made from the exceptionally pure plumbago or graphite mined in Borrowdale, Cumberland, where the deposits, originally extensive, were not completely worked out until 1850.

Not unnaturally William Wordsworth and his brothers borrowed cash from Ann Tyson to pay the charges on any letters they received. The total for a half-year varied a good deal. In 1786₁ it was as high as 4s. 6d.; in 1788₂ for Christopher alone it was 1s. 7d.; but in the following half-year it was 3s. 6d. Here are some of the payments made by the Overseers of the Poor for letters they received: 1d. from Kendal and from Cartmel; 3d. from Shap; 4d. from Dalton-in-Furness; 7d. from London and from Sunderland; 9d. from Whitehaven; and 1s. from London. These payments occur in late eighteenth century accounts. Thanks to the late William Heelis, I can cite some dated payments for letters addressed to Hawkshead, chiefly to John Gibson, Attorney. They are: 1d. and 2d. from Kendal, 1778–85; 3d. from Milnthorpe in 1780, from Ulverston in 1783, and from Broughton-in-Furness in 1785; 4d. from Millom in 1778, and from Dalton-in-Furness in 1781; 6d. from Shap in 1779; 8d. from Penrith in 1782, and from Egremont, Cumberland, in 1786; and 1s. 1d. from Cambridge in 1782. In one or two of these postal charges, particularly those from Shap, there seems to have been some irregularity. Mail coaches were introduced in 1784, and that from Manchester to Glasgow, which made stops at Kendal and Carlisle, first ran in 1786. A bill with a printed heading, kindly lent me by Major R. E. Porter, F.S.A., of the Rydal Estate Office, shows that in 1772 the Post Office in Hawkshead was at the Tanners' Arms; and very probably it was still there in the 1780s. The landlord and postmaster was Joseph Keen, a smith, of whom I shall have more to say later in other connections.

In Christopher Wordsworth's account for 1788₁ there is an entry in Ann Tyson's handwriting which I have copied as 'ped go ken', 9s. It means, I think, that she paid 9s. to cover his expenses when, alone or accompanied, he went to Kendal for some special purpose, possibly to consult a doctor, but that, of course, is a mere guess. The hire of a horse for the journey would not have cost more than 1s. 6d. at the most; so perhaps it is more likely that he was driven there and back in a two-wheeled chaise. But this speculation is leading nowhere.[1] Actually there is never any mention of a doctor in the Wordsworth accounts which appear in Ann Tyson's ledger. Nor is there any in those of her other boarders, except in Robert Greenwood's for his last seven weeks. In that she has entered 'Ped Mr Hodgen', 2s. 1d., meaning Matthew Hodgson, apothecary and surgeon. He and Charles Robinson, neither of whom had a medical degree, are often styled 'Mr' in Hawkshead documents such as the list of contributors to the S.P.G. collection in 1779.

Ann Tyson's half-yearly accounts were settled promptly on the return of the boys to school, apparently by the Assistant who was responsible for their final form. Thus her account for Richard, William, and John Wordsworth for 1785$_1$, amounting to £27. 7s. 11½d., was settled on 4 August, the boys having returned on the 1st; and that for William (nine weeks), John, and Christopher for 1787$_2$, totalling £20. 2s. 3¾d., on 24 January 1788, two days after Christopher's return.[2] Richard Wordsworth of Whitehaven also came back on 22 January, and his account for 1788$_1$ begins with the entry 'Cash due to Mrs Tyson on Settlement of Account this day', i.e. the 22nd, 18s. 1½d. It was different with Mr. Bowstead. He borrowed cash from Ann on five occasions during 1788$_1$, but never paid her anything at all until 24 January 1789, when she received £14. 1s. 0d. of the £19. 1s. 0d. he then owed her. She got the remaining £5 together with 5s. for a 'cart of Coal' he had just bought, on 25 February. His bill for 1789$_1$, which was limited to 'Board' and 'Washing', and amounted to £8. 3s. 0d., he paid by instalments in the following October, £4. 4s. 0d. on the 9th and the balance on the 31st. Ann herself kept John Sawrey waiting for his

[1] Mrs. Heelis reports to Gordon Wordsworth in a letter of 17 March 1920 that her husband 'came upon an account for the charity boys' *clogs*, paid to *Jo Keen*, shoemaker.' Footwear seems a more likely explanation for the expense of 9s. See above, pp. 109–10.

[2] In all these Colthouse accounts Ann charged for board at the rate of 6s. 4d. per week.

money. Her debt to him was £6. 18s. 1½d. on 3 December 1787; £7. 14s. 10d. on 4 August 1788, after paying him £3. 3s. 0d.; £4. 2s. 2d. on 19 February 1789. But as he was never in any hurry to pay his own debts, as she had reason to know, her tardiness in paying him had an element of justice in it. Apart from butchers' meat, her purchases appear to have been wholly or mainly on a cash basis.

Either there were no School Rules at Hawkshead laying down the hours in the evening by which boys had to be indoors or Wordsworth broke them, for, as I have already shown in commenting on the episode of the drowned man, shortly after his arrival at Hawkshead when the days were at their longest, he stayed out by Esthwaite Water one night until it was dark; and, during his first autumn, he says, it was his joy

> To wander half the night among the Cliffs
> And the smooth Hollows, where the woodcocks ran
> Along the open turf.
>
> (I.314–16 (1805))

These nocturnal wanderings by a nine-year-old new boy must have been both a worry and a nuisance to Ann Tyson, one would think. Just how he got into the house in the middle of the night we do not know.[1] In his later years he was in the habit of getting up at first light in the summer. His morning walks were early, he tells us, and

---

[1] Ann was probably not unduly worried about such a competent wanderer as Wordsworth. Writing to an Inspector of Schools late in life, on 17 December 1845, Wordsworth showed that he still did not begrudge shoe-leather:

Is not the Knowledge inculcated by the Teacher, or derived under his managemᵗ, from books, too exclusively dwelt upon, so as almost to put out of sight that which comes, without being sought for, from intercourse with nature and from experience in the actual employments and duties which a child's situation in the Country, however unfavorable, will lead him to or impose upon him? How much of what is precious comes into our minds, in all ranks of society, not as Knowledge entering formally in the shape of Knowledge, but as infused thro' the constitution of things and by the grace of God. There is no condition of life, however unpromising, that does not daily exhibit something of this truth. I do not relish the words of one of the Reporters (Mr Allen I believe whose notices are generally very valuable) in which he would reconcile the Parents to the expence of having their Children educated in school by remarking that the wear and tear of

> Oft, before the hours of School
> I travell'd round our little Lake, five miles
> Of pleasant wandering, happy time! more dear
> For this, that one was by my side, a Friend
> Then passionately lov'd . . .
>
> (II.349–53 (1805))

The reference is to John Fleming, who left school in 1785.[1] In Book V he adds:

> for the better part
> Of two delightful hours we stroll'd along
> By the still borders of the misty Lake,
> Repeating favourite verses with one voice,
> Or conning more.
>
> (V.585–9 (1805))

When morning school began at 6, they must have started on their round by 3.30 or very soon after. Occasionally Wordsworth was out earlier, for he tells us that

> before the vernal thrush
> Was audible, among the hills I sate
> Alone, upon some jutting eminence
> At the first hour of morning, when the Vale
> Lay quiet in an utter solitude.
>
> (II.360–4 (1805))

clothes will be less; and an equivalent thus saved in shoe-leather.—Excuse this disagreement in opinion, as coming from one who spent half of his boyhood in running wild among the Mountains. (*Wordsworth Letters: Later Years*, III, pp. 1268–9.)

[1] John Fleming was born Raincock, but took his mother's name on succeeding to the estate of his maternal uncle, at Rayrigg, Bowness in 1779. Wordsworth celebrates his friendship with Fleming in 'The Vale of Esthwaite' (1787), written after Fleming had gone to Cambridge ('Friendship and Fleming are the same', l. 545). During much of Fleming's minority, from 1780 to 1789, Rayrigg was in interesting hands; a John Gibson (not the Hawkshead attorney?) then agent for the le Flemings of Rydal, wrote on 23 November 1780, 'I am informed that Mr Raincock has Let Rayrigg to Farm to one Mr Wilberforce who is one of the members for Hull' (Record Office, Kendal). Wilberforce made summer visits to Rayrigg in 1782, 1783, briefly in 1784, and finally in 1788 from June to September. His diary notes a visit to Rayrigg by William Cookson (the poet's uncle) on 16 July 1787 (see *Life*, I, p. 179). See also pp. xviii–xix.

Hawkshead Church—Presbyterian or Quaker Meeting House—
Wordsworth's first vacation from Cambridge—Ann Tyson's dog—
'dedication walk'—Belle Grange and Belle Isle—John Christian
Curwen—regattas, dances—footpath over Claife Heights to Colthouse

In a letter to Stopford Brooke in 1890, J. H. Thorne[1] says that
Wordsworth in his old age, told him that on very wet or very hot
Sundays he and her other boarders went with Ann Tyson to the
Presbyterian Meeting House as it was nearer than the parish church.
As there was no such place of worship in Hawkshead parish at that
time or any other, and Wordsworth is not likely to have said there
was, one can only conclude that Thorne's recollection of their conversation was imperfect, in this particular at any rate. Not unnaturally it has been assumed that the Meeting House to which Ann and
her boys went was that of the Society of Friends at Colthouse; and
as there was no other, it must have been there if anywhere. But I find
it rather hard to believe that the boys ever went there, unless it was
very exceptionally. In his Statutes the founder of Hawkshead School,
Archbishop Sandys, laid it down that the Master, Usher, and
Scholars were to attend divine service in the parish church on
Sundays and Holy Days; and so far as the boys were concerned this
rule was reaffirmed by the Rev. James Peake, and was certainly in
force during Wordsworth's schooldays. Some really adequate
excuse for absence from church is likely, then, to have been
demanded, and to say that it was too hot to walk across the valley
from Colthouse could hardly have been acceptable; and anyhow the
boys were on holiday from midsummer to the beginning of August.
Nor am I at all sure that heavy rain, short of a cloud burst, would be
regarded as a sufficient excuse for staying away from church. There
is no reason to think that it excused boys from attendance at school;
and after all, Greenend, Colthouse, was only about half a mile from
Hawkshead Church. As for the local attitude to heavy rain, it was
embodied in my young days in a remark I heard then: 'It'll nut hurt
tha, lad, if thoo's weel hapt up [covered or wrapped up]; thoo isn't
med o' sawt [salt], is ta?' And though I do not wish to give details

---

[1] T.W.T. takes Mary Moorman's reading here (*Early Years*, p. 29); the letter is
signed, J. H. Thom. See Appendix II for a discussion of his intriguing recollection.

now, I must mention briefly that, during Wordsworth's time at Hawkshead School, the boys and the Colthouse Quakers were not on good terms with one another.[1]

The doubts I have felt bound to express in regard to her boarders do not, of course, apply to Ann Tyson. She was about seventy when she and Hugh moved to Colthouse, and if in after years, because of the heat or rain or for other reasons, she could not get as far as Hawkshead Church

> Her clear though shallow stream of piety,
> That ran on Sabbath days a fresher course
> (IV.216–17 (1805))

may well have led her to join the Friends in worship in their nearby Meeting House rather than miss it altogether. But it is as a church-goer that Wordsworth presents her in *The Prelude*. Writing of his return to Colthouse after his first year at Cambridge, he tells us that he 'had something of another eye' for people, and that

> With new delight,
> This chiefly, did I view my grey-hair'd Dame,
> Saw her go forth to Church, or other work
> Of state, equipp'd in monumental trim,
> Short Velvet Cloak (her Bonnet of the like)
> A Mantle such as Spanish Cavaliers
> Wore in old time.
> (IV.207–13 (1805))

He goes on to tell of the new pleasure he found in her 'Smooth domestic life,/Affectionate without uneasiness' (IV.213–14 (1805)), her talk, her business, and not least her piety. It was the summer of 1788, and she was seventy-five.

He had walked from Kendal by way of the Ferry, from which, he says,

> 'Twas but a short hour's walk ere, veering round,
> I saw the snow-white Church upon its hill
> Sit like a thronèd Lady, sending out
> A gracious look all over its domain.
> (IV.12–15 (1805))

[1] See below, pp. 246–9.

Like the buildings below it, Hawkshead Church was then roughcast and whitewashed. The roughcast on the tower was renewed in 1765; and then in 1785 the main body of the church was roughcast afresh, and the whole whitewashed, the work being done by two local wallers, Thomas Johnson and Thomas Mackreth, who charged 6 guineas for their labour and the lime they used, the only additional payments by the Churchwardens being 3s. to Samuel Holme for hair, and 2s. 10d. to Reuben Tyson for sand. Samuel Holme, as we have seen, was of Townend, Colthouse; and so was Thomas Johnson in 1767 (when he had a daughter Mahetable baptized) and for long after that date. Reuben Tyson, a farmer at Tockhow, on the way from Colthouse to Wray, was a son of John Tyson, an Outgate waller who was one of five adults to be baptized at Hawkshead on 3 September 1776, the others being his grown-up sons Reuben and Joseph, and his married daughters Ruth Satterthwaite and Deborah Martin. The whiteness of the church impressed itself not only on Wordsworth but also on two of the early tourists—Stebbing Shaw, the antiquary, who was at Hawkshead in 1787, and Joseph Budworth, who visited it for the first time some four or five years later. Shaw referred particularly to the 'milk-white tower' as part of a distant prospect of Hawkshead which greatly pleased him. In 1875-6 the whitewash and roughcast were replaced by pointing with cement plaster; and there were many who regretted the change. The 'gracious look' had been destroyed; the 'throned lady' had gone from her hill.

It has been stated that there is no hint in Wordsworth's writings that he ever set foot in Hawkshead Church. But at least four lines show, I think, that he was familiar with its interior. In *The Excursion*, in describing a church identical in the main with Grasmere, he says:

> Admonitory texts inscribed the walls,
> Each, in its ornamental scroll, enclosed
> Each also crowned with wingèd heads—a pair
> Of rudely-painted Cherubim.
>
> (V.150-3)

At one time there were such texts, painted by James Addison of

Hornby in 1687, in Grasmere Church; but they were whitewashed over as early as 1741, and black boards with texts on them hung on the walls instead; and never since then have they been visible. But there were also such texts in Hawkshead Church, twenty-six of them painted by James Addison in 1680 or slightly earlier, and a few more added by William Mackreth of Hawkshead in 1711–12, when he appears to have touched up some of the earlier paintings as well. And as these 'Sentances of Scripture decently Borderd & Florisht' were visible throughout Wordsworth's schooldays at Hawkshead, there can be little doubt that he was thinking of them when he wrote the four lines cited above. Actually not all the texts are enclosed in ornamental scrolls; there is, for example, an old stencil pilaster frame, almost certainly by Addison. And the number and positioning of the cherubs, which are represented by children's heads with large wings, are not always the same: sometimes there is only one crowning the text, and in a painting by Mackreth there is one above the lettering and one below it. Wordsworth's lines, then, are a simplified statement of what there was and is to be seen in Hawkshead Church in the way of mural texts. They were whitewashed over in 1794 or 1795 after the church had been re-pewed and a vestry added, but were revealed again in 1875–6 when it was restored. Some new texts, all or most of them reproductions, were painted then by William Bolton of Hawkshead under the direction of the architect, J. A. Cory. Finally, in 1954–5 there was an authoritative restoration of all the mural paintings in the church, including some newly discovered by Mr. E. Clive Rouse who was in charge of the work, the painting being done by Miss Janet Lenton, an artist who specializes in such reproductions.

On reaching Greenend, Wordsworth tells us,

> Glad greetings had I, and some tears, perhaps,
> From my old Dame, so motherly and good;
> While she perus'd me with a Parent's pride.
> *(Prelude, IV.16–18 (1805))*

His own joy at seeing her once again, both her and her rural dwelling, has been mentioned already, but only in so far as his narrative helped in the identification of the house to which he was returning.

Continuing, he says how delighted he was to take his place at what he calls 'our Domestic table'; maybe one of those massive oak long tables at which the entire household sat down together for meals, or rather more probably perhaps one of the later heavy oak oval or circular tables with four hinged leaves or flaps that could be let down, or raised, and supported by movable legs. Wordsworth then speaks of the joy with which he laid him down at night in his 'accustomed bed',

> That Bed whence I had heard the roaring wind
> And clamorous rain, that Bed where I, so oft,
> Had lain awake, on breezy nights, to watch
> The moon in splendour couch'd among the leaves
> Of a tall Ash, that near our cottage stood,
> Had watch'd her with fix'd eyes, while to and fro
> In the dark summit of the moving Tree
> She rock'd with every impulse of the wind.
>
> (IV.76–83)

I have nothing of my own to add at this stage; nor anything until I come to the 'dedication walk'. But may I linger yet awhile to cite what Wordsworth has to say about Ann's dog. It was a 'rough Terrier of the hills', he tells us, born and preordained to hunt the badger and unearth the fox; but having been from youth 'our own adopted' he had 'passed into a gentler service'. And when first as a schoolboy

> Along my veins I kindled with the stir,
> The fermentation and the vernal heat
> Of Poesy, affecting private shades
> Like a sick lover, then this Dog was used
> To watch me, an attendant and a friend
> Obsequious to my steps, early and late,
> Though often of such dilatory walk
> Tired, and uneasy at the halts I made.
> A hundred times when, in these wanderings,
> I have been busy with the toil of verse,
> Great pains and little progress, and at once
> Some fair enchanting image in my mind
> Rose up, full-form'd, like Venus from the sea

Have I sprung forth towards him, and let loose
My hand upon his back with stormy joy,
Caressing him again and yet again.
And when, in the public roads at eventide
I saunter'd, like a river murmuring
And talking to itself, at such a season
It was his custom to jog on before;
But, duly, whensoever he had met
A passenger approaching, would he turn
To give me timely notice, and straitway,
Punctual to such admonishment, I hush'd
My voice, composed my gait, and shap'd myself
To give and take a greeting that might save
My name from piteous rumours, such as wait
On men suspected to be craz'd in brain.

                          (IV.93–120)

During his stay with Ann Tyson in 1788 Wordsworth was working
on some of his translations, particularly from Virgil, and on fragmentary poems, parts of which became *Evening Walk*. Doubtless her
dog, which he thought of as his as well, was his 'off and on Companion' on many more walks than this which took him round
Esthwaite Water for the first time since his return to Colthouse.
   Speaking of this particular 'circuit of our little Lake' he says:

If ever happiness hath lodg'd with man,
That day consummate happiness was mine,
Wide-spreading, steady, calm, contemplative.
The sun was set, or setting, when I left
Our cottage door, and evening soon brought on
A sober hour, not winning or serene,
For cold and raw the air was, and untun'd:
But, as a face we love is sweetest then
When sorrow damps it, or, whatever look
It chance to wear is sweetest if the heart
Have fulness in itself, even so with me
It fared that evening. . . .
As on I walked, a comfort seem'd to touch
A heart that had not been disconsolate,
Strength came where weakness was not known to be,

> At least not felt; and restoration came,
> Like an intruder, knocking at the door
> Of unacknowledg'd weariness.
>
> (IV.129–48)

Musing, examining himself and life in general, he sat down in a sheltered coppice wood; and there he continued until it was dark, in lone contemplation, his dog somewhere in the offing engaged in his own pursuits.

At eighteen there was a certain discordancy in his life. The first hint of it is when he is referring to his arrival in the vale. 'The face of every neighbour whom I met', he says,

> Was as a volume to me: some I hail'd
> Far off, upon the road, or at their work,
> Unceremonious greetings, interchang'd
> With half the length of a long field between.
> Among my Schoolfellows I scatter'd round
> A salutation that was more constrain'd,
> Though earnest, doubtless with a little pride,
> But with more shame, for my habiliments,
> The transformation, and the gay attire.
>
> (IV.58–67)

A little later he adds:

> The very garments that I wore appear'd
> To prey upon my strength, and stopp'd the course
> And quiet stream of self-forgetfulness.
>
> (IV.292–4)

He is convinced that he loved more deeply all he had loved before; but, he explains,

> . . . a swarm
> Of heady thoughts jostling each other, gawds,
> And feast, and dance, and public revelry,
> And sports and games . . . these did now
> Seduce me from the firm habitual quest
> Of feeding pleasures, from that eager zeal,
> Those yearnings which had every day been mine,
> A wild unworldly-minded Youth, given up
> To Nature and to Books . . .
>
> (IV.272–82)

Sports and games he found less pleasing in themselves than as a 'badge glossy and fresh' of manliness and freedom. Social pleasures, conventional in pattern, seem to have appealed to him more, though he tells us that of manners put to school he took small note.

The discordancy was soon to be resolved. And here I quote once more before filling in a few details that have hitherto been wanting.

> . . . In a throng,
> A festal company of Maids and Youths,
> Old Men and Matrons staid, promiscuous rout,
> A medley of all tempers, I had pass'd
> The night in dancing, gaiety and mirth;
> With din of instruments, and shuffling feet,
> And glancing forms, and tapers glittering,
> And unaim'd prattle flying up and down,
> Spirits upon the stretch, and here and there
> Slight shocks of young love-liking interspers'd,
> That mounted up like joy into the head,
> And tingled through the veins. Ere we retired,
> The cock had crow'd, the sky was bright with day.
> Two miles I had to walk along the fields
> Before I reached my home. Magnificent
> The morning was, a memorable pomp,
> More glorious than I ever had beheld.
> The Sea was laughing at a distance; all
> The solid Mountains were as bright as clouds,
> Grain-tinctured, drench'd in empyrean light;
> And, in the meadows and the lower grounds,
> Was all the sweetness of a common dawn,
> Dews, vapours, and the melody of birds,
> And labourers going forth into the fields.
> —Ah! need I say, dear Friend, that to the brim
> My heart was full; I made no vows, but vows
> Were then made for me; bond unknown to me
> Was given, that I should be, else sinning greatly,
> A dedicated Spirit. On I walk'd
> In blessedness, which even yet remains.
>   (IV.316–45)

In the 1850 version of this Wordsworth adds that he saw the sea in

K

front and the mountains near, and mentions that the pathway leading him homeward wound through 'humble copse' and 'open field'.

I am convinced, and will try to prove, that he was returning to Colthouse over Claife Heights from Belle Grange;[1] this house is situated rather more than two miles north of the Ferry on the lake-side road to High Wray, which is a good mile further on. Its early history is bound up with developments during the last quarter of the eighteenth century on the Great Island in Windermere, previously known as Longholme, but called Belle Isle after Thomas English, a lover of all things Italian, purchased it in 1774. Long in the possession of the Philipsons, a well-known Windermere and Crook family, it had changed hands several times in the eighteenth century before English, who is said to have been a wealthy merchant, bought it. He proceeded to pull down the old buildings on it, and to cut down a great many fine trees so that he could have a formal garden on 'a slope in the bosom of the island'. These changes were condemned by Hutchinson, West, and Gilpin in their *Tours of the Lakes*. Undeterred, he set about building a large circular mansion— a 'bastard classic structure' is one description of it—and spent very lavishly on it. When it was well advanced he decided that to complete his Windermere estate he must have a dower-house, and as a site for it bought a little holding known as Sandbeds on the western shore of the lake. There, after clearances, he began to erect a small mansion in a less alien style, which became known as Belle Grange. It is said to have been built in 1778, but I doubt whether it was completed in that year.[2] Indeed, he may not have finished it at all, any more than he did his circular mansion, work on which had to be suspended when it was nearing completion. That was in 1779, it appears, and was due, it has been stated, to crippling business losses which resulted in his bankruptcy. Whatever the cause, his Windermere estate was offered for sale in the spring of 1781. One account says that it was purchased from his creditors by Henry Curwen of Workington Hall, another that it was bought for £14,000 by

---

[1] T.W.T. is enlarging here upon one of the suggestions canvassed by Knight and Canon Rawnsley (see *Poetical Works of Wordsworth*, ed. Knight, III, pp. 413–14).

[2] I have no details for the sale or building of Belle Grange (called by T.W.T. 'Bella Grange', though I have found so far no eighteenth-century authority for this).

Isabella Curwen, Henry's only daughter and sole heiress. In the following year, at the age of seventeen it is said, she married her first cousin John Christian of Ewanrigg, Cumberland, and Milntown, Isle of Man. And, unless I am sadly mistaken, it was this couple who were Wordsworth's hosts at Belle Grange on the night preceding his 'dedication walk'.[1]

John Christian, who was born in 1756, and whose mother was Henry Curwen's sister Jane, was the sixteenth lineal descendant of the Christians of Milntown, and the fourth of his family to be seated at Ewanrigg Hall, which was built by his great-grandfather Ewan Christian, who was followed there by two Johns. It is near Maryport, and only seven or eight miles from Cockermouth, with which the Christians had links. Ewan Christian's ninth daughter, Martha, married Robert Tubman, a Cockermouth mercer, and it was their only daughter Frances, Robert Tubman's sole heiress, who married first Samuel Irton of Irton Hall, and then the Rev. Reginald Braithwaite of Hawkshead. And John Christian's father, who was a barrister, had a brother Charles, an attorney-at-law, who by marriage acquired Morland Close, about two miles from Cockermouth. He was the father of Fletcher Christian of the *Bounty*, and of the Edward Christian who was Master of Hawkshead Grammar School for a time in 1781 [and 1782, see Appendix IV], and who in 1791, when he was a law professor at Cambridge, was counsel for John Wordsworth's sons and daughter in their suit against the first Earl of Lonsdale, as Sir James Lowther had become.

Isabella Curwen was John Christian's second wife; his first, whom he married in 1775, was Margaret, daughter of John Taubman of Nunnery, Isle of Man. She died in 1776 after bearing him a son John,

[1] The historical facts about the 'dedication walk' still remain elusive; from the piecemeal way in which Wordsworth constructed Book IV of *The Prelude*, it is not impossible that the account is not of a Hawkshead experience at all, or not simply of such an experience. (See Mary Moorman, *William Wordsworth: Early Years*, p. 57, for Wordsworth's report that the first voluntary verses that he ever wrote 'were written after walking six miles to attend a dance at Egremont'—six miles from Whitehaven.) While T.W.T.'s argument is not a proof that Wordsworth walked from a dance at Belle Grange—though the walk is a possible one—the importance of the discussion is to remind us of the impact of the Christian Curwens upon the area, not least, upon Wordsworth's Hawkshead. For the possibility that Wordsworth took Coleridge on this very walk in 1799, see Additional Notes, Appendix V.

who succeeded to his Milntown and Ewanrigg properties. By Isabella Curwen he had four sons—Henry, William, Edward, and John—and three daughters. They are included in the Curwen pedigree as, by virtue of the King's Sign Manual dated 1 March 1790, their father became John Christian Curwen, and assumed the arms of Curwen of Workington Hall. Whereupon his wife, an heiress on her father's death in 1778, conveyed to him all the property of which she was then possessed, including the Workington Hall estate, and Sandbeds, otherwise Belle Grange. The position in regard to the Great Island in Windermere is not quite clear, as it has been said, though mistakenly I think, that it had previously passed into his hands. In any event, he seems to have done nothing there until the early 1780s, when he completed the circular mansion, demolished the formal gardens, and from plans prepared by Thomas White, a leading designer of pleasure-grounds, laid out the whole island afresh, with a raised gravel walk a mile and a half long running right round it at the water's edge.[1] To make this possible an outrage was

---

[1] The sale of Belle Isle can be further documented by manuscripts now in the Records, the Castle, Carlisle. In 1781 the island was bought for Isabella Curwen for £2,000 by her trustees, Peter Taylor (see p. 305), and Christian. The negotiation, involving two smaller islands—Small Holme and Ing Holme for £47 10s. the pair—was settled by 17 October 1782, the whole transaction, according to Peter Taylor's accounts, having cost a little under £2,500. Taylor wrote to Addison, Christian's lawyer, on 4 July 1781:

> I have been by desire of Miss Curwen at Windermere, & find the House gone much out of repair, I mean the rooms wch were almost finished, the Windows wants [sic] almost reglazing & several other things will be necessary to be done to put it in only decent repair. . . I flatter myself when the Workmen begin with hopes y^t they wont be long in geting done, as the Young Lady seems anxious to be there. . . .

We know from a dispute about window tax that sometime during that same summer, 'the Ladies came to inhabit the Island in consequence of which, it became taxable, was taxed & accordingly paid' (W. Barton to Henry Addison, 25 October 1782). After Isabella's 'runaway marriage', in Edinburgh, 9 October 1782, apparently arranged by her trustees, the development of the island becomes the concern of her husband, John Christian. From Christian's personal account book we know that he was at Belle Island in October 1783 and paid Thomas White, the landscape architect, £52 10s. 0d. for 'Pland Imprvem^{ts}. W. &c.' He was there again in August 1784 and paid White £200 (White's 'improvements' to Belle Isle and to Workington Hall, had, by 1787, cost £2,426 5s. 4d.). In 1785 he was there, at least in the spring (see Appendix III), and probably again in September, when he paid a Captain Wilkes £14 0s. 6d. 'for Guns Belle Isle'; in the June of the following year boating interests

committed of which Wordsworth wrote in his *Guide to the Lakes*:

What could be more unfortunate than the taste that suggested the paring of the shores, and surrounding with an embankment this spot of ground, the natural shape of which was so beautiful! An artificial appearance has thus been given to the whole, while infinite varieties of minute beauty have been destroyed.[1]

Before that Belle Grange was their summer home. They were coming there at least as early as 1785, and it was during Wordsworth's schooldays, as he tells us, that 'Mr. Curwen', then John Christian, put a little fleet of swans on Windermere, not of the 'old magnificent species' of which there were two pairs on Esthwaite Water, but an attraction nevertheless until 'they were got rid of at the request of the farmers and proprietors [of fishing rights in the lake], but to the great regret of all who had become attached to them from noticing their beauty and quiet habits'.[2] John and Isabella Christian shared fully in the entertainments, which included dances at some of the larger houses. These summer gaieties were then a novelty in the Lake Country, dating back only to about 1780 I believe, and were due in the main to the influx of strangers.[2] Regattas were held, boats decorated, queens elected, hunts arranged,

become clear, 'To Cordage Curwen Yatch', £62 7s. 1d. Whatever the state of Belle Grange, it does seem evident that the house on Belle Isle had become an established Christian Curwen summer home by the mid 1780s.

[1] Dorothy, in her Journal for 8 June 1802, had made a comment that is earlier and rather more spontaneous:

Then we went to the Island, walked round it, and crossed the lake with our horse in the Ferry. The shrubs have been cut away in some parts of the island. I observed to the boatman that I did not think it improved. He replied: 'We think it is, for one could hardly see the house before.' It seems to me to be, however, no better than it was. They have made no natural glades; it is merely a lawn with a few miserable young trees, standing as if they were half-starved. There are no sheep, no cattle upon these lawns. It is neither one thing or another—neither *natural*, nor wholly cultivated and artificial, which it was before. And that great house! Mercy upon us! if it *could* be concealed, it *would* be well for all who are not pained to see the pleasantest of earthly spots deformed by man. But it *cannot* be covered. Even the tallest of our old oak trees would not reach to the top of it.

[2] See *Wordsworth's Poetical Works*, I, p. 319, and Additional Notes, Appendix V.

[3] One of these strangers was Wilberforce at Rayrigg who in 1782 had his mother, sister, and different college friends among his party: 'Boating, riding, and continual parties at my own house and Sir Michael le Fleming's, fully occupied my time until I returned to London in the following autumn.' (*Life*, I, p. 23.)

and there might be a play; but to the young ladies it seems to have been the dances that mattered most, though only too often 'there was such a scarcity of gentlemen' at them. My quotation is from a letter written probably in the summer of 1786, by Miss Mary Spedding of Armathwaite Hall at the foot of Bassenthwaite Lake, whose brother John was a school friend of Wordsworth's at Hawkshead. She was writing to Miss Martha Irton of Belmount, Hawkshead, with whom she had been staying earlier in the summer. Regarding the shortage of men at dances, she continues: 'so little Hawkshead still retains its superiority to my idea. I believe so great a majority of Beaux can seldom be boasted of in this part of the world'. There is a great deal of social gossip; in another undated letter she writes: 'I thought the Parkers were not much noticed by the Christians at the Hunt; a great change in Mr C's behaviour from the time I have seen them together before.' Perhaps the Christians had come to Windermere in 1786.[1] The Parkers mentioned can be identified as the Timothy Parker, aged twenty-nine, of the parish of St. James, Westminster, who in 1778 married Ann Hoskins, aged seventeen, at Bridekirk, which is two or three miles from Cockermouth. They had children christened there in 1779 and 1785, after which they moved to Coniston Waterhead, which became available after the death of Mrs. George Knott early in 1785, and their next child, William, was privately baptized at Hawkshead on 1 May 1787.

John Christian played a leading part in promoting the early regattas on Windermere, and as there was one in 1788 it is virtually certain that he and his wife were in the area in that year. In 1789 both are mentioned in documents relating to the proposed building of a new and larger Market House at Hawkshead. In one of them the land-holders, customary tenants, and principal inhabitants in the parish and manor were asked to say how much they would subscribe towards the cost; and among these who signed it was Isabella

[1] T.W.T. quotes these letters from 'A Lakeland Young Lady's Letters', S. Taylor, *Transactions of the Cumberland & Westmorland Antiquarian and Archaeological Society*, XLIII, 1943, pp. 96–116. House parties were frequent and the Christians illustrious throughout the Lakes area; Miss Spedding was as likely to have seen them at a Hunt in West Cumberland as at Hawkshead. She was Mary Spedding, 1768–1828, the elder of two sisters who, from time to time, fleetingly make an appearance in Dorothy Wordsworth's letters and Journals, and in James Losh's diary.

Christian, who promised £5. 5s. 0d. In another, a petition to the Lords of the Manor later in the year, it is stated incidentally that the inn at the Ferry and the ferriage had recently become the property of John Christian, Esq., M.P.; which shows that he acquired them earlier than has been stated.[1] To the inn, a two-storied building commonly called Great Boat, he later added a three-storied block which did not blend with it. In the 1790s, as John Christian Curwen, he bought Harrowslack and the Heald, between the ferry and what an indenture dated 1799 refers to as 'Sandbeds (otherwise Belle-grange)'. To Wordsworth's regret he made larch plantations on the steep slopes of these Furness properties of his which before had been 'scattered over with native hollies and ash-trees'.[2] But all was well in the end, for his son, as the larch matured, planted a great variety of trees and shrubs in its stead. Dr. Henry Lonsdale in the first volume of his *Worthies of Cumberland* (1867) devotes as many as 200 pages to John Christian Curwen, but all I can add here is that he is best remembered for his outstanding services to agriculture, particularly in Cumberland, where he himself farmed on a very large scale, in addition to being a principal coalowner; and as Member of Parliament for the county, in which capacity, as Lonsdale says, he was a distinguished member of the 'Old Minority' of Whig reformers.

Turning now to Wordsworth's memorable walk home soon after sunrise, let me say at once that there is an old right of way over Claife Heights from Belle Grange to Colthouse, and that by it the

---

[1] In a letter to Charles Udale, his agent at Ewanrigg, John Christian wrote as early as 17 November 1782, shortly after his marriage, 'Mr Greene has directions to make a purchase of the Ferry at Windermere . . .'. Entries in Christian's account book from 1786–92 show that George Robinson, ferryman, paid thirty guineas per year 'For the Ferry and Lands there near Belle Isle payable h. yearly.' In another note, of 24 May 1788, Christian tells Henry Addison, his lawyer, that 'the Ferry business is done'— though there is no context for this remark. (Unsorted Curwen papers, the Records, the Castle, Carlisle.) For earlier ownership of the Ferry, see Additional Notes, Appendix V.

[2] See *Guide to the Lakes*, 1926, p. 72. On an annotated estate map, John Christian, on the Heald, called here Furness Fell, has written, '1798 by the desire of my respected friend D[r] Watson Bishop of Llandaff I planted here 30 000 Larches'; on the lower slopes he has noted, 'Got the Medal for dibbling this with Acorns 1798'. (Curwen papers.) Curwen obtained the Heald through the Claife Heights Enclosure Act of 1794 for £6 per acre; the money went to pay for the Enclosure, the residue to the poor of the parish.

distance between them is almost exactly two miles. Partly footpath but mainly cart-track, it has been obscured or obliterated in places by plantations dating back no further than the nineteenth century. From Belle Grange it ascends steeply at first, and then more gently over Long Height, after which it proceeds by way of Rough Hows, skirting a small tarn, and passing just south of Renny Crags. The general direction is west-south-west, until on nearing Colthouse it turns north-west to ease the gradient, and comes out on to the road to High Wray at Crag, a furlong from Beckside. It and Greenend could have been reached a little more quickly on foot by leaving the track at the turn, and dropping down by the side of Spring Wood Ghyll. The highest point attained is about 700 feet above sea level, and from it there is a very fine view of the mountains in front and right round to the north-west, whilst to the south, and perhaps to the south-west in a favourable light, the sea is visible. Wordsworth would have the low early morning sun behind him, which would greatly enhance what he saw in front; and probably his feelings were heightened by the sort of night he had spent. There is just one thing in his description of the walk in the 1805 text which does not ring true. He speaks of it as being 'along the fields', which is incon-sistent with what he says of the nature and extent of the views it affords, and untrue of Claife Heights, which until the end of the eighteenth century were unenclosed fell held in common. Conscious of this no doubt, he struck out the offending phrase when he revised *The Prelude*, and spoke instead of his homeward pathway winding through humble copse and 'open field'. That is better; but even so I cannot regard his choice of the word 'field' as a happy one in that it does not convey the right impression.

Meeting with the discharged soldier and George Robinson, the ferryman at Great Boat—sheep-feeding in winter

Another change which Wordsworth made from the 1805 text of *The Prelude* is the provision of a new introduction to the story of his encounter late one night with a discharged soldier; and as it relates to the year 1788, and is relevant here and now, I will quote the passage with which it opens.

> . . . Once, when those summer months
> Were flown, and autumn brought its annual show
> Of oars with oars contending, sails with sails,
> Upon Winander's spacious breast, it chanced
> That—after I had left a flower-decked room
> (Whose in-door pastime, lighted up, survived
> To a late hour), and spirits over wrought
> Were making night do penance for a day
> Spent in a round of strenuous idleness—
> My homeward course led up a long ascent,
> Where the road's watery surface, to the top
> Of that sharp rising, glittered to the moon . . .
>
> (IV.370–81 (1850))

The verbal involutions here displayed might well have been avoided in view of the bare simplicity of the narration they preface. But whatever their faults, these lines have the merit of telling us something worth knowing, namely what Wordsworth had been doing shortly before he met the discharged soldier who made such a deep impression on him.

He had spent the day at a regatta on Windermere, and the night until a late hour at an indoor entertainment which followed it. As the place of assembly for these early 'meetings' as they were called was the Ferry on the Hawkshead side of the lake, it is safe to say that his way home lay up the hill, half a mile long and much of it steep, which rises from the lake shore just south of the Ferry to a point only a little short of Far Sawrey on the road to Hawkshead. In the 1805 text, which gives no reason for his being on this hill, he tells us that he 'slowly mounted up', and then that he 'slowly pass'd along' with 'an exhausted mind, worn out by toil'. These statements, and his reference in the 1850 text to a day spent in a round of strenuous idleness, suggest that he took an active part in the regatta, despite his dislike of emulation in sport unless it was tempered by some redeeming feature. They make one wonder, too, whether in the evening, whilst it was still light, there had been a procession of decorated boats, 'with a band of music aboard', such as John Christian is said to have organized in the late 1780s with the Ferry as the starting and finishing point. Little is really known about these early Windermere regattas. Speaking of his meeting with the discharged soldier,

Wordsworth says in the 1805 text that it was 'ere those summer months had pass'd away', and in the 1850 text that it was when they 'were flown'; two statements which can be reconciled by assuming that they were held at the end of August.

The indoor pastime in a lighted, flower-decked room that followed the outdoor events in 1788 was almost certainly at the Ferry Inn. In his poem *Windermere*, published in 1798, Joseph Budworth says in a footnote that the Ferry-house, as he calls the inn, was 'just hid in trees, amongst them, the wild cherry, of amazing magnitude'. This no doubt was the 'Great-Boat-tree' referred to more than once by the Rev. Charles Farish in his *Minstrels of Winandermere*, the preface to which is dated 1811. He was at Hawkshead School as a senior pupil from 1782 to 1784;[1] and in his poem, which consists

[1] Charles Farish was the only one of his family to go to Hawkshead School, and the venture was perhaps a result of the friendship between his older brother, William, the future Professor of Chemistry at Cambridge, and the headmaster of Hawkshead School, William Taylor. Charles was baptized in Carlisle on 1 September 1766, was at school there 1773–82, at Hawkshead 1782–4, then briefly at Trinity, afterwards at Queens' College Cambridge, and took his degree in 1788. He returned immediately to Hawkshead and became an Assistant to the then headmaster, Thomas Bowman, as is clear from Mr. Mingay's advertisements for his Military Academy (see above, p. 94). Farish, then, would be in Hawkshead for the opening of the Autumn Half, which, we know from Ann Tyson, began on or about 28 July 1788. There is every probability that Wordsworth also was in Hawkshead from that date until near the beginning of the Cambridge term. There are no accounts in Ann Tyson's ledger for board for William for that summer vacation, 1788 (though Mary Moorman, 'Ann Tyson's Ledger' and *Wordsworth: Early Years*, p. 107, and Mark Reed, following her, *Chronology: Early Years*, p. 87, misread the entry 'Board for 9 Weeks', £2. 17s. 0d., as an item for 1788; but it is unmistakably among the accounts for 1789: see footnote p. 143).

Fortunately, the administrators' accounts tell us more than has yet been noted. Thus: Ann has the Autumn Half account, 1788, for Christopher, amounting to £7. 14s. 9d. The settling of this is recorded in Uncle Richard's accounts for 16 January 1789; the entry reads: 'By Cash to Newphew Christ^r. to discharge his & NephewW^m's. Bill at Hawkshead' . . . £12. 18s. 0d. Thus, leaving out sundries, something less than £5. 3s. 3d. must have been for William's expenses at Hawkshead during the Autumn Half 1788 before his return to Cambridge. Expenses incurred before the school summer holidays belonged, of course, to the Spring Half, and were paid by Uncle Christopher (see Appendix V, note to p. 107), whose accounts record, on 19 August 1788, £14. 9s. 0d. for Hawkshead bills. £11. 9s. 9d. of this was for Ann Tyson—for Christopher's Spring Half and the weeks that William stayed with her on his glad return in June from his first year in Cambridge; the rest was for Hawkshead sundries—bookseller, shoemaker, surgeon, tailor and mercer. Two payments are recorded as for William: on 28 August Uncle Richard gave or

of a narrative interspersed with songs and a legend, he tells of a day-long 'pilgrimage' he and some of his school fellows made. On their arrival at Great Boat early in the morning George, the ferryman, unmoored the smaller of his ferry-boats, the more suitable for landing them 'far in Bowness-bay'; his daughter Edith brought them their 'ready breakfast', milk warm from the cows. We learn of

sent him 2 guineas, and on 18 September Uncle Christopher gave or sent the same amount. (These two payments are the only basis for the belief that Wordsworth visited Whitehaven and Penrith during the summer.) Though, on present evidence, the 1788 accounts do not tell everything about Wordsworth's movements during his first Cambridge vacation, they are not inconsistent with the notion that in that year also the pattern of the vacations of 1787 and 1789 was roughly followed.

Ann's ledger shows that after the school holidays in 1787 Wordsworth returned to her for nine weeks (probably arriving with Christopher around 5 August) before starting at Cambridge. We know that after that year in Cambridge, he returned straight to Hawkshead in June 1788 (*Prelude* IV), probably leaving with Christopher for the school holidays and again returning with him about 28 July (as explained at the opening of this note).

In 1789, whatever he did at the end of the Cambridge summer term (he spent some time at Forncett visiting his sister, Dorothy, and his Uncle William Cookson), he was back in Hawkshead for nine weeks with Ann Tyson at the beginning of the Autumn Half (3 August), buying himself an umbrella for 2s. and hiring a horse for 1s. 6d. (see p. 143). Two entries in the account of Uncle Richard of Whitehaven belong to this time: 16 September, 'By Cash remitted Nephew William to Hawks-head & Stamps' . . . £6. 6s. 6d., and immediately under this, 'By gave Servants for Wm.' . . . 3s. After 4 October or thereabouts Wordsworth appears to have gone from Hawkshead to Whitehaven, for the very next entry is a washing bill for him, 8s. (not entered until 5 November). He could only have stayed at his Uncle Richard's nine or ten days before returning to Cambridge by way of Penrith and a hasty visit on 14 October to his Uncle Christopher Cookson, who wrote on the 22nd to William's brother, Richard: '. . . believe me Dr. Richard there is nothing more I have at heart than to assist you & your Connections in every thing that is in my power—Your Bror. Wm. called here on Friday last in his road to Cambridge he looks very well. I should have been happy if he had favoured me with more of his Company, but I'm afraid I'm out of his good graces.' (MS. in private hands.)

These corrections of detail allow one to suggest that in his first Long Vacation from Cambridge, 1788, Wordsworth was in Hawkshead for more than the nine weeks which he is generally supposed (on the basis of a misreading) to have spent there; further, that he would not have spent any part of the school holidays in Hawkshead, and that for a considerable period his stay would overlap with the beginning of Charles Farish's time there as an assistant master. It could have been of autumn 1788 that Wordsworth wrote in his note on a borrowing 'from a short MS. poem, read to me when an undergraduate by my schoolfellow and friend, Charles Farish, long since deceased . . .' (*Wordsworth's Poetical Works*, I, p. 336). For a discussion of the 'short MS. poem', and some unpublished Farish poems later incorporated into the *Minstrels of Winandermere*, see Appendix I.

George's delight in 'woody Crowholme', which was the island nearest to his house; an island that, like Ferry Nab, was part of the Great Boat estate as it existed in the eighteenth century. The boys embarked, one taking the helm, another an oar, whilst a third 'the fishing tackle flings'. George landed them at Bowness.

At night, long after sunset, they made their way to 'Bowness point', which is Farish's name for Ferry Nab, and called loudly for George. On the point there was a ruined smithy that afforded shelter from the wind; and the Hawkshead carrier, arriving from Kendal, told them he had drunk many a stoup of ale in 'this same black-smith's castle'. There were other arrivals, early and late, including one or two more men with horses and carts, it appears. Then came George, who with 'measur'd oar' had rowed his ponderous boat across the lake, guided to the nab he sought by a lantern he kept burning there at night near to the ruined smithy. He came ashore and trimmed it carefully, and whilst he did so the boys helped to wheel the carts aboard, the horses having been loosed from the shafts for the crossing. George told them that once on a stormy night, when his 'little lighthouse' was buried under snow, the flame had not gone out. On the return journey he was guided to the mooring by his daughter Edith, to whom his usual signal was the raising of a light on board his boat accompanied by a loud call; and Farish pictures her as coming with 'cheerful haste' to the Great-Boat-tree, a light in her hand, her fluttering apron extended round the flame rashly but with skill. Her father said that when the mist was thick and black he had sometimes got her to keep on calling, and had shaped his course by her voice alone. We hear something, too, of his labours when the lake was frozen in its shallower parts; of how 'with battering maul and iron crow' he broke a way across, heaving with his hands the 'huge ice-boards' to either side, only to see them knit together again in his wake; and how, when the ice defeated him, he slid his massive boat ashore with hawser and rustic sleigh.

These details are all the more welcome as Wordsworth, though he must have known George very well, makes only one brief reference to him in his writings. It is when he is describing his return to Colthouse at the beginning of his first long vacation. Walking from Kendal on the highway linking it with Hawkshead he came at length to the top of a ridge from which he had a very fine view of Windermere gleaming in the noontide sun. And then, he says,

> I bounded down the hill, shouting amain
> A lusty summons to the farther shore
> For the old Ferryman; and when he came
> I did not step into the well-known Boat
> Without a cordial welcome.
> (*Prelude*, IV.5–9 (1805))

There is no doubt at all that the ferryman of whom Farish and Wordsworth wrote was the George Robinson I mentioned earlier as having been blinded in one eye when young by a potato wantonly thrown at him, and as having lost the sight of the other in or about 1794 in consequence of an accident he had when working as a turner, a trade he followed in addition to ferrying and innkeeping. After giving these particulars, and stating that the Rev. Reginald Braithwaite eventually procured for George the £10 pension to which he had become entitled, Joseph Budworth affords us a final glimpse of the blind old man, still physically strong, taking a walk up the hill leading past Satterhow to Far Sawrey. This 'pleasing sight', he says, 'filled my thoughts with the idea of a patriarch, led by two cherubs in *Heaven*'. George, he adds, 'calls himself *overlooker* of what is going on, and gives daily attendance'. The little girls may have been Edith's children; but he also had a daughter Agnes, seemingly younger, unless by any chance Edith is just Farish's name for Agnes, who was of marriageable age but unmarried in 1784.

Budworth is mistaken when he says that George Robinson owned Ferry-house. In 1707 the Great Boat estate, including the right of ferriage and two ferry-boats (but with the obligations of constant attendance during stormy weather and of keeping the boats in repair), was purchased by William Braithwaite of Satterhow; and it remained in the hands of his descendants until its sale to John Christian in [1786] or rather earlier.[1] The last Braithwaite to own it is said to be George Braithwaite of Harrowslack, who died on 10 October 1786, at the age of fifty-three. It must have been of him that the Rev. Eric Robertson was thinking when, in his *Wordsworthshire*

[1] T.W.T., following Swainson Cowper (*Hawkshead*, p. 248) had 1789 here. For some documents bearing on the Ferry, and not available to T.W.T., see p. 131, note 1.

published in 1911, he stated, without offering any proof, that the ferryman to whom Farish alluded as George was George Braithwaite. But the owner of Harrowslack and Great Boat never occupied Ferry-house or acted as ferryman during the last twelve years of his life.[1] His heir, Braithwaite Hodgson the elder, is said to be of Great Boat in an entry made in 1774 in the Hawkshead Parish Registers. He did not stay there long, however, as in 1776 and 1778 the same registers record the baptisms of children of Robert Robinson of Great Boat. The 1778 entry reads: 'George Son of Robert Robinson of Great Boat Ferryman Son of Thos: Robinson of Bowness Taylor by Marg^t. his Wife Daugh^t. of Geo: Dawson Millner The Mothers name Jeney Daugh^t. of Matthew Baisbrown Weaver at Bowness By Marg^t. Daugh^t. of John Gibson Born Octo^r. ye 21st Baptized ye 1st of Nov^r:'. The Robert Robinson and his wife thus identified by the Parish Clerk, John Hodgson, shoemaker, of Hawkshead Town, did not stay much longer at Ferry-house. Possibly then George Robinson, Farish's George, became occupier of the Great Boat estate.[2] Like Robert Robinson he was a Bowness man, evidently much older, almost certainly a near relative, and probably a widower. After he became totally blind, a son-in-law acted as ferryman. He and his wife lived at Ferry-house with George, who continued to let out rowing boats to Hawkshead Grammar School boys and others.

One of the obligations of the Trustees of the old Market Shambles at Hawkshead was to provide and maintain a 'coat-house' or shelter at the Ferry. There was one there in 1707, and in the 1760s it was still being kept in repair as a shelter for passengers in stormy weather. In 1789 it was stated to be disused and unneeded as there was then an inn at the Ferry, but the Lords of the Manor ruled that the need existed for a new and larger shelter, and the Trustees of the proposed Market House promptly circulated specifications for its building. The side walls were to be 32 feet long and 10 feet high, and the end walls 17

---

[1] But I show on p. 375 that George Braithwaite might have held the Ferry—as owner or ferryman—1782–6.

[2] Not so. The likely order of ferrymen is: Robert Robinson to 1778; Thomas Nicholson 1779–82; George Braithwaite 1782–6; George Robinson 1786 to at least 1794; his son-in-law—see pp. 131, 137–8, 375.

feet wide. There were to be two beams and two pairs of principals, and the roof was to be slated 'with the third Sort of Slate called Tom, all new Slate'. The door-opening was to be 9½ feet wide, and to have a stone arch; and the ground was to be cleared 'fit for the running of Carriages into the Coat-house'. The contract, which is dated 14 December 1789, was let to William Robinson of Braithwaite Fold in the parish of Windermere, waller, he being the lowest and best bidder for all the work, which he undertook to do for £15. He was another of the Bowness Robinsons, for Braithwaite Fold, the home in the seventeenth century of the Braithwaites who then owned Boat or Great Boat, was very near Bowness Bay. In Robertson's *Wordsworthshire* there is an interesting reproduction labelled 'Windermere Ferry Inn, as it was in Wordsworth's time (From an old picture)'.[1] It shows the cot-house or cotehouse built in 1790, and John Christian Curwen's rather later three-storey addition to the inn. But it also shows the nature and extent of the older buildings, though not, I think, the wild cherry-tree 'of amazing magnitude'.

Before describing his meeting with the discharged soldier, Wordsworth tells us that on his way home from the Ferry, up Briers Brow and on to Far Sawrey, 'all was peace and solitude', and that the silence of the night was broken only by the murmurings of a brook 'in the valley'; the distant murmurings, I may add, of Wilfin or Sawrey Beck, which descends from Claife Heights between the two Sawreys and then flows down a little valley into Windermere by way of Sawrey Townend and High Cunsey. It was moonlight, and presently where the road turned sharply, he suddenly saw the 'uncouth shape' of a man of uncommon tallness, stiff and lank, and lean, in military garb, faded but 'yet entire', seemingly half sitting and half standing, his back against a milestone. In a glen hard by, we are told, there was a village, its houses visible among the scattered trees, scarcely 'an arrow's flight' away. That is enough, almost more than enough, to identify the spot as the third milestone from Hawkshead, just round a sharp bend in the road to the Ferry as it is on the point of leaving Far Sawrey.[2] Wordsworth, as soon as he saw the strange figure, slipped back into the shade of a thick hawthorn from which he

---

[1] Similar to the photograph reproduced in Plate 6.
[2] There is no milestone now: see Additional Note, Appendix V.

could 'mark him well' whilst he himself was unseen; and there for a long time he remained, filled with a mingled sense of fear and sorrow. The old soldier never moved, but from time to time 'groans scarcely audible' passed his lips.

Wordsworth, who was only eighteen it must be remembered, at length subdued his fears, and left the hawthorn's shade to hail the stranger, who slowly rose, and with a lean and wasted arm returned his salutation; and in answer to his questions told of service in the Tropic Islands, from which he had returned a bare ten days ago and been discharged, and 'now was travelling to his native home'. On hearing this, Wordsworth looked towards the nearby houses, but there was no light in any of them. None are here awake, he told the poor man, so we must retrace our steps, for

> . . . behind yon wood
> A Labourer dwells; and, take it on my word
> He will not murmur should we break his rest;
> And with a ready heart will give you food
> And lodging for the night.
>
> (IV.455–9)

Straightway they started, and with 'ill-suppress'd astonishment' Wordsworth beheld the tall and ghostly figure moving at his side, slowly, but without pain it seemed. As they walked together he asked his companion about the hardships he had endured, questions better spared, he says in the 1850 text. The discharged soldier replied calmly and concisely, and as if he remembered the 'importance of his theme but felt it no longer'. After that they passed in silence through the gloom of the wood; and then 'turning up along an open field', they reached the cottage door.

Evidently they travelled back about a quarter of a mile on the road to the Ferry and then branched off to Briers, where at that date there were two principal houses and two cottages. They stood at a short distance from the road and at a rather higher level, the site being that later occupied by Brierswood. In 1788 one of the main houses was owned and occupied by Thomas Hodgson, a descendant of the Braithwaites of Briers, and the other by William Taylor, who was born in it, and lived there only part of the time as he had business interests in Manchester; but I cannot say who the occupants of the cottages were. On reaching the one he sought, Wordsworth knocked at the door, he tells us, and called aloud

> . . . My Friend, here is a Man
> By sickness overcome; beneath your roof
> This night let him find rest, and give him food,
> If food he need, for he is faint and tired.
>
> (IV.484–7)

Turning to the old soldier, he entreated him

> . . . that henceforth
> He would not linger in the public ways
> But ask for timely furtherance and help
> Such as his state requir'd.
>
> (IV.489–92)

To this the poor man replied that his trust was in the God of Heaven, and in 'the eye of him that passes me'. The cottage door, says Wordsworth, was speedily unlocked,

> And now the Soldier touch'd his hat again
> With his lean hand; and in a voice that seem'd
> To speak with a reviving interest,
> Till then unfelt, he thank'd me; I return'd
> The blessing of the poor unhappy Man;
> And so we parted. Back I cast a look,
> And linger'd near the door a little space;
> Then sought with quiet heart my distant home.
>
> (IV.497–504)

He had some three miles to go, which at the end of such a day may have seemed a long way.

Wordsworth does not say how he had come to know so well the Far Sawrey labourer to whom he turned for help and was not refused it; nor whether their friendship was an old one, or as recent as the summer of 1788, when 'with another eye', he tells us,

> I saw the quiet Woodman in the Woods,
> The Shepherd on the Hills.
>
> (IV.206–7)

On the same theme he had just said:

L

A freshness also found I at this time
In human Life, the life I mean of those
Whose occupations really I lov'd.
(IV.181–4)

The woodman's no doubt was one, the shepherd's another. As a school-boy he certainly took some interest in shepherding, for Miss Mary Hodgson remembered him telling her father when, at Green-end in the 1840s, the two old men were talking about farming past and present, that, during his schooldays at Hawkshead, he had often seen sheep being fed on young holly shoots in winter, on Claife Heights in the neighbourhood of Colthouse, and at or near Tockhow. The practice, a very ancient one, was then dying out.

The best authority for it is the Rev. Thomas West in his *Antiquities of Furness* published in 1774. 'Whilst the villains of Low Furness', he writes, 'were employed in all the useful arts of agriculture, the woodlanders of High Furness were charged with the care of flocks and herds, which pastured the verdant sides of the fells, to guard them from the wolves which lurked in the thickets below; and, in winter, to brouse them with the tender sprouts and sprigs of the holly and ash. This custom has never been discontinued in High Furness; and the holly-trees are carefully preserved for that purpose, where all other wood is cleared off; and large tracts of common pasture are so covered with these trees, as to have the appearance of a forest of hollies. At the shepherd's call the flock surround the holly-bush, and receive the croppings at his hand, which they greedily nibble up, and bleat for more. . . . The mutton thus fed has a remarkable fine flavour.'[1] To this excerpt I will add another, taken from the 5th edition, published in 1835, of Wordsworth's *Guide to the Lakes*. Commenting on the sylvan appearance of the Lakeland valleys, he adds that it is 'heightened by the number of ash-trees planted in rows along the quick fences, and along the walls, for the purpose of browsing the cattle at the approach of winter. The branches are lopped off and strewn upon the pastures; and when the cattle have stripped them of the leaves, they are used for repairing the hedges or for fuel.' Ash was used for this purpose in the Fieldhead and Outgate districts of Hawkshead Parish as late as 1850 if not later.

[1] p. xlv.

Final accounts 1789—Wordsworth's presentation to the Library—Ann Tyson's will and her last years

With the account of his meeting with the discharged soldier Wordsworth ends Book IV of *The Prelude*, which he entitled 'Summer Vacation'. He must have left Colthouse very soon after, as Mrs. Mary Moorman in her biography *William Wordsworth, The Early Years*, published in 1957, says that he spent some weeks at Penrith and Whitehaven before returning to Hawkshead for a further two or three weeks at the beginning of October 1788. There is no indication of all this in Ann's ledger. On the other hand it contains a short account amounting to £3. 0s. 6d. that throws light on his stay with her during his second long vacation (1789). It is headed 'Mr Wm Wordsworth', and the main item is 'Board for 9 Weeks', £2. 17s. 0d. which is what she had charged him for the same period in 1787. The bill is not dated, but it occurs with others that are: on the opposite page are Christopher Wordsworth's accounts for 1789₁ and 1789₂, and on the same page are those of Richard Wordsworth for 1789₁ and 1789₂.[1]

---

[1] For a discussion of what accounts there are for 1788, see above p. 134, note. T.W.T. is the first to establish that the short account headed 'Mr Wm Wordsworth' and totalling £3. 0s. 6d. belongs to 1789; but he seems unaware that this is a correction of the only other (so far as I know) published reading of this entry. This is in Mary Moorman's article 'Ann Tyson's Ledger' (1951) where the account is assigned to the date 6 January 1789 and said to represent 'William's stay with Ann Tyson during . . . the summer of 1788'. This reading has hitherto remained unchallenged. But there is no '6 January 1789' evident at all—see photograph, Plate 8. The account is undated, but it is quite firmly placed among accounts for the Autumn Half, 1789.

Christopher's account for the whole of that Autumn Half, 1789, and William's for nine weeks of it, were as usual payable at the beginning of the next Half; and it has not been noted that they are entered in Uncle Richard's accounts for January 1790:

> 1790. Janry 19th. By Nephew Christrs. Exps. for Board
>   &c at Hawkshead   9. 17. 9
>   By Do. for pocket Money   15. 0
> 19th. By Nephew William's Exps.
>   Do. [i.e. at Hawkshead]   6. 1. 8

As Ann's charge for Christopher's board was £8. 0s. 10½d., his extra expenses were

The only other entries in William Wordsworth's 1789 bill are horse hire, 1s. 6d., and an umbrella, 2s. As a schoolboy he occasionally went for long rides just for the pleasure of them, but only once, and that in his last nine weeks, does the cost of his hiring a horse appear in Ann Tyson's ledger, presumably because he dare not have it entered in his account. His purchase of an umbrella at Hawkshead in 1789 rather surprises me, as in most places, though not perhaps at Cambridge, a man was still regarded as effeminate if he carried one. In London the first man to do so was Jonas Hanway soon after his return to England in 1750; and though ridiculed by all and sundry, and abused by the cabmen, he persisted in the habit. After a time the coffee-houses began to keep a common umbrella for the use of their customers, and before Hanway died in 1786 it was not unusual to see a man with one in London. The frame, I need hardly say, was covered with oilcloth. At a vestry meeting at Hawkshead on 21 January 1783, it was unanimously agreed that the Churchwardens should purchase an umbrella for the Minister's use to shelter him in walking with the corpse to the grave. These churchyard umbrellas, which were very big and cumbersome, had a leather covering, and cost about 2 guineas. The one at Hawkshead was repaired in 1797, the charge for material and work being 1 guinea.

The appeal for books for a New or Modern Library at Hawkshead School was launched by the Rev. Thomas Bowman in the summer of 1789, and among those who responded to it in that year were the four undergraduates 'admitted at Cambridge from this School in 1787'. They were Robert Hodgson Greenwood of Ingleton, William Wordsworth of Cockermouth, Thomas Holden Gawthrop of Sedbergh—all of whom had boarded with Ann Tyson—and 'John Millar of Presall', who is the John Miller of Lancashire who entered Jesus College in October 1787, and graduated 8th Junior Optime in 1791. Their gift, a joint one, was *The History of Ancient Greece* by John Gillies, LL.D., 2nd edition, 4 volumes, 8vo., London, 1787, and *Jerusalem Delivered*, an Heroic Poem by Torquato Tasso, translated from the Italian by J. Hoole, 6th edition, 2 volumes, 8vo.,

small compared with William's, whose board was, as we have seen, £2. 17s. 6d.; but Christopher was a schoolboy of fifteen, William an undergraduate about to start his second year at Cambridge.

London, 1787. As Wordsworth had studied Italian under Agostino Isola during his first year at Cambridge, it is more than likely that it was he who suggested the second book.

Ann Tyson was seventy-six when she ceased to be a 'Household Dame' in December 1789, ten and a half years after Richard and William Wordsworth had first come to board with her and Hugh. Shortly before her retirement she made her will, signing it on 3 November 1789. Drawn by John Gibson, the Hawkshead attorney, it begins: 'IN THE NAME OF GOD AMEN I ANN TYSON of Hawkshead in the county of Lancaster widow being aged and weak in body but of sound and perfect Mind Memory and Understanding (praised be God for the same) and mindful of my Mortality do make publish and declare this my last Will and Testament in manner and form following . . .' She named as her executors her 'good friends' the Rev. Reginald Braithwaite of Belmount and the Rev. Thomas Bowman of Hawkshead, and to each of them she bequeathed a guinea. Out of her personal estate they were to pay her just debts and her funeral and testamentary expenses; and they were to repay themselves if they spent any money of their own in carrying out the provisions of her will. To her niece Eleanor Nevinson she left 'such and so many of my Household Goods and Furniture as she shall have occasion for in the opinion of my said executors or the survivor of them'. The rest of her 'Goods Chattels Money Securities for money and personal estate' she devised upon trust to her executors, who were to convert the whole into money which, after ensuring that all just claims on her Estate had been met in full, they were to place at interest on real or personal securities, and pay the interest thereon to her niece Eleanor Nevinson or apply it for her maintenance and support during her natural life. And should the need arise through illness or other cause they were to call in at their discretion a part or the whole of the 'principal money' for use to the same end, after taking into account the said Eleanor Nevinson's 'own private and independent property'. On her decease, what remained of the principal, assuming she had not made provision for its disposal in her last will and testament or other deed, as she was entitled to do, was to be divided and paid by Ann Tyson's executors, or the survivor of them, to the next of kin of her late mother Eleanor otherwise Ellen

Braithwaite afterwards Troughton and originally Leathom 'as if my said Mother had died Eleanor otherwise Ellen Leathom sole un-married and intestate'. Eleanor Nevinson died unmarried at the age of seventy-three in one of the cottages at the How in Hawkshead Field on 17 March 1812. By then the Rev. Thomas Bowman, Master of Hawkshead Grammar School, had become the sole executor of Ann Tyson's will.

After her retirement as a 'Household Dame' in December 1789 Ann Tyson continued to live at Greenend, Colthouse, for the rest of her days, in company with a niece who can have been no other than Nell Nevinson. As already stated, Miss Mary Hodgson's father, Braithwaite Hodgson, son of Thomas Hodgson of Briers, Far Sawrey, saw something of both when he attended Hawkshead Grammar School from about 1790 to 1797. During the earlier part of this period Nell (whose name he did not recall) worked at the School House for the Rev. Thomas Bowman, who as yet was un-married. He provided a mid-day meal for local boys who, like Braithwaite Hodgson, lived too far from the school to go home for dinner, and it was mainly in connection with this that Nell was employed as a daily help. Subsequently she stayed at home with her aunt, who was in failing health, and looked after her. Braithwaite Hodgson's mother was then in the habit of sending Ann little presents of potted char, rum-butter, cream-cheese, early lamb, and the like—why I do not seem to have discovered; and when he was riding to and from school, as he did in his later years, she sometimes entrusted him with the delivery of her gifts. He was very good about it, and, he said, had reason to be, as when he called with them Mrs. Tyson quite often had something for him. Once it was a pocket-knife, and a very good one too; and on another occasion it was a spinning-top. And nearly always she gave his pony 'a bite', or a lump of sugar after she found out that it liked one. But her memory was bad, he said, and she was apt to tell him the same thing each time he called, more particularly that her husband had been at the Grammar School when he was a boy, though only in the Writing Master's class. And towards the end she would forget what she was going to say, and have to be prompted by her niece.

To Philip Braithwaite she seems to have spoken of her long term of service at Rydal with Mr. and Mrs. Michael Knott. At any rate, it was from him that Miss Mary Hodgson heard of it, as well as of Ann's later visits to Bonaw with Mr. and Mrs. George Knott, but not, I think, of her occasional entertainment of their son William after she ceased to board him. That information is more likely to have come from her father, as the two were boys together at Hawkshead School, and within a year of being the same age. One other thing Miss Mary learnt from Philip Braithwaite was that two or three years before her death Ann had a visit from her one-time boarder Robert Greenwood of Ingleton. At the time he was on an equestrian tour of the north of England with two young gentlemen, probably sons of Lord Stamford if they were then old enough. Greenwood had not intended their staying the night at Hawkshead, but on hearing that Thomas Garnett, formerly second Assistant at the Grammar School, was landlord of the Red Lion he at once announced a change of plan. As a result, Ann saw rather more of him than seemed likely when he first called; which delighted her, as he had been one of her favourites. Philip Braithwaite, who did not know him, happened to look in on Ann whilst he was there. 'Philip', she said, 'this is Robert, t'lad wi't' flute'. They completed the introduction themselves. And then Philip found some reason for not staying more than a minute or two.

Among the entries made in the Hawkshead Registers for the year 1796 is this: 'Ann Tyson of Colthouse Widow Died May 25 Buried 28 in Church Yard Aged 83'. As she was baptized on 2 June 1713, the age ascribed to her would seem to be correct. Her grave, which is almost sure to have been to the north-east of the church, is unmarked by any stone. But William Wordsworth saw fit to write her epitaph when he first composed *The Prelude*; and it is fitting that I should conclude with it.

> The thoughts of gratitude shall fall like dew
> Upon thy grave, good Creature! While my heart
> Can beat I never will forget thy name.
> Heaven's blessing be upon thee where thou liest,
> After thy innocent and busy stir
> In narrow cares, thy little daily growth
> Of calm enjoyments, after eighty years,

And more than eighty, of untroubled life,
Childless, yet by the strangers to thy blood
Honour'd with little less than filial love.

(IV.19–28)

PART TWO

More Local Inhabitants

More Local Inhabitants

WHO was Matthew? Twice in his old age Wordsworth answered that question, in the same strain each time, but with some difference in detail. Writing to Professor Henry Reed on 27 March 1843, he says: 'The character of the schoolmaster, about whom you inquire, had, like the "Wanderer", in "The Excursion", a solid foundation in fact and reality, but, like him, it was also, in some degree, a composition: I will not, and need not, call it an invention—it was no such thing; but were I to enter into details, I fear it would impair the effect of the whole upon your mind; nor could I do it to my own satisfaction.' And in a prose note dictated to Miss Isabella Fenwick he says: 'This and other poems connected with Matthew would not gain by a literal detail of facts. Like the wanderer in the "Excursion", this schoolmaster was made up of several, both of his class and men of other occupations.' My quotations are from Grosart's *Prose Works of William Wordsworth*.[1]

Wordsworth's statements apply to the little cycle of poems entitled *Matthew*, *The Two April Mornings*, and *The Fountain* which he wrote in 1799. They arose, though far from simply, out of his memories of certain men he had known during his schooldays at Hawkshead, and of his reflections thereon. Judging from the poems themselves, it would appear that these men were old, and that he regarded them with affection; whilst he himself speaks of 'several', which should mean at least three. He would say no more about them; but there can be no harm in my suggesting who they might have been. The men I have in mind are John Harrison, schoolmaster, Thomas Cowperthwaite, ironmonger, and John Gibson, attorney. In any event, they were an essential part of Wordsworth's Hawkshead, and must have a place in this study of it.[2]

[1] See vol. III, pp. 376 and 161.

[2] William Taylor, headmaster of the Grammar School, who died in 1786, may have supplied the death-bed motif at the opening of Wordsworth's 'Address to the Scholars of the Village School of ——', but T.W.T.'s discussion properly shows that we should think of a village teacher rather than a grammar school master. Mary

*Oral gleanings about John Harrison, schoolmaster—discovery of John
Ireland's MS. autobiography—history of Thomas Deason's house—
Ireland's account of Harrison as a schoolmaster—ancestry of Harrison—
Emma Harrison—Wordsworth's compositions—Agnes Ford—Henry
Ainslie*

In 1906 I made inquiries at Hawkshead to try and find out whether
there was any truth in a statement I had just heard that at, or in
connection with, the tercentenary of its Grammar School in 1885
fresh light had been thrown on Wordsworth's schooldays there. I
soon learnt that the Rev. John Allen, who was Vicar of Hawkshead
at the time, had been active in the matter, and had new information
to impart that he had got mainly or entirely from the senior
Governor of the school, Thomas Bowman, J.P. of Roger Ground.
Born in 1806, he was the only son of the Rev. Thomas Bowman,
Master of the Grammar School from 1786 to 1829. John Allen's
son, Dr. William E. L. Allen, confirmed this, but was not disposed
to add anything except that he himself was a pupil at the Grammar
School in the tercentenary year. And so it came about that it was
Isaac Postlethwaite (1843–1912), shoemaker and caretaker of the
Town Hall, who first told me that the schoolmaster Wordsworth
had written so much about was not at the Grammar School, but
had a little school of his own in Hawkshead. He remembered Mr.
Allen saying this, and that his name was Harrison. For further
particulars he referred me to Miss Mary Hodgson; but as it happened she knew nothing about this schoolmaster.

During the following year I gleaned a little more about him.
Arthur Brydson told me that he had heard members of the Benson
Harrison family say that he was a distant kinsman of theirs who had
failed more than once in business before he became a schoolmaster,
and that Wordsworth as a boy at Hawkshead School had known him
quite well. My other informant in 1907 was the Rev. Reginald M.
Samson, Headmaster of Hawkshead Grammar School from 1883

Moorman has wondered whether the inspiration behind these Matthew poems might
be the same packman who is known to be behind the pedlar/wanderer figure of the
Excursion (Wordsworth: Early Years, pp. 51–2). In the light of T.W.T.'s research this
now seems less probable.

until its closure in 1909. He recollected something of what had been said about schoolmaster Harrison in the tercentenary year, since when he had heard no more. What he told me was that Harrison, who belonged to a well-known local family, had been in the neighbourhood as a boy and young man, but had then gone away, to Manchester or Liverpool he thought, and been employed there in business. He had married his master's daughter. On her death, however, he had returned to Hawkshead, where for a great many years he had a private school, mainly for boys either not old enough or not clever enough to go to the Grammar School. He was an old man when Wordsworth was at school. The rest of my note suggests that Samson had this information direct from Thomas Bowman of Roger Ground.

Then came the discovery by my sister Sarah (1873–1938) that Mrs. Isabella Ireland, a widow who then lived at Elph How, Staveley, near Kendal, had in her possession a manuscript auto-biography that contained a good deal of information about eighteenth-century Hawkshead. It was the *Memoir of My own Life* by John Ireland which I mentioned earlier; a bound manuscript of 106 pages (plus a few that were blank), begun, he says, in April 1803, and finished in October 1805. Mrs. Ireland had found it after her husband's death in his desk, together with some notes on early woollen mills in and near Kendal. As she had not seen it earlier, or heard him speak of it, she concluded that he could not have had it long before he died. She did not think he was descended from the writer, but, as she said that both his father and his grandfather had been woollen manufacturers in Kendal and Staveley, I had doubts on this point, and it was not until more than forty years later that I discovered them to be groundless.[1] I first saw the *Memoir* in January 1908, and was allowed to make notes from it both then and in the following August, and finally in January 1909. I still remember how surprised and delighted I was to find so much in it about

---

[1] This interesting MS. I have been unable to find. Mrs. Isabella Ireland was the second wife of George W. Ireland, probably connected with the firm of Simpson and Ireland who in 1858 operated at Barley Bridge Mill, Staveley, and Kent Street, Kendal. In 1885 G. W. Ireland's Kendal mill was on Lowther Street; the firm of John Ireland and Co. is listed as a separate company with the address, 'Sand Area Mills, Low Mills'. See also below, p. 171.

schoolmaster Harrison, or 'Mr. John' as Hawkshead preferred to call him. But before I say more about him I must deal with John Ireland's boyhood.

In his autobiography he says that he was born at Hawkshead on 2 February 1734, and the Parish Registers record the baptism there of 'John Son of John Ireland Waler' on 4 March 1734. That is on the old reckoning, when for all legal purposes the year began on 25 March: on the new style, which dates from 1752, we should say that he was born and christened in 1735. He had a sister Mary about two and half years older than he was, and a brother Edward almost exactly two years younger. Their home was in Hawkshead itself, in two old cottages thrown into one, but used in part by their father as a workshop and store, cottages that were thatched with 'ling and brackens and moss toppings'. Ling, I need hardly say, was the usual local name for heather; whilst moss-toppings were the top sods or turfs cut from a peat-moss, and thoroughly dried to kill the herbage. At the time there were still several thatched cottages in Hawkshead, apparently behind what at a later date became the Queen's Head and the Brown Cow, and it was not until the 1790s that the last two of them were pulled down.

Young John was only eight years old, he says, when his father died; and that is correct, for John Ireland, waller, was buried at Hawkshead on 12 May 1743. His widow Elizabeth then moved into a small cottage at Outgate, and was still of 'Outy^t' when she married Edward Atkinson on 6 November 1749. During the intervening six and a half years she earned a living by spinning wool, and never once had a penny from the parish. Mary, who had little or no schooling, was able to help from the start, first by carding the wool for her mother, and then by spinning as well; and so long as he lived at home John sometimes gave a hand with the carding.

John's account of his own schooling is as follows. During the year before his father died he began attending a little school in Hawkshead where the boys were taught by Mr. Deason, who was Parish Clerk and had been Usher at the Grammar School, and the girls by his daughter Miss Alice Deason. It was held at their house, and there were both morning and afternoon sessions. He was allowed to continue at this school after his father's death, but his mother

applied for his admission to the Grammar School as a Sandys
Charity boy. Her application failed on the ground that he was 'not
far enough on'; she was told, however, to renew it when he was.
Then, in the year after his father's death, Mr. Deason died, and as a
result John got no more schooling for a time. But after a while Mr.
Harrison, who was always known as Mr. John, came to board with
Mrs. Deason; and he restarted the school her husband had taught.
Young John attended it, and at the age of ten was admitted from it
to the Grammar School as a Sandys Charity boy, which meant that
he was boarded and clothed, as well as educated, free of cost. He did
not like the Writing Master as much as he had Mr. John, and
though he did fairly well, he considered, he left after one year
whereas his election was for two. And at the age of eleven he was
apprenticed to Robert Addison, a weaver who lived first at Knipe
Fold and then at Roger Ground.

Thomas Deason, who had been Usher at the Grammar School
for at least thirty years before he opened a little school of his own,
and Parish Clerk for nearly as long, was buried at Hawkshead on
24 March 1743, which means 1744 by the way we reckon now. But
it is of his property[1] rather than of him that I would speak, for it
was in the house in which he lived and died that John Harrison
subsequently boarded and had his school for nearly forty years,
either from the autumn of 1744 or from the following January.
Rebuilt in 1689, the house still stands at the foot of Vicarage Lane
its front facing the Grandy Nook Arch, its north side windows
looking out on to Ann Tyson's cottage on the other side of the lane.
On Thomas Deason's death his customary estate, including the peat-
mosses and bracken-garth mentioned earlier, passed to his eldest
son, the Rev. William Deason of Stokesley in Cleveland, who on
30 May 1744, conveyed it to his only surviving sister Alice, in
consideration of his 'natural love and affection for her, and for her
better preferment in the World, and for the sum of Five Shillings
in money'. On the following day, however, Alice Deason the
younger, spinster, conveyed the estate to her mother, Alice Deason
the elder, widow, for the same nominal sum, 'to provide for her for
the term of her natural life'. On Mrs. Deason's death on 8 September

[1] This was T.W.T.'s own house for some twenty years, c. 1936–56, see p. 361.

1767, at the age of eighty-two, her daughter having predeceased her, it descended to her grandson, the Rev. Thomas Deason of Stokesley in Cleveland, who first let it to Myles Robinson, house-carpenter, and then sold it to him in April 1771 for the sum of £131. 5s. 0d. in money 'and also for Diverse other good Causes and Valueable Considerations'. The buyer, who had to borrow most of the money on mortgage and later found difficulty in repaying it, was officially admitted to the estate at a Court Baron for the Manor of Hawkshead held on 26 November 1771, on payment of the 'Customary Admission Fine', which was fixed at twice the annual Lord's Rent, and amounted in his case to 1s. 1d. He was then twenty-eight and had been married five years. As holder of the estate he was called upon to serve as Churchwarden for the Hawkshead Quarter in 1782, and as Overseer of the Poor for the same quarter two years later.

In 1744 the Deason property in Hawkshead Town consisted of a dwelling house with eight principal rooms, and a large upper room or loft having an outside entrance only; a block of outbuildings in the rear, including shippon, stable, and barn; an orchard still further up what is now known as Vicarage Lane, and situated between it and the Town Beck; 'one little parcel of Ground called Dunghil-stead' on the opposite side of that lane, near the cottage afterwards occupied by Hugh and Ann Tyson; and 'the ancient usuall occupation way . . . through Edward Satterthwaites Garden' to the Town Beck to get water. Clearly there was room in the house, or in it and the loft, for both Alice Deason's class of girls, which according to John Ireland was never large, and for John Harrison's boys' school. Sometime prior to 1771 the orchard was sold, and half a dozen cottages, five of them small and very varied in design, were built on the rising site it had occupied. Myles Robinson altered the outbuildings just enough to provide for himself a workshop and sawpit; but the stable, where Mr. John kept his horse or pony, was not affected by this change; nor was the barn. There was still room in the house for him and his school, for the Robinsons' family was limited to four girls born between 1767 and 1776, and the second of these died when she was eighteen months old.

It is not known who took over Alice Deason's girls' school after

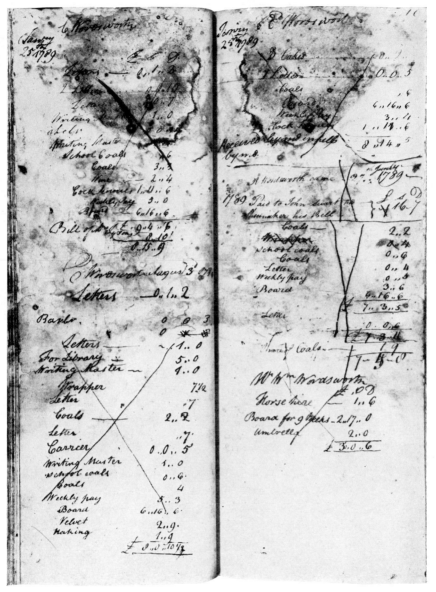

8. Ann Tyson's accounts for the two school Halves, 1789, for Christopher and William Wordsworth, and their second cousin, Richard.

9. A Hawkshead schoolboy? A pencil sketch in Wordsworth's verse note-book, MS. 3, containing the *Vale of Esthwaite*, written 1786–7.

her death, but it continued, and round about 1775 to 1780 a Miss Whinfield was teaching it in or near Grandy Nook, probably at Myles Robinson's as he needed every penny he could get. Two Miss Whinfields are commemorated on an upright stone set against the north wall of the church, namely Dorothy, who died on 3 May 1800, aged sixty-nine, and Catherine, who died on 22 March 1808, aged sixty-five. They were daughters of 'Mr.' Reginald Whinfield, a Hawkshead mercer, and may not have been too badly off, as in 1779 they contributed 2s. between them to the parish collection for the S.P.G. They were then living in Hawkshead Town, apparently somewhere near Grandy Nook but not in it.

According to John Ireland, who goes out of his way to outline the course of Mr. John's life, he was a native of the parish of Hawkshead, and attended its Grammar School when he was a boy; after which he worked for Richard Ford, manager of the Cunsey Furnace, and later became his 'private Clerk'. He lived with Mr. and Mrs. Ford, and tutored their sons, "Mr. William and his brother", before they were old enough to go to school. Then 'him and Mr. Richard differed over something', and he went off to Liverpool, where for some years he was in a shipping business. He married, but never had any liking for the place; and when his wife died early in life he returned, and lived first at Coniston and then at Hawkshead. He had three children, and brought at least two of them with him, a little girl and a baby boy, the latter of whom, John Ireland says, was with a foster-mother at Coniston. Mr. John himself set up as a yarn merchant, but the Kendal buyers were too smart for him, and soon had him out of business. It was then, or shortly afterwards, that he came to board with Mrs. Deason, and reopened the school her husband had taught during the last few years of his life. A little later he lost his only daughter, who was the eldest of his three children. About this time Miss Alice Deason had hopes that he would marry her; vain hopes, for 'he had no thoughts that way', it appears.

His chief recreation was fishing, and John Ireland liked to go with him whenever he could; but after he was apprenticed to Robert Addison, who housed, fed, and clothed him, his chances were few, as his master, though very good to him on the whole, made him work long hours, and it was only rarely that he had a whole evening

M

free. In his old age Mr. John still went fishing, we learn; on his pony as a rule, and often with two or three boys running alongside him, ready to take a turn in looking after it whilst he fished, and maybe hoping for a ride. Even in his early years as a schoolmaster he had a horse or pony, for John Ireland speaks of his riding over to Outgate and Sawrey where, in addition to Hawkshead, he held evening classes for those who could not read and write, and who wished to be able to do so. Held in a different part of the parish each year, they were attended chiefly by young women and older girls who had never been to school, or only for a very short time; but he also had a sprinkling of men and boys at them. John Ireland's sister Mary was among those who learnt to read and write at the classes held at Outgate; and I noticed that when she married Richard Bragg, a hatter, at Hawkshead on 26 August 1755, both were able to sign the register. From about 1750 there was a notable increase in the proportion of Hawkshead brides who could sign their names.

Reverting to the Fords, John Ireland says that after Mr. John's return from Liverpool he and Richard Ford were very good friends; and that William Ford, whom he had taught as a small boy, 'thought the world of him', and often had him to stay. William Ford married a Harrison of the same family as Mr. John, and their two little girls, afterwards Mrs. George Knott of Coniston Waterhead and Mrs. Henry Ainslie of Grizedale, were great favourites of his. But rich and poor were alike to Mr. John: he was the same to everybody whatever their station or calling. He had a friendly greeting for all, and time for 'a few words' if they had. He took an interest in their daily doings and cares; inquired about any who were old or ailing, and made a point of visiting them when he could; and advised and helped those who were in doubt or difficulty. 'Many people', says John Ireland, 'thought a great deal of him, and had a very real affection for him.' But there were some, he adds, who said that with the chances he had when he was younger he ought to have done much better for himself.

During his last year or two as a schoolmaster Mr. John was not very well at times, and it was evident that he could not go on much longer; but what caused him to retire just when he did was the death of George Knott. He then felt he must go to Mrs. Knott, his niece, as John Ireland now plainly states, adding that Mr. John was about seventy-five at the time, and that she had asked him more than once before to go and live with her and her husband at Coniston Waterhead. He helped by teaching one or two of her older children, and no doubt would have remained with her for the rest of his life; but she herself died in the following year, and in the end he went to a son in Liverpool. The last time John Ireland saw him was at the bicentenary of the Grammar School in 1785, when he had two grandsons in the school. That is the end of Ireland's account of Mr. John; but before reviewing it I may as well add at this point that one of the grandsons is likely to have been the Richard Harrison of Liverpool who subscribed 10s. 6d. to the New Library Fund in 1791; that George Knott, as already stated, died on 4 January 1784, and his wife Catherine, eldest child of William and Catherine Ford, on 6 March 1785.

John Ireland says nothing about Mr. John's parentage, but the clues he provides, together with entries in the Hawkshead Parish Registers, make it certain that he was the John, son of 'Mr.' Richard Harrison of Coniston Waterhead, who was baptized at Hawkshead on 13 September 1709, and who was, therefore, aged seventy-four when he gave up his little school there after teaching it for thirty-nine years. His father, who was baptized at Hawkshead on 26 September 1676, was the eldest of the three sons of Lancelot Harrison and Lancelot was the only known son of the Richard Harrison who settled at Coniston Waterhead at the end of the Civil Wars. This earlier Richard is mentioned several times in Miss M. L. Armitt's *Rydal*, published in 1916. His father, it appears, was a Richard Harrison of Martindale who married Jane, daughter of the William Fleming who died in 1600 possessed of the manors of Rydal, Coniston, and Beckermet in West Cumberland. He was succeeded by his son John, who lived first at Coniston and then at Rydal, where from 1633 if not earlier his nephew Richard Harrison acted as his agent. Squire John was a Roman Catholic, and Richard Harrison and his wife and their son Lancelot are listed as such. The squire's family consisted of two daughters, and a son William who was only fourteen when his father died in 1643. The management of the Rydal demesne and household was then entrusted to Richard

Harrison, whose wife and son seem to have assisted him. An account of his responsibilities, anxieties, and troubles during the Civil Wars, when he was imprisoned for eight weeks, will be found in Miss Armitt's book. And there, too, some information is given of the struggle for the possession of Rydal following the death of Squire John's son William in 1649. Here I need say no more than that Daniel Fleming, afterwards Sir Daniel, who eventually obtained it, in spite of the opposition of Richard Harrison acting in the interest of Squire John's daughters, bore his opponent no rancour. He attended Richard's funeral and was on visiting terms with his son Lancelot; and his daughter Catharine was godmother to Lancelot Harrison's son and heir, Richard, father of Hawkshead's Mr. John, who thus turns out to be a kinsman, though rather distant, of the Flemings or le Flemings of Rydal and Coniston.

Mr. John's father, the second Richard Harrison of Coniston Waterhead, was one of the Twenty Four for the parish of Hawkshead from 1716 to his death in 1761, but he was never called upon to act as Churchwarden or Overseer of the Poor. Much the same may be said of the contemporary Myles Sandys of Graythwaite. In parochial documents Richard Harrison is usually styled 'Mr.': in one, however, the list of Sidesmen elected in 1751, he appears as 'Rich: Harrison gent'. The Agnes Scale he married on 29 June 1704, can be identified as the Agnes, daughter of John Scale of Dale Park, who was baptized at Hawkshead on 9 November 1681. She belonged to a family, mainly statesmen but occasionally rising above that class, who were fairly numerous in the seventeenth century in the Satterthwaite Quarter of Hawkshead parish and the neighbouring part of Colton. By her Richard Harrison had five children in addition to John, namely Elizabeth in 1705, Richard in 1707, Emmy in 1716, Catherine in 1719, and Robert in 1721. As we have seen, Catherine married William Ford; but I can add nothing about the rest, except that Robert died young, and that Richard did not succeed his father at Coniston Waterhead, which passed into the hands of William Ford. Mr. John's mother was buried at Hawkshead on 20 January 1763, and his sister Catherine Ford on 7 July 1765.

Richard Ford's two eldest sons, William and John, were baptized at Hawkshead on 17 January 1728, and 25 April 1729, respectively;

and, as John Harrison tutored them before they went to school, he cannot have gone to Liverpool much before 1736. Even so, there would still be time for his courtship and marriage, the birth of his three children, and the death of his wife before he returned to Coniston, apparently in the latter part of 1743, or very early in 1744. My notes do not make it plain whether he came back to Monk Coniston or to Church Coniston. Monk Coniston is the more likely of the two; but if by any chance he chose Church Coniston, then a chapelry in the parish of Ulverston, the baby boy he brought with him could be the 'Willm Son of John Harrison of Ulverstone Gent' who was baptized at Hawkshead on 30 July 1744. The father of this child, however, may well have been the John Harrison, attorney, who had two or three children christened at Ulverston from 1747 onwards as his wife was Mary, eldest daughter of Myles Sandys of Graythwaite and of Esthwaite.

In the present context it is not Mr. John's sons who matter, but his eldest child and only daughter, who according to John Ireland died fairly soon after her father became a schoolmaster in Hawkshead. There is one, and only one, entry in the Parish Registers that could relate to her; an entry which records the burial at Hawkshead on 9 April 1746, of 'M^s. Emmy Harison a Minor'. If this was Mr. John's daughter, which is almost certain, as the date is right, and the Christian name that of one of his sisters, the prefixed 'M^s.' is understandable. Because of it the only alternative would appear to be that Emmy's father was the Rev. John Harrison, Curate of Finsthwaite from 1724 or 1725 to 1741, and then Vicar of Hawkshead until his death in 1761. And that possibility can be ruled out, I consider, as there is no mention of any wife or children of his in the registers of either place.

There can be little doubt, I should say, that Emmy Harrison, who must have been somewhere about eight years old when she died, is the child Emma to whom Wordsworth refers in 'The Two April Mornings'; and that this poem is based in part on his recollection of John Harrison, and of something the old schoolmaster once told him. Living as he did so close to Mr. John during his earlier years at Hawkshead School, Wordsworth must have known him well; and seeing that the old man was friendly and ready to talk, and the young boy eager to hear what his elders could tell him, it would be strange indeed if they had not conversed with each other at times. Besides, Ann Tyson must have had an interest in Mr. John, and not least because he was Mrs. George Knott's uncle; and no doubt she would have something to say to Wordsworth about him, and possibly a good deal, since that seems to have been her habit. As I have shown, Ann was less than four years younger than John Harrison, and like him a native of the parish.

It would seem that Wordsworth had John Harrison in mind, though perhaps not him alone, when in 1798 he composed the poem entitled 'Address to the Scholars of the Village School of ——.' In a manuscript variant of this poem the following lines occur near the end:[1]

> He taught in this his humble state
> What happiness a man of worth
> A single mortal may create
> Upon a single spot of earth.
> Among the distant stars we view
> The hand of God in rain and dew
> And in the summer heat,
> And Matthew's little works we trace
> All round his happy native place
> In every eye we meet.
> The neat trim house, the cottage rude
> All owed to Matthew gifts of gold,
> Light pleasures every day renewed
> Or blessings half a century old.

I can think of no one in Hawkshead during Wordsworth's school-days there to whom these lines apply better than they do to Mr. John.

[1] See *Poetical Works of Wordsworth*, ed. de Selincourt and Darbishire (1947), IV., p. 451. In a manuscript used for the preparation of his volume of 1842 when this poem first appeared, Wordsworth's title was 'The Schoolmaster', and the present title was the sub-title (see verse MS. 102, Dove Cottage Library). The year of composition was attached to the poem, as it was for at least one other poem in this MS.: Wordsworth appended '1789', clearly a slip for 1798 or 1799. Indeed, on other grounds the probable date of composition seems to be the winter and spring of these two years, 1798–9, when Wordsworth was in Goslar. It was at this time that his imagination was deeply involved with Hawkshead and he was drafting some of the great passages that are now chiefly found in Books I and II of *The Prelude*.

The same may be said of certain verses in two manuscript elegies on Matthew, evidently written about the same time.[1] From the first I will quote only these lines:

> A schoolmaster by title known
> Long Mathew penn'd his little flock
> Within yon pile that stands alone
> In colour like its native rock.
>
> Learning will often dry the heart,
> The very bones it will distress,
> But Mathew had an idle art
> Of teaching love and happiness.

The second elegy reads:[2]

> Ye little girls, ye loved his name,
> Come here and knit your gloves of yarn,
> Ye loved him better than your dame
> —The schoolmaster of fair Glencarn.
>
> For though to many a wanton boy
> Did Mathew act a father's part,
> Ye tiny maids, *ye* were his joy,
> Ye were the favourites of his heart.
>
> Ye ruddy damsels past sixteen
> Weep now that Mathew's race is run
> He wrote your love-letters, I ween
> Ye kiss'd him when the work was done.

Could these be references to anyone but Mr. John? I doubt it, but gladly leave the decision to others, remarking only that Matthew, though a composite figure, was not an invention.

Having justified, I hope, the space already given to John Harrison, I feel I can say a little more about him by way of comment and explanation. He never held any parochial office, nor did he contribute to the parish collection for the S.P.G. in 1779, or to any of the earlier Briefs that came to light when the old Register Chest—a box-cavity three feet long hollowed out of a massive oak beam of

---

[1] *Ibid.*, p. 452.   [2] *Ibid.*, p. 454.

more than twice that length—was opened in 1954. Briefs were parish collections authorized by the Sovereign as head of the Church for some special purpose, usually the relief of distress resulting from fire, flood, or other calamity. Those preserved at Hawkshead are mostly undated, but the names of the contributors show that they belong to the period 1735–70. Either John Harrison or Mr. Harrison is mentioned in at least three or four of them as having given 6d. (as against Hugh Tyson's and Alice Deason's 1d. or 2d.); but I decided that he was the Vicar, the Rev. John Harrison. The absence of Mr. John's name from all parochial lists troubled me until I realized that as he was never a householder in the parish but only a boarder, he was, of course, not liable to be called upon either to hold office or to contribute to the maintenance of the church, the poor, and the highways, or even to a Brief.

His youngest sister Catherine and her husband William Ford were married in 1751, and after living for a short time first at Grizedale and then at Ulverston they joined her parents Richard and Agnes Harrison at Coniston Waterhead not later than the spring of 1754; and there, as we have seen, all four died in the 1760s, the last of them, William Ford, in 1769. It would, then, be at his own old home that Mr. John often stayed with his brother-in-law, and his sister so long as she lived, and that he first got to know their daughters Catherine and Agnes. When Catherine died in the spring of 1785 Agnes was not married, but in 1782, 1783, and 1784 she had planted no fewer than 77,100 trees on the Grizedale Hall estate, which was part of her inheritance. She began with 19,100 oak trees, and is reported to have said: 'No oak can grow so crooked but it falleth out to some use.' Her marriage at the age of twenty-three to 'Henry Ainslie, gentleman, of Kendal', afterwards Dr. Henry Ainslie, Physician to St. Thomas's Hospital, London, took place at Colton on 9 August 1785.[1] In the register entry she appears as 'Agnes Ford of Colton', but for the previous two or three years, if not more, she had been living at Ford Lodge, Grizedale, and at least once had invited Mr. John to go and live there too. John Ireland's reference to this is of the briefest, and it is impossible to infer from it just when she asked him. Whenever it was, he declined. Perhaps his final

[1] For comments on this marriage, see letter dated 13 Aug. 1785, Appendix III.

decision to go to a son in Liverpool was influenced by her impending marriage to Henry Ainslie, but I have no evidence for this.

By his marriage, Henry Ainslie (1760–1834) acquired not only the Grizedale Hall estate but also a large holding in the Newland Co., in whose affairs he took an active interest, mainly by correspondence, for he and his wife spent very little time at Grizedale. By George Knott's will the 'sole management and direction of the concern' were entrusted to his steward Matthew Harrison, under whose control its position, previously unsatisfactory, rapidly improved. In 1812 he bought the Knotts' majority shareholding in the company for upwards of £34,000, whereupon it became Harrison, Ainslie & Co. On his death in 1824 in his seventy-second year he was succeeded in the management by his only surviving son Benson Harrison (1786–1863), who in the preceding year had married Dorothy Wordsworth as his second wife.[1] Matthew was not baptized at Hawkshead, and I do not know how he was related to Mr. John. That his descendants should have thought that the old schoolmaster had failed more than once in business before taking to teaching is not surprising; apart from his venture as a yarn merchant I think it would be truer to say that he had failed to profit from his opportunities, and that he had neither taste nor talent for business.

During his thirty-nine years as a schoolmaster at Hawkshead I doubt whether he ever earned enough to keep both himself and his pony unless it was during the period when he was holding evening classes as well as teaching in the day-time. The fact that he always had a horse or pony suggests that he was not wholly dependent on his earnings; and John Ireland, though he does not say so in so many words, clearly implies that he never troubled, and had no need to trouble, about money as he had some private means. They could have come from his wife if, as the Rev. R. M. Samson had heard, she was his master's daughter; and that, I should think, is the most likely source. But later, following his father's death in 1761, he may well have benefited under his will.

And that ends what I can usefully say about John Harrison, schoolmaster, perhaps the most important of the Hawkshead men from the memory of whom Wordsworth fashioned his Matthew.

[1] See Additional Notes, Appendix V.

Seemingly he was neither a gay nor a witty man, nor a rhymester.
To one who was all of these I turn next.

Churchend—the early Cowperthwaites—burials in Hawkshead Church
—Hugh Cowperthwaite—Thomas, ironmonger—Isaac Swainson's
rhyme—links in trade between Kendal and Hawkshead—two other
rhymes—the church clock—Cowperthwaite's elegiac rhyme?—'The
Fountain'—couplets in the Register Chest—an old account book

On one occasion Miss Mary Hodgson came upon Wordsworth in
Hawkshead churchyard, and he then told her that in his earlier years
at the Grammar School he often went up there on summer evenings,
and that sometimes old men sitting against the church wall would
talk to him, and invite him to share their seat. He was referring to
the long stone bench set against the east wall of the church almost as
if it were part of it; a bench that affords fine views of the Vale of
Esthwaite, the long line of Claife Heights, and in the farther distance
some of Westmorland's mountains. Both place and seat have been
known as Churchend at least from the middle of the eighteenth
century; and for as long or longer Hawkshead folk have sat there
and talked on fine summer evenings. The bench is continued on the
south side of the church for about two yards at present, but evidently
extended at one time as far as the south porch, near which vestiges
of it remained until the restoration of the church in 1875–6. Its
original purpose was to provide somewhere to sit, if need be, whilst
parish officers transacted secular business, and notices were read or
cried and sales called after Sunday, Holy Day, or Market Day
service. Lists of assessments, however, were read in church 'in the
time of divine Service', and then signed by the minister to certify
that this had been done; after which they had to be 'allowed' by
two magistrates.

Set upright against the east wall of the church, and towards its
northern end, is a tombstone bearing this inscription:

In Memory of Thomas Cowperthwaite late of
Hawkshead Iron-monger, who departed this
Life the 6th Day of July 1782, in the 72[d] Year
of his Age. His facetious disposition, together

with his other good qualities, made him
respected by a numerous Acquaintance;
who to perpetuate his Memory, have caused
this Stone to be erected.

At that date facetious meant gay, witty, humorous, amusing. It was not used then in the sense jocose. The relevant entry in the Parish Registers for 1782 reads: 'Mr Thos. Cowperthwaite of Town Ironmonger Died July ye 6th Buried ye 8th in C^h. yard Aged 72'. He is the 'Thomas Son of Hugh Cowperthw^t of Hawksh^d Town' who was baptized at Hawkshead on 22 September 1709, just nine days later than John, son of Richard Harrison of Coniston Waterhead. It is more than likely that both were among the old men who during Wordsworth's early years at Hawkshead often sat on Churchend on summer evenings, and I feel it is appropriate that the memorial to Thomas Cowperthwaite should be there.

His father is the 'Hugh Cowpthwaite fil. W^m. de Haukeshead field head' who was baptized at Hawkshead on 5 February 1683/4. He had an older brother William who was not christened there, and two younger brothers who were—Leonard on 25 March 1688, and John on 9 February 1689/90. John was buried in the church on 23 February 1693/4, as an elder sister Agnes, 'fil .W^m. de fieldhead', had been on 14 April 1683. This last is the earliest mention in the Parish Registers of any Cowperthwaite of Fieldhead; and William cannot have stayed there more than twenty years, as beyond doubt he is the 'William Cowprthwaite of Tockhow' in Upper Claife who was buried in the church on 11 August 1704. Yet the family gave its name to an intake at the northern extremity of Hawkshead Fieldhead; the 'Intack' from which the stones were got for the rebuilding of the Market House in 1790, as is shown in a bill for 15s. presented to the Trustees on 14 February 1791, and paid by them on 26 November 1793. William Cowperthwaite was succeeded at Tockhow by his son William, who had a daughter Katherine, baptized on 3 June 1724. The elder William's son Leonard seems to have lived at Tockhow too. Anyhow, it is certain that he is the 'Leonard Cowp^{r}thw^t of the Tockhow' who died unmarried at the age of twenty-seven, and was buried in the church on 13

December 1715. He left the interest on £20 for the benefit of the poor of Fieldhead and Claife.

This legacy, and the four intramural burials just noted, can hardly be regarded as indications of wealth. From 1605 to 1704 more than 1,100 burials, mainly of statesmen and their families, are noted in the Parish Registers as having taken place in the church, where the normal place of interment was under the ground on which the pews stood; ground that was bare earth except for a covering of rushes renewed annually, originally on St. James's Day. There was little falling off in the number of such burials until about 1740, after which a decline set in. But it was not until 1793–4, when the church was re-seated with pews more costly to remove and put back, and the fee for intramural burial raised from 3s. 4d. to 5 guineas that the old practice virtually ceased, except for a very occasional burial in the chancel, the charge for which was advanced from 6s. 8d. to 10 guineas.

Hugh Cowperthwaite of Town, who was neither married nor buried at Hawkshead, had six children baptized there: William in 1707, Thomas in 1709, Margaret in 1719, Hugh in 1721, Henry in 1723, and Prudence in 1725. Margaret and Henry died in infancy; and of the rest, only Prudence was married at Hawkshead, and only she had children baptized there. Her marriage took place in 1751, and was to John Suart, a Hawkshead currier whom I mentioned earlier. In addition to the six children named in the Hawkshead registers, Hugh Cowperthwaite may well have had others, born in the ten-year gap between the christenings of Thomas and Margaret, and baptized wherever he was then living. There are three Cowperthwaites, John, Mary, and Agnes, who are difficult to account for if they were not his children. John married Sarah Myers at Hawkshead in 1733, but is not mentioned again in the Parish Registers. Mary wedded Daniel Fisher, hatter, of Far Sawrey, at Hawkshead in 1741, and was buried there in 1748. And Agnes, the most likely of the three to have been one of Hugh's family, was interred at Hawkshead on 26 April 1778, when she was described in the register entry as 'Mrs Agnes Cowperthwaite Spinster Gallabarrow'. 'Cathrine Wife of Hugh Cowerthwte Town', apparently his only wife, was buried at Hawkshead on 5 October 1756. He stayed on for another two or three years at least, but was no longer there in

1765, when Thomas, the ironmonger, seems to have been the only male Cowperthwaite in the parish.

In 1721 Hugh Cowperthwaite, who is sometimes styled 'Mr.', was an innkeeper, and this he continued to be for a great many years, all or most of the time as landlord of the Red Lion, Hawkshead's leading inn. In 1737, when the churchwardens decided to buy the Communion wine locally, they got it from him and three others, and his bill for it amounted to 12s. 0d. In 1719 he was Overseer of Highways for Fieldhead, where the Cowperthwaites must have retained a customary holding of some sort; and in 1720 he was both Churchwarden and Overseer of the Poor for the Hawkshead Quarter. Later he filled these offices a second time, being Overseer of the Poor in 1736/7 and Churchwarden in 1744. His elder brother William of Tockhow was Overseer or Surveyor of Highways for the High End of Claife in 1720, and Churchwarden for the Claife Quarter in 1723; but there is no mention of him in Hawkshead records after the baptism of his daughter Katherine in 1724, and it is probable that he did not stay much longer in the parish.

The only parochial office Thomas Cowperthwaite ever held was that of Surveyor of Highways for Fieldhead in 1752. His, or his father's holding there, must, I think, have been Cowperthwaite Intake, which in 1790 was in the hands of William Benson of Skelwith, and did not, it seems, form part of any of the Fieldhead farms. Thomas's house in Hawkshead Town cannot have been one of the ancient tenements whose occupiers were called upon in turn to act as churchwardens and overseers of the poor. From the Churchwardens' Accounts I have noted only two entries in which his name appears, both records of payments, the first in 1754 of 2s. 6d. to 'Mr Cowperthwte for Nails', the second in 1756 of 2s. 3d. to 'Thos. Cowperthwte for Nails'. In the lists of subscribers to Briefs that happen to have been preserved he is nearly always styled 'Mr.', and his usual contribution was 2d. during the period 1756 to 1770. In 1765, when there was an appeal for subscriptions towards the cost of replacing the old 'great' bell and two smaller ones by a ring of six, he gave 5s. 0d. and Agnes Cowperthwaite 1s. 0d. And to the S.P.G. collection in 1779 he contributed 2s. 0d. It is clear that he had no children, unless by any chance they were baptized elsewhere and did not survive very long. On the other hand, the 'Mrs. Elizabeth Cowperthwaite of Town Widow', who died at Hawkshead on 1 September 1799, aged 85, can hardly have been anybody's widow but his.

And now for the four or five rhymes that have come to light, and that appear to be his; and first as to the evidence that he wrote them. Two of them date themselves, either exactly or approximately; and the dates are right. Two I have seen as they were written, and compared the handwriting with Thomas Cowperthwaite's signature. I thought the handwriting was his, but I am not an expert in this field, and cannot vouch that it was. The Rev. John Allen, Vicar of Hawkshead from 1875 to 1892, who found three of the rhymes in the old Register Chest and made copies of them, was of the same opinion, as I discovered in 1949 when some valuable papers and notes of his were placed at my disposal by his son Dr. William Allen. Added to which there is the evidence that rests in the first place on a sentence occurring in a letter written on 2 April 1784, by a Hawkshead schoolboy named Isaac Swainson to his father Joseph Swainson, a Kendal wool merchant, to whom he had sent or was sending a rhyme linking Hawkshead and Kendal. The sentence reads: 'Wm Suert has got by heart a lot of his Uncles rhymes, some are very witty'. Isaac was born at Kendal on 30 November 1770, and his mother Margaret, daughter of Isaac and Margaret Rawlinson of Lancaster, died eleven days later, aged twenty. His letters to his father show that he boarded at Hawkshead with a Mr. and Mrs. Suart, or Suert as he writes, at the foot of Church Hill, doubtless John, the currier, and his wife Prudence. The William he mentions was the eldest of their three sons, and a shoemaker by trade, as I mentioned earlier. Baptized at Hawkshead on 30 January 1757, he was married there to Ann Wilson in 1780; and amongst their many children was a son Cowperthwaite born in 1794. Thomas Cowperthwaite was, of course, William Suart's uncle.

The rhyme Isaac Swainson sent his father was this:

> Hawkshead and Kendal are bound up together
> Firstly by Wool and Lastly by Leather.
> Both Live by their Trade in fair or foul Weather,
> And pay scanty heed to Mighty Folks Blether.

My thanks are due to the late Joseph Swainson of Stone Cross, Kendal, for allowing me to copy this rhyme from an old family Memorandum Book, and to copy also extracts from five letters written by Isaac Swainson from Hawkshead in 1784-5. That was in 1906. In 1949 I found the author's version of this rhyme in the church safe at Hawkshead. The first two lines were the same, and the third and fourth read:

> They live by their Trade in fair and foul Weather,
> And pay scanty heed to the Mighty Ones Blether.

Hawkshead market was at its most important during the second half of the eighteenth century. According to John Ireland, woollen yarn was offered for sale there that had been brought from near and far, even from the Duddon Valley and over Dunmail Raise. He himself was a buyer of it from the time he became manager of Braithwaite's Stramongate Mill in Kendal; and after he set up as a woollen manufacturer on his own account in part of the very extensive Low Mills just south of the town—the whole of which property, with its four water-wheels on the river Kent, John Ireland & Sons acquired in 1805—he attended Hawkshead market almost every week to buy 'garn' as it was called locally. During the great frost in the early months of 1785, when there were heavy falls of snow as well, 'he had garn brought from Hawkshead on sleds [sledges designed for goods transport]', he says, 'to keep his own and other weavers in work'. He mentions, too, that the handloom weavers on Kendal Fellside, who normally got their yarn from the wool-badgers,[1] 'went to Hawkshead with a sled to get a supply, pulling the sled themselves both there and back'. Such was the dependence of Kendal on Hawkshead market for woollen yarn. The wool-link between the two places was the first both in time and importance. Leather was a later and much less important link: indeed it is not until the second half of the eighteenth century that one hears of Hawkshead being a mart for it. I know nothing of Kendal buyers of leather during this period, but mention has already been made of visits to Hawkshead market by Daniel Satterthwaite, a Cockermouth saddler, and of his subscription

[1] Wool buyers, middlemen between the farmer and the weaver or manufacturer.

towards the cost of rebuilding the Market House in 1790. And at least by the end of the century Hawkshead became noted for its 'clog-whangs' and 'shoe-whangs', which were still spoken of by old people when I was young. These were leather laces for clogs and high shoes, for *whang* like *thong* is descended from Old English *thwang*. Cowperthwaite's rhyme begins well, but the last two lines are not up to the standard of the first two. Who the 'Mighty Folk' or 'Mighty Ones' were is anybody's guess. Mine is that they were the leading Whig and Tory politicians, for whose utterances a certain contempt may have been felt in both Hawkshead and Kendal, though the only evidence of it I have is John Ireland's reference to them, and the pleasure with which he quotes the Rev. William Taylor as saying that he could 'scarce tell the difference between Whig and Tory'. Blether, I may say, is the local dialect name for voluble or loquacious nonsense.

The second rhyme in the author's handwriting that I found in the church safe proved to be one the Rev. John Allen had previously seen and copied. Except that his copy had a semicolon instead of a full stop at the end of the third line, it was identical with the original, which read:

> M.th.w H., our widow'd Surgeon,
> Of late has had a heart felt urge on
> To gain the Hand of F.n.y I.t.n.
> That he'll succeed is more than Certain.

I have already dealt with Matthew Hodgson and Fanny Irton, and need only add that the precise date of their marriage was 10 January 1778.[1]

The most important rhyme from our present view-point was discovered by the Rev. John Allen, who noted that it was written on a 'piece of grocery paper', and perfected only after three or four attempts. It then read:

> True time I tell, the Sundial said,
> When Sol his Rays sends from the Sky.
> If he's a Bed, the Clock replied,
> You cannot even Tell a Lie.

[1] See above p. 11.

10. The ruined Station above the Ferry in 1970: built by the Rev. William Braithwaite who acquired the land under the Claife Heights Enclosure, 1794–9.

11. *West view across Windermere, looking over the Great Island. From the Hill above the Ferry House.* By Joseph Farington, engraving published 1789. Apparently West's No. 1 Station.

Allen copied two of the discarded lines, the beginning of a rhyme that was then abandoned it seems. They are:

> Full well we know the Clock tells Lies;
> To mend its Ways they've tried in vain.

In other words, they have tried in vain to reform it. I wish Thomas Cowperthwaite had finished this rhyme. John Allen copied another; and though it has no particular interest or merit, it may as well be recorded here. It runs:

> When Sol sends forth his glorious Rays
> I tell the time the Gnomon says,
> But when his Face is hid from Earth
> Then truth to tell I'm nothing worth.

The sundial, which was, and still is, at the north-east corner of the churchyard, bears the inscription 'Lat. 54° 50' Anno Dom. 1693'. Standing on a somewhat weathered sandstone pedestal, it has a copper dial engraved with the hours, but the copper gnomon, whose shadow used to indicate the time, was wrenched off at the beginning of this century, and has never been replaced.

The clock that was in the habit of telling lies was the church clock, to which, in his poem 'The Fountain', Wordsworth refers as

> the crazy old church-clock,
> And the bewildered chimes.

It was a twenty-four-hour clock whose works were old and worn when he was at school, and one of whose main faults was that of striking the wrong hour. In the eighteenth century it had three new faces, the chief cost of which was the painting, the first in 1710, the second in 1741, and the third in 1787, which was Wordsworth's last year at Hawkshead School. The second face had been painted and coloured by a local decorator: the third was painted white, with black list and numbers, by the carpenter who made it. In 1723 'a pig of lead to ye clock' cost the churchwardens 18s. 0d., and now and again they had to buy a new clock-rope or string. But from about 1740 to his death in 1767 Thomas Burton, a son of the Samuel

N

Burton who produced some well-made grandfather clocks at Hawkshead, and himself a clocksmith as well as a blacksmith, kept the church clock in repair at very small cost. After that Joseph Keen, smith, innkeeper, and postmaster, who already looked after the bells, took over the repair of the clock. His later bills include 1s. 5d. in 1778 for 'striken part of clock repeard'; 1s. in 1784 for 'repearing the clock severel times'; and 3s. in 1787 for 'repearing the clock many diffrent times'.

By 1778, however, other help was at hand if needed, as Thomas Armstrong, a twenty-three-year-old clockmaker who afterwards made long-cased clocks at Hawkshead, had come there from the chapelry of Egton-with-Newland in Low Furness. In 1780 he was paid 7s. 6d. for work done on the clock on 7 and 8 March in that year. The details are as follows:

> to laying the pallets deper in the Swing
> Wheel and Scraping the Same   1s. 0d.
> Repairing the Stricking part as to
> Striking true Numbers &c.   1s. 6d.
> all parts whatsoever thear to
> belo[n]ging taken down and
> thorowly Cleand.   5s. 0d.

Ten years later the same clockmaker was called upon to overhaul the clock and make all necessary repairs to it, evidently a big undertaking, as the Churchwardens' Accounts for 1791 record the payment of £5. 4s. 7d. to 'Mr Thomas Armstrong for Repairing Church Clock in 1790 as pr. Note'.

No doubt it was better for a time, but at a Vestry Meeting held on 17 January 1804, it was resolved 'that the clock being very old and irregular, bc altered from a twenty-four-hour clock to an eight-day clock; and that a clocksmith be employed for the same.' It was laid down that all worn and defective parts were to be repaired or replaced at the same time, and that all new material, other than wood, was to be supplied by the clocksmith. He was to do all the work required except the carpentry; and for work and materials he was to receive the sum of 18 guineas, which sum was to be raised by levying a Church Rate. The maker of the 'new' clock, as it was called when paid for, was William Bellman of Broughton-in-Furness, a clockmaker of greater repute than Thomas Armstrong. It remained in use until 1876.

There is one other rhyme that, despite appearances to the contrary, I am inclined to attribute to Thomas Cowperthwaite; though if it was his, let me say at once that I know of it only from a copy found in the church safe among papers relating to the rebuilding of the Market House in 1790. Apparently it had been used as a marker by someone consulting them. Later I identified the handwriting beyond reasonable doubt as that of the Rev. George Park who was Vicar of Hawkshead from 1812 until his death on 12 July 1829. Born at Hawkshead on 20 March 1779, and educated there, he was the youngest of the three sons of George Park of Town, saddler and ironmonger. Though only three when Thomas Cowperthwaite died, he is almost certain to have heard of him and his rhymes during his boyhood. The one that he wrote out differs from the others that have come to light, for it reads:

> The last of my Name in this Conny Spot,
> That's what I'm destined to be;
> My Course it's near run, decided my Lot,
> And there's no one to rue it but me.

Conny, a variant of *canny*, is here used in the sense good, a meaning not found in Scotland.

The rhyme is a puzzling one. The last line, I take it, means that the writer alone was sorry and sad that he would be the last of his name in the place where he lived. As I have pointed out already, Thomas was the last male Cowperthwaite to live at Hawkshead, or anywhere else in the parish. But what of the Mrs. Elizabeth Cowperthwaite, almost certainly his wife, who lived until 1799? Though not of his blood, she was a Cowperthwaite by name in virtue of her marriage. If she was his wife, she may have intended to return to her native place when he died; if not, it is possible that she did not come to live at Hawkshead until after his death. Or it may be that he did not think of her as a Cowperthwaite. That his sister Prudence did not die until 1800 is irrelevant as she was married to John Suart; and Miss Agnes Cowperthwaite had been laid to rest in 1778.

The Cowperthwaites were not an old Hawkshead family, though before William's coming to Fieldhead in 1683 or slightly earlier there are solitary mentions in the registers of a Stephen Cowperthwaite in 1613 and of a George in 1661; nor were there ever many of them in the parish. So the fact that Thomas was the last male Cowperthwaite to live there can hardly be regarded in itself as likely to cause general regret. What his 'numerous Acquaintance' felt when he died was the loss, not of the last male member of a small local family, but of a companion whose gaiety and wit, 'together with his other good qualities', had won their respect and esteem. Unfortunately there is no information available as to what those other good qualities were.

The Rev. George Park, though only fifty when he died, outlived his father, his two brothers, and his wife; but he had an unmarried sister Elizabeth who resided at Hawkshead until her death in 1843, and a son who, as the Rev. George Park, M.A., was Vicar of the parish from 1834 to 1865; besides which there were Parks of another family living there in 1829 and for long afterwards. He cannot, then, be regarded as the author of the sad little rhyme known only in his handwriting. Nor can I think of anyone more likely, except Thomas Cowperthwaite. The style is his, and the sentiments are natural to an old man, even a gay old man, who was nearing his end, and who had no descendants, and few relatives about him, none of them of his name *and* blood. That he should have been rueful at times does not, of course, belie the fact that he was esteemed for his gaiety and wit. And as to the inaccuracy in his rhyme to which I felt bound to draw attention, surely that is but a trifle.

Wordsworth, who was twelve when Thomas Cowperthwaite died at the age of seventy-two, seems to have been pondering more on him than on anyone else when he composed 'The Fountain', a poem cast in the form of a conversation it will be remembered. In it Matthew, the 'dear old Man', the 'grey-haired man of glee', is said to be seventy-two, and his days to be 'almost gone'. Wordsworth suggests that they match the water's pleasant tune

> With some old border-song, or catch
> That suits a summer's noon;

> Or of the church-clock and the chimes
> Sing here beneath the shade,
> That half-mad thing of witty rhymes,
> Which you last April made!
>
> (ll.11–16)

Again, in the closing verse, Wordsworth says:

> And, ere we came to Leonard's rock,
> He sang those witty rhymes
> About the crazy old church-clock,
> And the bewildered chimes.
>
> (ll.69–72)

A good part of the poem consists of Wordsworth's reflections on old age. They are put into Matthew's mouth, and may be based in part on what he had once heard from Thomas Cowperthwaite. Matthew then continues:

> If there be one who need bemoan
> His kindred laid in earth,
> The household hearts that were his own;
> It is the man of mirth.
>
> My days, my Friend, are almost gone,
> My life has been approved,
> And many love me! but by none
> Am I enough beloved.

Whereupon Wordsworth breaks in with these lines:

> Now both himself and me he wrongs,
> The man who thus complains!
> I live and sing my idle songs
> Upon these happy plains;
>
> 'And, Matthew, for thy children dead
> I'll be a son to thee!'
> At this he grasped my hand, and said,
> 'Alas! that cannot be'.
>
> (ll.49–64)

With this last line Wordsworth, for the second time in the Matthew poems, expresses his belief that for a dead child or children someone else's child can be no replacement.

As already stated, there is no record of Thomas Cowperthwaite's marriage in the Hawkshead registers, nor any indication that he ever had any children. But then there is no mention of him in any Hawkshead document after his baptism in 1709 until 1752; and considering the comings and goings of other Hawkshead Cowperthwaites it would not be strange if he were living somewhere else in the 1730s and 1740s, when he could have had two or more children who died young. If he had, the memory of them may well have been with him more as he neared his end than it had in the years between when he still had health and vigour. As Wordsworth, in the person of Matthew, says in 'The Fountain', the wiser mind

> Mourns less for what age takes away
> Than what it leaves behind.
>
> (ll.35–6)

John Harrison lost his little girl, and John Gibson (to whom I am coming next) a son at the age of twelve, but neither a second child so far as I know. So it is possible that Wordsworth was thinking of Thomas Cowperthwaite when he referred to Matthew's 'children dead'. Another doubt which remains in my mind is whether Thomas was capable of writing longer and more ambitious rhymes than the ones I have cited as his. Quite possibly he was; but it is only fair that this doubt should be stated.

When the old Register Chest was opened I had hopes that something more by Thomas Cowperthwaite might turn up. Instead I found two rhymed couplets, obviously not his, and not in his handwriting I thought. They were written on the lower half of a folded sheet of paper, on the other side of which were three receipts for sums of money brought in by Henry Wilson, probably the Henry Wilson of Bank Ground, Monk Coniston, who was a Churchwarden. The receipts, which were dated 26 December 1754, had been made out by John Hodgson, Parish Clerk, and two of them were signed by George Braithwaite, then Churchwarden for the Hawkshead Quarter. The first of the couplets, which were in a more educated handwriting, read:

> To please the Ladies I've done what I can
> For nothing now but black breaches makes yᵉ Man.

And the second was:

> They have a Dark Lanthorn of the great Spirit
> Which none can See by but those that do bear it.

The second seemed familiar, and proved to be an adaption or mis-quotation of two lines in *Hudibras*, the seventeenth-century satire by Samuel Butler which is directed against the Puritans. What he actually wrote, including the two preceding lines, was this:

> Whate're men speak by this New Light,
> Still they are sure to be i'th' right.
> 'Tis a dark-Lanthorn of the Spirit,
> Which none see by but those that bear it.[1]

The first couplet may well be from the same poem, a new edition of which by Dr. Zachary Grey appeared in 1744. 'Many of its brilliant couplets', it has been said, 'have passed into the proverbial commonplaces of the language. . . .'

One more discovery, this time by H. S. Cowper, towards the end of the last century, may be mentioned, though it, too, is scarcely relevant. It is of a poem running to twenty-one verses which some-one has copied into the leather-bound account book recording the distributions in the years 1707–61 of the interest on two charitable bequests by George Rigg, Parish Clerk, for the benefit of the sick, poor, and of the aged of the Bailiwick of Hawkshead. The poem has been printed by Cowper in his *Hawkshead*, published in 1899,[2] but as the author of it does not seem to have been identified I will summarize it here, with the addition of a full-stop now and again. It is about a hermit who lived in a wood, in a 'spacious grot' beside a rill; 'the hermit of the vale', as the neighbouring shepherds called him. 'Grave Contemplation on the roof', we are told, 'had fix'd her awful seat'. His beard was 'silvered o'er with age', and his hoary locks 'in careless order' down his back did flow. His body felt no foul disease; 'his bosom felt no care'. His 'Custom'd meal' was a plate of herbs; his table was of oak. There is no mention of chair or bed: indeed it is stated that a death's head and an hour glass 'his

---

[1] *Hudibras* (Oxford, 1967), I, 1, 496–500.   [2] Pp. 451–3.

furniture composed'. Yet should a pilgrim stray from his path through the wood he 'glad receiv'd him at his board', or led him on his way. At cock-crow—for he had a cock—he wakes,

> And oer the Dew besprinkled lawn
> His morning ramble takes.

And whilst he 'views the earth beneath', the glowing sky above,

> No passion touchd his beating heart
> But pure celestial love.

Here city lords are urged to think of this, 'and Learn from him to Live'. When night falls he ascends the 'mountain high',

> And thence with raptur'd eye observes
> The stars that gild the sky.

After which he 'pours celestial hymns of praise' to God the King of all. Then once, whilst the moon still 'viewed' him, and 'disfused her conscious light around',

> The pious hermit seiz'd with joy
> Unusual joy I trow
> Seemed in a trance to mount the skies
> Relieved from mortal woe.

In short, he died, as the closing verse makes plain. Why anyone should want to copy the poem is a mystery. 'The handwriting', says Cowper, 'appears to be about 1750, and is very similar to that in which the accounts were kept about that date; though it may not be the same.' On inspecting it, I decided that it was not Thomas Cowperthwaite's.[1]

---

[1] The account book appears to have been in the keeping of the Hodgson family; first, John Hodgson, Parish Clerk 1744–85, used it for the Rigg charity accounts until 1761; then an Elizabeth Hodgson wrote in it miscellaneous accounts, chiefly for the sale of caps, hats, bonnets; in addition to the poem there is a draft ill-spelt letter by one A. [? Gragg] asking for a place in the 'Queain School'—possibly Hawkshead Grammar School, founded by Royal Letters Patent dated 10 April 1585, the twenty-seventh year of the reign of Queen Elizabeth. For the Hodgsons, see pp. 197–8.

John Gibson, attorney—his wife, Elizabeth Sandys, and her family—
duties as Clerk to the Vestry—church chest and school chest—Clerk to
the School Governors—Clerk to the Market House Trustees—pranks
—reminiscence of Joseph Budworth

There are lines in *Matthew* that make one wonder who Wordsworth
had in mind when he wrote them; lines such as

> Poor Matthew, all his frolics o'er,
> Is silent as a standing pool
>
> (ll.17–18)

and again

> The sighs which Matthew heaved were sighs
> Of one tired out with fun and madness
>
> (ll.21–2)

but also

> Yet, sometimes, when the secret cup
> Of still and serious thought went round,
> It seemed as if he drank it up—
> He felt with spirit so profound.
>
> (ll.25–8)

To these lines a verse may be added from an elegy he wrote at much
the same time but did not publish:

> Yet when his hair was white as rime
> And he twice thirty years had seen
> Would Mathew [sic] wish from time to time
> That he a graver man had been.[1]

And one more verse may be appended, this time from his 'Address
to Scholars of the Village School of ——':

> Oh true of heart, of spirit gay,
> Thy faults, where not already gone
> From memory, prolong their stay
> For charity's sweet sake alone.
>
> (ll.65–8)

[1] *Wordsworth's Poetical Works*, IV, p. 453.

Each time the man in the forefront of his mind could well have been John Gibson, the Hawkshead attorney his father consulted about customary tenements in the Lordship of Millom; a man whose quips and pranks delighted generations of Hawkshead schoolboys, to whom he was known familiarly as 'Little John'. In any event, I want to set down what I know of him.

Born in 1728 or the latter part of 1727, John Gibson may have been a younger son of the 'George Gibson & Margaret Holme of ye Birks in Millom' who were married on 22 November 1711, at Hawkshead (as were 'Thomas Fox & Isabel Gibson of Millom' in the following summer), though why at Hawkshead I cannot say. He was not baptized there, the earliest mention of him in the Parish Registers being on 27 April 1758, when 'John Gibson of this Parish Gentleman and Elizabeth Sandys Spinster' were married by licence. His bride was a daughter of the Samuel Sandys of Roger Ground who died at Colthouse on 22 July 1755, and was interred on the 25th in the Friends' Burial Ground there, of which he had been a trustee at least since its enlargment in 1704. In the Register of Burials at Colthouse he is described as an 'ancient Friend and writer of the Records of Hawkshead Meeting', of which he was clerk for more than forty years according to Elizabeth Satterthwaite.[1] 'He was often put on to delicate appointments for dealing with delinquents', she says, 'so we may judge that he was tactful'. He travelled a little in the ministry. In 1737 he 'had a concern to visit Friends' Meetings in Cumberland'; and in 1750 the minutes of the Colthouse Preparatory Meeting note that 'Our Antient ffriend Sam: Sandys hath signified unto us that for some time he hath felt drawings upon his Mind to visit the Meetings of ffriends in the countie of Cheshire and some of the Western parts of this Nation'. He was also appointed in his old age to attend the Yearly Meeting for the Northern Counties. The only known son of William and Elizabeth Sandys of Roger Ground, he succeeded his father there in 1694, but did not marry until rather late in life. He and his wife Mary, who in her latter days was of Colthouse and was buried there in November 1772, had two sons, Samuel and William, and a daughter Mary in

[1] See Elizabeth J. Satterthwaite, *Records of the Friends' Burial Ground at Colthouse* (1914), p. 40.

addition to Elizabeth; but Mary died in 1752 and William in 1756, as the Colthouse register shows. Samuel was of Roger Ground when Elizabeth was married, and was not a Quaker, at any rate in the early 1760s, as will appear on a later occasion.

Such was the family to which John Gibson's wife belonged. Yet she was pregnant when he led her to the altar—no uncommon thing in the district generally—for their eldest child, 'John Son of Mr John Gibson Attorney Colthouse' was baptized at Hawkshead on 4 September 1758, just over four months after their marriage. A second son, 'Samuel Sandys Son of Mr John Gibson, Town', was christened on 21 September 1760. After that the interval between birth and baptism was much longer, for 'Mary Daughter of Mr John Gibson, Greenend' was not christened until 14 March 1773, and 'George Graham Gibson Son of Mr John Gibson Colthouse' until 25 April 1774. George must have been about seven when he was baptized, as his age is given as twelve when he died of a fever on 26 June 1779. By then his parents had moved to Roger Ground, perhaps into the Sandys house there, as Samuel had left Hawkshead some years before. There is no further information to be had about Mary, or about her brother John, but Samuel's name reappears in Hawkshead records in 1789. In that year 'Samll Sandys of Roger Ground . . . now at Kendal' subscribed 10s. 6d. to the New Library Fund at Hawkshead School, where he had been a pupil; and in the same year 'Samuel Sandys Gibson', as he signed himself, promised to contribute £1. 1s. 0d. towards the cost of replacing the old Market Shambles at Hawkshead by a new Market House.

When John and Elizabeth Gibson's children were young it looks as if they had a relative of his, probably a niece, living with them for a time, as at Hawkshead on 24 October 1772, 'Margaret Gibson of this Parish Spinster' was married to the Rev. Matthew Postlethwaite of Millom. John Gibson's beautiful handwriting seems to have served as a model for the bride, judging from her signature in the marriage register. Robert Gibson, one of the witnesses and very likely her father, made his mark.

On religious and other grounds, John, the attorney, and his wife appear to have been an oddly assorted couple; but whatever the truth about that, their marriage endured until his death on

9 July 1800, at the age of seventy-two. He was buried in Hawkshead churchyard, in a grave unmarked by any stone. His widow, who lived for a further eighteen years, was interred in the Quaker sepulchre at Colthouse, the precise date being 23 December 1818. In the register of burials there her age is given as 'abt 96', and it is indicated that she was not a member of the Society of Friends.

John Gibson did not subscribe towards the cost of providing a ring of six bells for the church in 1765, or of building the new Market House in 1790. And he did not contribute to the collection for the S.P.G. in 1779, or to any save one of the parish 'gatherings on Briefs' of which I have seen particulars. The solitary exception was when, at an unspecified date, there was a collection 'for a brief in Wiltshire by fire'. On that occasion 'Mr Gibson' gave 2d., and the parish as a whole £1. 3s. 5d., of which 13s. 2d. was obtained in the Hawkshead Quarter from eighty-seven householders, an average of just over 1¾d. each. John Gibson, I may add, was never called upon to serve as Churchwarden, Overseer of the Poor, or Surveyor of the Highways; but it was hardly to be expected that he would, as he was Clerk to the Vestry, at any rate in his later years and for a considerable time. His duties as such included the recording, transcription, and circulating of the detailed specifications agreed upon for the repewing of the church and the addition of a vestry; work, of which more will be said on a later occasion, that was eventually undertaken in 1793-4. From time to time the Overseers of the Poor employed him to fill up the indentures of parish apprentices, paying him 1s. 6d. for each. And in 1789 he received £6. 6s. 0d. from the Churchwardens for 'regulating the Papers in the Church Chest', in other words calendaring them, which he did very well, as I have good reason to know. The 'Church Chest' in which they were then kept was the chest with three locks and three keys provided for the safe keeping of the register in accordance with an ecclesiastical mandate of 1603. The massive oak beam cambered on the top from which it has been hollowed out, probably the middle portion of a discarded tie-beam as J. F. Curwen first pointed out, is 6 feet 8 inches long, but the length of the oak-banded box-cavity is only 3 feet.

There is a chest of the same type, but smaller and flat on top, in the Grammar School. Its former use is disclosed in the minutes of a Governors' Meeting held on 2 March 1784, when one of the resolutions passed was that 'three Locks with three Keys to the same [be] provided for the Chest containing the Deeds Writings Escripts and Muniments belonging to and concerning the said School'. John Gibson was Clerk to the Governors, and the minutes are in his handwriting. I found them in a leather-bound volume inscribed 'Account Book of the Rev. Thomas Sandys Charity'; a charity founded in 1717 for the benefit of poor boys, who were to be housed, fed, clothed, supplied with certain books, and taught at the Grammar School to write and cast accounts. Of the early trustees of this charity some were Governors of the school and others not; but by 1780 the composition of the two bodies had become identical, except that the Master of the Grammar School in virtue of his office was a Sandys Charity Trustee. This development probably explains the use of the Trustees' account book—they took it in turn to act as treasurer—by the Clerk to the Governors as well. What matters at the moment is that it contains in his handwriting a calendar, evidently made in or about 1784, of the contents of the School Muniment Chest. He headed it 'A Schedule of the Deeds, Writings, Books, Papers and Securities relating and belonging to the Lands, Revenues, Goods, and Possessions of the Free Grammar School, of The Most Reverend Father in God Edwin by Divine Providence sometime heretofore Archbishop of York Primate of England and Metropolitan, in Hawkshead in the County of Lancaster'. This schedule completed, John Gibson went on to calendar under the same heading the title deeds, securities, and other muniments held by the Trustees of the Thomas Sandys Charity, whose capital resources had been considerably increased in 1766 by the addition to them of a surprisingly large gift made in his lifetime by William Dennison, a former Writing Master. The entries in the calendar number fifty-one in all.

In 1789 John Gibson became Clerk to yet a third body, the newly appointed Market House Trustees. The appeal they launched is in his handwriting; and so are the detailed specifications for the new Market House and the Cote House at the Ferry. As it happens, these documents were the first extensive example of his work that I came upon, and I was impressed by the precision and clarity of their phrasing, as well as by the beauty of his penmanship. The writing of 'warning letters' to tenants of stands and shops in the old Market Shambles who still had not paid their arrears of rent, in some instances of long standing, was entrusted, not to him, but to an Ulverston attorney. There was no other in Hawkshead until the arrival of George Jackson, who is first mentioned in 1794 as the highest bidder for the lodging suite at the western end of the upper storey of the new Market House; and evidently the Trustees had reason to think that John Gibson was not the best man to instruct to write such letters. What the reason was will be less obscure presently.

When Wordsworth visited Greenend, Colthouse, in the 1840s, he and his host Braithwaite Hodgson, who was eleven years his junior, and was meeting him for the first and only time, got talking about their school days at Hawkshead and people they had then known. Miss Mary Hodgson recalled two of them by name, and one of the two was John Gibson, the attorney, to whom they both referred as 'Little John'. For a while they regaled each other with recollections of his quips and pranks—a phrase I originally borrowed from her; but her memory of what they said about him was dim, she confessed, apart from one or two details. She remembered only one prank of his, and that imperfectly. He once made a very man-like scarecrow, she said, and leant it against a roadside gate, choosing a dark but not pitch-black night, and a spot near Hawkshead where passers-by would not be too infrequent. From a hiding-place close to the gate he greeted them in a disguised voice, and continued to talk to them if he considered it worth while. They all thought it was the 'man' leaning against the gate who was speaking. Some took him to be an old soldier or a wandering beggar, others a local man who was either drunk or a bit moonstruck; at least that is what 'Little John' said when relating the conversations he had had with the various passers-by. Whoever they imagined the figure was, he did his best to confirm them in their belief by what he said and the way he said it. He was a very good mimic, it seems. But the prank is hardly likely to have been popular with the victims of it; and anyhow he lacked an audience, unless there was one concealed with him. I fancy there was; but Miss Mary did not say so.

A thing she clearly remembered was Wordsworth's tribute to John Gibson's cleverness in proving this or that, and then completely demolishing his proof, leaving you just where you were to think things out for yourself. The example of this which he gave is summed up in my original notes in the one word 'obstinacy'. I doubt whether I was impressed at the time; but lately I have come to think what a strong case could be made out for the virtues of obstinacy, and yet how easy it would be to show that these virtues were either vanities or stupidities. Be that as it may, the choice of subject is an interesting one; and it is interesting to know that Wordsworth remembered it in his old age. Though strict proof is out of the question, I feel almost sure he had the frolicsome and clever little attorney in mind as he wrote that Matthew, when 'he twice thirty years had seen', would wish from time to time that 'he a graver man had been'. John Gibson was sixty when Wordsworth came to Colthouse in 1788 to spend most of his first long vacation with Ann Tyson; and, as he then 'had something of another eye' for those he had known as a schoolboy, his friendship with 'Little John' may well have matured sufficiently for the latter to tell him of his occasional regrets.

In a long and entirely irrelevant footnote to the third edition of his *Fortnight's Ramble to the Lakes*, which appeared in 1810, Joseph Budworth, a retired soldier who was well acquainted with Hawkshead, tells of a meeting with John Gibson, then on the verge of seventy. His account is a revealing one, and I shall quote it in full.[1]

Having one day in November 1797 gone through more than my usual exercise, dined at Ambleside, and taken beyond par of Stout Beer, I resolved to set off to Hawkshead, although I had never walked there in the direct road. The night was dark and windy, and my judgment equally so: I was advised not to go, but was too foolishly wise to hearken to reason, and immediately started. By good luck I got over the narrow bridges of Rothay and Brathay; and I may truly say by good luck; for the diminutive battlements are more calculated to trip a man into the water than to protect him, in darkness from it. After some time pursuing what I thought a right course, but meeting great unevenness and fresh obstacles, I judged I was bewildered in the stone quarry, which I had often observed but never

[1] Pp. 168–72.

been at; and knowing the peril that would in such purgatory surround me, I thought it prudent to arrest my course, and to conduct myself like a man who was benighted in a labyrinth. My situation, with the freshness of the wind, had completely expelled the fumes of liquor. I had roared lustily without being heard; and, as the mind was again my commanding officer, I deliberately made it up to make my quarters as bearable as possible for the night, cautiously heaving the lead, and moving on, until I came to two narrow rocks, where I determined to bring-to, that I might stir about between them in safety, with my umbrella for my canopy and only extra covering. I might have been in my prison two long hours, when I heard the distant sound of a man singing, and was rejoiced to find the wind brought it louder and louder to me; and, when sufficiently near, I hove out a tremendous signal of distress! which, as he afterwards said, quite electrified him, and echoed like thunder; and I was answered by 'What! what's the matter?'

Rambler. A Stranger, and lost in the quarry.

G – b – n. Necromancy, by G.—! Where the d. . . l are you? I can't see my finger; but old G——n will ever lend a hand to damsels in distress, or quarry-bound mortals.

Ramb. I dare scarcely move, not knowing my station.

G – b – n. But I do, man and boy, these fifty years; and if you can't come to the mountain, the mountain shall soon be at you; and beest thou a spirit of health, or goblin damn'd I will speak to thee.

Presently he fell, and I hoped he were not hurt.

G – b – n. No; from this very reason, 'Naught's ne'er in danger', or I might have been; and if I can't extricate you from durance vile, I'll share in it; for there is not a road round the country that I have not slept in. Sing on, and the voice of gladness will soon reach you.

And it soon did.

G – b – n. I am quite happy to meet you in the regions of darkness; for, had it been day, drunken G——n might have passed unnoticed; now he is the good Samaritan; and, although a tale that is told, he is ever happy to pour oil into other people's wounds, and wine into his own.

Assuring him how rejoiced and obliged I was, and to prove it, if he would pilot me back to Ambleside, we would sup together.

G – b – n. As to that, Sir, I am at your service; and if I cannot eat with

you, it will do your heart good to see me drink; but, as I groped
the way to you, it will require double skill to steer out again.
Lay hold of my coat; don't pull hard; it is as old as the hills,
and the flap as tender as a chicken.

After many slips and tacks, we got into the right road, and, before the
people were gone to rest, reached my old quarters [the Salutation Inn, his
current quarters being at Hawkshead].

G – b – n. And now we have brought you to anchor, allow me to claim
a glass of grog before supper, and as many after as my little
carcase can contain: 'for grog is the liquor of life—the delight
of a Hawkeshead attorney.' It was my bosom-friend for many
years, and should constantly be my night-cap, but for such
light reasons (smacking his pocket) as these: we are worse than
poor, we are pennyless, and the crocodiles say I deserve to be
so; and what care I what they say? when a man ceases to value
himself, he careth not what others palaver about him.

His company was for a short time sparkling; but, as grog was the only
part of supper he tasted, and that as copiously as his glass could be replenished, he was soon put to bed. The next morning at breakfast he requested
to have a glass of brandy, and I ordered one for myself; he drank his
immediately, and, on my going to the window, emptied mine too. Telling
him that 'fair play was a jewel', he assured me, in the most pathetic tone,
and heaving up his shoulders, that it was *irresistible*; and the best mode of
settling it, according to *law*, would be, to order the two glasses in point to
be replenished; but, as I was preparing for departure, he requested I would
think on the Samaritan, and lend him a trifle, which he promised faithfully
to repay after he had gained a suit he was to bring on at the next assizes.
His request was too small to be denied; and had it been larger, and I could
with prudence on his account have given it, he was fully entitled to share
my purse, and should have done it. I afterwards learned, some soldiers
marching in that day, he soon squandered his money with treating them;
and at night, as many of them were obliged to sleep up on straw, he
declared it would be the pride of his heart to fare as such brave fellows
did, and he slept amongst them.
Several chapters might be filled with his pranks, and those eccentricities
the man of genius is often impulsed by, especially when devoted to
liquor; and probably, had he lived in a city, where he would have met a
reciprocity of intellectual communication, instead of an obscure village,

o

such might not have been his failing; he began his profession with fair
prospects, and might have had as good practice as most in the county; but,
as he said, 'I am buried in these mountains, and never wished to quit them,
till I became too old and foolish to succeed any where; and, having passed
the *Rubicon*, if that celebrated stream flowed with brandy, instead of
classical water, by great Cæsar himself—I'd drink it dry.'

Two minor points of interest in this welcome 'irrelevancy', which
in a sense is a tribute to both men, is that John Gibson was singing
as he walked the roads on that dark and windy November night in
1797, and that until late in life he was fond of the neighbouring
mountains. It is possible, then, that Wordsworth had him in mind,
and not Thomas Cowperthwaite, when writing those lines in 'The
Fountain' which speak of his proposal to Matthew that they should
match the water's pleasant tune with some old border-song, or
catch, that suits a summer's noon; possible, too, and perhaps
probable in this instance, that he was thinking of John Gibson, and
not the much older John Harrison, who in any event was wedded
to his pony, when telling in 'The Two April Mornings' of travelling
merrily with Matthew to pass a day among the hills. I have but one
more thing to say. It is that, wittingly or unwittingly, Wordsworth
composed 'Little John's' epitaph, a trifle prematurely it is true, when
he wrote:

> Oh true of heart, of spirit gay,
> Thy faults, where not already gone
> From memory, prolong their stay
> For charity's sweet sake alone.[1]

---

[1] 'Address to the Scholars of the Village School of ——', ll. 65–8. Confusingly, a
John Gibson was apparently factotum for the le Flemings of Rydal Hall. In the
Record Office, Kendal, there are letters written by this Gibson on Rydal business, 1780–4, and spasmodic accounts, 1777–84; he paid out housekeeping bills,
servants' wages, hired a new cook, interviewed farmers wanting tenancies, saw to it
that neighbours, like the Bensons of Dove Nest, did not cut down Rydal timber, sent
off pots of char to Sir Michael's friends, arranged that Mr. Reginald Braithwaite in
his new house at Belmount received the larches he had been given to replace trees
that had died; he was generally useful. But it hardly seems the kind of attorney's
work which we know Hawkshead Gibson was doing in 1783 (see p. 241). Handwriting suggests, though it does not confirm, that there were two John Gibsons in
the area.

'The Two Thieves'—essential dates of Daniel and Dan Mackreth—
Matthew Jackson—Betty Jackson—marriages of Frances Jackson—
number of old people buried at Hawkshead

Though not without biographical interest, Wordsworth's poem 'The Two Thieves; or, the Last Stage of Avarice', is hardly more than the facile versifying of a plain tale. After an introduction that is little to the point,[1] he begins:

> The One, yet unbreeched, is not three birthdays old,
> His Grandsire that age more than thirty times told;
> There are ninety good seasons of fair and foul weather
> Between them, and both go a-pilfering together.

The old man, who is in his dotage, is called Daniel; the child remains unnamed. Daniel, we are told, had always 'cherished his purse', as thousands before him had done; but he went 'something farther than others have gone' along the path they, too, had trod:

> And now with old Daniel you see how it fares;
> You see to what end he has brought his grey hairs.

He and his grandson sally forth hand in hand early in the day, and hunt through the streets, each in turn leading. If they see chips on the carpenter's floor, or a cart-load of peats at an old woman's door,

> Old Daniel his hand to the treasure will slide!
> And his Grandson's as busy at work by his side.

The child but half knows the wrong he is doing, his grandsire not at all. Everyone smiles at their plots and their wiles, and neither rich nor needy check them, for they know that old Daniel has a daughter at home

> Who will gladly repair all the damage that's done;
> And three, were it asked, would be rendered for one.

---

[1] The introduction is in praise of the engraver, Thomas Bewick; Wordsworth's intention in the poem is surely to parallel the anecdotal (and moral) effectiveness of Bewick's tailpieces in such volumes as *Quadrupeds* (1790) and *British Birds* (1797).

Wordsworth then concludes:

> Old Man! whom so oft I with pity have eyed,
> I love thee, and love the sweet Boy at thy side:
> Long yet may'st thou live! for a teacher we see
> That lifts up the veil of our nature in thee.

The poem was composed in 1800; and in a note on it, dictated to Isabella Fenwick in his old age, the author says:

This is described from the life, as I was in the habit of observing when a boy at Hawkshead School. Daniel was more than 80 years older than myself when he was daily thus occupied under my notice. No book could have so early taught me to think of the changes to which human life is subject, and while looking at him I could not but say to myself, We may, any of us, I or the happiest of my playmates, live to become still more the object of pity than the old man, this half-doating pilferer.

The only entry in the Hawkshead burial registers that could relate to him was made in 1788 and reads: 'Daniel Mackreth of Town Shoemaker Died Dec^br 8 Buried 10 in Church Yard Aged 91'. From what Wordsworth says he should have been older than that, and in fact he was, for the only relevant baptism at Hawkshead between 1690 and 1700 was that of 'Daniell Mackreth fil. John de Sawrey infra' on 10 July 1693. That would make him nearly seventy-seven years older than Wordsworth, but not more unless his christening was delayed, which is unlikely, though his sister Barbary's must have been. He was not married at Hawkshead; but between 1726 and 1738 he had half a dozen daughters baptized there, and then two or three sons, including William on 26 May 1743. During the whole of this time, and for the rest of his life, he lived in Hawkshead, and twice, I noticed, he subscribed 1d. to a Brief. Of his daughters, at least two of whom died young, Elizabeth never married; and it is safe to say that it was she who recompensed neighbours for any losses they sustained as a result of his and his grandson's pilferings. She died on 12 September 1785, at the age of 51. Evidently she had been caring for her mother as well as her father, in proof of which the following registration, made in 1786, may be cited: 'Elizabeth Wife of Daniel Mackreth of Town Shoe-maker Died Jan^ry 4, Buried 6 in Church Yard Aged 85'.

Their son William, the only one who lived in Hawkshead during the last quarter of the eighteenth century, is the 'William Mackreth of this Parish Shoemaker' who married 'Agnes Askew of this Parish Spinster' at Hawkshead on 19 June 1775; and he is the William Mackreth who repaired Richard and William Wordsworth's shoes during their early years at Hawkshead School. He had only one son, who was entered in the register of baptisms on 22 June 1777, as 'Dan Son of William Mackreth Town'. Clearly this child was the grandson with whom old Daniel went pilfering. He would be three near the end of Wordsworth's first year at Hawkshead, and a little before his third birthday his grandsire would be first more and then less than thirty times as old. The difference between their ages was eighty-four years, and not as Wordsworth says (in a phrase reminiscent of Thomas Cowperthwaite) 'ninety good seasons of fair and foul weather'. Old Daniel, who received a few, usually seven shillings a year from parochial charities during the last twelve years of his life, must have ended his days with his son William, and therefore under the same roof as Dan; but by then the one must have been past pilfering and the other have outgrown it. 'William Mackreth of Town Innkeeper and Shoemaker' died on 8 September 1798, aged fifty-five.

So far as I know Wordsworth never mentions 'Fine Matthew', but his school fellow Isaac Swainson has this to say of him in a letter dated 14 November 1784:

There was a stir here three days since as Fine Matthew as they called him was being buried, having died at the age of 100. Matthew Jackson was his right name and he lived at Outgate. It is not two years ago Mrs. Suert says since he got married again, it was his third wife and she is nigh on 70.

The Parish Registers show that 'Matthew Jackson of this Parish Widower and Francis Jackson of this Parish Widow' were married at Hawkshead on 10 December 1782. Both made their marks. The wedding was reported in the *Cumberland Pacquet* on 17 December; and in its issue of Friday, 27 December, the *Morning Chronicle, and London Advertiser*, had this notice of it:

Tuesday the 17th instant was married at Hawkshead, by the Rev. Mr. Braithwaite, Mr. Matthew Jackson, of Out Yeat, near that place, (commonly called *Fine Matthew*) 97 years and six months old, to Mrs. Frances Jackson, of the same place, 67 years of age, whose former husband had been dead almost four months.

I found a copy of the paper containing this notice in the church safe at Hawkshead in 1951. There the Rev. Frank D. Stones, Vicar of Hawkshead from 1927 to 1940, discovered a manuscript account of the wedding; and as it is fuller than the *Cumberland Pacquet* report, and has never been published, I will summarize it here from notes I made in 1932.

Matthew Jackson, it states, was ninety-seven years of age, and not far short of ninety-eight. He lived at 'Birkway by Outyeat', and since his previous wife died 'fourteen or maybe fifteen years ago' his daughter Betty had looked after him. Until he was past ninety he carried on his trade, which was weaving, and she spun the wool for him. Unmarried, she was the same age, or very near it, as his bride, both being about sixty-five. The latter, who also lived at Outyeat, and was named Frances Jackson, had been a widow for only four months. There was a very big attendance at the wedding, people of all classes being there, including several from a distance. The banns had been called, and everybody had been talking about it. Betty got the old man safely to church; but though he had been married twice before he could not follow the service, and the Parish Clerk had to show him what to do, and tell him what to say. As soon as the couple were united, his new wife took charge of him, and one of the first things she had to do was to stop him taking a glove a gentleman had laid down. In their greed for money, the writer says, Matthew and Frances Jackson were well matched. He had never earned a lot, but it was 'reckoned he had saved, and had a bit put by, and that was why she wanted to marry him', and was in a hurry about it too. Admittedly, however, this was 'no more than hearsay'. The bride, we are told, 'had a settlement of £6 a year', but no information is given as to how or why that had come about. This settlement is also mentioned, without the source of it being given, in the *Cumberland Pacquet*. And there, as well as in the manuscript account, it is stated that Frances asked onlookers how long they thought Matthew would live, and that when they replied 'Three or four years', she exclaimed 'O Lord, so long think ye?' She and Matthew gave a little party in the evening; but next morning they were hard at work, she spinning, and he carding the wool for her.

As 'Ann Wife of Matthew Jackson Outyeat' was buried on 30 October 1767, he had in fact been a widower for fifteen years when he married Mrs. Frances Jackson on 10 December 1782. His own death and burial were registered in 1784 in these words: "Matthew Jackson of Birkray Died November ye 9th Buried ye 11th in Church Yard Aged 100'. Not improbably he was a son of the John Jackson of Birkray who was Churchwarden for the Hawkshead Quarter in 1740; but as he was not baptized at Hawkshead I could not confirm this, nor make sure of his age, which is not likely to have been more than ninety-nine, when he died. As he was not a native of the parish, he may not have been entitled to poor relief at its expense: anyhow, he did not receive it. And even if he was a careful spender, he does not seem to have been miserly, as in 1779, at the age of ninety-four or somewhere near it, he contributed 6d. to the parish collection for the S.P.G., whilst at a rather earlier date he and a William Jackson of Outyeat each gave 1d. when there was a parish gathering for sufferers from a fire in Wiltshire.

A Betty Jackson, almost certainly Matthew's daughter of that name, who was a pauper when she died unmarried at Outyeat on 3 December 1805, 'Aged 88', was in receipt of poor relief, at first occasionally and then regularly, from the year 1782–3 (May Day to the following 30 April) until her death. For most of the time she lived in a small cottage at High House, and until she was over eighty tried to maintain herself by spinning; but like many others she was hard hit by the sharp rise in prices in the 1780s and 1790s. She often had help with her house-rent, which was £1. 1s. 0. a year; and in 1796–7 she had a weekly allowance of 6d. Now and again she had help 'in Necessity', which means in sickness; and occasionally things were provided for her such as shifts at 2s. 1d. and 2s. 6d., clogs at 2s. 4d. a pair, and wool cards at 5s. 2d. a pair. If the age ascribed to her when she died is correct she would be sixty-five when her father married Mrs. Frances Jackson in December 1782.

According to the Parish Registers, 'Frances Jackson of Outyeat Widow' was seventy when she died on 20 March 1789. She had been a widow for just over four months when she married 'Fine Matthew', for her previous husband, her first, was the ' William Jackson Weaver Outyeat' who died on 3 August 1782, 'Aged 88'. Proof of this lies in an earlier entry in the Hawkshead registers recording the marriage by banns on 27 July 1772, of 'William Jackson of this Parish Weaver and Frances Pepper of this Parish Spinster'. A third entry registers the burial on 27 May 1771, of 'Hannah Wife of William Jackson Outyeat'. Frances Pepper, then, remained single until she was well over fifty, after which she married a widower of seventy-eight or thereabouts, and then, following his death, a twice widowed man whose age at the time was given as ninety-seven. She was not baptized at Hawkshead, and I cannot say for certain in which year she was born, or who her father was. It is very likely, however, that she was a daughter of the Pharaoh Pepper whose infant son Pharaoh was buried at Hawkshead on 11 April 1726. There were Peppers at Sawrey and at Satterthwaite in the second half of the seventeenth century; but Pharaoh was not baptized at Hawkshead; nor did he have any children christened there.

There is quite a chance that Frances Pepper's two husbands were brothers: both were of Outgate, both were weavers; and it can be said of William Jackson, as of Matthew, that he was not baptized at Hawkshead. True, there was a 'William Jackson fil. John de Eltarwater pke' christened there on 6 February, 1693/4; but that is a record of the baptism of William Jackson of Law Park Skelwith, a statesman who died on 9 April 1784, 'Aged 91', and was buried in Hawkshead Church two days later. In the Poor Accounts for the Hawkshead Quarter payments in the year 1782–3 to William Jackson of £2. 0s. 0d. for his house-rent and 7s. 6d. 'in Necessity' are noted. In the following year, however, when he was living at Ulverston, he was again helped, and so cannot have been William of Outgate, who died, as we have seen, on 3 August 1782. Like Matthew, he managed to the end of his life without parish relief. Why the elder of these two Outgate Jacksons was 'commonly called Fine Matthew' I have never been able to discover. Though it is not strictly parallel, the case of William Wilson, a boarder at Hawkshead Hill, may be cited. In 1797, when his death and burial were registered, the entry reads: 'William Wilson of Hill, commonly call'd Fleming a Pensioner Died Feb^ry 4 Buried 6 in Churchyard a pauper'. In the Poor Accounts for the Hawkshead Quarter he is referred to as William Fleming in 1794–5, and simply as 'Sir William' in the two following years.

In all, a considerable number of very old people were interred at Hawkshead in the 1780s. In 1785, for instance, nine of the twenty burials registered were of persons aged from eighty to eighty-nine. And in the next three years the following interments and ages were recorded:

1786   Edward Thwaites, How in Hawkshead Field, 86.
1786   Anthony Sawrey, Townson Ground, Monk Coniston, 89.
1787   Eliner Scales, Near Sawrey, Widow, 88.
1787   George Rigg, Hawkshead Town, 90.
1787   Mary Denison, Crofthead, Colthouse, Widow, 98.
1788   Mary Moore, Hawkshead Town, Widow, 90.
1788   Agnes Benson, Skelwith Fold, Widow, 92.

And that, with the two Mackreths and three Jacksons previously cited, must suffice as proof that longevity was far from uncommon in the parish of Hawkshead when Wordsworth was a schoolboy. The reverse of the picture is that there were too many deaths in infancy and childhood.

John Hodgson, Parish Clerk—his well-kept and informative Parish Register—the church pitch-pipe—John Pepper, Dog Whipper

When Miss Mary Hodgson came upon Wordsworth in Hawkshead churchyard he told her of his delight when new to Hawkshead school in watching the old Parish Clerk giving the psalm-singers their keynote on the pitch-pipe: he did so, it seems, with such an air and flourish. Though Miss Mary was a bit uncertain about it, there is no doubt that Wordsworth was speaking of John Hodgson, shoemaker, who 'entered Parish Clark Hawkshead on Wednesday ye 28th of March, 1744', in succession to Thomas Deason, schoolmaster, deceased, and held the office until his own death on 16 January 1785, at the age of seventy-six, but had some help towards the end from his successor, George Pennington, another shoemaker. John Hodgson, whose widow Elizabeth died on 19 January 1786, aged eighty, was one of the old men who sat on Churchend on summer evenings. His house was either in the Market Square or just off it.

The Hawkshead registers have rarely been other than well kept, but naturally the amount of detail included in the entries has varied. When John Hodgson was responsible for them they were often very, and at times unusually, informative as to where people lived, what they did, and precisely who they were. His registrations show that during his term of office charcoal-burning, which had brought Irishmen to the district, was on the decline, and slate-quarrying on the increase; that there were still a good many weavers in the parish, and a fair number of tanners and curriers; that shoe-making and hat-making were important minor industries; that with the exception of the landlord of the Red Lion all the inn-keepers followed trades as well; and that several of the shop-keepers had second strings to their bows, one of the grocers being a farrier as well, and one of the mercers a glazier, whilst the only bookseller was also a hatter.[1] Each of these items of information may be trifling in itself; but together they help in building up a picture of Hawkshead in these years.

In his later years, and especially in 1778 and 1779, John Hodgson made baptismal entries in the registers that may be described as genealogical. That made on 1 November 1778, when 'George Son of Robert Robinson of Great Boat' was christened has been cited earlier, and soon one or two others will be quoted. So here I will give only the following example, the year being 1782, by which time the old man's handwriting had become very shaky:

George the Son of William Benson of How Husbandman Son of George Benson of How Ditto Son of William Benson of Skelwith by Elis: his Wife Daught of William Rigge of Hawksh^d field. The Mother's name Ann Daught of Mr Benjamin Brown Troutbeck by Elis Daught of M^r

---

[1] The administrators' accounts show that Sarah Todhunter received money for hats, and William T. payments for books; but this does not make 'M^r. Todhunter' into a hatter; see above, p. 91, n. 3.

Geo: Longmire of Limefoot in Applethwaite. Born Friday yᵉ 12ᵗʰ Baptized Sunday yᵉ 14ᵗʰ day.

Such entries, of which there are a good many, add to the general picture; and once in a while some searcher of the registers has reason to bless the man who made them.

The pitch-pipe on which John Hodgson gave the psalm-singers their keynote is now on exhibit in Hawkshead Church, together with other articles formerly in use. It has ten notes from C to E, including A and B sharp. They are engraved on a brass plate bearing the date 1764. The Churchwardens' Accounts for that year, which are in John Hodgson's handwriting, show that it was supplied by Isaac Holme, about the best of Hawkshead's many carpenters, and that he charged 7s. 6d. for both it and a plan of the vestry it was proposed to build. About the same time he prepared a plan for the re-pewing of the church. But neither of these improvements was put in hand until four or five years after his death, which took place in 1789 at the age of fifty-three. The pitch-pipe he made was in regular use until 1828, when an organ was installed in the gallery which then existed at the west end of the church. Isaac Holme's handwriting was notably good, and for a short time in 1781 when Joseph Varty was ill he acted as Writing Master at the Grammar School. Another who did a little teaching was George Pennington after he became Parish Clerk. His pupils were pauper children, for whose education the Overseers of the Poor evidently felt responsible.

John Pepper was appointed Dog Whipper in 1772 for a period of ten years at 5s. 0d. a year, his duty being to see that there were no dogs in church during the hours appointed for worship, and if necessary to remove any that had slipped in with or to their masters. The Churchwardens supplied a dog-whip, and had bought a new one in 1769 at a cost of 2s. 3d. These facts are given because of their bearing on a story of Wordsworth's schooldays at Hawkshead that Dr. William Allen used to tell. It related to a man named or nick-named Pharaoh, who was Dog Whipper at the time; a rather simple old man for whom some of the dogs were a little too clever. In particular, they were apt to slip into church with the Grammar School boys: a dog would get between a pair of them for instance, and so protect itself from the lash of his whip. On the whole

Pharaoh liked the 'young gentlemen', but at times he suspected them of encouraging the dogs, and of aiding them by distracting his attention. So in the end he reported the matter to the Master of the Grammar School. And that, he said, did a 'power o' good', for on calling at his favourite inn on the following evening he found that some of the 'young gentlemen' had left the price of a quart of ale for him. It looks as if Pharaoh was but another name for the John Pepper who was appointed Dog Whipper in 1772, and that John was a son of the Pharaoh Pepper first mentioned in the Hawkshead registers in 1720. For the preservation of the story down to the time of the tercentenary in 1885, when Dr. Allen first heard it, we appear to be indebted to Thomas Bowman of Roger Ground, who was then seventy-nine.

George Park, Saddler—the Park family and the 'Nab', Rydal— ironmonger's business—parish offices—the Rev. George Park—Tom Park—Wordsworth's fishing expedition—Fletcher Raincock's account —John Martin, weaver

In a prose note on his Duddon sonnets Wordsworth says:

I first became acquainted with the Duddon, as I have good reason to remember, in early boyhood. Upon the banks of the Derwent, I had learnt to be very fond of angling. Fish abound in that large river,—not so in the small streams in the neighbourhood of Hawkshead; and I fell into the common delusion, that the further from home the better sport would be had. Accordingly, one day I attached myself to a person living in the neighbourhood of Hawkshead, who was going to try his fortune, as an angler, near the source of the Duddon. We fished a great part of the day with very sorry success, the rain pouring torrents; and long before we got home, I was worn out with fatigue; and if the good man had not carried me on his back, I must have lain down under the best shelter I could find. Little did I think then it would have been my lot to celebrate, in a strain of love and admiration, the stream which for many years I never thought of without recollections of disappointment and distress.[1]

[1] See *The Prose Works of William Wordsworth*, ed. A. B. Grosart (1876), III, pp. 98–9. Wordsworth continues the note with a recollection of visits to Broughton, near the Duddon estuary; at least one of these was in a college vacation—presumably 1788 or 1789. For the Smiths of Broughton, see p. 303, note.

As an angler during his early years at school, Wordsworth is said to have owed more to Tom Park and his father George than to anyone else in Hawkshead; but before considering the claims that have been made in this respect I had better say more than I have done as yet about George Park and his family. He is described as 'George Park of the Parish of Penrith Saddler' when on 9 February 1767, he married Elizabeth Parker of the parish of Hawkshead, spinster. Both signed the register, and I have noted that her hand-writing was good and his very good. From the start they lived in Hawkshead, and had children baptized there as follows: Mary (who died in infancy) on 24 June 1767; Thomas on 12 February 1769; John on 13 September 1771; George on 25 April 1779; and Eliza-beth, usually called Betty, on 16 December 1781. When George was christened the entry reads:

George Son of George Park of Town Saddler Son of John Park of Nab in Rydal Husbandman by Mary his wife the Mother's name Elisabeth D^r. of Thos. Parker of Town Currier by Elisabeth [h]is wife D^r of John Hodgson of Town Butcher Born March ye 20th Baptized April ye 25th.

The mother, Elizabeth, whose father at one time kept the Eagle and Child as well as being a currier, died on 29 November 1782, aged thirty-eight, and George Park never remarried.

Born in 1743, he was the youngest of the three sons of John Park of the Nab in Rydal, a statesman whom Miss Armitt describes as 'ambitious, as well as prosperous', and who certainly kept adding to his patrimony, mainly by a succession of relatively small purchases, the largest being the acquisition in 1735 of the Rydal farmhold with dwelling house known as Hart Head. His first wife, who died in 1730 after bearing him a son John and a daughter, was Dorothy Knott, a sister of the Michael Knott with whom and his wife Susannah (née Fleming) Ann Tyson was in service before her marriage. By his second wife Mary, whose family name Miss Armitt does not give, John Park had two sons, William and George. On his death in 1748 he left the Nab, and lands adjacent to it that he had bought, to his eldest son John; and to George, the youngest, who was then only four, he left Hart Head, and part of the tenement known as Hobsons or Causeway Foot, but his widow Mary was to have possession of them first, and for as long as she lived. As a result, George Park did not come into his inheritance until either 1759 or 1760, when he was admitted to it on paying a Fine of £5. 16s. 8d., Lord's Rents, Fines being much higher in the Manor of Rydal than in the Manor of Hawkshead. On his marriage, however, he preferred to settle at Hawkshead as a saddler; and in 1769 he sold his Rydal property.

In the following year his half-brother John died, and the Nab was sold to provide for his widow and infant daughter, who shortly afterwards moved to London. The buyer was William Park, George's elder brother; and he remained there until his death in 1825 at the age of eighty-four. His only son being an idiot, he was succeeded by his daughter Mary and her husband John Simpson, who had been living with him ever since their marriage, and whose daughter Margaret had become the wife of Thomas De Quincey in 1816. The not very happy story of these occupants of the Nab is available in Miss Armitt's *Rydal*,[1] which tells of their impoverishment as a result of spirited if unwise litigation with the manor concerning wood-rights. And all I need add here is that in the 1820s the Rev. George Park of Hawkshead, the saddler's youngest son, had a mortgage of £500 on the Nab; that early in 1829 he lent his cousin John Simpson a further £250, mainly to meet the costs of yet another law-suit; that at his own request he was repaid the whole of the £750 shortly before his death on 12 July in that year out of a loan of £1,400 procured by De Quincey, who for the purpose of borrowing had become phantom owner of the Nab; and that to repay this loan the Nab estate, so long in the possession of the Parks, was sold by auction in 1833.

George Park, originally of Rydal and then of Penrith, was a saddler in Hawkshead from his marriage early in 1767 until his death, at the age of fifty-four, on 23 July, 1797. His two elder sons after leaving the Grammar School, where they do not seem to have progressed beyond the Writing Master's class, learnt and followed their father's trade; but Tom, as we saw earlier, was drowned in Esthwaite Water 'by falling through the Ice' on 18 December 1796, aged twenty-eight, and John was only forty when he died on

[1] See pp. 352–60 and 675–704 for the major part of M. L. Armitt's discussion.

25 January 1812, the year in which his younger brother George returned to Hawkshead as Vicar of the parish.

The Poor Accounts for the Monk Coniston and Skelwith Quarter include a payment in 1793 of 8s. 8d. to 'George Parke for Cartgeer for the Farm at Sandground', then a Poor House for the Hawkshead and Monk Coniston Quarters of the parish. Otherwise he appears in parochial accounts as a vendor of what may be termed iron-mongers' sundries, in which he dealt, as a side-line, from an early date. He supplied the Churchwardens with a clock-rope at 2s. 3d. in 1772; another at 3s. 3d. in 1779; a cog for the clock, 10d., in 1786; a hang-lock, 10d., in 1783; screws, and nails, and spikes at various times; even corks and candles on occasion; and unspecified articles for which his bill totalled £1. 4s. 9½d. in 1773, to give but one example. The Overseer of the Poor for the Monk Coniston Quarter in 1788-9 had a pair of wool-cards from him, which cost 5s. 3d.; and late in 1791 the Trustees of the new Market House spent 9s. 3d. with him on locks and candlestick-sheaves. In the 1780s he rented one of the 'five small rooms occupied as repository shops' on the upper floor of the old Market Shambles. This is revealed in the 'Ould Butcher House Acct.', which is dated 30 June 1788, and goes back no further than 1784. It shows, too, that the rent of his shop was £1. 10s. 0d. a year.

His house in Hawkshead Town must have been one of the ancient tenements whose holders (and virtual owners) were obliged to serve in turn as churchwardens and overseers of the poor, or in certain circumstances to provice an acceptable substitute. At any rate, in 1773 he became Churchwarden for the Hawkshead Quarter of the parish, and in 1774 Overseer of the Poor for the same Quarter. Moreover, in the latter year he continued in office as Churchwarden for the Hawkshead Quarter in place of a Mrs. Braithwaite whose turn it was to fill it; and in addition he took over the duties of Surveyor of the Highways for Hawkshead, a district that included Hawkshead Field but not Fieldhead. Thus for one year he held the three offices simultaneously, which so far as I can discover no other Hawkshead man has ever done. But it may be that he was not so ready to give of his money as he was of his time, for in 1779 his contribution to the parish collection for the S.P.G. was no more

than 3*d.*, whereas Hugh Tyson gave 6*d.* and Isaac Holme 1*s.* 0*d.*
And it is noticeable that his son George, who was at the Grammar
School from about 1789 to 1797, never subscribed to the New
Library, and that on leaving he did not give it a book or a donation.
This son, born on 20 March 1779, became Vicar of the parish in
1812 until his death on 12 July 1829. Five years later, another Park,
his nephew, was Vicar.

This third and last of the George Parks of Hawkshead, the Rev.
George Park, M.A., Vicar of the parish from 1834 to 1865, was
born in 1804 and died in September 1865. He matters here because
he was Miss Mary Hodgson's main source of information about
Wordsworth's acquaintance during his schooldays with the earlier
Hawkshead Parks, and her only source of any importance apart from
her father. When she saw the poet in Hawkshead churchyard he
was reading the inscriptions on the Park gravestone (and looking up
now and again, apparently at the view). It is a large, flat stone in
the northern part of the churchyard, and commemorates George
Park, the saddler, his wife Elizabeth, their sons Thomas and John,
and their daughters Mary and Elizabeth, the latter of whom did not
die until 5 April 1843. Their son George is not mentioned on it as
there is a memorial to him and his wife Ann, 'daughter of the late
Robert Peel of Ardwick near Manchester Esquire' inside the church
on the north wall. Wordsworth did not speak to her of the Parks,
and she did not like to ask him why he was interested in them. But
when she had a chance she mentioned the matter to the Vicar; and
briefly this is what he told her.

During his first few days at Hawkshead, Wordsworth became
acquainted with Tom Park, who was then at the Grammar School,
and finding that he was a keen angler made inquiries from him
about the local fishing. So Tom offered to take him with him, and
to show him the different becks and tarns in which fishing was
free. Then meeting one evening with his old schoolmaster, who was
just starting off to fish, Tom asked if he and another boy, a new
boy at the Grammar School, could come with him, and was told
that they might. That was how it started. Afterwards, for as long as
Tom was at school, he and Wordsworth often went fishing together, sometimes with his father or his old schoolmaster, whom

Miss Mary could not identify or name, but usually just the two of them by themselves. The Rev. George Park then went on to claim that it was his grandfather, George Park the saddler, who carried Wordsworth, then a small boy, a good part of the way back from the Duddon Valley, where they had gone to fish. The claim, whether justified or not, shows that some knowledge of this episode was in local circulation long before Wordsworth's account of it appeared in print. Miss Mary Hodgson's informant also said that both he and his father knew Wordsworth personally.

She was inclined to believe all she heard from the Rev. George Park about Wordsworth's association with Tom Park and his father, or so I thought when she was reporting what he said. But she admitted that her father was sceptical on some points, or at least not wholly convinced. He himself had been at the Grammar School from about 1790 to 1797, and had then known Tom Park, who at that time was more noted, he said, as a skater than as an angler. He did go fishing though, and as his father was very fond of it, and a good fisherman, Tom might have been keen on it for a time when he was a small boy. Anyhow, after Wordsworth made a name for himself as a poet, Tom's brother George, then Vicar of Hawkshead, and his sister Betty, used to talk about their 'poor brother's' friendship with him when they were at the Grammar School together, and especially of Wordsworth's first year or so at Hawkshead when Tom often took him fishing, and took him skating as well when there was any to be had. They may have exaggerated a little, but Braithwaite Hodgson, I gathered, thought there was some truth in what they said; and, for what it is worth, that is my own view.

But according to Miss Mary, her father did not remember George Park, or Betty at this period, ever saying anything about their father taking Wordsworth as a small boy to fish with him in the Duddon, and having to carry him on their homeward journey; and, as I shall show in a moment, it is virtually certain that he never did. Nor did Braithwaite Hodgson recall their having mentioned Tom Park's old schoolmaster, and that the two boys sometimes went fishing with him. On the other hand, Miss Mary, who was twenty when Betty Park died in 1843, thought she had heard her

P

say that he was the village schoolmaster who had taught Tom before he went to the Grammar School. By that time, however, Betty may well have been influenced by what her nephew, the Rev. George Park, was saying; and his claims must, I fear, be disregarded unless there is sound corroboration of them; and in this instance, as in the preceding one, it is lacking. Nevertheless, it might possibly be true that Tom Park and William Wordsworth sometimes went fishing with John Harrison, whose school Tom is almost certain to have attended before going to the Grammar School.

Proof that it was someone other than George Park who was imprudent enough to take Wordsworth with him when he went to fish in the upper waters of the Duddon has been furnished by Fletcher Raincock, a school fellow and friend of Wordsworth's, who went up to Cambridge a year before he did, and was a barrister later in life. Some of his recollections were recorded in her Memorandum Book by a Miss Saul of Lancaster, who on investigation turns out to have been a first cousin of his. Among other things she noted from him was 'Wordsworth's Fishing Expedition to the Duddon Valley', in which it is stated that he went with 'one Martin, a weaver', who had to carry him most of the way home. This information, together with the substance of a very long reminiscence of his school days by Fletcher Raincock, was passed on to me in 1907 by Peter Polding Platt, then Headmaster of Windermere Grammar School, and tenant of the cottage at Tarn Hows known as Rose Castle. It was not news to Arthur Brydson I found, for in his younger days he had heard precisely the same thing from Mrs. Benson Harrison, whom he reported as saying that Wordsworth when telling her had added that he specially wanted to go to the Duddon Valley because of what Hugh Tyson had told him about it.

In 1949, when studying the Hawkshead Parish Registers, I concluded that 'one Martin, a weaver', could be identified for certain as the 'John Martin of Outyeat Weaver' who died on 17 March 1805, 'Aged 63 Years', and equally certainly as the 'John Son of John Martin at Wat^{r}son ground' who was baptized on 13 July 1742. When he was a boy his father, who was a waller, and whose eldest son and fourth child he was, lived in turn at Waterson Ground, Sand Ground, Borwick Ground, and Fieldhead. After remarrying in 1782, he eventually died at Sand Ground in 1798, 'Aged 92'. His son John was married on 19 March 1764, to Deborah, daughter of John and Ruth Tyson of Outyeat, a couple who did not have their children baptized. All were christened as adults however, Sarah, wife of Thomas Wishert, in 1774, and the rest, including Deborah Martin, in 1778. She and her husband had six children baptized at Hawkshead, the eldest in 1764, the youngest in 1782. The first two were born at Sand Ground, and the remainder at Outyeat, where John Martin was living when he took Wordsworth to fish near the source of the Duddon, their journey, I take it, being by way of Little Langdale and Wrynose. Wordsworth tells us that he attached himself to 'a person living in the neighbourhood of Hawkshead', not in Hawkshead; which is true of John Martin but not of George Park. How was it, though, that he knew of the Outgate weaver's intention, seeing that he lived a mile away, and had no need to come through Hawkshead? One possibility is that he learnt of it from John Martin's brother-in-law Thomas Wishert, a much older man who had once been a soldier and was then a packman; a man who, when not on his rounds, seems to have been fond of talking to Grammar School boys, and telling them of his experiences. Of him I shall have more to say presently.

The Raincocks—Peter Platt—burning of MSS. at Rayrigg—rescue of Fletcher Raincock's reminiscence—expedition to the raven's nest—John Benson—boating on Coniston—Thomas Usher, waller—Will Tyson—Mr. Walker of Yewtree—Edward Birkett and the other boys —payment for raven's heads—the Tarns—attempt to arrest Jonathan Castlehow—Francis and Richard Castlehow—Poor Accounts—note in the Westmorland Gazette*—William Tower's account—Ullswater Castlehows—William Tower's register—punishment for the Hawkshead boys*

Fletcher Raincock, whose long reminiscence of his school days at Hawkshead I shall be giving in three parts, and with such additions to it as I can usefully make, was the second son of the Rev. William Raincock, a Cambridge graduate who married Agnes, eldest daughter of the Fletcher Fleming of Rayrigg, Windermere, who died in

1770. He was Rector of Ousby and Vicar of Bromfield, both in Cumberland, but he and his wife lived in Penrith, where all their children were baptized, John on 14 May 1768: Fletcher on 25 March 1769; William on 28 March 1770; Agnes on 21 December 1771; Christopher on 12 July 1775; and George on 8 February 1779. John, the eldest, succeeded to the Rayrigg estate on the death in 1777 at the age of twenty-four of his mother's only brother Fletcher Fleming; and in consequence he changed his name to Fleming by deed-poll in 1779. He left Hawkshead school in 1785, and Fletcher in 1786, both proceeding to Cambridge; whilst William, who was a few weeks older than Wordsworth, and 'a fine spirited lad' he tells us, stayed on until 1788, and then went to sea. With their younger brothers I am not concerned at present, and with John only as father of Jane Isabella Fleming who was living at Rayrigg in 1899, and died there on 2 January 1902, aged ninety-three.

The Rev. William Raincock, oldest of the three sons of John Raincock of Penrith, was baptized there on 12 December 1734 and died in 1787. He had a sister Mary, christened at Penrith on 10 November 1737, and married there on 1 September 1763, to George Saul. She and her husband afterwards lived at Lancaster, where they had two sons and six daughters baptized in the years 1767 to 1780. It was one of their daughters who included some of Fletcher Raincock's reminiscences in her Memorandum Book, but I do not know which. After graduating as 2nd Wrangler in 1790, and being called to the Bar, Fletcher Raincock practised on the Northern Circuit; and Peter Platt discovered from a letter addressed to Miss Jane Fleming that when he was briefed to appear at Lancaster he generally stayed with his Saul relatives there. His home from the age of thirty, and probably earlier than that, was Liverpool. He had an aunt there, his mother's sister Barbara, wife of Thomas Lake, a merchant; and for her second husband his mother married a Liverpool man named William Bolden. She died there on 15 July 1809, and Barbara on 17 May 1817. Fletcher Raincock, who was a bachelor,[1] continued to reside in Liverpool until his death on 17 August 1840. He was buried there, as his mother had been, his grave being close to hers in St. James's churchyard. There is a memorial

---

[1] Perhaps not: see Alphabetical List, Appendix IV.

to him in Windermere Parish Church in the form of a bust with a long inscription, which gives details of his father, mother, and maternal grandfather, and then states that he was 'Fellow of the Society of Antiquaries, formerly Senior Fellow of Pembroke Hall, Cambridge, Recorder of Kendal, and one of her Majesty's Council at law for the County Palatine of Lancaster'. He was Recorder of Kendal from 1818 to 1840; the last of an unbroken line stretching back to the incorporation of the borough in 1575, for on his death the office was abolished. He was a Penrith and Hawkshead friend of Wordsworth, who in a letter to Basil Montagu of 1 October 1844, mentions him as one of his *intimate* associates' at Cambridge.[1]

It was purely by chance that Peter Platt saw a copy of Miss Saul's record of his long Hawkshead reminiscence. Soon after he became tenant of Rose Castle he was told that it had been built by the Castlehows, who were wallers as well as thieves, and used by

[1] There is a MS. note on Fletcher Raincock by J. Gibson in his *Epitaphs and inscriptions on tombstones and monuments in Liverpool churches*—(III, p. 78) which is derived from the two following notices:

In Rodney-street, likewise, lived Fletcher Raincock, one of the most remarkable characters of his day. He had few equals in a legal capacity, and no superiors in literary attainments. He had a most gluttonous appetite for books, and read everything, old and new. He was a regular 'curiosity shop' in the variety of his knowledge, and could produce all sorts of odds and ends at a moment's notice, from all sorts of ancient authors, unknown to and never heard of by other people. This made him a most agreeable companion, his conversational powers being tremendous, and set off, rather than impaired, by a spice of originality and eccentricity, just enough to draw a line between him and the common herd of ordinary and every-day people by whom he was surrounded. Like Yorick, 'he would set the table in a roar', by the combined wit and wisdom which he had ever at command.

(James Stonehouse, *The Streets of Liverpool*, 1869, p. 151.)

Mr. Counsellor Fletcher Raincock resided in Rodney-street. He had an immense chamber practice. He was the agent for the Lowther family at their Appleby elections. He was a man with very plain face and ungainly gait. On one occasion, in cross-examining a female witness, who had used once or twice the then newly-coined word 'humbugging', Mr. Raincock inquired what she meant by 'humbugging'? 'Whoi if oi war to ca' yer a handsome mon, that ud be humbugging.'

(James Aspinall, *Liverpool a few years since*, 3rd ed. 1885, p. 41.)

The Liverpool directories indicate that Raincock's address at least in 1805 was 1 Alfred Street; while in 1839 it is 69 Rodney Street. In 1843 there are two Sotheby catalogues for the sale of Raincock's collection of coins and medals and for his 'Numismatalogical Library'.

them in connection with their plunderings; and, although Hawkshead's historian, H. S. Cowper, informed him that there was no truth in either statement, he mentioned the Castlehows to some pupils of his who shortly afterwards visited him in his retreat. To his surprise one of the boys said his father knew about them, and about some Hawkshead Grammar School boys who were friendly with them. He had it in writing, the boy explained, and added that it was something he had picked up at Rayrigg after it had been thrown away from burning but had not been burned. That would be in 1902, Peter Platt thought, after the death of Miss Fleming, when a great mass of papers and letters were turned out and burned. And oddly enough in 1952 Mr. George H. Pattinson, whose grandfather George H. Pattinson bought the Rayrigg estate in 1913, told me about the destruction of a great many documents, some eighteenth century in date, following the death of Miss Jane Isabella Fleming, the last of the Rev. John Fleming's family. They were turned out from chests in the attic, he said, into the farmyard, and burned there; but owing to the strong wind some were scattered and afterwards retrieved.

At the second time of asking Peter Platt was allowed to see and borrow the little batch of papers picked up at Rayrigg by the father of one of his pupils. It contained a copy, for which Miss Jane Fleming had asked, of Miss Saul's recording of Fletcher Raincock's long Hawkshead reminiscence; a note on Wordsworth's fishing expedition to the Duddon Valley; and two letters addressed to Miss Fleming by the copyist, the first from Blundell Sands on 11 September 1899, and the second, in which there is a reference to 'my great aunt's Memorandum Book', on 22 November in the same year, this time from Cheltenham. The writer, who either possessed or had access to the Memorandum Book, signed the first letter 'Your loving niece Dot', but the chances are that she was a granddaughter of George and Mary Saul, and neither a Fleming nor a Raincock. From this letter Peter Platt either noted or inferred that Miss Jane Fleming had asked for a copy of her uncle's stories of the Castlehows, of which she evidently knew, because of what had just appeared about this family in Cowper's *Hawkshead*, which was published in 1899. As Miss Fleming was then ninety, or more probably ninety-one, it is hard to believe that she would trouble. But unlike her sister Barbara, who died in 1897 at the age of eighty-nine, she was mentally alert almost to the end of her life, and interested, though she rather soon forgot things again. And according to my sister Sarah, who saw her twice in 1900, she had a companion who read to her when she was in the mood to listen, and now and then wrote a letter for her; a Nurse Addison, I think it was, who had first gone to Rayrigg to look after Miss Barbara.

Though the particulars I have given of the recording and passing on of Fletcher Raincock's long reminiscence of his school days at Hawkshead are not always as precise as they might be, I have no doubts as to the authenticity of the copy of it that was picked up at Rayrigg, and of which Peter Platt kindly lent me a very full summary in 1907. The narrative, I may say, is devoid of dates, and the ages of the Grammar School boys mentioned in it are not given. To a large extent these omissions can be remedied, and it will help, I think, if I state now, and leave the proof till later, that the opening episode, a hazardous climb on the Yewdale Crags, must have taken place early in 1783 when John Benson was not quite fourteen years old.

One day Bill Raincock and Jim Machell, a friend of his, when scrambling on these crags caught sight of a raven's nest with eggs in it, but it was on a high ledge, and they did not think they could reach it. On getting back to Hawkshead they told Fleck, in other words Fletcher Raincock, about it; and they also told John Benson, a Skelwith boy who was good at crag-climbing. He went with Bill Raincock to have a look at it, and having seen the position of the nest, and studied the ledge it was on near the top of the crags, he said he thought he could reach and take the eggs, but he would have to be roped, and hauled up after he had got them. So he arranged with Tom Usher, a young waller, to come with them, and to bring a strong rope long enough for the job and a short gavelock with him. In addition to John Benson, the boys in the party were Fleck and Bill Raincock, Ted Birkett, who was a friend of Fleck's, and Bill Wordsworth as the Raincock boys called him. Jim Machell did not go as he was not very well that day. On the way they were joined by Young 'Tailor' Tyson, who was also out in search of birds' eggs, in the scarcer of which he did a good trade with some of the Grammar School boys. It was carried on, Fleck said, through his brother John when he was in the Writing Master's class, 'which we boys always called Joe's, the Writing Master then being one Joseph Varty'. Will Tyson, when he heard that Tom Usher and his party were going to the Yewdale Crags, said he would come with them, and he did; which was just as well as things turned out.

On reaching Yewdale they all climbed to the top of the crags near where the nest was, and after John Benson had been roped he started off along the ledge, a wallet on his back for the eggs, a short, stout stick in his hand to fend him off the rock face when he was being hauled up. The going, with Tom Usher keeping the rope fairly taut and moving along at the same pace, was easy at first, but later there were two or three places where the ledge was awkwardly narrow. John was successful, however, in negotiating each in turn. Then, as he neared the nest, a new difficulty arose: the rock above him projected a bit. He still moved forward though, slowly, a little at a time. But in the end, almost within reach of the eggs, he was beaten: the rock projection was too big, and he dare not venture another step. When Tom Usher became aware of this, he called to him to make his way back as best he could to where the rock above him did not stick out so much. John Benson did not respond, however. His confidence had gone, and he was afraid to turn round, or to back for a few yards, or even feet. Assurances and encouragement were of no avail, and as Tom was certain that it was unsafe, because of the protruding rock above him, to try and haul him up from where he stood, he decided that they must get more help. It would have to be from a good cragsman, he said, and even so he would need to be roped.

So he asked Will Tyson to go down to the farm below, and to inquire if there was anyone who could and would give a hand in trying to rescue a crag-fast boy, John Benson of Skelwith. The farm was Yewtree, and the family then living at it bore the name of Walker. They knew John Benson, but Mr. Walker had no liking for Grammar School boys on account of their molesting Quaker children on their way to and from school at Colthouse, and his reply to Will Tyson was that if one of the boys was crag-fast they must first seek help from their friends. Whereupon Will hurried back, and then set off on the way to Hawkshead to tell Mr. Matthew Harrison, steward to Mr. Knott of Coniston Waterhead. He was nearly related to John Benson, and used to let him and his friends have a boat when they went over for a row on Coniston Water. Young Tyson had hopes that Mr. Harrison would see to it that John was rescued, and as quickly as possible; but he could not find him either at Mr. Knott's or at his own home, which was not far away. He made contact with his man, however, though only to learn from him that his master was absent from home, and would not be back till night. After telling the man of John Benson's predicament, and that someone must be found to rescue him from it, Will Tyson was advised to go on to Frank Castlehow's and ask him to help, as he was about the only one nearby who might be able to free the crag-bound boy. Not knowing what else to do, Will said he would, and the man offered to lend him his horse. Tom Usher had sent the two youngest boys, Bill Wordsworth and Bill Raincock, with Young Tyson, and at this stage Will told them to go back and say that Mr. Harrison was not at home, and that he himself was going on to Frank Castlehow's on horseback.

Frank Castlehow lived near Hawkshead High Cross, by the little tarn there, in a house he had built for himself, for like Tom Usher he was a waller. It was a good mile further on, and little more than a mile from Hawkshead. The Castlehows had a bad name for stealing, but up to then nothing had been proved against them. It was uphill all the way for Will Tyson, and he was some time getting to Castlestead even though he was on horseback. Frank Castlehow, a big, powerful man, was at home when he arrived, and on hearing of John Benson's plight he said that he and his son Jonathan, who was also at home, would come along at once, and see what they could do for the boy. Jonathan, who was only about fifteen at the time, looked more like a grown man than a boy. After sending Will Tyson off, they made a bee-line for the Yewdale Crags; and, though he was on horseback, they got there almost as soon as he did. They scaled the crags faster than he could; and, after taking a look at the spot, Frank Castlehow roped his son Jonathan, and let him down on to the ledge not far from where John Benson was standing.

In no time, or so it seemed, Jonathan had him back to where he could easily be hauled up; and Tom Usher and Frank Castlehow did the rest. 'I don't know how he managed it,' Tom Usher said afterwards; and Will Tyson added: 'He's a masterpiece at anything like that, Jonathan is.'

The long wait on the crags till help arrived was terrible, Fleck said, and for John Benson it must have been a truly awful ordeal. The only detail I have noted is that Tom Usher kept talking to him, and that Ned Birkett and Fleck, as soon as they realized why Tom was doing this, followed his example. Poor John was in a sad state when at last he was hauled up to safety; but thanks to Frank Castlehow, who tended and cared for him, he soon recovered sufficiently for the party to start on their descent of the crags, down which he was carried by the two wallers in turn, for Tom Usher, though much the smaller of the two, was also a strong man, and very sure-footed on the crags. Will Tyson, who had gone on in advance, was waiting at the foot with the horse he had borrowed; and one way or another they got John Benson safely to Mr. Matthew Harrison's. They wanted him to stay the night there, but he would not hear of it: he must get back, he said, to the Hawkshead relatives who boarded him during the week, some Bensons who had a farm not far from the school. So they all went on again, up the long ascent to Hawkshead High Cross. By then it was dusk, and as they neared the summit of the hill Frank Castlehow said they must all come into his place, and have a bite and sup before going on. They did, and apart from John Benson the boys had a 'rare good meal'. After thanking the Castlehows for all they had done, the party then dropped down to Hawkshead and dispersed. Tom Usher, who lived near the Bensons with whom John boarded, saw him home.

He never went crag climbing after ravens' eggs again; nor did Fleck. But soon afterwards Ted Birkett and two of his Carlisle friends, Francis Graham and Edmund Atkinson, went up the Yewdale Crags, and saw that the nest and eggs were still there. They made no attempt to reach them, however, and in the end it was Kit Gilpin, 'an older boy', who secured the eggs. He was a farmer's son, and about the best in the school at reaching ravens' nests on high ledges. They are usually built, I may say, where the rock above projects enough to afford some protection from the weather.

Having come to the end of the first part of Fletcher Raincock's reminiscence, I may as well add what I can about those who took part in the Yewdale Crags escapade, other than the Castlehows, about whom there is more to come. John Benson, with whom it seems natural to start, was a son of John and Eleanor Benson of Skelwith Fold, who had him baptized at Hawkshead on 25 April 1769. His father, who owned Bull Close as well, and was Church warden in respect of it in 1769 and Overseer of the Poor in 1772–3, is perhaps best described as a superior statesman. Born in 1731, he was a son of Leonard Benson of Skelwith and his wife Agnes, *née* Birkett, who can be identified as the 'Agnes Benson Widow Skelwith Fold' who died on 5 January 1788 'Aged 92', and was buried in the church on the 8th. He himself was one of the Twenty Four for a good many years, and after the church was pewed afresh in 1794 he purchased two pews, one for Skelwith Fold and the other for Bull Close. Moreover, he was one of the very few statesmen who subscribed in 1789–90 towards the cost of building a new and enlarged Market House, his contribution being £1. 1s. 0d. He and his wife had a good many daughters, but apart from Leonard, who lived for only three months, John seems to have been their only son. He and his father died in the same year, as appears in the following inscription on a head stone in the northern part of the churchyard: 'In Memory of Mr. John Benson of Skelwith Fold, who departed this life on the 15th day of January 1819, aged 87 years, Eleanor, his wife died on the 28th day of September 1805 aged 73 years. Mr. John Benson their son, died on the 17th day of July 1819 aged 50 years. Elizabeth his wife died on the 22nd day of June 1845, aged 79 years. Also of Eleanor Jackson their daughter, and widow of Thomas Jackson Esq. of Waterhead Ambleside, born 14th August, 1790, died 4th January 1861'. Following his early marriage, John Benson lived for some years at Aldingham in Low Furness, but having no information from the registers there I cannot say whether Eleanor was his only child or not. She returned to Aldingham after her husband's death, and died there, but was buried at Hawkshead where, in the northern part of the churchyard there is a flat-topped tomb with a cross on it and the simple inscription 'Eleanor Jackson 1861'. H. S. Cowper once told me that it was she who had the John Benson head stone cut and erected. Her father, she said, was a quiet man whose main pleasure was in country sports and pastimes.

There is no mistaking the Hawkshead farmhouse at which he boarded during the week when he was a schoolboy, for the Parish Registers and other records show beyond doubt that it was the How in Hawkshead Field and could have been no other. It was the home at that time of George Benson and his wife Isabel, and also of their married son William, who was having children christened in the 1780s. John does not seem to have been a very near relative of theirs. At any rate, George's father was the William Benson of Far Skelwith who in 1712 married Elizabeth, daughter of William Rigge of Hawkshead Field. This couple had four sons baptized at Hawkshead, namely James in 1713, William in 1715, John in 1718, and George in 1720. James succeeded his father, but died at the How in 1779. John, after being at school at Lowther under a Mr. Wilkinson, entered St. John's College, Cambridge as a sizar in 1740 at the age of twenty-two. George acquired an estate in Hawkshead Field at an early age, and because of his ownership of it he was called upon in 1741 to act as Overseer of the Poor for the Hawkshead Quarter. In the same year he married Isabel Ashburner, who must have been about thirty-five, as when she died in 1786 her age was given as eighty. In 1745 he was Churchwarden 'for his wifes estate at how', and later he was elected one of the Twenty Four. He did not die until 1802, but after the re-seating of the church in 1794 it was his son William who bought one of the new pews for the How, the price of which was £6. 10s. 0d.

Matthew Harrison, steward to Mr. George Knott, the ironmaster, and his successor in January 1784, as sole manager of Knott, Ainslie & Co., otherwise the Newland Co., was certainly very closely related to John Benson, but only in virtue of his marriage early in 1781 to John's sister Mary, who was then twenty-four. She and her husband lived at Monk Coniston until they moved to Newland, which is near Ulverston, in 1787. They had daughters christened at Hawkshead in 1781 and 1782, but the registers do not name the

house in which they were then living. They give it, however, as
Townson Ground when, in March 1786, their eldest son Benson
was privately baptized. Fletcher Raincock's incidental reference to
Matthew Harrison's loan of a boat to John Benson and his friends
when they fancied a row on Coniston Water might mean that on
occasion he himself was one of the company; and I am tempted to
think that William Wordsworth may have been another. True,
there is no mention of his boating on this particular lake in either
the 1805 or the 1850 text of *The Prelude*; but the two citations which
follow are proof enough that he did.

The first is from a prose note dictated to Miss Isabella Fenwick
on his *Extract from the conclusion of a poem, composed in anticipation of
leaving school*:

The beautiful image with which this poem concludes suggested itself to
me while I was resting in a boat along with my companions under the
shade of a magnificent row of sycamores, which then extended their
branches from the shore of the promontory upon which stands the ancient
and at that time the more picturesque Hall of Coniston, the Seat of the
Le Flemings from very early times.[1]

It is on the western side of the lake, and rather more than a mile from
its head. My second citation is from a passage, recently printed by
Ernest de Selincourt, which Wordsworth at one time intended to
include in *The Prelude* after line 144 of Book II, 1805 text. It refers
to the same place, and says:

> Thither we repair'd,
> 'Twas even a custom with us, to the shore
> And to that cool piazza. They who dwelt
> In the neglected mansion-house supplied
> Fresh butter, tea-kettle, and earthen-ware,
> And chafing dish with smoking coals, and so
> Beneath the trees we sate in our small boat
> And in the covert eat our delicate meal
> Upon the calm smooth lake.[2]

[1] See *Prose Works of William Wordsworth*, ed. A. B. Grosart (1876), III, p. 4.
[2] These lines are found in MSS. V and U and are printed in *The Prelude* ed. de
Selincourt and Darbishire (1959), p. 582.

Evidently boating on Coniston Water was more than just a change from boating on Windermere, and for that the caretakers at Coniston Hall were largely responsible.

The young waller, Tom Usher, who played such an essential part in the Yewdale Crags escapade, is the 'Thomas Son of Tho:ˢ Wishert Outyeat' who was baptized at Hawkshead on 30 March 1754. The local people did not take to the surname Wishert, and converted it into Usher, probably more quickly in speech than in written records. From the start there was a tendency to change it, as, when Thomas Wishert, a comparative newcomer to the parish, married Sarah Tyson of Outgate in 1746, his name is entered in the register as Thomas Ushirt. He and his wife had five children, but before the youngest was born in 1757 he had joined the army, as we shall see later, leaving Sarah to cope as best she could. She and her family had an allowance from the parish of 2s. 6d. a week, later reduced to 2s. od., in addition to which her house-rent of £1. os. od. a year was paid for her. Even so, she must have had a struggle to maintain herself and her five children; and it is not surprising to find that when her second son, Isaac, died of small-pox in 1762 at the age of eleven he was buried at the expense of the parish. Tom, her third son, was apprenticed to a waller as soon as he was old enough, most likely to her eldest brother John, who like his father before him followed that trade.

Early in 1776 'Thomas Usher of this Parish Waller and Ann Newby of this Parish Spinster' were married at Hawkshead. In one of his genealogical entries made in 1779 John Hodgson says that Ann's father was John Newby, a mariner. She and Tom had children baptized at fairly regular intervals from 1776 to 1795, and the registrations show that they lived in turn at Keen Ground, Gallowbarrow, the How, and Walker Ground, and that they were at the How when a daughter and a son of theirs were christened in 1782 and 1784 respectively. Their father's surname was given in 1782 as Wishirt and in 1784 as Wishert; and the Churchwardens' Accounts for 1783 record a payment of 14s. 2d. to Thomas Wishert and John Tyson jointly for work done by them on two separate occasions. But after the death on 16 January 1785, of John Hodgson, shoemaker, and Parish Clerk for more than forty years, Tom's surname invariably appears in Hawkshead records as Usher. He and his wife cannot have had much in reserve as in 1787-8 Ann Usher had an allowance from the parish of 1s. 6d. a week for eleven weeks, and in the following year Thomas Usher had the same allowance for one week.

More work was coming his way, however, for on 14 December 1789, it was announced that the contract for all the wallers' work needed in building the new Market House had been awarded to Thomas Johnson the Younger and Thomas Liket, both of Ambleside, and Thomas Usher of Walker Ground. The work contracted for seems to have been completed in 1790, but in the three following years there were substantial payments to Tom by or on behalf of the Market House Trustees. Then in 1793 he and his partner, Thomas Johnson the Younger of Ambleside but originally of Colthouse, secured the contract for all the wallers' work involved in adding a vestry and re-pewing Hawkshead Church, for which they were to receive £36. The work, which was finished before the end of 1794, must have been done wholly or mainly by Tom, as payment for it was made (in driblets) to him alone. It is doubtful whether the Churchwardens had fully discharged their debt to him when he died at Walker Ground on 23 July 1796, at the age of forty-two. His eldest son John, who was the second of his ten children, was only seventeen at the time, and obviously could not succeed his father straightaway; but when he was married rather less than two years later the Parish Clerk described him as a waller. Apart from this small gap, if it should be regarded as such, the Hawkshead Ushers have been wallers and builders without a break from Tom's day to the present time; for which reason, as well as for his own sake, I am glad that some of his handiwork is so readily visible in Hawkshead. Immediately after his death his widow was granted a pension of 1s. 0d. a week; and 'in Necessity' she received additional help from the Overseers of the Poor to the extent of about £4 a year in 1798-9 and 1799-1800. In 1808 she was living in Ulverston.

There is little I can add about Will Tyson, or to what I said earlier about his brother John, whose mention by Fletcher Raincock was merely incidental. They were sons of William Tyson, the Gallowbarrow tailor who repaired the Wordsworth boys' clothes during their earlier years at Hawkshead School. He was not a native of Hawkshead, nor were any of his children: indeed there are only four entries in the Hawkshead registers that relate to him and them. The first two arise out of the deaths of his son John, aged twelve, in 1782 and his daughter Emmy, aged seventeen, in 1783. The other two record the marriage in April 1784 of 'William Tyson of this Parish Taylor and Sarah Swainson of this Parish Spinster', and the birth and baptism in September 1784 of 'John ye Son of Wm Tyson Junior of Gallabarrow Taylor'. There is no later mention of young Will in other Hawkshead documents, nor of his father after 1787.

The Mr. Walker of Yewtree to whom Will Tyson went first in his search for help would be the 'George Walker Yewtree' who had a son George baptized at Hawkshead in November 1759. He was Overseer of the Poor for the Monk Coniston and Skelwith Quarter in 1757-8, Churchwarden in 1788 as a substitute for George Law, Esquire, of Brathay, and again in 1789, this time in respect of his own estate, which took its name from a giant yew tree whose trunk, a mere shell when it was blown down in the great gale of 22 December 1894, was nine feet in diameter in the eighteenth century. An earlier 'George Walker de Yewtree' was Churchwarden in 1726; and in 1688 a Richard Walker of 'Yew Tree in Tarn Hawes (Yewdale)', who is mentioned in George Fox's *Journal*, was buried in the Quaker sepulchre at Colthouse. Though none of the later Walkers of Yewtree were Friends, it may be that some memory of him and what he endured was still alive among them a hundred years after his death. If not, it is difficult to understand why the George Walker with whom we are concerned had no liking for Grammar School boys because they 'molested' Quaker children going to and coming from school at Colthouse. As will appear more fully on a later occasion,[1] the offenders were small boys who contended, not without some reason, that they were only playing 'English and Scotch'. But was this, I wonder, the only or main objection that the owner of Yewtree had to the things Grammar School boys were apt to do. There might well have been others closer at hand.

Of the boys mentioned by Fletcher Raincock, and not identified

[1] See below, pp. 247-8.

as yet, his brother William's friend Jim Machell is undoubtedly the 'James Penny Machell, Son of John Machell Esqre, of Penny Bridge', who was baptized at Ulverston on 4 January 1771. He was the eldest of the four sons of John Machell, originally of Hollow Oak, Colton, who in 1767 married Isabel, daughter and co-heiress of William Penny (1708–88) of Pennybridge Hall. He later went to Rugby School, and Mr. A. R. Tatham, Honorary Secretary of the Old Rugbeian Society, was good enough to tell me that he entered it in September 1783. So the Yewdale Crags enterprise cannot have taken place in any later year. The month would be February or March, for it is then that the female raven lays her eggs; and for a long time I thought the most likely year was 1782. But Edward Birkett's participation shows, as I was rather slow to discover, that the attempt could not have been made until 1783. In the *Carlisle Grammar School Memorial Register, 1264–1924*, a copy of which the Headmaster, Mr. V. J. Dunstan, kindly lent me, it is stated that Birkett, the eldest son of Henry Birkett of Carlisle, '*armiger*',[1] was admitted to the school in January 1773, and left before Christmas, 1775; and further, that he was readmitted on 1 May 1780, and left before Christmas, 1782. It seems to be certain, then, that he did not come to Hawkshead School until January 1783. As Edward Joseph Birkett he was admitted to Christ's College, Cambridge, in April 1786, at the age of nineteen, and went into residence in the following October, at the same time as Fletcher Raincock went up to Pembroke. Edward Birkett, then, was much the oldest of the boys involved in the Yewdale Crags escapade, but was at the time new to Hawkshead School.

His friend Edmund Atkinson was the fourth son of James Atkinson of Carlisle, 'armiger', and was first admitted to the Grammar School there on 1 March 1773, a few weeks later than Edward Birkett, like whom he was readmitted in 1780, but not until September. The two appear to have been exact contemporaries, and it is not unlikely that they entered Hawkshead School at or about the same time. Francis Graham is different: he was not at Carlisle Grammar School, and apparently he is the 'Fra^s. Graham of Dalston,

---

[1] An alternative for a squire, i.e. one entitled to bear heraldic arms. For Birkett, see also Alphabetical List, Appendix IV.

Cumberland', who contributed 10s. 6d. to the New Library Fund in 1792. For no apparent reason Miss Saul mentioned that his father was a soldier. I have no information about the Kit Gilpin, said to have been an older boy and a farmer's son, who eventually secured the raven's eggs, and can only suggest that possibly he might have been the Christopher, son of Christopher and Elizabeth Gilpin, who was baptized at Kentmere on 15 December 1767, and who was therefore a good deal older than Fletcher Raincock and John Benson though not as old as Edward Birkett. But whilst the age is about right, there is no evidence, so far as I know, that he ever was at Hawkshead School.

William Wordsworth was the youngest of the boys present when John Benson got crag-fast. He does not mention this hazardous venture in *The Prelude*, but tells instead of a solitary experience:

> Oh! when I have hung
> Above the raven's nest, by knots of grass
> And half-inch fissures in the slippery rock
> But ill sustain'd, and almost, as it seem'd,
> Suspended by the blast which blew amain,
> Shouldering the naked crag; Oh! at that time,
> While on the perilous ridge I hung alone,
> With what strange utterance did the loud dry wind
> Blow through my ears! the sky seem'd not a sky
> Of earth, and with what motion mov'd the clouds!
>
> (I.341–50)

That, we are left to infer, was one of the severer ways in which Nature would frame a 'favor'd Being'.

In his *Guide to the Lakes* Wordsworth says: 'I recollect frequently seeing, when a boy, bunches of unfledged ravens suspended in the churchyard of H[awkshead], for which a reward of so much a head was given to the adventurous destroyer'.[1] The Churchwardens' Accounts show that for ravens the payment per head was 4d. Cowper worked out that between 1730 and 1797 the total number whose destruction was rewarded was 421, an average of rather more than six a year.[2] In some years the number destroyed was much larger, the highest being 24 in 1780, when Wordsworth had not

[1] Ed. de Selincourt (1926), p. 122.   [2] *Hawkshead* (1899), p. 434.

long been at Hawkshead, 19 in 1772, and 18 in 1769. The number
was 14 in 1773, in which year, according to the Rev. John Allen, the
Parish Clerk was instructed, 'on request being made by the School
Master, to pay no Varmen Rewards to the Scholars for Ravens
& c'. I failed to find any statement to this effect in the Vestry minutes,
but do not doubt its authenticity.[1] The payment for carrion crows,
which are very rarely mentioned in the Churchwardens' Accounts,
was 2d. a head, whilst for foxes it was from 5s. 0d. to 6s. 8d., and
for fox cubs at least 2s. 6d. No payments are recorded for eagles,
marts, badgers, or otters, which were sometimes classed as vermin.
The need to destroy ravens, powerful birds who could live sixty
years or more, arose from their attacks on lambs, a serious matter in
the Lake Country, where fell sheep were of paramount
importance.

After this digression, excusable I hope since it is not wholly
irrelevant, I will turn without more delay to the second part of
Fletcher Raincock's reminiscence. In Peter Platt's summary the
boys now concerned were said to be those Frank Castlehow entertained after the Yewdale Crags rescue, and two or three of their
friends whose names were not given. The first statement in the
narration was that Frank Castlehow continued to invite these boys
to a meal, admittedly only occasionally, but they made the most
of it to their school fellows. It was nearly always at night when they
were returning from Coniston, or from what Fletcher Raincock
called the Coniston Tarns where, he said, they sometimes bathed
on summer evenings, and skated by moonlight in frosty weather.

The tarns he referred to would be the three in Monk Coniston
which ceased to exist as such when, in the nineteenth century, the
much larger, single sheet of water commonly known as Tarn Hows
was formed by building a dam across the beck flowing out of the
lowest of them, and so raising the water-level in the upland depres-
sion where they were situated under Tom Heights. This spot, which
owes some of its present attractions to man's intervention, is still
known locally as the Tarns. Originally part of the farmhold registered in 1598 as Tarnhouse and in 1656 as Tarnhows, it was added
to the Coniston Waterhead estate by George Knott, who appears

[1] A letter of Richard Benson, 3 November 1773, confirms this: see Appendix III.

to have purchased the whole of the Tarnhows property, which extended southwards almost to Waterhead House, and westwards to the Yewdale Beck. Before the raising of the water-level, the Three Tarns, as they were sometimes called, can hardly have been an ideal place for bathing and skating, for in course of time they had been reduced in size by silt, with the result that there was a good deal of marshy ground on and near their edges. But doubtless both activities could be pursued there: in fact I have heard of people skating on the High and Low Tarns, which because of their altitude and shallowness froze quickly in really cold weather. A nearby alternative to them was High Cross, otherwise Wharton Tarn, close to Frank Castlehow's house, and the boys may have gone there occasionally. It is not very likely, though, that Fletcher Raincock was thinking of it when he spoke of the Coniston Tarns.

After a year or two, he continued, an attempt was made to arrest Jonathan Castlehow by a party of men including the Parish Constable, who had a warrant to take him, and Joseph Varty, the Writing Master, who at the time was a 'leading office holder' in the parish. The time of year was autumn, and it was just after nightfall when they approached Frank Castlehow's house. From one of their number, who had gone earlier and had been watching it, they learnt that Jonathan had returned home not long before, and had not left the house again; so they decided to close in on it at once. As they did so, they caught sight of a figure slipping away from it; a man, they assured each other, of Jonathan's height and build. 'Aye, and the clothes were his', said one who had been closer to him than the rest; 'I'll swear they were.' Without hesitation they gave chase, guided mainly by the noise their quarry made in fleeing from them. The night was not pitch-dark, however, and at least once or twice they caught sight of him, or thought they did. The pursuit, in which their best runners were not being left behind even if they did not seem to be gaining ground, took them down into Yewdale by way of Tarn Hows, presumably the farmhouse so named; and from there through Upper Yewdale and Tilberthwaite into Little Langdale, and on to Fell Foot at the head of that valley, where their quarry, giving up the attempt to outrun them, was taken without any trouble. But it was not Jonathan Castlehow they had caught: it was his sister Ruth dressed in his clothes; a strapping young woman two or three years older than he was, and nearly as tall. Having recovered her freedom, for the Constable had no warrant to arrest her, and her breath, she turned on them and roundly abused them for having frightened her, and caused her to run all the way to the bottom of Wrynose, to avoid being seized and perhaps killed by what from their behaviour as they approached her father's house she took for a band of robbers. The truth, of course, is that her flight in Jonathan's clothes was a ruse to give him time to get right away, for the Castlehows had discovered that the Parish Constable and several other men were coming to arrest him. The attempt must have been made in the autumn of 1784, when 'Mr' Joseph Varty was Churchwarden for the Hawkshead Quarter, and when another of the Castlehows was successfully arrested, as we shall see very shortly.

Francis Castlehow was not baptized, married, or buried at Hawkshead, but he appears to have lived in the parish, perhaps not continuously, from 1764, when he had a daughter Margaret christened at Hawkshead, to 1789, when his daughter Elizabeth, who was two years younger than Margaret, was married there to 'John Point of the Parish of Ulverston Husbandman'. Margaret, however, was said to be of Ulverston when she was married there in 1787 to William Wainman of Urswick, another husbandman. Both she and Betty, to use her baptismal name, were born whilst their parents were living at High House. And so was Jonathan, who was christened at Hawkshead on 31 December 1768, and would therefore be only a little over fifteen when he rescued John Benson, and not quite seventeen when he was in danger of being arrested. He was described as a husbandman when he and Anne Steele, both of the Parish of Ulverston, were married at Ulverston on 28 September 1789; but when in the following year their first child, born on 30 June was baptized at Hawkshead on 15 August he was registered as 'Isaac Son of Jonathan Castlehow of Oxenfell Slater', i.e. slate-quarryman, -river, or -dresser. 'Ann, D^r of —— Castlehow, Ulv. — poor', baptized at Ulverston on 1 April 1793, was a daughter of Jonathan and his wife. Isaac married Sarah Jackson at Lowick in

1817, and had several children christened there. Ruth Castlehow, who was born before her parents moved to High House, Hawkshead, was six or seven years older than Jonathan, and not two or three as Fletcher Raincock thought. On 18 August 1788, 'Joseph Slee of this Parish Husbandman & Ruth Castlehow of this Parish Spinster' were married at Hawkshead. He signed the register, she made her mark, and one of the two witnesses was Isaac Slee, her husband's father. In the following year 'Ruth Wife of Joseph Slee of Sawrey ground Labourer Died in Childbed April 17 [and was] Buried 19 in Church Aged 28'. Evidently her husband had been allowed to borrow some Charity Money on bond and at interest as in the Poor Accounts repayments by him are recorded of 1, 3, and 2 guineas in the year 1790–1, and of a further 2 guineas in 1792–3. He later remarried, and when he had daughters baptized at Hawkshead he is described in 1798 as 'of Oxenfell Husbandman', and in 1801 as 'of Arnside Labourer'.

The house Frank Castlehow built for himself near High Cross Tarn is named in at least three entries in the Hawkshead registers. The first two record the baptism of 'Jane Daughter of Francis Castlehow Scalesteads' on 28 December 1773, and the burial of 'James Son of Francis Castlehow Scalestead' on 28 February 1777, whilst the third, which was made in 1779, reads as follows: 'Francis Son of Francis Castlehow Scalestead Waller Died Feb. ye 23rd Buried ye 25 in C^hyard Aged 3 years Chink cough'.[1] There can be little doubt that Scalesteads or Scalestead is the house Fletcher Raincock called Castlestead, and that an aged informant of Cowper's referred to as Frankhousesteads, a place, he said, that was reputed to be haunted by fairies. Cowper himself found the remains of a small house, and one of the oldest and best of his informants described it as the Castlehows' hiding place. That hardly makes sense, as it was not far from the highway between Hawkshead and

---

[1] Presumably a whooping cough. A northern form of 'chink' is 'kink', and a note in West's *Guide to the Lakes* (4th ed. 1789, p. 303) explains 'kink-cough', (a coinage which, incidentally, the *O.E.D.* does not note): '*Kink*, is to be thrown into the convulsions which we observe in the highest degree of coughing or laughter. Hence the cough in children which always put on this strained appearance is called the *Kinkcough*. From an ignorance of this etymology, though with some reference to the sound, we find the word wrote *chin*, or *kink-cough*.'

Coniston. Anyhow, the evidence I have set out points to its having been the dwelling place of Frank Castlehow and his family for a number of years in the 1770s and 1780s. He was employed to do waller's work by the Churchwardens, as their accounts for the years beginning at Easter 1773, 1782, and 1783 reveal. The payments I have noted are:

1774 To Francis Castlehow as pr. note..............0. 2. 0.
1782 To Francis Castlehow as pr. Bill in part........1. 4. 4½
1783 To Frank Castlehow as pr. Note
 & latter end of his Bill ....0. 19. 0.

The second and third of these entries show that round about the date of the Yewdale Crags rescue the Churchwardens picked on him to do a substantial amount of work for them, which suggests that he was not then regarded as a robber or thief.

There was another Castlehow, Richard by name, who appears to have been a younger brother of Frank, though documentary proof that he was is lacking. On 16 May 1767, he was married by licence to Hannah Grigg at Hawkshead, and in the register, which he just managed to sign, both are stated to be 'of this Parish'. They had no children baptized at Hawkshead, and he is not mentioned again until 1784 in any of the parochial records. In that year he was granted a certificate stating that his place of 'Legal Settlement' was the Parish of Hawkshead, which meant that he was entitled to receive Poor Relief there should he ever be in need of it. This information occurs in the Poor Accounts for the Monk Coniston and Skelwith Quarter for the year 1784-5, the relevant entries being:

June 16. Paid Reckoning at Stampers
 upon a consultation with Mr Brathwaite,
 Mr Jackson and Mr Varty concerning
 Richd Castlehow as to giving
 him a Certificate ....0. 1. 0.
June 18. Drawing a Cert: for
 Richd Castlehow and attending
 the execution thereof by the
 Churchwardens and Overseers ....0. 6. 8.

June 19. Paid Thos. Stamper Journey to
 Mr Taylor to get the Cert:
 allowed and for expenses at the
 signing thereof by the Churchwardens
 and Overseers ....0. 3. 6.

The Rev. Reginald Brathwaite of Hawkshead and Mr. Taylor of
Finsthwaite were Magistrates; Mr. George Jackson was then Over-
seer of the Poor for the Monk Coniston and Skelwith Quarter; and
Mr. Joseph Varty, as we have seen, was Churchwarden for the
Hawkshead Quarter.

The decision reached at Thomas Stamper's on 16 June, after what
cannot have been a very long consultation since the reckoning was
only 1s. 0d., was as noteworthy, I consider, as the celerity with
which it was implemented; for the Hawkshead Churchwardens and
Overseers of the Poor very rarely consented to their parish being
certified as the Place of Legal Settlement of a man born and bred
elsewhere. They did so in 1762, in the case of Oliver Otley who had
come from Keswick; in 1773, when the applicant was Anthony
Harrison, originally of Haverbrack in the parish of Beetham; and in
1782, after Thomas Armstrong, clock-smith, had moved to Hawkshead from the chapelry of Egton-with-Newland in the parish of
Ulverston. Moreover, the cost of maintaining and assisting the poor
had risen in the Hawkshead Quarter from £43. 19s. 8d. in the year
1774–5 to £134. 2s. 5d. in 1782–3, and in the Monk Coniston and
Skelwith Quarter from £39. 1s. 3d. to £93. 19s. 9d. in the same
period; and the steep rise was continuing. Such was the background;
and yet in June 1784, the Churchwardens and Overseers were prepared to let Richard Castlehow have a Certificate of Legal Settlement, and even saw that he got it as speedily as possible. There could
scarcely be stronger proof that they did not then regard him as a
robber or thief, or otherwise undesirable inhabitant of the parish.

Less than three months later, however, he was arrested, as a further
entry in the Poor Accounts for the Monk Coniston and Skelwith
Quarter reveals by recording the payment on 7 September 1784, of
13s. 0d. to John Robinson, then Parish Constable, 'for apprehending
Richard Castlehow and bringing him before Mr Brathwaite who

committed him'. He is not mentioned again in these accounts, but
the Poor Accounts for the Hawkshead Quarter include a payment
on 4 October 1784, to Thomas Stamper 'for going to Finsthwaite
on Richard Castlehow's Account', doubtless to Mr. Taylor, the
magistrate recently mentioned. They show, too, that in 1786–7 the
Overseer spent 1s. 3d. on 'Bread at different times for Castlehow
Wife', and that in 1791–2 he gave her 6d. But neither in the Poor
Accounts nor in the Churchwardens' is there any record of a payment to John Robinson for 'failing' to arrest Jonathan Castlehow in
the autumn of 1784. There must have been some expense in connection with the proceedings, but evidently the parish was not asked
to bear the cost of them, which perhaps was just as well for those
concerned.

In the *Westmorland Gazette* of 29 January 1887, there is a contribution to 'Notes by the Way' by a writer who signed himself
'W.S.', but whose identity is unknown to me. Castlehow 'Intack',
he says, on the border of Hawkshead Moor, was named after a man
Castlehow who 'something less than a century ago' built himself a
rude dwelling there of which only the foundations remain. He
'helped out his living by plundering his neighbours'. After a while
they took action, and a party of them, 'with a Constable no doubt',
visited his house with intent to arrest him. Standing at the head of
the stairs with a pitchfork in his hand, he defied them; but in the
end he was taken without bloodshed. On search being made, much
stolen property was found in his house. He was taken to Hawkshead, and lodged there in the local 'Black hole'; but from this he
escaped and there was a chase after him across the meadows. The
leading pursuer grabbed him by the back of his breeches, and in the
ensuing struggle his 'waistband string' broke, and his breeches
dropped down. Helpless as a result, he was returned to the lock-up,
and this time securely confined. His sister, who lived with him,
reproached him for not stealing things more worth while—if he
must steal at all. That his thefts were petty seems to be amply proved
by the fact that he was not tried for them at the Quarter Sessions.
On this point I consulted the Lancashire County Archivist, Mr. R.
Sharpe France, who kindly replied: 'I have searched the Quarter
Sessions Order Books, the Indictments, and the Recognizances

through the years 1784 and 1785 but cannot find any trace of Richard (or Francis) Castlehow.' He was probably committed for only a short period as could then be done by an individual magistrate.

The rude dwelling on the border of Hawkshead Moor mentioned in this note was close to the old fell road to Satterthwaite, and about a mile from Hawkshead, and 700 feet above sea level. Cowper says of it that it had been 'a small one of two or three rooms',[1] but adds that the only room sufficiently preserved to be measured was about 9 yards by 5, which is by no means small. If it had stairs, as the note assumes, there must have been an upper room as well. The house was built rather earlier than 'W.S.' thought, and on what at the time was unenclosed fell, as Cowper makes clear. The same point was stressed, and given a wider application, by an early nineteenth-century writer identified by the Rev. John Allen as William Towers of Sawrey. I found the first sheet of a manuscript of his, but only the first unfortunately, among John Allen's papers. It was headed 'The Castlehows', and the writer, after mentioning Richard and Francis by name, went on to speak of the rough dwellings they hastily erected for themselves when he was a boy, Richard on Hawkshead Moor, Frank by Hawkshead High Cross. Both were put up, he said, 'on what was then open fell occupied in common by a number of landholders in the Hawkshead Quarter of the Parish'. They were built without permission, and when the Steward of the Manor, Mr. Atkinson of Dalton,[2] found out about them he ought to have ordered them to be pulled down again, and the ground made good. As it was, the Castlehows were allowed to stay in them, but 'were never Admitted as Tenants of the Manor'. After they had 'finally gone away' their houses were 'thrown down', and when the open fells on which they had stood were enclosed the stones were used by the men who built the containing walls.

At the foot of the sheet a new paragraph began with the statement that the Castlehows came to Hawkshead 'from the other side of Kirkstone', and were said to have sprung from a long line of statesmen. There was no room for more, but this one sentence is enough to suggest that they were an offshoot of the Castlehows of Water-

[1] H. S. Cowper, *Hawkshead* (1899), p. 230.
[2] Father of John A.; see Alphabetical List, Appendix IV.

side on the Cumberland shore of Ullswater in the chapelry of Watermillock; a family of statesmen whose name is preserved in Castlehow or Castlehows Point near Watermillock House and about two miles from the foot of the lake. I have not seen the Watermillock registers, but the Castlehows of Waterside are mentioned in *Tom Rumney of Mellfell (1764–1835). By Himself as set out in his letters and diary*, which was edited by A. W. Rumney, and published at Kendal in 1936. Tom, who inherited Mellfell, a high-lying Watermillock estate, when his elder brother Anthony was drowned in Ullswater in 1798, thereupon came home from London; and in 1806 he married Elizabeth Castlehow who, it is stated, 'came off an old statesman's family, settled at Waterside', and apparently was of Waterside herself. And the 1829 Directory compiled by Parson and White lists two Castlehows in the neighbourhood of Ullswater, namely Thomas, a yeoman farmer in the chapelry of Watermillock, doubtless at Waterside, and John, a tenant farmer in the parish of Askham. John died on 27 December 1832, aged sixty-one, and was buried at Askham; but he was not baptized there.

As all the information given by William Towers is first-hand and little of it available elsewhere, I had better identify him more fully, and date him precisely. Born at the Crag, Colthouse, and baptized at Hawkshead on 11 February 1759, he was a son of David Towers, hat-maker, earlier of Hawkshead Town, whose wife Alice died just two years later. As a boy, William was at Hawkshead Grammar School; after which he learnt and followed his father's trade of hat-making. In or about 1784 he married Jane Beck of Sawrey, who was three years younger than he was, and came of a family that ranked higher than the Towers. He and his wife settled at Hawkshead Hill on the road to Coniston, and within half a mile of High Cross. They had two sons born there, James in 1785 and Thomas Beck in 1787, and were still 'of Hill in Hawkshead' in 1791, when 'Mr Willm. Towers' subscribed 10s. 6d. to the New Library Fund at Hawkshead School. But in 1800, when they had a seven-month-old son baptized, he was registered as 'William Son of William Towers of Near Sawrey Gent'.[1] Evidently the elder William, or more probably his wife, had inherited enough to enable him to retire at an early

---

[1] Called 'Yeoman', 1799: see Additional Notes, Appendix V.

age. In the Hawkshead Church safe I unexpectedly found evidence of how he had used his leisure during the following years when, in 1950, I came upon a notebook of his consisting of single sheets stitched together and then bound; for it contained, firstly excerpts from the Hawkshead Parish Registers from their beginning in 1568 down to 1802, together with additions to some of the later entries, and secondly, statistical tables giving the monthly and yearly totals of baptisms and burials, of males and females separately, from 1568 to 1812, and of marriages from 1568 to 1752. Cowper, who later compiled some statistical tables down to 1704, was clearly unaware of the existence of this notebook; nor has it been mentioned by any other writer. With it were two loose sheets of notes by Towers on a few of the persons mentioned in the registers; but I did not notice or find anything about the Castlehows. So far as I am aware, William Towers' account of them never appeared in print; and there is no telling what happened to the rest of his manuscript. He and his wife continued to live at Sawrey, and are said to have built Towerbank, where she died on 7 November 1824, aged sixty-two, and he on 16 April 1836, at the age of seventy-seven.

Although I have not seen an account of Richard Castlehow's trial, it seems safe to say that he was convicted, and sentenced to a term of imprisonment. If that was his punishment, it follows that he was found guilty only of petty larceny, which was defined at that date as the theft of property of the value of 1s. od. or less; for had it been more valuable his crime would have been grand larceny, the penalty for which was then death by hanging. It will be remembered that the pettiness of Castlehow's thefts was mentioned by 'W.S.' in his note published in 1885; and that it was Castlehow's wife, not his widow, who had a little assistance in the form of poor relief in 1786–7 and again in 1791–2. I cannot, then, support Cowper's supposition, based as it was only on a very vague tradition, that the Castlehows were a band of robbers of whom Richard was the head, or his suggestion that they may have used their 'hill shelters', as he calls them, 'as rendezvous for sheep-stealing forays, and possibly for actual highway robberies'. More to the point, I consider, is his admission that he could get no precise information even from the oldest inhabitants about their criminal activities, for if these were limited to stealing things worth 1s. 0d. or less it is hardly likely that more could be gleaned about them a hundred years later than is found in 'W.S.'s' note, except of course from written records. Strangely for him, Cowper's account of the Castlehows is ill informed, and tendentious in that he heads it 'The Castlehow Robbers', and omits from his summary of the note just mentioned what the author of it had to say about the pettiness of Castlehow's thefts.

The third and last part of Fletcher Raincock's long reminiscence tells only of happenings at school, but as they arose out of the failure to arrest Jonathan Castlehow I will mention them here and now. When Fleck and the others, said Miss Saul, heard of the ruse that had enabled him to escape, and that Mr. Varty had been one of the men who went off in pursuit of his sister instead, they decided to write some verses about it. Here Bill Wordsworth was foremost among them, he being better at verse-making than any of the rest. But afterwards, though all had a hand in the game, it was Fleck and Ted Birkett who took the lead; and it was they who kept it up the longest. What they did was to recite the verses when Mr. Varty was within earshot, at first loudly enough for him to hear, but later they varied their tactics, sometimes raising and lowering their voices so that he heard only snatches of the verses, usually the parts they most wanted him to hear. He did nothing whatever to stop their game, but when the Master, Mr. Taylor, heard of it he very soon put an end to it. Fleck and Ted Birkett had to report to him every hour when the school was not in session, and each time he issued paper to them, and made them write out the verses in full, and to his complete satisfaction. That went on for a week or more; after which he summoned all the boys concerned to his study. Mr. Varty was there, and the Master told them to apologize to him, and to ask his pardon. This he granted; and they plagued him no more.[1]

---

[1] Budworth, in *A Fortnight's Ramble to the Lakes* (1810), p. 201, comments on how in 1797 he 'walked the complete round of the Lake Windermere from Hawkshead, by Newby-bridge, Bowness, and Ambleside. Once with Mr. Varty, an Usher at the Free-school; we started from the market-house, he wheeling a circumferenter before him the whole of the way, and without stopping for one moment, reaching the market-house again within six and a half hours, thereby ascertaining the distance to be twenty-six miles five furlongs.' Varty was probably never Usher: see Appendix IV.

Miss Saul added that the boys were not beaten; but apparently she did not say how, if at all, the lesser offenders were punished. Before the boys were allowed to go, Mr. Taylor warned them that if they visited the Castlehows again, now that one of them had been arrested for thieving and Jonathan suspected of it, they would be expelled from the school. They heeded his warning, Fleck said, and never afterwards went to Frank Castlehow's.

The Wanderer of the Excursion—James Patrick—inoculation— 'The Ruined Cottage'—Thomas Wishert—his daughter Sarah— letter of Isaac Swainson—David Moore—other Scotchmen

In the First Book of *The Excursion*, which is entitled 'The Wanderer', Wordsworth says of this title figure:

> We were tried Friends: amid a pleasant vale,
> In the antique market-village where was passed
> My school-time, an apartment he had owned,
> To which at intervals the Wanderer drew,
> And found a kind of home or harbour there.
> He loved me; from a swarm of rosy boys
> Singled out me, as he in sport would say,
> For my grave looks, too thoughtful for my years.
> As I grew up, it was my best delight
> To be his chosen comrade. Many a time,
> On holidays, we rambled through the woods:
> We sate—we walked; he pleased me with report
> Of things which he had seen; and often touched
> Abstrusest matter, reasonings of the mind
> Turned inward; or at my request would sing
> Old songs, the product of his native hills; . . .
>
> Still deeper welcome found his pure discourse:
> How precious when in riper days I learned
> To weigh with care his words, and to rejoice
> In the plain presence of his dignity!
>   (I.52–67 and 73–6)

He was born of God-fearing parents on a small hereditary farm among the hills of Athol, we are told. From his sixth year he tended cattle in the summer and went to school in winter; and afterwards, as a youthful herdsman, he borrowed what books he could, and now and again bought one. Urged by his mother, he later taught a village school for a short time, but resigned, and became a packman instead. In this way of life he continued till he had made 'provision for his wants'; whereupon he retired. But still, staff in hand, he liked to walk the public roads and the wild paths; and in summer he would often leave his home and journey far, revisiting scenes that 'to his memory were most endeared'.

This is not the literal truth, as Wordsworth himself makes plain, more especially in a prose note on the leading characters and scenes in *The Excursion* that he dictated to Miss Isabella Fenwick in 1843. After stating that books were Southey's passion, he adds that '*wandering*, I can with truth affirm, was mine; but this propensity in me was happily counteracted by inability from want of fortune to fulfil my wishes.' He then goes on:

But had I been born in a class which would have deprived me of what is called a liberal education, it is not unlikely that, being strong in body, I should have taken to a way of life such as that in which my 'Pedlar' passed the greater part of his days. At all events, I am here called upon freely to acknowledge that the character I have represented in his person is chiefly an idea of what I fancied my own character might have become in his circumstances. Nevertheless much of what he says and does had an external existence, that fell under my own youthful and subsequent observation.

Then he mentions two packmen,

An individual, named Patrick, by birth and education a Scotchman, followed this humble occupation for many years, and afterwards settled in the town of Kendal. He married a kinswoman of my wife's, and her sister Sarah was brought up from early childhood under this good man's eye. My own imaginations I was happy to find clothed in reality, and fresh ones suggested, by what she reported of this man's tenderness of heart, his strong and pure imagination, and his solid attainments in literature, chiefly religious, whether in prose or verse. At Hawkshead also, while I was a school-boy, there occasionally resided a packman (the name then generally given to this calling), with whom I had frequent conversations upon what had befallen him, and what he had observed during his wandering life, and, as was natural we took much to each other . . .[1]

In a pencilled note Mrs. Wordsworth says that 'Sarah went to Kendal on our mother's death, but Mr. P. died in the course of a year or two.' The Penrith registers record the baptism on 20 January 1775, of 'Sarah d. of M^r. John Hutchinson, Tobacconist, & Mary his wife', and the burial on 2 April 1783, of 'Mary, wife of Mr Hutchinson, Tobacconist'. Sarah, then, was eight when she went to live with the Patricks in Kendal; and as James Patrick did not die until 2 March 1787, she had nearly four years 'under this good man's eye'.

The two are depicted together in a charming little scene that Wordsworth wrote in 1802, but omitted from the final version of *The Excursion*. The scene is Hawkshead, the packman, in this version, called Patrick Drummond, who in his boyhood had herded cattle on a Perthshire hill-side for forty pence a year.

> We were dear Friends; I from my childhood up
> Had known him, in a nook of Furness Fells
> At Hawkshead, where I went to school nine years.
> One room he had, the fifth part of a house,
> A place to which he drew from time to time
> And found a kind of home or harbour there.
> He was the best Old Man! and often I
> Delight to recollect him, and his looks,
> And think of him and his affectionate ways.
> In that same Town of Hawkshead where we dwelt
> There was a little girl ten years of age,
> But tiny for her years, a pretty dwarf,
> Fair-hair'd, fair-fac'd, and though of stature small
> In heart as forward as a lusty child.

That introduces the pair of them; and it is all that concerns me here.[2]

I need hardly say that the references to Hawkshead are not to be taken literally, but one or two facts about James Patrick's later life, gleaned from the Penrith registers and Nicholson and Axon's *Older*

---

[1] *Prose Works of William Wordsworth*, ed. A. B. Grosart (1876), III, pp. 196–7.

[2] For the whole of the 'charming little scene' see *Wordsworth's Poetical Works*, V, pp. 405–8.

Nonconformity in Kendal (1915), may not come amiss. He was already settled in Kendal, it would seem, in August 1762, when he bought from a Mr. Archibald Lyle for £2. 2s. 0d. the seat or pew numbered 23 in the chapel in the Market Place erected in 1723 by the 'Protestant Dissenting Congregation of Presbyterians', whose principal Ministers during the eighteenth century were Dr. Caleb Rotherham from 1716 to 1752 and his son Caleb from 1754 to 1796. The chapel seated 200, and when it was built the pews were sold to help to meet the cost; and until the end of the century at least they were all privately owned. On 2 November 1763, 'James Patrick, Batch. of Kendal psh. & Mary Robison, spr. of this psh.' were married by licence at Penrith. He was then either forty-seven or forty-eight and his bride thirty-eight, according to the ages ascribed to them when they died. In the following year he subscribed £2. 2s. 0d. to the fund, amounting in all to £100, for 'discharging the mortgage on the Parsonage House in Finkle Street', and for repairing the chapel.

On 21 December 1766, Margaret, daughter of 'Mr.' James Patrick, Stricklandgate, was baptized at the chapel; and on 23 November 1767, she was buried in the chapel graveyard. The registers note that she 'died the 22nd of the small-pox by inoculation', which means that she was deliberately given a mild form of the disease so that she would be immune for the rest of her life from the severe and dangerous form of it. Introduced about 1720, inoculation was general in England during the second half of the eighteenth century: thus at Hawkhscad in 1797 no fewer than twenty pauper children were inoculated at a cost to the parish of £2. 10s. 0d. The risk was small, for at the worst only about 3 in 1,000 died of the induced small-pox. James and Mary Patrick were very unfortunate to lose Margaret as a result of having her inoculated. She was their only child, it appears from the registers, though there was a James Patrick junior among those enrolled as Special Constables in 1786 when the Kendal journeymen weavers were trying to improve their lot, and when outrages were attributed to them. This younger James is said to have been a member of the Market Place congregation, and there is little doubt that he is the James Patrick who with others signed on Christmas Day, 1788, a new set of rules for conducting the business of the chapel, for by then the elder James was

R

in his grave. A headstone set against the chapel wall bears this inscription: 'Near this place are buried John Patrick of Barnard Castle who died May 10, 1763. aged 51 years. Margaret the daughter of James and Mary Patrick who died Nov. 22. 1767. in her infancy. James Patrick of Kendal who died March 2. 1787. aged 71 years'. John Patrick may have been an elder brother of James the one-time packman, and the younger James a foster son of his namesake, and maybe a son of John. That is guesswork, however. In the burial register, in an entry dated 5 March 1787, James Patrick of Kendal is described as a 'Linen-draper', which may well have been his occupation during all or most of the twenty-five years he lived in the town. His wife Mary sold the pew he had bought in the chapel of his choice to a Mr. Waith for £2. 2s. 0d. in 1798. Probably she then returned to Penrith for the Registers there record the burial on 16 December, 1810, of 'Mary Patrick, widow, Town-end, aged 85'.

Wordsworth's conception of an aged packman whose character, convictions, feelings, and thoughts on 'Nature, Man, and Society' were the author's own, or what he thought his would have been had he followed the same calling, first found literary expression in 'The Pedlar', which began as an addition to 'The Tale of Margaret' or 'The Ruined Cottage', a poem first composed at Racedown and Alfoxden 1797-8. Mary Hutchinson asked to see a copy of it, and in writing to her from Alfoxden on 5 March 1798, Dorothy Wordsworth says: 'The Pedlar's Character now makes a very, certainly the *most*, considerable part of the Poem.' It was given greater unity by putting the story of Margaret's afflictions and sufferings into the pedlar's mouth, and at one time Wordsworth considered publishing it as a separate work; but in the end, and after a good deal of revision, it became the First Book of *The Excursion*, the site of the ruined cottage being removed for this purpose from a flat common in Dorset or Somerset to a tract of open moorland near Hawkshead. And that is all I need say, except that in the original, but not the final, version the packman is referred to as the 'venerable Armytage', and that he is stated to have been born of 'lowly race' on Cumbrian hills, and to have been a shepherd there before he adopted a wandering life.

From Wordsworth's creations in his own image I can now turn to packmen he may have known in the flesh during his schooldays at Hawkshead. Judging from the Parish Registers, and to a lesser extent from his own statements, men of this calling must have been a fairly common sight there in his boyhood; and on the evidence at present available it would seem that he saw more of them then than he ever did as a grown man. In the registers they are almost always described as Scotchmen wherever they were born and bred, and in 1779, the year in which Wordsworth entered the Grammar School, one crops up straight away in a baptismal entry made on 3 January, the beginning of which reads: 'John Son of Thomas Wishert Gallobarrow Waller Son of Thos. Wishert a Soldier & Scotchman . . .' He is, of course, the Thomas Wishert who, as a relative newcomer to the parish, married Sarah Tyson of Outgate in 1746. As stated earlier, they had five children. All of them were baptized at Hawkshead, John in 1747, Jane in 1749, Isaac in 1751, Thomas in 1754, and Sarah, after their father had joined the army, in 1757. In the baptismal entries his surname appears successively as Ushirt, Whichit, Wishirt, Wishert, and Whishirt. In each he is said to be of Outyeat, but in none is his occupation recorded.

Towards the end of 1753 he must have applied for Hawkshead to be certified as the Place of Legal Settlement of himself, his wife, and their children, as in the church safe I found a document which ran as follows:

The Examination of Thomas Wishart of Outyeat within the Division of Hawkshead with [Monk] Conistone and Skelwith in the County Palatine of Lancaster Shoemaker Taken upon Oath this Eighth Day of January 1754 touching and concerning the last place of legal Settlement of him the said Thomas Wishart his wife Sarah and their three Children John aged Six Years Jane aged four Years and Isaac aged two years before us Myles Sandys and James Machell Esquires two of his Majesty's Justices of the Peace and Quorum of and for the County Palatine of Lancaster aforesaid This Examinant being first duly sworn deposeth and saith That he was bound an Apprentice about Sixteen Years ago to one John Steel then of Abby Holm otherwise Holm Cultrum in the County of Cumberland Shoemaker, that he served him as an Apprentice under an Indenture in the

Parish of Abby Holm . . . for the Term of three Years and a half and upwards and inhabited in the said Parish during the said Term . . . and at the
Expiration of the said Term . . . removed from thence into the Parish of
Kirkbride in the said County of Cumberland and there resided with his
said Master under the said Indenture and served as an Apprentice about a
Year and a half but saith that his said Master was a Certificate Man during
the time he so resided with him in the said Parish of Kirkbride and further
saith that he hath not gained any legal Settlement since that time and
further also saith that his said Master dyed at Kirkbride aforesaid about the
End of the said Year and a half and that at his Death he the said Thomas
Wishart and the Widow of the said Master came to an Agreement for the
Remainder of the Term under the said Indenture and that by Virtue of the
said Indenture he apprehended himself bound to serve for the term of Six
Years from the Commencement of the said Indenture.

The statement is signed by the two magistrates as having been taken
and sworn before them, and Thomas Wishart, who could not write,
made his mark.

It was not until three years later that he was granted the Certificate
he sought, following a visit by the Overseer of the Poor for the
Hawkshead Quarter for the year 1756-7 to Abbey Holm and
Kirkbride in north-west Cumberland. This investigation cost the
parish £1. 1s. 0d., and Thomas Wishart's oath a further 2s. 0d.
When he got his Certificate he seems to have joined the army almost
at once, as his wife had 2s. 6d. a week in poor relief for the last quarter
of 1756-7, and from then onwards for some years, together with
extras such as 'her Lying in' when Sarah was born, and her house
rent. If, as is probable, Thomas Wishart was twelve when he was
apprenticed to John Steel, he would be thirty-one when he became
a soldier very early in 1757, and fifty-three when on 3 January 1779,
John Hodgson described him as 'a Soldier & Scotchman'. How many
of the intervening years he spent in the army is uncertain; but it
may be significant that when his wife was buried on 3 September
1776, she was not registered as such but merely as 'Sarah Wishert
Pauper from Outyeat'. The Poor Accounts for the Hawkshead
Quarter for 1776-7 might have been more informative, but I failed
to find them.

Another uncertainty is where he lived when he was not travelling with his pack. It may have been in Hawkshead Town in 'the fifth part of a house', but equally well it may have been at Outgate with his unmarried daughter Sarah. On 19 September 1783, she gave birth to a son, who was christened on 5 October, and entered in the registers as 'Thomas Bastard Child of Sarah Wishert of Outyeat'. Not long afterwards, and certainly before the end of 1783, the Overseer of the Poor for the Hawkshead Quarter paid 3s. 0d. 'For Sarah Ushard to Mʳ Gibson [attorney] for a Warrant', and £1. 1s. 0d. 'To Thomas Ushard Journey to Liverpool'. The object of this expenditure appears to have been to 'father the Child'; and I rather think it was Thomas Wishert senior, and not his son Thomas, who made the journey to Liverpool. In 1784 the Overseer paid 1s. 5d. on 20 May for 'one Gill of Brandy and one Quart of Ale For Sarah Usher to stop the Ague', and 2s. 4d. on 31 July 'for one Bottle of Wine for Sarah Usher by Doctor Robinson's Order'. In 1787-8 she was provided with 'a pair of Stock Cards' at a cost of 5s. 0d.; and in 1792 she is described in the Parish Registers as a pauper when 'John Bastard Son of Sarah Usher', born on 13 January was baptized on 26 February. On this occasion her lying-in cost the parish £1. 1s. 0d., and assistance for twelve weeks a further 6s. 4d.; and from then onwards she had a 'pension' of 6d. a week until 1800, when it was decided at a Vestry Meeting that it should be discontinued. On the whole, then, it seems unlikely that her father boarded with her. In the registers her age is given as eighty-eight when she was buried at Hawkshead on 30 December 1846, but in fact she was eighty-nine when she died.

The only other certain reference to Thomas Wishert is in the first of Isaac Swainson's letters from which I have excerpts. Writing to his father Joseph Swainson of Kendal on 2 April 1784, this Hawkshead schoolboy said: 'Thos Wishert the old Soldier whose stories I have often told you about cannot go on his rounds any more because of his legs being so bad. I gave him 2d. I had left of my weekly money as he is very poor now and not able to keep himself.' With this statement I will link a bare mention by John Ireland of *John* Ushirt, a Hawkshead packman who sometime between 1785 and 1788 called on him in Kendal to give him a message from Hawkshead. I did not connect this Hawkshead packman with

Thomas Wishert, the old soldier mentioned by Isaac Swainson, until I studied the Hawkshead registers some forty years later; but it then became clear that he was Thomas Wishert's eldest son, unless by any chance John Ireland was thinking of the father but misnamed him John, which is unlikely as he must have known the family well in his youth. 'John Wishert of this Parish and Margaret Martin of this Parish' were married at Hawkshead on 26 February 1770; but as they had no children baptized there the registers furnish no information as to where they lived or what his occupation was. His wife Margaret died on 10 December 1802, aged sixty-three, and was buried at Hawkshead on the 13th. In 1822 he was being boarded at the expense of the parish at Roger Ground. He died there at the age of ninety-one (not ninety-two as stated in the registers), and was buried at Hawkshead on 21 September 1837, leaving no descendants as far as can be ascertained.

What happened to his father, who was still under sixty in 1784, is a question as yet unresolved. Judging from the Poor Accounts that are available he was never in receipt of parish relief at any time up to 1800; whilst the Thomas Usher who had small sums from the Parochial Charities Fund in 1784 and 1790 was undoubtedly his son Tom, whose widow Anne and a young daughter of his later received grants from this fund. Moreover, Thomas Wishert, 'Soldier & Scotchman' was not buried at Hawkshead. It may be, then, that his legs improved sufficiently to enable him to continue as a packman. In any event, Wordsworth is almost certain to have known him. But if his stories related mainly to his soldiering days it is doubtful whether they would appeal as much to the future author of *The Excursion* as they evidently did to Isaac Swainson, who later enlisted and, as a Kendal inscription states, was a Lieutenant in the 66th Regiment of Foot when he died at St. Domingo on 31 March 1796, aged twenty-six. Thomas Wishert, however, is likely to have been the first packman Wordsworth encountered at Hawkshead, and it could have been he who, in the poet's own words,

> from a swarm of rosy boys
> Singled out me, as he in sport would say,
> For my grave looks, too thoughtful for my years.

According to Arthur Brydson, the packman with whom Wordsworth became intimate at Hawkshead was a young, not an old, man. He learnt this from Mrs. Benson Harrison, who had heard speak of him when she was living at Rydal Mount and afterwards, but could not recollect his name. From entries in the Hawkshead registers I should say it was David Moore, who can be identified without any doubt as the 'David Moore, travelling Mech^t, of Ulverston', who was married there by licence on 11 October 1779 to 'Mary Park, of Torver, Spinster'. A daughter of Edward and Margaret Park of Brocklebank Ground, she was baptized at Torver on 19 June 1759; and her first born, 'John s. of David & Mary Moor', who died at an early age, was christened there on 5 March 1780. David Moore was not a native of Ulverston, and I do not know for certain where he was born. There are indications, however, that he was the 'David s. of John Moor, Malster', who was baptized at Gressingham, eight miles north-east of Lancaster, on 25 July 1756; and that he had an elder brother John, not christened there, who was of Broughton-in-Furness when on 15 April 1771 he married Jane Taylor at Hawkshead, and, I may say, signed the register. He and Jane, I take it, were the parents of the 'John Moor of Ulverston, Travelling Chapman', who was married there to 'Eleanor Coward, Spinster by Licence', on 3 June 1805. Anyhow, this couple had four children baptized at Ulverston, John in 1806, Jane in 1808, 'Ellinor' in 1809, and William in 1811 (when they were living at Penny Bridge), the father, whose surname is usually entered as Moore, being described first as a pedlar and then as a mercer.

The registrations at Hawkshead in which David Moore's name appears extend from 1782 to 1790, and here they are in full.

1782   Peggy Daugh^t. of David Moore Town a Scot[c]hman Born May ye 11th Baptized Sept ye 8th.

1784   John ye Son of David Moore of Town a Scotchman Died Sept. ye 19th Buried ye 21st in C^{h}yard Aged 4.

1784   Edward ye Son of David Moore Town a Scot[c]hman Born July ye 24th Baptized Nov:^{r} ye 14th.

1786   Mally Daughter of David Moore of Town Born Jan^{ry} 20 Baptized June 25.

1789   David Son of David Moore of Town Mercer Born July
24ᵗʰ 1788 Baptized May 3ᵈ 1789.

1790   William Son of David Moore of Town a Scotchman Born
Feb.ʳʸ 13 Baptized March 14.

In 1787 the Overseer of the Poor for the Monk Coniston and Skelwith Quarter paid 1s. 6d. 'To David Moore for a Neckcloth for
Henry Hodgson'. And among the Hawkshead tradesmen whose
bills John Wordsworth and his executors were called upon to pay
was David Moore, mercer, a fact noted by Gordon Wordsworth
in the article he contributed to the *Cornhill Magazine* for April
1920.[1]

In the light of these records there can be little if any doubt that
David Moore was the packman, residing occasionally at Hawkshead
while Wordsworth was a schoolboy there, with whom he had
'frequent conversations', and of whom he remarked that, 'as was
natural, we took much to each other'. Judging from the time that
elapsed between birth and baptism of all but one of his Hawkshead
children, it rather looks as if David went far afield with his pack;
and if that was so he should have had a good deal to tell Wordsworth
'upon what had befallen him, and what he had observed during his
wandering life'. His home was in Hawkshead Town, as the registers
repeatedly state; and it may well have been of him that the poet
was thinking when he wrote of Patrick Drummond that at Hawkshead 'One room he had, the fifth part of a house'. That might have
sufficed at first, especially as he was away from home so much, but
hardly when he had four or five children. Where he settled his wife
and family after Hawkshead ceased to be his headquarters I do not
know, for I have no information about him or them subsequent to
William's baptism in 1790.

There were yet more packmen Wordsworth might have known
during his schooldays at Hawkshead, and it is only fair that some
reference should be made to them. Another of the genealogical
entries John Hodgson made in the registers in 1779 reads: 'Hannah
Daughter of John Watson Far Sawrey Shoemaker Son of John
Watson a Scotchman by Hannah his Wife The Mothers name Mally

[1] P. 417.

D^r. of Bartholomew Purcel an Irishman Born Jan ye 28 Baptized Feb ye 21st'. When I copied this registration my interest was in Bartholomew Purcel, and I regret to say I have no notes on the elder John Watson. The next relevant entry in the registers is one made in 1782: 'John The Son of Francis Watt, a Scotchman, Born July ye 5th Baptized Octo: ye 27th.' Like David Moore, and at much the same time, this packman evidently found accommodation for his wife in the parish whilst he was away on his rounds. But there the similitude ends, for Francis Watt is mentioned in the registers on this one occasion only. It is possible that he was a Scot.

The same may be said of Niel Matheson, another visiting pack-man. His name does not occur in the registers, but in the church safe I found a bill of his in copper-plate handwriting, clearly his own. Dated 'Hawkshead', and on the next line, 'Jany. 18, 1786', it was made out to 'Mr Giles Bolton' and paid by him on the same day. It was as follows:

> Bot. of Niel Matheson for Thos. Walker a poaper
>
> | | £. s. d. |
> |---|---|
> | To 5 yds Duffle at 2/7 pr y^d | 0 12 11 |
> | To Trimmings for D^o | 0 2 1 |
> | | £0 15 0 |

Before 'Jan^y.' there was a faint 'May' in another hand; but probably it was only a reminder that the cost of the duffle and trimmings should be included in the Poor Accounts for the year ending 11 May 1786. The purchaser, Giles Boulton, was a Hawkshead tailor; and as he was elected Churchwarden for the Hawkshead Quarter at Easter, 1783, and for the Monk Coniston with Skelwith Quarter a year later, it is not unlikely that he was Overseer of the Poor for one or the other during the year 1785–6.

That makes six packmen Wordsworth could have known when he was a schoolboy at Hawkshead. And possibly there was one more, for in 1787, just after he had left for Cambridge the following entry was made in the parish registers: 'William Jamieson a Tradesman from Paisley in North Britain Died Nov^{br} 16 at Red Lion, Town. Buried the 18th in Church Yard. Aged 49.' The difficulty about this entry arises from the use of the word 'Tradesman', which occurs in no other registration during the second half of the eighteenth century. The usual local meaning at that date was a man who had served an apprenticeship to a trade or craft such as weaving or carpentry, and then followed it as a means of earning his living. As applied to William Jamieson, however, it almost certainly meant that he was a trader of some kind; and that being so, there is a chance that he was a 'Scotchman' as well as a Scot, for if not, it is hard to see what brought him to Hawkshead.

William Rigge—the slate business—hostility to Grammar School boys and their 'revenge'—David Huddlestone—John Hubbersty

When William Wordsworth and his wife had tea with the Braithwaite Hodgsons at Greenend, Colthouse, in the 1840s, and the two men afterwards talked of their school days, and people they had then known, Wordsworth spoke of William Rigge of Walker Ground, a Quaker slate merchant commonly called 'Slaty' Rigge, perhaps to distinguish him from the William Rigg of Greenend who died in 1786, aged eighty-three. William of Walker Ground, who married Agnes Warriner in Hawkshead Church in the summer of 1734, buried her in the Quaker sepulchre at Townend, Colthouse, in May 1781. He himself died on 22 March 1791, and was interred at the same place, the records of which state that he was 'abt 84' at the time of his death. Till then he was head of the firm of William Rigge & Son of Hawkshead, who produced and marketed Coniston green slates, his partner being his only known son Thomas of Keen Ground, which like Walker Ground, is on the western side of Esthwaite Vale and near Hawkshead Town. Green slates, the hardest and costliest of all roofing slates, were got by the Rigges and others largely from quarries on Coniston Old Man and at Tilberthwaite in the chapelry of Church Coniston, but also on Holme Ground Fell and at Hodge Close in the Monk Coniston and Skelwith Quarter of Hawkshead Parish. Writing in the 1770s of this cluster of quarries, Thomas West says that they were 'the most considerable slate quarries in the kingdom', and that the principal of them were then in the hands of a Hawkshead firm of Rigge, meaning William Rigge & Son, who exported 1,100 tons a year and upwards.[1]

From the quarries it was carted to Kirkby Quay at the head of Coniston Water and piled there. A little fleet of sailing boats then carried it down the lake to Nibthwaite Wharf, from which it was carted either to Penny Bridge or to Greenodd, and there loaded from piles on to ships doing a coastal trade, and carried on them to ports in different parts of the country. The total cost of transport from the quarries down to the sea was from 6s. 10d. to 7s. 10d. a ton. I cannot give its exact prices at the various points. But Cowper[2] quotes Bishop Richard Watson of Calgarth, Windermere, as saying in 1786 that Westmorland roofing slate sold in Kendal at from £1. 3s. 4d. a ton for the coarsest sort to £1. 15s. 0d. a ton for the finest, and that gives some idea of the cost of Coniston green slate in the 1780s if allowance is made for the fact that it was dearer than the blue slate Westmorland produced. The Hawkshead Church-wardens paid William Rigge 1s. 6d. a load for slate in 1781, but neither the weight nor the quality is specified. Earlier they had twice paid him 2s. 0d. a load for it.

At Greenend Wordsworth seems to have spoken of William Rigge of Walker Ground merely as an old Quaker slate-merchant who was for ever complaining of things the Grammar School boys did, and of the noise they made at their games; after which, if Miss Mary

---

[1] A conversation about the slate trade, showing more of the connections between people in Wordsworth's Hawkshead, is reported by John Gibson (of Rydal) to Sir Michael le Fleming in a letter of 21 May 1783: 'On the 4th. Inst. Edward Barrow and I called upon Mr. Thos. Rigge and I read him that part of your Letter respecting the Carriage of the Slate down the Water, and he did not seem agreeable to let him have it. He said he would be glad to comply with your request as much a[s would be?] convenient, but he hoped you would excuse that of the Water Carriag[e...?] Year, as Mr. Kirby and his Father had been Employd. in it from their first sending them down the Water, and that he Kirkby had Built a new Boat for that purpose only Two or Three years since. And also that Edwd. Barrow had his Horses in such ill Condition, that he would write to you about it. I Beg leave to say that the scruple respecting the Boat may be remedied by you taking it at a reasonable Price, which may be to the same purpose as Building a new one (And if Desired) Edward Barrow may Employ the same Men to Row the Boat.' (The Record Office, Kendal.) The Mr. Kirkby here would of course be David Kirkby of Thwaite (see above, pp. 65–6), and the Water, Coniston.

[2] *Hawkshead*, p. 293, citing Watson's *Chemical Essays*.

Hodgson remembered rightly, he mentioned ways in which they retaliated against 'Old Slaty', as they called him. One was to line the road as he approached, and gaze at him in stony silence as he rode past, for he was always on horseback. Thinking he would end this, he one day stopped and greeted them, but instead of replying verbally they sprang to attention and saluted him. That was more than he could bear, for he disliked anything military; and, being by nature an irascible man, he struck out at them with his riding whip; whereupon they broke silence with cries of 'Shameful, sir, shameful!' He rode off, but quickly returned and apologized to them for losing his temper and striking. And then, said Wordsworth, he spoiled the good impression he had made by telling them that failure to restrain his anger was hurting him more than the lash of his whip could have hurt any of them. Wordsworth, then a new boy, witnessed the incident, but had no part in it.

Another example of retaliation against 'Old Slaty' that Miss Mary Hodgson recalled him giving was an individual effort by David Huddlestone, a farmer's son from Langdale who boarded at Townend, Colthouse. Having discovered by observation through the windows and door where William Rigge sat in the Friends' Meeting House, and that he was in the habit of putting his hat under his seat, this 'quiet but purposeful elderly boy', to use the description of him attributed to Wordsworth, thought it might be possible to set a 'clock hen', otherwise a broody hen, on some eggs under the seat before anyone arrived for the meeting, or on the evening before. And with the aid of another boy he somehow succeeded in doing it, with the result that 'Old Slaty' again hurt himself by failing to restrain his anger, and according to report was asked to leave the meeting. He was also known to the boys as 'Mr. Tompeg', a name that originated with John Hubbersty, the son of a Kendal attorney. This boy, who was at Cambridge when Wordsworth first went to Hawkshead School wrote 'Old Slaty' a letter which began 'Mr. Tompeg, Sir,' and ended 'Your humble servant Dobbin'. It purported to be from his old mare, whom he rode to the Meeting House on Sunday as well as to the quarries on week days, and after pointing out that he in his great wisdom considered that one day in seven should be set apart for rest and reflection, it asked that she, too, should have one day of the week free from the labour of carrying him on her back. 'Tompeg' is compounded of the names then given to two kinds of slate: *Tom* to the 'third sort' or coarsest of the roofing slates, the finest being known as London and the second as Country; and *Peg* to the very small slates sometimes fixed on the walls of houses to make them more waterproof. And in south Westmorland, I may add, country children used to call any draught horse 'Dobbin' if they did not know its real name.

Both these boys became well known. David Huddlestone is 'David Son of David Huddlestone of Low-brick-how in Little Langdale' who was baptized at Grasmere on 6 February 1765/6. His parents' eldest son, he was one of a large family, all of whom were born at Low Birkhow and christened at Grasmere. When he was married there on 25 December 1790, he was described in the registers as a 'Banker's Clerk', and was in fact employed in the Kendal bank opened by Messrs. Maude, Wilson, and Crewdson on 1 January 1788. Rather surprisingly he became one of the proprietors of this bank, just when I do not know,[1] but on 8 February 1812, it was stated in the local press that the partnership between T. H. Maude, C. Wilson, W. D. Crewdson, and D. Huddlestone had been dissolved. The reason was the retirement of Tom Maude from banking. David Huddlestone remained a partner for a further eleven years when, on 11 January 1823 it was announced that he had 'retired from a lucrative situation in the Kendal Bank where he had been laboriously employed for upwards of thirty years, and . . . fixed upon a beautiful situation amongst the lakes of Ellterwater for his future residence'. Having built Elterwater Hall for his own occupation—his wife died at Kendal in 1815—he then turned his attention to the manufacture of gunpowder, and to this end he and his partners built works at Elterwater, which 'commenced operations in December 1825', and two or three years later were producing from 4,000 to 6,000 pounds of powder a day. In 1824 the company that bore his name had erected a school for the township of Great and Little Langdale 'in consideration for a plot of land given them for the use of their mill'. Nor was gunpowder making his

[1] At least by 28 November 1810; see Chandler, *Four Centuries of Banking*, II, pp. 76–7.

only activity during the latter part of his life, for in the 1829 Directory it is stated that he 'raises large quantities of fine blue slate' in Troutbeck Park, an estate of some 2,000 acres. He died at Elterwater Hall on 27 October 1832, and was buried at Grasmere.

John Lodge Hubbersty, to give him both of his baptismal names, was the second son of Zachary Hubbersty, a Kendal attorney who after his marriage to Phillis, daughter of John Lodge of Barnard Castle, lived at Fallen Yew, Underbarrow, where she died in 1781 at the age of sixty-one, and he in 1789, aged fifty-four. The New Library records show that both their sons were at Hawkshead school by noting that in 1797 'Messrs. Zachary and John Lodge Hubbersty, formerly of this School', presented *An Ecclesiastical History Ancient and Modern*. By J. L. Mosheim, D.D. Translated from the original Latin by A. Maclaine, D.D. (New edition. 5 vols. 8vo. London, 1774). On 30 June 1777, at the age of eighteen John was admitted as a Sizar at Trinity College, Cambridge, of which he became a Scholar in 1779. In the following February, however, he migrated to Queens' College, and it was from there that as 9th Wrangler he graduated B.A. in 1781. In the same year he was elected to a Fellowship, and from then until his death in November 1837 he was first a Fellow and later a Senior Fellow of Queens' College, Cambridge, for he never married. On 20 December 1782, he was admitted at Lincoln's Inn, and in due course became a barrister. Not content with that, he became an M.D. in 1796, but chose the law as his profession, and was Recorder of Lancaster from 1799 to 1837, and Deputy High Steward of the University of Cambridge. And in a summary that is cited in Venn, a work to which I am largely indebted for information about him, it is also stated that he was 'a cotton-spinner and a bankrupt'.[1]

There is a memorial by Flaxman in Kendal Parish Church, the inscription on which reads:

Sacred to the memory of Zachary Hubbersty of Great Winchester Street, London, Esquire, who died on the 23rd September 1797, in the 41st. year of his age, leaving a disconsolate widow and six children. Few equalled and none excelled him in professional knowledge, and strict integrity; and of whom the learned and virtuous Lord Eldon in a letter of Condolence

[1] See J. A. Venn, *Alumni Cantabrigienses* (1940–54).

to the deceased's brother observed, 'His loss is not more to be lamented by his family than by the profession, of which he was an ornament and an honour'. Also of Phillis Sarah Hubbersty his second dau. who in the following year lost her life by falling into the sea from the pier in Whitby harbour. This monument is erected by John Lodge Hubbersty Esqre . . . who has never ceased to lament the loss of the best of brothers and friends.

Specifications for the new Market House—uses of it—Jenny Rigg's tale—family of Nanny Holme—Jenny Rigg's subsequent life—connection with T.W.T.'s family—origin of Nanny's Stone

In the Second Book of *The Prelude* the following passage occurs in the 1805 text of the poem:

A grey Stone
Of native rock, left midway in the Square
Of our small market Village, was the home
And centre of these joys, and when, return'd
After long absence, thither I repair'd
I found that it was split, and gone to build
A smart Assembly-room that perk'd and flar'd
With wash and rough-cast elbowing the ground
Which had been ours. But let the fiddle scream,
And be ye happy! yet, my Friends! I know
That more than one of you will think with me
Of those soft starry nights, and that old Dame
From whom the stone was nam'd who there had sate
And watch'd her Table with its huckster's wares
Assiduous, thro' the length of sixty years.

(II.33–47)

For 'joys' the word 'sports' is substituted in the 1850 text.

The return to Hawkshead of which Wordsworth speaks was almost certainly his visit in 1799 in company with Coleridge. He had not been there since 1789, the year when it was proposed to pull down the dilapidated Market Shambles, a two-storey building measuring 47 feet by 18 ft, and to build a new Market House which was to be 75 feet by 23 feet, and to include a yarn market as well as shambles on the ground floor, and a Great or Court Room, commonly called the Assembly Room in the 1790s, on the upper floor, with Lodging Suites at either end. These proposals were submitted to the Lords of the Manor in the autumn, and new trustees appointed and a subscription list opened at about the same time; and then on 14 December the contracts for the work involved were assigned. They show that the length of the building had been increased to 78 feet 'without the walls', and the breadth to 25 feet 5 inches in the middle and 24 feet at the two ends. The dimensions of the Great Room are given as 30 feet long, 25 feet 9 inches wide, and 14 feet high from floor to ceiling, and of each of the Lodging Suites as 20 feet square. There was to be a staircase of blue flags at the west end, and the whole of the exterior was to be rough-cast. The Lords of the Manor, who were to receive 6d. a year rent for this larger building, were assured that it could be erected without 'incommoding the public or interrupting private property'. But to make room for it the great stone which had stood at the higher or southern end of the Market Square, and evidently quite close to the original Market Shambles, had to be got out of the way.

The uses to which the Great Room was put during the early years of its existence appear to have been limited. Manor Courts were held there once a year, or oftener if need arose. But when the Twenty Four met to transact parish business, which happened three times a year, it was agreed in 1790 that it should be at the Red Lion on Easter Tuesday, the Tanners' Arms on the Tuesday after Trinity Sunday (later altered to Whit Tuesday), and the King's Arms on St. Stephen's Day; whilst the rules of the Amicable Society of Hawkshead, a Friendly Society established in 1792, show that its annual feast and monthly meetings were held at one or other of the local inns, the choice being made by members at the previous meeting, and falling first on the house kept by Giles Boulton, tailor and inn-keeper. When the Market House trustees first let the Lodging Suites they asked the tenants to allow their rooms to be used in connection with the Great Room on special occasions. This request became a requirement when, on 24 November 1794, the suite at the western end was let to Mr. George Jackson, attorney, for a term of seven years, beginning on the 12th of May following, at a rental of £3. 19s. 0d. a year, this being the highest offer made for it. It was then stipulated that the trustees should have the use of

12. Hawkshead Church from the east end, a photograph taken before 1875 when the white rough-casting was removed. Churchend, the stone seat running the breadth of the church, supports the tombstones on the church wall.

13. Hawkshead Grammar School, founded 1585. The school was rebuilt c. 1675; and repaired

the entrance-room or kitchen and ·of the parlour or sitting-room on 'every Ball-night, or Assembly, in the Court or Great-room, [and] at the general Anniversary Hunt; as also on any other public Night whereon the said Great Room is so made use of. But if on more than two nights in any one year the trustees have the use of his rooms, the tenant is to have 10s. 6d. deducted from his rent for every night over and above two; and in any event he is to be indemnified by the trustees against damage done on any such occasion.'

Shortly before my mother's marriage, which took place in 1873, her grandfather John Wilson, with whom she was then living at the Causey, Windermere, engaged a young girl named Jenny Rigg, a Hawkshead farmer's daughter, to help in the house and with the women's work out of doors; and before she had been with him very long it was noticed that she used a simile unfamiliar to the rest of his household. An example of it my mother cited was: 'It'll cost as mich ta git shut on it as Nanny Staen (or t'rocking staen) did.' Asked about it, Jenny explained that it was an old saying in her family, and dated back to the building of the present Market House, to make room for which a great stone at the top end of the Square had been broken up and removed. An old body who sold ginger-bread and parkins, small cakes and pies, and other confections was accustomed to set them out on this stone, she said, and when she heard that it was to be broken up she made a fuss, saying that her living and that of her family depended on it. Always known as Nanny, she came from Sawrey, and had a string of daughters, all unmarried, who baked the things she sold. A Mr. Rigge, a wealthy slate-merchant who had something to do with rebuilding the Market House, asked her how much the stone was worth to her, and when she replied 6d. a week, he offered to give her that sum for the rest of her life: she was very old, and he thought it would save further trouble, at no great cost to himself. 'But what about my daughters?' Nanny asked. 'No', he said, 'the offer is for your lifetime only.' In the end she accepted it. But, according to Jenny, the joke was that she lived to a very great age, getting on for one hundred. Mr. Rigge died before her, but as long as she was alive someone had to go on paying her 26s. a year out of the money he

s

left. Hence the saying that it would cost as much to get rid of it as Nanny's stone did; a saying that undoubtedly prolonged the period over which some memory of her and it survived.

A year or two later, when the work my father was then doing took him to Far Sawrey on several occasions, he learnt that Nanny had lived there, and that her surname, which Jenny Rigg did not know, was Holme, but he could not discover her husband's name or occupation, or anything else that was new about her and her daughters except that they had a pony and cart, and that her baptismal name and that of one of her daughters was Ann. In the Concordance at the end of Eric Robertson's *Wordsworthshire*, which was published in 1911, the old dame mentioned in Part II of *The Prelude* is identified as Nanny Holme, but there is no reference to Nanny in the body of the work, and no information in the Concordance as to who she was or where she lived.

The Hawkshead Parish Registers, I found, furnish a number of details about her that supplement the traditional story of her and the great stone that bore her name. To begin at the end, there is this entry, made in 1805: 'Ann Holme of Far Sawrey Widow Died May the 10ᵗʰ Buried 12ᵗʰ in Church Yard Aged 95 years'. It undoubtedly relates to Nanny, for though there was a contemporary Ann Holme of Far Sawrey, her sister-in-law in fact, she was described as a spinster when she died in June 1795, at the reputed age of eighty, an underestimate by four years as she was baptized on 24 December 1710, as 'An Daughter of Clement Holme of Sawrey'. This Clement Holme was of Cunsey Forge when his son John, who became Nanny's husband, was christened on 23 September 1705. As he and Nanny were not married at Hawkshead I do not know her maiden name, but there are indications that she may have been the 'Ann Daughter of Thomas Atkinson of Hawksᵈ. Town' who was baptized on 22 April 1711. If she was, she would be ninety-four when she died. Anyhow she and her husband, who is more than once described as a tailor, settled at Far Sawrey, and remained there for the rest of their lives, he dying of a 'decline' on 4 September 1779, at the age of seventy-four. He had twice been Surveyor of Highways for the Low end of Claife in 1740/41 and in 1759/60.

He and Nanny had five children christened at Hawkshead, the

eldest, whose baptismal name is not entered in the registers, on
19 March 1733/4. The remaining four were girls, whose baptisms
were recorded on the following dates: Agnes on 29 May 1737;
Dorothy on 1 January 1739/40; Ann on 5 May 1744; and Jane on
19 January 1747/8. Though they all lived to a good age, none of
them ever married. Jane died on 14 October 1806; Dorothy on
23 October 1809; Ann on 26 January 1814; and Agnes on 25 March
1814. They are all registered as being of Far Sawrey or Sawrey when
they died, and are believed to have carried on Nanny's business
when she became too old and after her death. Clement Holme,
Nanny's father-in-law, is stated to have been a pauper, and his
widow Agnes a pensioner, in the register entries recording their
burials on 7 February 1732/3 and 8 October 1735, respectively; but
neither John, her husband, nor Nanny herself was ever in receipt of
poor relief, it would seem, nor were any of their daughters.

The Mr. Rigge, a wealthy slate merchant who, according to the
traditional tale, compensated Nanny for the loss of the great stone
in the Market Square on or beside which she set out her stock-in-
trade, can only have been Thomas of Keen Ground. He was one of
the Market House Trustees appointed in 1789, and subscribed 5 gns.
towards the cost of rebuilding. Moreover, the Parish Registers
record that he died on 4 November 1798, which is about six and a
half years before Nanny did. Jenny Rigg, on whose version of the
traditional story I have relied since my father confirmed it, was a
daughter of James Rigg of Outgate, farmer, and his wife Mary,
and was baptized on 19 December 1858. Her father, who had earlier
farmed at Low Wray, was a son of John Rigg of Outgate, a 'clogger'
remembered long after his death as the maker of the Hawkshead
Great Clog, which in Cowper's day was exhibited in the Brown
Cow Inn, and was, he says, 'twenty inches in length, eight inches
wide at the bottom, and sixteen inches from welt to welt across the
front'. It was made for an Outgate mole-catcher named John
Watterson or Waterson, who had one elephantine foot, the other
being normal. Jenny Rigg (Jane in later life) cannot have been more
than fourteen when she first went to the Causey. She stayed there
in the service of John Wilson for several years, and subsequently
became the second wife of his grandson John, the eldest son of

Thomas Wilson of Windermere. With him she emigrated to Ontario, where his uncle George Wilson had by then acquired more land than he could farm, and had offered him some of it if he would go out. Not long after their arrival, however, he was killed in a railway accident, and Jenny came home again, and eventually settled at Violet Bank, Hawkshead, after living for a time with various relatives in turn, including my parents at a time when my mother needed help.

And now for a word or two about Nanny's Stone. The fact that it was also known as the Rocking Stone suggests that it was what geologists term a 'perched block', that is a large piece of rock which had fallen on to a glacier, and been carried downwards on it as it advanced, and then, when the ice melted, left stranded, poised on a pinnacle or an edge. There is ample proof of glaciation in the vicinity: the two round green hills known as Keen Ground High and Charity High, situated between Hawkshead and Hawkshead Moor, are of morainic origin; boulder clay is not uncommon; and rocks rounded and striated by glacial erosion certainly occur. But whilst 'Nanny's Stone' probably got where it did as a result of glacial action of one kind or another, there is no evidence, apart from its other popular name, that it was perched and could be rocked. Sometime after 1805 in a re-working of the passage relating to it in *The Prelude* there is a line which reads: 'Gone was the old grey Stone; that 'Stone of Rowe.'[1] The allusion, which the poet finally rejected, is one I do not understand, and on which I have seen no comment; but I doubt whether it has any local significance.

> *Extract from 'Lines left upon a Seat in a Yew Tree'—Joseph Budworth —the Rev. William Braithwaite—Satterhow—at Cambridge—the Waterside boggle—removal of seat and tree—Braithwaite's activities in the parish—re-pewing the church and other alterations—division and sale of pews—gift of a hearse*

Another Far Sawrey resident of whom Wordsworth wrote, this time at greater length in both verse and prose, was the Rev. William

[1] 'Rowe' was Helen Darbishire's reading in 1959; it is a good guess, but one cannot feel certain about it as the word is cramped towards a margin. 'Rowe' is not a name in the Hawkshead Parish Registers.

Braithwaite of Satterhow, who can be identified from what
Wordsworth tells us of him as the recluse with whose habits and
character he is concerned in an early poem entitled 'Lines left upon
a Seat in a Yew-tree, which stands near the lake of Esthwaite, upon
a desolate part of the shore, commanding a beautiful prospect'. The
poem was begun in 1787, whilst he was still at school; completed in
1797, and published in 1798; but in the form we have it only the
opening lines can have been written in boyhood. Following them
there is a description of the poor man that I will quote for the sake of
those who are not familiar with the poem.

Who he was

That piled these stones and with the mossy sod
First covered, and here taught this aged Tree
With its dark arms to form a circling bower,
I well remember.—He was one who owned
No common soul. In youth by science nursed,
And led by nature into a wild scene
Of lofty hopes, he to the world went forth
A favoured Being, knowing no desire
Which genius did not hallow; 'gainst the taint
Of dissolute tongues, and jealousy, and hate,
And scorn,—against all enemies prepared,
All but neglect. The world, for so it thought,
Owed him no service; wherefore he at once
With indignation turned himself away,
And with the food of pride sustained his soul
In solitude.—Stranger! these gloomy boughs
Had charms for him; and here he loved to sit,
His only visitants a straggling sheep,
The stone-chat, or the glancing sand-piper:
And on these barren rocks, with fern and heath,
And juniper and thistle, sprinkled o'er,
Fixing his downcast eye, he many an hour
A morbid pleasure nourished, tracing here
An emblem of his own unfruitful life:
And, lifting up his head, he then would gaze
On the more distant scene,—how lovely 'tis
Thou seest,—and he would gaze till it became

Far lovelier, and his heart could not sustain
The beauty, still more beauteous! Nor, that time,
When nature had subdued him to herself,
Would he forget those Beings to whose minds
Warm from the labours of benevolence
The world, and human life, appeared a scene
Of kindred loveliness: then he would sigh,
Inly disturbed, to think that others felt
What he must never feel: and so, lost Man!
On visionary views would fancy feed,
Till his eye streamed with tears. In this deep vale
He died,—this seat his only monument.

(ll. 7-47)

With the didactic ending of the poem I am not concerned here.

In a prose note on the poem dictated to Miss Fenwick in 1843 Wordsworth, after stating that it was composed in part at school at Hawkshead, goes on to say:

The tree has disappeared, and the slip of Common on which it stood, that ran parallel to the lake, and lay open to it, has long been enclosed, so that the road has lost much of its attraction. This spot was my favourite walk in the evenings during the latter part of my school-time. The individual whose habits and character are here given was a gentleman of the neighbourhood, a man of talent and learning, who had been educated at one of our universities, and returned to pass his time in seclusion on his own estate. He died a bachelor in middle age. Induced by the beauty of the prospect, he built a small summer-house on the rocks above the peninsula on which the ferry-house stands. . . .

This property afterwards past [sic] into the hands of the late Mr. Curwen. The site was long ago pointed out by Mr. West in his *Guide* as the pride of the Lakes, and now goes by the name of 'The Station.' So much used I to be delighted by the views from it, while a little boy, that some years before the first pleasure-house was built, I led thither from Hawkshead a youngster about my own age, an Irish boy, who was a servant to an itinerant conjurer. My motive was to witness the pleasure I expected the boy would receive from the prospect of the islands below, and the intermingling water. I was not disappointed. . . .[1]

[1] *Prose Works of William Wordsworth*, ed. A. B. Grosart, III, pp. 8-9. The first two sentences of the extract here refer particularly to the yew tree and its immediate surroundings on the shores of Esthwaite. Wordsworth then digresses to comment on

Joseph Budworth, in a footnote to his poem 'Windermere', written in November 1797 and published in the following year, refers to the same rocky hill above the Windermere ferry peninsula.

Since the commencement upwards of 40,000 different plants, besides acorns, have been planted. The Rev. Mr. Braithwaite of Satterhow, the liberal owner, spares no expense. The features of the hill, the constant verdure, the apparent falling of small rocks, unite in a grand effect; and I do not hesitate to say, are unequalled by any object of the Lake; and as a scene in winter is unrivalled.[1]

This statement, together with Wordsworth's prose note, and what can be gleaned from the Hawkshead Parish Registers, prove beyond doubt that the unhappy man described in 'Lines left upon a Seat in a Yew-tree' was the Rev. William Braithwaite of Satterhow; and all I need do now is to outline the story of his life, and say more about his activities in the 1790s.

His parents were the 'Willi^m. Braithw^te. Satterhow Far Sawrey and Agnes Grisedale Hawkes^d.' who were married by licence at Hawkshead on 8 July 1751, his father being a grandson of the William Braithwaite of Satterhow, yeoman, who in 1707 purchased the right of ferriage across lake Windermere, the two ferry boats then in use, and other property that went with the right of ferriage. William and Agnes Braithwaite had three children: William who was baptized on 29 November 1753; Margaret, who was born two years later, and died in 1769; and Ann, who was about ten years younger than her brother. When Margaret was christened on 28 November 1755, her father was stated to be of High Satterhow,

Braithwaite and his Windermere property. But he does have one further comment about the yew tree: in a draft for his *Guide to the Lakes* (see W. J. B. Owen, ed., *Lyrical Ballads 1798*, 1967, p. 128) 'the remnant of a decaying yew tree' 'yet to be seen', and the 'seat from which the solitary humour of the framer may not unfairly be inferred . . . the boughs had been trained to bend round the seat and almost embrace the Person sitting within allowing only an opening for the beautiful landscape.'

[1] Joseph Budworth's comment is amplified by a footnote added to West's *Guide to the Lakes* (8th ed., Kendal, 1802): 'In consequence of the act for inclosing Claif-Common, the late Rev. W. Braithwaite purchased the ground including this station, and erected an elegant and commodious building thereon, for the entertainment of his friends, called *Belle-View*; he also planted the adjoining grounds, and altered the direction of the road, which was rugged and unsafe, and rendered it more convenient by carrying it nearer the margin of the lake.' See also Additional Notes, Appendix V.

a house situated on Briers Brow about midway between Far Sawrey and the ferry. There is a ground floor plan of it in Cowper's *Hawkshead*.[1] The place was then (1898) in ruins, 'but especially interesting', says Cowper, 'as showing a complete yeoman's house of apparently the early seventeenth century, with large additions, probably late in the same century'. The whole house had mullioned windows, of limestone in the older part, and of oak in the newer, each with an iron safety bar. Not far away was Low Satterhow, a farm that seems to have been tenanted at the relevant date by the 'John Braithw^te. Farmer Satterhow', who was buried at Hawkshead on 10 February 1777. In recent years High Satterhow has been largely rebuilt.

As a boy young William evidently attended Hawkshead Grammar School, as among former pupils who subscribed to the New Library Fund in 1790 was the 'Rev^d. Willm. Braithwaite, M.A., Satterhow, Hawkshead', his contribution being £1. 1s. 0d. He then proceeded to St. John's College, Cambridge, whose Admission Registers, which have been edited, with notes, by Sir Robert Forsyth Scott, state that he was born at Hawkshead, Lancashire, but name neither his father nor his school. He was admitted sizar on 8 July 1772, and pensioner on 3 November in the same year, having gone into residence on 8 October. He never became a Scholar of the College; and ruled out the possibility of being elected a Fellow by not taking the Mathematical tripos, then the only avenue to an Honours Degree and academic preferment. This undistinguished record does not disprove Wordsworth's assertion that he was 'a man of talent and learning'. He himself had a very similar one when, from 1787 to 1791, he was at the same college, the only difference being that he was admitted a Foundress Scholar early in his first term, for he, too, did not take the Mathematical Tripos, and so lost the chance of obtaining a Fellowship. After graduating in 1776, William Braithwaite took Holy Orders, but neither Scott nor Venn says when or where he was ordained.[2] It seems certain, however, that he was not offered a Living until some years later, in fact not

[1] P. 153.
[2] R. F. Scott, *Admissions to the College of St. John in the University of Cambridge*, Part IV, 1767–1802 (1931); Venn, *Alumni Cantabrigienses*, part II, (1940–54).

until Wordsworth's schooldays were all but over. And that may well have been the crowning disappointment which led him to turn away indignantly from the world, and with the 'food of pride' sustain his soul in solitude. This withdrawal seems to have taken place sometime between 1780, in which year he became an M.A., and 1785.

Just when his father died I cannot say: he was not buried at Hawkshead, and the probate abstract of his will is not in the Lancashire Record Office at Preston. But his name does not appear in the detailed account, dated 16 August 1779, of a 'Parish Collection . . . on his Majesty's Letter for the use of The Society for the Propagation of the Gospel in Foreign Parts', whereas that of 'Mrs. Braithwait Satterhow' does, together with the sum she gave, which was 1s. 0d. Her name and contribution were entered, I found, not under 'Claife Division', but in the columns headed 'Hawkshd. fd. and Fieldhd.'; and an examination of the names adjacent to hers showed beyond dispute that she was then a householder in Hawkshead Town. And because of the situation of the aged yew-tree under which her son built himself a seat, it looks as if he, too, was living at the time at Hawkshead, which he certainly did when nearing his end.

Thanks in the first instance to Cowper, it is known that the little strip of common on which the tree stood was at Waterside in Claife, towards the head of Esthwaite water, and about two and a half miles from Satterhow, but little more than a mile from Hawkshead on the opposite side of the valley, and less than a mile from Colthouse, which is on the same side. It is where the road from these two places to the Ferry runs close to the water's edge; and the lovely distant view to which Wordsworth refers in the poem is of the mountains of southern Lakeland, seen as the eye ranges from west to north; a more comprehensive view than a low lying position usually affords. When William Braithwaite made and used his yew-tree seat the only habitation anywhere near it—and it was quite close— was the Claife Poorhouse, which for the past hundred years and more has been known as Waterside Cottage. From there for a quarter of a mile or so in the direction of Near Sawrey, the road was believed to be haunted, and Cowper has a good deal to say about the Waterside boggle, which he considered to be the most widely known, most feared, and least explicable of the apparitions reported to have been seen on the road along the margin of Esthwaite Water. It appeared to night pedestrians in a variety of shapes, but in the stories told of it, the narrator usually likened it to a large white calf, fox, or dog, or to a strange beast, neither calf nor donkey, that had something in common with both. It appeared suddenly from nowhere discernible; and when closely approached, disappeared just as suddenly leaving no trace; following which, says Cowper, there would be 'a sound resembling that of a cartload of stones being emptied into the lake, or sometimes into the road'.[1] These details suggest that the Waterside boggle should be classed as a barghest, an apparition that was greatly feared because the sight of it was held to be a portent of death.

But Cowper also mentions two spectres in human shape said to have been seen at Waterside, one being a man in light blue, of whom no other particulars are given, and the other an old woman in a wide-brimmed bonnet who figures in a story told by a nineteenth-century Vicar of Hawkshead, identified by Miss Mary Hodgson as her father's friend George Park the younger, who was minister from 1834 until his death in 1865. He was walking home from Sawrey one moonlight night, he used to say, when at Waterside he suddenly saw a woman in an old-fashioned bonnet walking in front of him in the direction he was going. He caught her up, and, thinking she was sure to be a parishioner, he bade her 'good-night'. Getting no response, he half turned to see who the unsociable old body was; and to his horror he saw, in Cowper's words, 'a death-like face with goggle eyes, which gleamed like the red bull's eye at the back of a carriage lamp'. Then suddenly she vanished, seemingly through a wall-gap a yard or two ahead. On looking through it, however, he could not see her anywhere. It was early spring, and there was a light covering of snow on the ground; but no foot-prints in it were visible on the other side of the wall, and only his own on the road they had come. Such was the vicar's story, which I have no excuse for quoting except that it helps to show what an uncanny place Waterside was considered to be.

The 'Act for dividing, alloting and enclosing the Commons, or

[1] See Cowper's *Hawkshead*, pp. 328–30, for a discussion of the Waterside boggle.

waste lands, called Claife Heights or Claife Commons', dated 34 Geo. III (1794), but not passed till 1799, applied to Waterside, which was allotted to Greenend, Colthouse, then in the hands of William Taylor. Fenced in the early years of the nineteenth century, his allotment or intake seems to have been a strip about a mile long on the lowest slopes of Claife Heights and at their foot, with his Poorhouse about midway between its northern and southern extremities. The greater part of it was to the east of the road, and of this all the higher land later became Waterside Wood. William Taylor evidently left the aged yew-tree and the seat beneath it as he found them; but when Braithwaite Hodgson took over Greenend about 1820 he quickly got rid of both. He did so, Miss Mary Hodgson said, to prevent his cattle poisoning themselves, as he found that they were given to nosing round the old tree, probably out of curiosity. Dr. William Allen (1865–1950) gave as an added reason that the seat was haunted by the ghost of a hermit who had once made it his abode; a statement that is hardly surprising in view of the reputation Waterside had. Not far from the site of the yew tree Braithwaite Hodgson destroyed was another, Cowper says, which in his day was sometimes identified by enthusiastic visitors, and even pointed out, he believed, by local inhabitants, as 'Wordsworth's Yew'.[1]

In my view Wordsworth's poetic description of the recluse of the yew-tree seat is essentially true, but not necessarily strictly factual in every particular, as in the opening lines of the poem he says that this lonely yew tree was far from all human dwelling whereas, as I have said, it was close to the Claife Poorhouse, though distant from all other habitations. It is probable that Wordsworth first became acquainted with the Rev. William Braithwaite during his last two years at school, after his great friend John Fleming had left, and when his favourite evening walk was to Waterside, crossing Smooth Beck on the way, no doubt the 'sparkling rivulet' alluded to in line 3. Almost certainly he would have heard about him earlier, for it would be strange if Ann Tyson, not to mention others, did not talk to him of this descendant of a long line of local statesmen who was so untypical of his class, at any rate at that time in his life. How

[1] *Hawkshead*, pp. 416–17.

well Wordsworth knew him is a question to which I have no answer. So I will pass on to point out that he was still alive when 'Lines left upon a Seat in a Yew-tree' was first published,[1] despite this Wordsworth wrote: 'In this deep vale/He died—this seat his only monument.' Why Wordsworth called the Vale of Esthwaite, which is open and wide, a deep vale is hard to understand.[2]

It seems safe to say that William Braithwaite's life as a recluse ended in 1787, for in that year, as Sir Robert Scott notes in his *Admissions to St. John's*, he was instituted Vicar of Burton Pedwardine, Lincolnshire, on 5 September, and Vicar of Riseley, Bedfordshire, on 15 October. It is not known who presented him to either of these benefices, which he held in plurality till within a year of his death. Unless it was during the first two years, he did not reside in either parish, but appointed a curate in each to serve in his stead. In the 1790s, however, he entered more and more fully into the life of his native parish. His subscription in 1790 of a guinea to the New Library Fund at Hawkshead School has been mentioned already. And in 1789 or 1790 he signed an appeal addressed to and circulated among the 'Landholders, Customary Tenants, and Principal Inhabitants of the Parish and Manor of Hawkshead', adding after his signature that he would give 5 gns. towards the cost of building the proposed Market House. Only the Lords of the Manor, besides William Matthews, a London merchant, and George Law,[3] a newcomer from Ulverston, promised to give or gave more than he did.

[1] The poem was published in *Lyrical Ballads* (1798), and was largely written, whatever its Hawkshead origins, in the first half of 1797. T.W.T. here, in the search for literal correspondences, perhaps does not sufficiently take into account the literary traditions behind this poem. Wordsworth's own unpublished note on it (see p. 258 above, note 1) seems indeed to suggest that he inferred the character of his recluse from the characteristics of the yew tree seat. The rather stereotyped figure is descended from a long tradition of literary melancholy; the use of an actual seat in a yew tree as the basis for an emblem of such a figure is typically Wordsworth's. In poems slightly later than this one, and notably in *The Prelude*, the Hawkshead figures more fully emerge into a particular, though never literal, clarity.

[2] Again T.W.T. makes perhaps an over-literal response; but it is interesting to compare A. Walker's comment on Hawkshead: 'Its situation . . . is pretty—it is in a narrow well enclosed vale, at the head of a Lake called Ested Water.' (*Remarks . . . Tour from London to the Lakes*, London, 1792, p. 58.)

[3] Also a merchant; see Additional Notes, Appendix V.

Nor was it long before he became an active participant in parish affairs, for in 1792 he was chosen as one of a committee of ten, consisting of the minister, three Churchwardens, and six landowners, who were to supervise the work of re-pewing the church, adding a vestry, with a room beneath it big enough to house a hearse, effecting other improvements within the church, and making two new approach roads to it from the Market Square. The main work, namely reseating and the provision of a vestry, had been resolved upon, and agreed to by a majority of parishioners, as early as 1763, when it was stated that the 'common forms or seats', which were backless, were 'old, decayed, and in a ruinous condition'; but nothing was done then. Nor was it in 1778, even after every detail had been thrashed out in the previous year, including the appointment of an arbiter should clamour or dispute arise over the allocation of pews. In 1792, however, when the decisions reached in 1778 were approved after slight revision and with some additions, application was made on 27 November for a faculty to carry out the work; and it was in this application, a copy of which I found in the church safe, that the committee of ten were named, apparently for the first time. The faculty was granted on 1 May 1793, and on the following 30 July detailed specifications were drawn up. As we saw earlier, John Usher and his partner Thomas Johnson of Ambleside secured the wallers' work, which they undertook to do for £36. The accepted tender for the joiners' work was one of £188 put in by Oliver Barrow of Cartmel and George Taylor of Ulverston.

The specifications included in the contracts were full and precise, and one of the tasks of the committee would be to see that there was no departure from them. Among those relating to the pews was this: they were to be of 'red deal without sap' (a late substitution for Riga deal), except for the soles and floor joists, which were to be of oak. The soles were to be 5 inches square and 'properly supported from the surface of the Burying Ground', the joists 4 inches wide and $2\frac{1}{2}$ inches thick, the pews 3 feet 6 inches high, with floors 1 inch thick, and seats 1 foot broad and $1\frac{1}{2}$ inches thick; and if they had doors, as all the statesmen's pews were to have, the door-frames must be $1\frac{1}{4}$ inches thick, and the panels, which were to be raised on the outside $\frac{3}{4}$ inch thick. There were other pew measurements and specifications, but I have quoted enough, I think, to show that in supervising the reseating of the church the committee had more to do than to ensure that the pews were erected according to a plan prepared in 1777 that neither Cowper nor I could find.

Besides re-pewing and the addition of a vestry,[1] which was to have a window with a sash and a 'Fashionable grate with freestone hobs and slabs', the work to be done in church included moving the pulpit to its earlier and present position against the second pillar of the north arcade, and improvements to it, among them the provision of a 'sound-board'; the removal to fresh sites of the reading-desk and font; taking up the flooring flags in the middle and side aisles, and relaying them properly between the soles of the new pews; and paving with new flags the 'Ile in the W. end of the Church'. Outside, the only constructional work to be done was the making of two regularly ascending roads from 'the Public market place or street . . . with a Breast Wall to the said street'. Each road was to be 12 feet wide, and to have a gate into the churchyard. The decision to have these roads was taken soon after the Churchwardens had been authorized on 11 May 1792, to purchase a parish hearse. The church had to be ready for use on Christmas Day, 1794.

In the eighteenth century the only properties in the parish that were assessed for church and other rates were the ancient customary estates or tenements, and it was the holders of these, commonly described as the owners, who alone had the right to have pews in the 'body' of the church, which should mean the chancel and nave, but is clearly a reference to the nave only in the vestry minute dated 24 March 1778. It was then decided, and the decision was adopted in 1792, that the pews to be erected there, were to be shared equally by the four Quarters of the parish, though there had been a consecrated chapel at Satterthwaite since before 1650, and in 1766 it had been licenced for baptisms, marriages, and burials. The way in which the pews were to be divided between the Quarters was agreed upon in 1777, confirmed in 1778, and adopted in 1792. The names of the Quarters written on pieces of paper were to be put into one hat, and the numbers 1, 2, 3, 4 written on other slips into

---

[1] Wordsworth disliked this: see Additional Notes, Appendix V.

a second hat. A disinterested person was then to draw a name with one hand and a number with the other; after which pews were to be chosen in the following order:

1	2	3	4
2	3	4	1
3	4	1	2
4	1	2	3
1	2	3	4

The drawing made in 1778 gave the Quarter corresponding to these numbers as Satterthwaite no. 1, Claife no. 2, Hawkshead no. 3, and Coniston with Skelwith no. 4. Whether it was held to be still valid in 1794 is not clear. What is certain is that the Satterthwaite Quarter, which included Grizedale, Dale Park, Rusland, and Graythwaite, got its full share of the statesmen's pews though it did not need them. From what is said later, it appears that there were twenty-one rows of seating, with four pews in each row, two on either side of the middle aisle. The rows must have been very close together, and the pews only long enough to hold three or four people without crowding.

The division into 'private shares, of the pews allotted to each Quarter, and the method of paying for them, were settled at a 'General public Vestry meeting' held on 17 December 1794. The Monk Coniston and Skelwith resolution was that the 'proprietors of ancient messuages [in the Quarter] should pay the expense of erecting the pews; and should be entitled to them as marked and numbered in the order they have unanimously chosen them.' Then follows a list signed by all the proprietors, a few of whom held two ancient 'tenements' (for example John Benson, Bull Close and Skelwith Fold) and in consequence paid for and were entitled to two pews. The Hawkshead resolution, which has twenty-one signatures, was that the pews belonging to the Quarter should be 'sold to ratepayers of the Quarter. No person to buy two sittings until every ratepayer has had opportunity to buy one. Sale to be 14 Jan. next. Expense of erecting pews to come out of proceeds; surplus to be returned'. The Claife resolution was to the same effect. It has only ten signatures, possibly because Upper Claife, and Colthouse especially, had been a Quaker stronghold, and still was, though to a less extent. With regard to the Satterthwaite pews, Thomas Bellingham, Chapelwarden, stated that it was 'the sense of the said Quarter' to let them for one year, but nothing about paying for their erection. No exception seems to have been taken to his statement; which rather suggests that these pews had been let before, perhaps to statesmen in other Quarters who wanted more seats in the nave than their own pews afforded.

At the auction on 14 January 1795, it was resolved to sell by pews those marked H. 1 to 21 and C. 1 to 21. For C. 15 'W^m. Braithwaite Satterhow' paid £9. 0s. 0d., and for C· 16 'W^m. Braithwaite for Town End Mich¹. Satterthwaite' paid £9. 15s. 0d., the highest price any of the Claife pews realized, the lowest being £1. 11s 0d., and the total for the Quarter £109. 19s. 6d. as against £125. 11s. 0d. for the Hawkshead Quarter. At the beginning of the eighteenth century, when there were Satterthwaites at Townend, Greenend, Beckside, and the Crag, all of them were Quakers, but I am not sure whether the Michael who was at Townend, Colthouse, in the 1790s was a member of the Society of Friends. Whether he was or not, there is no doubt whatever that the Rev. William Braithwaite of Satterhow bought C. 16 as well as C. 15. Being a bachelor he had no need of a second pew, and I fancy his main motive in buying it was to swell the Claife total, about which he may well have been anxious, seeing that the resolution to sell the pews bore only ten signatures.

Of the other pews, it was resolved in 1792 that eight in the south aisle and seven in the north aisle should be reserved for 'the common use of the Parish'; that there should be 'a pew for common use without a door on each side of the passage into the intended vestry'; and that the Churchwardens' pew, after it had been moved to the wall on the south side of the gallery stairs, should be 'in common without a door'. There was to be a new pew for the Churchwardens with a door, and three pews in the gallery for the psalm-singers. No mention is made of pews in the chancel, or of who might use the remaining pews in the side aisles, or of where the Grammar School boys sat or were to sit; but at a vestry meeting on 3 December 1794,

14. The Writing Master's book-plate in John Gillies' *History of Ancient Greece*, a gift from four boys admitted to Cambridge from Hawkshead in 1787.

15. The large school-room on the ground floor, Hawkshead Grammar School, after the 1891 restoration. Wordsworth's name, shown here, is carved into the desk by the door.

when it was decided that the pews should be painted a light stone colour on the outside and upper railing, it was also agreed that the little pew erected where the pulpit had stood should be 'appropriated' to the Master of the Grammar School. Its founder, Edwin Sandys, Archbishop of York, ordained in 1588 that the 'scholemaster, usher, and schollers, shall sytt together in some conveniente place in the chauncell', and the senior boys still sat there in the 1790s both before and after the re-pewing. As a new boy in 1790, Braithwaite Hodgson had to sit at the east end of the south aisle facing the chancel, his seat being a backless form; and doubtless it was from one of these that Wordsworth when he was new to the school found pleasure in watching the Parish Clerk give the psalm-singers their keynotes on his pitch-pipe, for the gallery could be seen from there with no more movement than a turn of the head. When Braithwaite Hodgson was at school the rest of the boys sat in the south aisle in a body, and after the re-pewing he himself had a seat there, but never advanced far enough to have one in the chancel. Needless to say I had this information from Miss Mary Hodgson, whose inquiries from her father had resulted from what Wordsworth had said when he was at Greenend.

It is doubtful whether the wide, regularly ascending roads to the church were ever made, and all but certain that the parish hearse was never purchased. There is no further mention of it in the Vestry Minutes, and none at all in the Churchwardens' Accounts up to 1800, beyond which I did not look. On the other hand, as Cowper discovered,[1] there are several entries at the end of an older account book which begin:

Hawkshead From the 30th of May 1796 The Hearse belonging to the Bailifwick and Division of Claife lent out
   29th Augt 1796 to Cartmel with the Corpse
     Of Mrs Taylor of Hawkshead . . . . 5s. 0d.

The same charge was made when the hearse was lent on 31 March 1797, to take the corpse of Agnes Vickers of Oxenfell to Grasmere; but a later entry reads: '1799 Oct[br] 12 for carrying the Corpse of John Kirkbys Wife from Knipefold to Tottlebank 2 Days, 7s. 6d.'

[1] *Hawkshead*, p. 437.

T

Tottlebank in the neighbouring parish of Colton has a Baptist chapel founded as early as 1669, and it must have been there that the burial service took place. But it is strange that the hearse was required for two days when one sufficed for a burial at Cartmel.

What I am leading up to is a memorandum I found among the loose papers preserved in the church safe at Hawkshead. It was headed 'Claife Hearse May 30 1796', and was in the handwriting of George Pennington, Parish Clerk from 1785 until his death in 1802. It read:

The Revd Mr Braithwaite of Satterhow stated this day that the Hearse he had lately given to the Claife Division of the Parish and which was now housed at Colthouse was to be lent as well to Inhabitants of the Hawkshead and Conistone Divisions who lived at a distance from Hawkshead. That for the present no charge was to be made for it for burials there but only if the Corpse was carried outside the parish for burial when the charge was to be Five Shillings That a separate account was to be kept of any monies received for its use and That the borrower was to pay for any damage done to it while on loan to him.

This memorandum, which affords further proof of the Rev. William Braithwaite's generosity, makes no mention, it will be noticed, either of the Satterthwaite Division of the parish or, of the burial ground attached to Satterthwaite Chapel.

The Twenty Four—parish administration—bequests for charity—rise in cost of assisting the poor—renting of Sand Ground—clothes for paupers—pauper children—refusal of smaller statesmen to undertake parish duties—introduction of payment

Not later than 12 May 1796, the donor of the hearse had become a Sidesman for the Low End of Claife. The Twenty Four, as the Sidesmen were usually called, are referred to as early as 1585 when, as the result of a petition from Hawkshead, commissioners appointed by order of Queen Elizabeth met there as instructed, and examined on oath 'all the head parishioners and also XXIIII personnes of the most auncient substanciall and best credyte chosen and appoynted for the well government and oversighte of the said parish and church'. And that, the oldest, is as good a definition of the Twenty

Four as any. It is not known who chose and appointed them in the first instance, but from 1694 onwards there is ample evidence that it was the Sidesmen themselves who filled vacancies as and when they arose through death or retirement, the changes being noted on some but not all of the lists entitled 'Sidesmen in being'. During the eighteenth century fresh lists were entered in the parish books in 1704, 1716, 1736, 1751, 1766, 1783, and 17 May 1796, and it is in the last of these that the Rev. William Braithwaite's name appears for the first time. There is reason to think, though, that he was appointed Sidesman for the Low End of Claife in 1793 in succession to his kinsman George Braithwaite formerly of Harrowslack.

Consisting mainly of superior statesmen, but with a sprinkling of gentry including the head of the Sandys family seated at Graythwaite, the Twenty Four must have enhanced the prestige and added greatly to the strength of the parochial administration; whilst the fact that they were a permanent body whose composition changed only gradually must have done much to ensure stability and continuity of policy and practice. And these things mattered the more since parish officers normally served for one year only, and then never again or not till long afterwards; and since Churchwardens, who ranked first among them, were elected, not on the ground that they were specially suitable, but because, as holders of ancient customary estates, it was their turn to fill the office for a year. It was contrary to canons 89 and 90 for Churchwardens to serve for longer than that at a time, and they rarely did so at Hawkshead in the eighteenth century, and then only in exceptional circumstances. But it was very common for retiring Churchwardens there to hold office in the following year as Overseers of the Poor for the same Divisions of the parish.

Bishop Francis Gastrell in his *Notitia Cestriensis*, after naming these Divisions, adds: 'for wch there are four Churchw. chosen by Min. and 24'. He had this information early in the 1720s from the Rev. William Bordley, who was minister from 1720 to 1742, and a native of the parish, his father, also the Rev. William, having been Master of the Grammar School from 1647 to 1669. Choosing merely meant deciding whose turn it was in each of the several Quarters (about which there was a mistake, almost immediately corrected, in

1721), and approving a substitute on the rare occasions when this was necessary. It appears that the minister and Twenty Four continued to nominate the Churchwardens up to and beyond the end of the eighteenth century. The same is true, I believe, of the Overseers of the Poor, who came into being in 1601, when it was enacted that every parish must maintain or relieve its own poor, the cost to be met by laying a rate, for in the same act magistrates were directed to appoint in each parish three or four substantial persons being householders to act, along with the Churchwardens, as Overseers of the Poor. As they were accused of relieving their friends too generously, it was subsequently laid down that fresh Overseers must be elected each year. At Hawkshead in the eighteenth century the statesmen served in turn for one year for the Quarters of the parish in which they had an ancient customary messuage. The only difference from Churchwardens I noticed was that being a dissenter was not necessarily a bar as the following note shows: 'Mr Sandys has promised ye 24 to be Overseer of ye poore for Walkergr^d. Being a Quaker he C^{ld} not be Churchw^n'. It refers, I found, to Samuel Sandys of Roger Ground, 'the ancient Friend and writer of the Records of Hawkshead Meeting' who died in 1755. As owner, or more correctly holder, of a customary estate at Walker Ground he served as Overseer of the Poor for the Hawkshead Quarter for the year beginning 12 May 1719. Sometimes the unnamed 'occupiers' of an estate are listed as having been Churchwardens or Overseers in place of the owners or holders. This happens, too, in the lists (available for the years 1716 to 1767) of Surveyors of the Highways, parish officers who also seem to have been elected by the Twenty Four. From seven to ten, not all of them statesmen, were appointed each year for districts such as Low End of Claife, Hawkshead Fieldhead, and Skelwith. But I do not remember seeing their detailed accounts, or any mention of the Surveyors prior to 1713, though they are believed to have existed during the latter part of the seventeenth century. In the second half of the eighteenth century they were elected to office on St. Stephen's Day.

In 1721 the Twenty Four agreed and promised that each and everyone of them should and would forfeit a shilling if he failed to appear in Hawkshead Church at the time appointed by usual notice for their meeting there to transact parish business, or send a reasonable excuse for his absence, allowed to be sufficient by the majority of the Twenty Four then and there assembled. They agreed and promised, too, that Sidesmen should and would each forfeit a shilling if they absented themselves 'without an excuse or reason given & allowed as above mencon'd' from either of the two usual parish meetings held on the feast of St. Stephen and Tuesday in Easter week. It was further agreed that the forfeits or fines received should go 'towards the defraying of the expences of such of the Said four and twenty as shall at the severall appointed times appear'. Then follow the signatures of all the Twenty Four, and a note saying that George Banks then retired and William Kirkby was elected in his place. The church at 10 o'clock in the morning continued to be the place and time of meeting for the transaction of parish business at least until the 1760s. But in or about 1790, when the forfeit of a shilling for non-attendance at meetings was either reaffirmed or reintroduced, it was laid down that the forfeitures were to be expended each time for the benefit of the 'House' where the meeting was held. As we have seen, that was the Red Lion on Easter Tuesday, the Tanners' Arms on the Tuesday after Trinity Sunday, and the King's Arms on St. Stephen's Day. The Twenty Four still met at other times as well, and doubtless it would be at one or other of the inns. Even when they met in church it was their custom to resort to one afterwards to refresh themselves before they parted; a custom not peculiar to Hawkshead.

It was the duty of the Twenty Four to help and advise the parish officers, and to see that they fulfilled their duties. The clearest proof of the latter is in the minutes of their meeting on 31 May 1725, when the sixteen Sidesmen then present resolved that if any parish officer neglected the duties of his office to the detriment of any of the several Divisions of the parish, or refused or failed to render his account when lawfully summoned to do so, or if any person whatsoever misapplied parish money, he was to be presented, in other words brought before the proper ecclesiastical or civil court, at the expense of the whole parish. It was then decided to present forthwith William Dixon of Dixon Ground, Church Coniston, tanner, who was not a parishioner, and George Harrison of Coniston

Waterhead, yeoman, who was, and that the cost to the parish was to be laid as a Poor Rate. The charges to be preferred against them were not recorded. Later in the century it was noted that 'Sam Sandys Overseer of ye Poor (for the Hawkshead Division) for 1764 gave no account at all', but nothing is said about his being presented. He was Samuel of Roger Ground, son and heir of the 'ancient Friend' lately mentioned, and had been Churchwarden for the Hawkshead Division for the previous year, and as such had produced an account at the end of his term of office. When elected Churchwarden, he was not a member of the Society of Friends; but neither was he a baptized member of the Church of England, it would seem.

The laying of Poor Rates required magisterial sanction, but in other financial matters the Twenty Four were the ultimate parochial authority. They approved the laying of Church Rates, for example, and settled the rateable values of the various customary estates; and the investment of charitable bequests could be made only with their consent or on their direction. The earliest proof of the latter is in the following minute:

Be it Remembered that so many of us as are here present (ye 26 Day of Decemb^r 1726) viz: of ye 24 do freely give our consents yt ye 10 li left to ye poor & ye 10 li to the minister by ye Last Will & Testant of Geo: Banks of Bank-groung [*sic*] shall be let out by the Churchw^{ns} & Overseers of ye poor of ye Bayliffewick as ye said Will directs with prop^r securities for the same & ordr our names to be subscribed as followeth.

The number of signatures is fourteen and beneath them, in a different hand from the minute are the words: 'pray rememb^r the fines then spent'. The testator, George Banks of Bank Ground, Monk Coniston, was a member of the Twenty Four from 1702 or earlier until his retirement in 1721, and was Churchwarden in 1716. The poor who were to benefit from his first £10 bequest were those of the Bailiwick of Hawkshead, which comprised the Hawkshead and Monk Coniston-with-Skelwith Divisions of the parish, with the possible exception of Brathay. The interest on the minister's £10 was to be paid to him annually for preaching a sermon on Easter Monday.

In the 1750s all but one of the charitable bequests for the poor of the Bailiwick of Hawkshead or some part of it were consolidated into one fund, which in 1758 is stated to have amounted to £208. 8s. 0d., including George Banks' £10 and another of £5 for the minister for additional sermons. It was the sum total of twelve legacies, by far the largest of which was the £126 left by George Rigg, Parish Clerk, in 1706 or 1707. The consolidation was the work of the Twenty Four, or of the Sidesmen for the two Divisions concerned. And the same may be said of the framing of a new description of the poor who were to benefit; a description contrary to George Rigg's in that it ruled out those in receipt of parish relief. This change was made in or before 1770, from when there was an annual distribution in church in the month of April. The interest available was £8. 0s. 8d., of which 12s. 9½d. was due to the minister. A record of the sums paid and to whom in the years 1770 to 1830 is preserved in an account book entitled 'Objects of Charity', and I noticed that old Daniel Mackreth (of 'The Two Thieves') received 7s. 0d. in each of the years 1778 to 1781. At that time and later the recipients were given a good dinner at the Tanners' Arms before they went home, the ringing of the church bell being the summons to it as it had been to the distribution. The cost of the dinner, I need hardly say, did not come out of charity money: it was met by private benevolence.

During the short time the Rev. William Braithwaite was one of the Twenty Four—for he died early in 1800—'Mr' John Jackson of Bank Ground, who for many years had been a Sidesman for the Monk Coniston and Skelwith Division, invested £50 in 3% Consols in the names of the Rev. Reginald Braithwaite, Minister of Hawkshead, Joseph Varty, Overseer of the Poor for the Division above named, and Edward Backhouse, Churchwarden for the same Division, the indenture being dated 4 May 1798. It declared that the stock was to be held by them and their successors in office in trust, and that every half year, in the vestry of Hawkshead Church, they should 'pay and divide the dividend to such poor widows and other necessitous poor persons within the said division, who should have their legal settlement there, and should not receive any weekly pension besides an allowance for house rent. . . .' It provided that 'the parish clerk of Hawkshead should have sixpence for opening the church door and ringing the church bell on the day of such half yearly distribution, and should also have a reasonable allowance for making a fire on those days in the vestry'. As provision was made by the donor for the continuance of the charity, the Twenty Four readily approved his directions, but later decided that the distribution should be annual and at Candlemas, a time of year when a fire in the vestry would be very welcome. The aged poor of the same Quarter of the parish had long shared on Christmas Eve the annual rent (less two small charges) of an estate at Oxenfell which had been purchased with money left for their benefit by Miles Sawrey in 1713. With accrued interest his legacy of £50, contingent on the death of his daughter Margaret during her minority, had amounted to £72 when it came available; that was enough to buy the Oxenfell farm.

Three grave issues faced the Twenty Four during the closing years of the eighteenth century: the height to which the cost of poor relief had risen; the passing in 1796 of a new Poor Law Act that was calculated to increase the cost still further; and the threatened breakdown of the accustomed system of parochial administration owing to the difficulty, acute in the Hawkshead Quarter, in maintaining the necessary succession of Churchwardens and Overseers of the Poor. Indeed the later 1790s were critical years, for it is true to say, I think that the turn of the century coincided with the beginning of the end of the old order.[1]

Judging from the figures for the Bailiwick of Hawkshead, which are the only ones available for the period, there was a sixfold increase in the cost of maintaining and assisting the poor during the last quarter of the eighteenth century, the rises being from £43. 9s. 8d. for the year 1774–5 to £259 17s. 8½d. in 1799–1800 for the Hawkshead Quarter, and for the same years from £39. 1s. 3d. to £254. 17s. 6¾d. for the Monk Coniston and Skelwith Quarter. Two contributory causes were the very sharp rise in the cost of living, and the growing competition of factory-produced woollen yarn with that spun at home. A third reason was that Hawkshead had never fully conformed to the Poor Law Act of 1723, which in the interests

---

[1] See Additional Notes, Appendix V, for Wordsworth's deep concern over the operation of the Poor Law, and for Dorothy Wordsworth's description of a dignified pauper's funeral.

of economy had laid it down that the poor were to be maintained in workhouses, and that those who refused to enter one were to be denied relief. No notice seems to have been taken of the new legislation for almost forty years; whilst even after a poorhouse for the Bailiwick of Hawkshead was established in 1762, and one each for the Claife and Satterthwaite Quarters some years later, many of the poor were still relieved in their own homes. Nor was the cost of this form of assistance kept as low as it might have been had economy been the only consideration. As we have seen, Sarah Usher was allowed wine, brandy, and ale when she was ill. And entries in the Hawkshead Poor Accounts relating to pauper funerals in the 1790s include payments, not only for coffin, shroud, and grave digging, but also for 'bidding' to the funeral, that is sending a man round to inform and invite all neighbours living within a certain distance of the deceased's home; for 'waiting' or 'waking', in other words keeping vigil as long as the corpse lay unburied; and for the 'arval', or ritual funeral feast, of which all who were bidden, usually two from each house 'in the bidding', must partake, as it was in honour of the deceased, and was often spoken of as his or her arval. According to custom, it consisted of ale, oat bread and white bread, and sometimes cheese, and was not thought of as refreshment as has sometimes been stated. In short, a pauper's funeral differed little if at all from that of a statesman or his wife, assuming that the death occurred at home.

No poorhouse in the Bailiwick of Hawkshead was ever built for that purpose. What happened in the year 1762-3 was that a number of poor persons were boarded with Anthony Sawrey of Coniston Waterhead, who at the time was one of the Twenty Four. He was paid for housing and maintaining them, and authorized to make use of their services in any way he could. Soon afterwards they were transferred to Jonathan Park of Loanthwaite in the Hawkshead Quarter, and later to Gawen Williamson of Hawkshead Hall, who in 1784-5 received £75 from the Hawkshead Overseer, and a like or nearly equal sum from the Monk Coniston and Skelwith Overseer. Then came a change of policy; the customary holding of Sand Ground, rather more than a mile north-west of Hawkshead, was rented at £17 rising to £18 a year. It comprised a farmhouse, cottage, outbuildings, enclosed land adjacent to them, common rights, and its flock of herdwick sheep that lived all the year round on a portion of the open heights they had won for themselves by driving intruders away from it. It was known as their 'heaf', and because they were strongly attached to it, and would give endless trouble if taken elsewhere, they were treated as part of the customary holding, and were let or sold with it. Sand Ground, including its 'hefted' sheep, having been rented, it appears to have been farmed under the direction of the Overseers, for there is no mention thereafter of a 'Master of the Poor House'; and their accounts for 1789–90 and the following years show payments for several cows, a horse, and a cart, and for seed needed to grow oats, potatoes, turnips, peas, and beans. I noticed also that they paid for 'chatts', or small potatoes. After washing, and boiling in their skins they were probably fed to pigs at Sand Ground as part of their swill.

Wool was bought for spinning, and John Tyson paid for weaving the yarn, or such of it as was not used for knitting stockings. In addition there were purchases of blue, brown, and white duffel, a coarse woollen cloth with a thick nap, the blue a favourite choice for men's jackets and boys' suits, the white stated to be for men's breeches; white kersey, a coarse cloth, narrow and usually ribbed, made from long wool, and commonly used for men's breeches; 'pladding', sometimes called 'Scotch Stuff', a twilled woollen cloth with a checkered pattern; flannel, the dialect and the original name for which was flannen; striped 'linsey', probably linsey-woolsey, for women's petticoats; linen and the coarser 'harden', both made from long staple fibres of flax, for shifts and shirts; 'blue harden', which was generally used before printed cotton became available, for protective and working clothing such as women's aprons and 'bed-gowns', and men's 'kytles', otherwise short, unlined jackets; and lastly tow cloth, which was made from the shorter, thicker fibres of flax.

Ready-made clothes are rarely mentioned in the Sand Ground accounts, the chief exception being the strangely named 'bedgowns', which were worn only by day, and certainly not in bed, where shifts then sufficed for clothing. Round about 1800 they were loose-fitting dresses of the button-through type which a generation or two later were sometimes called overalls. Women on farms commonly wore them (after removing one or two other outer garments in hot weather) for work in the fields such as haymaking, and when milking cows, feeding calves, and the like; and some, it appears, for certain indoor jobs, including washing, baking, and butter-making. They are said to have been of ankle-length at one time, but in the Windermere district, for which I happen to have particulars, the long bedgowns worn during the first half of the nineteenth century reached only to the knees or just below, whilst the short bedgowns, which came into fashion during the late part of this period, were hip-length jackets very similar to men's 'kytles', As to Cumberland, John Richardson, a dialect poet born in 1817, tells us that

> Aw t'women fwok hed bedgoons lang
> Wi'tails 'at to their knees hung doon . . .

and Alexander Craig Gibson, his junior by a year, speaks of 'yan o' them skipjacks o' fellows 'at ye see weearin a lal jacket like a lass's bedgoon'. The mention of 'bedgowns' in the Sand Ground accounts is the earliest I have seen. My remaining notes on Hawkshead's Poorhouse being sketchy, all I will add by way of detail is that its inmates, whose number varied from twenty-three to twenty-five in 1796–7, normally wore clogs, as most working men and women did, statesmen and their wives included; and that like the majority of their neighbours they slept on chaff beds devoid of sheets but with blankets for coverings.

Some at least of the pauper children were provided with shoes as well as clogs; and if they were 'put out' parish apprentices, as several were, the sum of £2. 10s. 0d. was given with each, 'for clothing' it was stated in one entry. At Hawkshead pauper apprentices were scarcely ever sent out of the parish, though early in the 1780s two sisters were indentured to the master of a newly established cotton mill at Backbarrow on the river Leven. Later, doubts were felt as to whether he should be allowed to keep them. In the end the Overseer for the Hawkshead Quarter agreed to their staying at Backbarrow; but no other poor children were ever sent there; and at a Vestry Meeting on 19 April 1808, it was ordered that 'such Paupers as are put out Parish Apprentices be not indentured to Persons making use of or getting their Living by Cotton Mills, Factories, or Works of a Similar Nature.' Thus Hawkshead refused to share in what was the worst inhumanity arising out of the Industrial Revolution, namely the sending at an early age, mainly from the southern agricultural counties, of a great number of pauper children to work in cotton mills, and their neglect and pitiless exploitation by the masters of these mills. Conditions in them were a little better after the passing of the Morals and Health Act in 1802, but it was not until 1819, following the introduction of steam power which increased the strain of the work, that the Cotton Mills Act restricted the employment of children to those who were nine years of age and upwards, and their working week to seventy-two hours, presumably twelve hours a day on six days a week as Saturday was not as yet a half-holiday. No more need be said.

Despite the almost intolerable burden of the Poor Rates there is evidence of avoidable expenditure by the parish on the poor children for whom it had to provide. In 1786, for instance, the Hawkshead Overseer went to Backbarrow 'to order Elinor Preston to take her child to Mr. Kelletts of Long Sleddale to be cured of a scabbed head', and later he paid this gentleman £1. 1s. 0d. for curing the boy. Evidently his mother, though no longer living in the parish of Hawkshead, had her place of legal settlement there. But why was she ordered to take her son all the way to Long Sleddale, and why to a man whose fee was equal to that of a fashionable West End Physician? The likely explanation is that after medical treatment had failed to cure the scabs, it was decided to try a 'wise man' who by incantations or other magical means might be able to 'charm' or 'wish' them away. But what an expense for the parish to incur on behalf of a poor child no longer living there! Then in 1797, doubtless with the approval of the Twenty Four, as many as twenty children were inoculated at a total cost of £2. 10s. 0d. though, so far as I could discover, there were no deaths from small-pox in the parish that year. The Hawkshead Poor Accounts also contain payments in the early 1790s to George Pennington, Parish Clerk, and Mary Elleray for 'schooling' poor children, but not many, nor for long at a time, judging from the sums they received. The expenditure here exemplified I have called avoidable in that it was not called for in the Poor Law Act of 1723, the object of which was to secure, in the interest of ratepayers, the strictest economy in the relief of the poor.

The Poor Law Act of 1796 repealed the workhouse test, and thereby made it legal once more to relieve the poor in their own homes; but as Hawkshead had only partially ceased to do so, this reversal had little immediate effect there, though in time it led to the closure of the several poorhouses belatedly established in the parish; Sand Ground was closed by 1820. The new Act sanctioned higher scales of relief, no doubt owing to the greatly increased cost of living; but at Hawkshead, where the poor had been treated more generously than the 1723 Act intended, there is little sign of a general rise in the amounts granted to individual poor persons by way of weekly pensions and allowances in necessity. Nevertheless the total expenditure on the poor during the closing years of the eighteenth century continued to increase, in the Hawkshead Quarter, for example, by more than £35 in the last four years. This increase cannot be attributed to a clause in the 1796 Act that permitted for the first time the granting of poor relief to augment wages no longer adequate to support a family, for in the Bailiwick of Hawkshead it is clear that this clause was ignored, wisely and rightly I should say. The Poor Law assessments on the little customary tenements in the Bailiwick, most of them very small it must be remembered, already averaged some £12 to £13 a year each; and the statesmen, impoverished by now through no fault of their own, could not in fairness be called upon to subsidize low wages as well as to relieve the aged, infirm, and sick, and poor widows and children. In the district generally, whenever the head of a family, or his wife, or maybe some other key member of it, was laid low by illness or injury, neighbours would each take a small present as an indication of their readiness to help if needed. This taking of a token present was called 'owning' the family, 'aanin' 'em' as dialect speakers put it; and was expected of 'aw i't'nebber-raa', all in the neighbour-row, including those, if any, who had been having 'differences' with the afflicted family. As no complaint is registered in the Vestry Minutes of the extremely high cost of relieving the poor, it may be that this, too, was regarded as an obligation to unfortunate neighbours which must be fulfilled. Providing money to supplement inadequate wages is not likely to have been seen in the same light.

When the Rev. William Braithwaite became one of the Twenty

Four the breakdown of the accustomed method of electing parish officers was already in progress. The earliest indisputable evidence of it occurs in the list of Churchwardens for 1791, all styled 'M^r' it may be noted; for two of them were substitutes, William Stephenson, the tallow chandler, for the Hawkshead Quarter in place of William Waterson, and William Benson of Skelwith 'for Mr Laws estate at Brathay'; whilst the other two, William Fisher for Claife and Thomas Bellingham for Satterthwaite, had held the same offices in the preceding year, and Thomas Bellingham in the year before that. He continued in office in 1792; and so did William Stephenson, this time as substitute for John Atkinson of Outgate. Unfortunately lists of Churchwardens, hitherto unbroken since 1716, are available for only two more years in the eighteenth century, namely 1795, when Thomas Bellingham's name appears once more, and 1797 when, as in 1795, the Claife Churchwarden was George Barker. In the later year Edward Backhouse was Warden for Monk Coniston and Skelwith in lieu of Edward Parke of Skelwith; and he, Edward Backhouse, as an indenture recently mentioned shows, filled the same office in 1798. Though one cannot be certain, it looks as if it was mainly the smaller, poorer statesmen who declined to serve as Churchwardens when it was held to be their turn to do so, the reason, if I may hazard a guess, being that they were anxious to avoid being called upon to become Overseers of the Poor in the following year, as the office of Overseer, unlike that of Church-warden, had developed into an unduly burdensome one.

I never did more than glance now and again at early nineteenth-century records, but in 1801, I noticed, William Stephenson was paid 10s. 0d. for his services for one year as Churchwarden for the Hawkshead Quarter, and £3. 3s. 0d. for having acted as well as Overseer of the Poor for the same Quarter, and again for one year, probably 1800–1. These payments can certainly be regarded as an innovation. William Stephenson died on 10 July 1807, at the age of seventy-eight, and on 14 June in the following year it was recorded as the unanimous opinion of the Vestry, apparently a Select Vestry, 'that it is expedient a person properly qualified should be appointed Overseer of the Poor of the Bailiwick of Hawkshead for such Time as may be agreed on at a General Meeting'. Soon afterwards a more fundamental departure from the eighteenth-century pattern of parochial administration seems to have taken place, for whereas the Charity Commissioners in a Report published in 1820 say that in each of the parishes of Cartmel, Dalton-in-Furness, and Kirkby Ireleth the management of parochial affairs was vested in the Twenty Four, they make no such statement regarding the parish of Hawkshead, or that of Ulverston; which at least suggests, even if it does not prove, that they had been more 'progressive'.

Will of Thomas Sandys—descendants of Sandys—purchase of a habitation for the Sandys Charity boys—business transactions of the Trustees—accounts for the Charity boys, board and school—property investments—William Braithwaite's wood planting and summer-house—death and will of William Braithwaite

With that I will return to the eighteenth century, and to the Rev. William Braithwaite, about whose place in local life during the 1790s there is more to say. In the muniment chest at Hawkshead School I found a substantial leather-bound volume inscribed 'Account Book of the Rev. Thomas Sandys Charity', and from it that the one-time recluse had been a trustee of this educational foundation. As such he first signed the annual accounts on 9 March 1792, and he continued to do so up to and including 1799. The Rev. Thomas Sandys, Curate of St. Martin's-in-the-Fields, Lecturer of St. James', Westminster, and absentee Rector of Tunstall-in-Holderness, and of Wighton, also in the County of York, by will and two codicils signed and sealed on 19 August 1717, and proved on 17 December in that year, bequeathed to

the free Grammar School in Hawkshead Parish in Forness Fells in Lancashire £800 to be so disposed of & settled for Perpetuity by the Trustees of the said School that ye yearly Interest of it may be imployed to such Uses of the poor Children born in that parish and taught in the School aforesaid as shall be more particularly mentioned in a Codicil hereunto annexed.

The reference is to the first codicil, in which the testator says his 'further Will & Desire' is that the interest be employed to maintain such a Number of poor Children and in such proportion for providing them with Necessaries in Lodging Diet Clothes & Books as the Trustees of the Free School aforesaid in their Discretion shall think fit and the Yearly Income alloted for the Children will well bear ... that in choosing the poor Children for this Charity a special Regard to be had to such as are Orphans and to those whose poor Parents live at so great a Distance from the School that they cannot conveniently give them School Learning ... more particularly ... that out of the said Yearly Interest Provision be made for teaching the Children to write and cast accounts & for buying them not only School Books and Bibles Whole Duties of Man &c at or before their leaving off School that they may by God's Blessing the better answer the End of this Charity.

These excerpts from Thomas Sandys' will and first codicil are from a copy in the Account Book preserved at Hawkshead. Copley Christie, in his *Old Church and School Libraries of Lancashire* (printed for the Chetham Society in 1885),[1] states that in the first codicil attached to Thomas Sandys' will he desired provision to be made for modulating the poor children's voices by teaching them to sing psalms; and that the religious works to be bought for them were 'Bibles with the Common Prayer, Beveridge's *Exposition of the Church Catechism* and Gibson's *Sacrament of the Lord's Supper*'. Clearly the Hawkshead copy is at fault, as Copley Christie consulted the original; but he omits *Whole Duty of Man*. Sandys left £10 to Hawkshead to buy the same books for distribution among poor families in the parish, and £5 each to Tunstall and Wighton, where the poor were to have the benefit of a free issue of all save Dr. Beveridge's *Exposition*. The preferential treatment accorded to Hawkshead in this respect may not have been fully appreciated there, as in 1789 the Curate of Rusland in the Satterthwaite Quarter of the parish informed his Bishop: 'I have neither expounded the Church Catechism myself, nor used any printed exposition of it. And I have reason to believe that should I attempt anything of the kind, it would not be acceptable to my congregation; no such thing having been practised in this country for a long time.'

In the Hawkshead copy the first codicil concludes as follows:

[1] New Series, VII, p. 163.

Lastly my Will and Desire is that Mr Myles Sandys of Easthwaite in the parish of Hawkshead and his heirs successively, my Cousin Edwin Sandys Citizen of London and Heirs successively, the Vicar of Hawkshead for the time being, the Master of the Free School for the time being and my Cousin Samuel Sandys of Roger Ground near Hawkshead be by this my special Nomination and Appointment of the Number of Trustees for the well ordering of the Charity and for applying it to the several Uses mentioned in this Codicil.

To Mr. Myles Sandys and Cousins Edwin and Samuel Sandys 'to each of them I give a Ring of a Guinea Value set with a Chrystal to be valued over and above in Token of my good Affection and of my Gratitude to them for executing the Trust I repose in them'. He also authorized the Trustees, whether of his nomination or not, to spend not more than twenty shillings yearly 'on their refreshment when they met on business concerning the Charity'.

The 'Mr Myles Sandys of Easthwaite', who heads the list of Trustees nominated by the testator, was born in 1696 and died in 1766. Sixth in line of descent from Anthony of Esthwaite, youngest brother of Archbishop Edwyn Sandys, he succeeded to the estate relatively early in life. His mother was also a Sandys, she being Ann, daughter and eventually sole heiress of Myles of Graythwaite, who was descended from Christopher, another brother of the archbishop. As a result, Myles of Esthwaite, Captain of Militia and a Justice of the Peace, later became of Graythwaite as well as of Esthwaite and went to live at Graythwaite Hall. He was High Sheriff of Lancashire in 1725, and Deputy Lieutenant of the County on four occasions. He was succeeded by his eldest son Myles, who died without issue in 1792, aged seventy-two, and was in turn succeeded by his nephew Myles, eldest son of his next brother Thomas by Ellen, daughter of Captain Samuel Sandys of Skirton. Born in 1762, the last mentioned Myles, who duly became a Trustee of the Rev. Thomas Sandys Charity, married in 1790 Elizabeth, daughter of Sir John Dalrymple of Oxenford Castle, near Edinburgh, whose sons James and North were at Hawkshead School with the Wordsworths.[1]

---

[1] See Alphabetical List, Appendix IV, for notes on James, North, and Robert Dalrymple. Their older brother, John, was also at Hawkshead, and subscribed to the New Library, 1789.

U

'Edwin Sandys Citizen of London' cannot be identified as surely as 'M^r' Myles of Esthwaite. It is very likely, though, that he was Edwin, younger brother of the Thomas of Esthwaite who married Anne of Graythwaite. Their father was Thomas Sandys of Simon House, third and last surviving son of Samuel of Esthwaite, who was a grandson of the archbishop's brother Anthony. This Thomas, who died in 1680, eventually became possessed of the Esthwaite estate, but does not appear to have lived at Esthwaite Hall except when young. His son Edwin had male issue, but West, writing in 1774, referred to them as 'since extinct'. Samuel of Roger Ground, the third Sandys nominated by the Rev. Thomas as a Trustee, is undoubtedly the 'ancient Friend' buried at Colthouse in 1755. He was a son of the 'Willm Sandes of Rogerground' named in 1669 as one of the Trustees of the Friends' Burial Ground at Colthouse; and it is all but certain that he was a grandson of the Samuel Sandys of Roger Ground who died in Lancaster Castle in 1663 whilst a prisoner there for his 'testimony against tithes', and whose corpse was carried through the country, possibly to Colthouse for burial though proof of that is lacking, with a paper fixed to the coffin telling 'in great Capital Letters' how he had offered up his life as a witness to the 'truth of God as it is in Jesus', and for an example and encouragement to 'all that shall be in the truth', and a warning to their persecutors to bear in mind the dreadful Judgement Day, and the sentence of everlasting punishment that Christ would then pass on them. The Hawkshead registers afford information about the wives and children of this Quaker martyr, and tell us something of a nearly contemporary Thomas Sandys or Sands of Roger Ground; but I could not trace for certain the descent of either, their Christian names being common among the Hawkshead Sandys, and the early registrations lacking in detail. As to the Rev. Thomas Sandys, Curate of St. Martin's-in-the-Fields, I can add nothing to what he himself said in the first codicil to his will about his kinship to two of the Sandys he nominated as Trustees of the Hawkshead charity he founded, or relate him to Myles Sandys of Esthwaite, whose name precedes theirs in his list of nominees.

Among other bequests, the Rev. Thomas Sandys left £200 to Queen's College, Oxford, to which he referred as 'the Place of my

Education'; but in the final clause of his will he stipulated that for not less than five or more than seven years after his death, which took place on 28 November 1717, the interest on this £200 and on the £800 bequeathed to Hawkshead was to be at the disposal of his executor, the Rev. Robert Grisedale of St. Martin's-in-the-Fields, for the purposes of his will, and for such other uses as might be inserted in a codicil to it. There were three of these additional uses, and first priority was given to the provision, if it was found to be practicable, of a 'Convenient habitation for the poor Children to be educated in Hawkshead School'. In their 1820 report the Charity Commissioners say they had no means of ascertaining the use made of the reserved interest; but they overlooked the existence among the muniments of the Thomas Sandys Charity Trustees of a deed listed by John Gibson in 1784 or thereabouts. In his schedule it is dated '16ᵗʰ Novʳ. 1725', and described as 'Admittance to Myles Sandys Esqʳ. and others of a Messuage in Hawkshead from John Mackreth dated 15ᵗʰ Novʳ. 1724'; which shows that the house was bought just before the seven years had expired, but that the Thomas Sandys Charity Trustees were not entered on the manorial roll as the owners, or more correctly the holders, of it until a year later. Another deed of theirs calendared by John Gibson affords indirect proof that the purchase from John Mackreth also included a 'Dale of Peatmoss called Stang Moss in Claife'. From their accounts it appears that the charity first became fully operative in 1726.

The habitation in Hawkshead provided for the Sandys Charity boys cannot have been satisfactory, as at the beginning of 1730 the Trustees laid out £135 in the purchase of a customary tenement at Gallowbarrow, between the town and Hawkshead Hall. It comprised a dwelling house and outhouses, the latter including a barn; a garden and at least two small closes of land; a peatmoss at the Tarns, and a bracken-garth at Sand Intake: the lord's rent was 1s. 0½d. a year, and the corn tithe rent 3½d. a year: admittance was on 13 April 1730, the day on which the purchase deed was executed. Cowper, who clearly regarded it as the first and only 'Charity House', says that it formerly bore an inscription, which he quotes, giving particulars of the Rev. Thomas Sandys and his bequest, and bearing the date 1749.[1] The

_____
[1] *Hawkshead*, p. 36.

boys were housed there several years before that, and probably from 1730, but not, as we shall see, in the 1780s and 1790s. In 1731 George Satterthwaite left £20 to the Grammar School Governors, and directed that it should be continued as a stock, and the interest applied 'for and towards the further maintenance and education of the charity boys going to the said School'. Then in 1766 came William Dennison's gift of £400 for the same purpose. It was about that time, I believe, or very soon afterwards, that the Grammar School Governors, with the addition of the Master, became the Trustees of the augmented Thomas Sandys Charity. Apart from the Master, the two bodies had been nearly identical in composition for some considerable time, but not in their function and procedure, which continued to be different until 1863.

In 1772 the Thomas Sandys Charity Trustees bought from Clement Satterthwaite for £135. 1s. 0d. 'a Close of Land called the High—near Hawkshead': the lord's rent was 6d. a year, and admittance not till 28 November 1775. It was the more southerly of two rounded hills of morainic origin that lie between Hawkshead and Hawkshead Moor, and was called Little High when Samuel Sandys of Roger Ground sold it, together with other property, to William Satterthwaite in 1731 whilst for the past hundred years or more it has been known as Charity High. This close of land, which was from four to five acres in extent, was not a particularly good investment, as at the time it commanded a rent of only £4 a year, whereas the Sandys Trustees were getting $4\frac{1}{4}$% on the £700 lent by them to Fletcher Fleming of Rayrigg, Windermere, and others in 1768, and on the £270 lent to John Moore Esq. and others in 1770. In 1780, by a majority of 4 to 2, they decided 'to purchase Stock in the Public Funds with the whole of the money then at Interest', the result being the investment, of £970 in the $4\frac{1}{2}$% stock of the Kendal Turnpike Trust, the annual income from which amounted to £43. 13s. 0d. The sum of £43 previously on loan to the Rev. Reginald Brathwaite, who as minister of Hawkshead was an *ex officio* Trustee, was left in his hands as it could be got at once in case of need; and the interest on this at 10d. in the pound produced a further £1. 15s. 10d. a year.

That was still the position when the Rev. William Braithwaite was elected a Grammar School Governor and a Sandys Charity Trustee. In 1796, however, the Kendal Turnpike Stock was sold, and £1,000 invested in 3% Consols; and as they then stood at 56½ the amount of stock secured was £1,735. 7s. 1d., on which the interest was £52. 1s. 2d. a year. The switch raised the annual income of the trustees to over £60, for at the time the Gallowbarrow property was let on lease at £4 a year, and the High at £4. 10s. 0d. The increase in total receipts was timely in view of the sharp and continuing rise in prices in the 1790s, but not really sufficient to offset the mounting cost per head of maintaining the Charity boys, and some reduction in their number appeared to be inevitable. And here the Trustees were in a dilemma as they were receiving more and more applications for admission to the benefits of the Charity as the number of poor widows grew. That probably accounts for a step taken on 2 March 1796, when 'At a Meeting of the Governors for Hawkshead School . . . it was unanimously agreed & resolved that in future no Boy shall be admitted into the Charity for which they are Trustees under the Age of nine years, & that, cœteris paribus, a Preference shall be given to a Candidate of the Age of ten years.' If, as I believe, a legacy of £21 bequeathed to the Trustees in 1794 by John Scales, late of Soho, Birmingham, was treated as income not capital, it would for a while ease their position. The Charity Commissioners do not mention it, nor does Cowper. A John Scales, probably of Rusland, was a Trustee in the 1770s and for a year or two afterwards, but I do not know whether he and the John Scales of Birmingham were identical or not.

Originally there were eight Trustees of the Thomas Sandys Charity, four nominated by the founder (for Edwin Sandys, citizen of London, did not serve), and the other four by the Grammar School Governors. At the end of the eighteenth century the number was the same, and for 1796, when I happen to have noted all their names, they were the Myles Sandys of Graythwaite who succeeded his uncle in 1792; the Rev. Reginald Brathwaite, minister of Hawkshead since 1762; the Rev. Thomas Bowman, who became Master of the Grammar School in 1786; John Machell of Hollow Oak, Colton, in whose name the Kendal Turnpike investment was made; William Taylor of Briers, Far Sawrey, and Manchester, yeoman and merchant; John Jackson of Bank Ground, Monk Coniston, another yeoman who was also a merchant; Reginald Brathwaite's stepson, Edmund L. Irton, and the Rev. William Braithwaite of Satterhow, Far Sawrey. According to custom, the Trustees took it in turn to act as treasurer for a year, Reginald Brathwaite being ready to deputize for anyone unable or unwilling to undertake the work. And, as had always been the case, they met as a body but once a year, to receive and pass the treasurer's accounts, to elect poor boys to the benefits of the Charity, and to transact any other business. That done, they treated themselves to a very good dinner on the twenty shillings the Rev. Thomas Sandys had authorized them to spend; and from 1788, when detailed, as distinct from summary accounts, first become available, till 1842 they never once spent less, no matter what the attendance was. In the 1790s the permitted expenditure would still cover the cost of a good deal to drink as well as to eat, and it may be that the diners tended to become convivial; a supposition not necessarily in conflict with the presence among them, as a leading figure, of the Rev. Reginald Brathwaite, for writing of him in 1791 Adam Walker, the natural philosopher, after a reference to his hospitality, remarks that 'his kindness and hilarity providentially soften the gloom and vigour of the country.'[1]

The first detailed account of the Trustees' expenditure and income is dated 26 February 1788, less than five months after Wordsworth left Hawkshead School, which is the reason why I chose it for transcription in full. The charity boys were then boarded with Benjamin Jackson, and had been for some time as an entry in the account book made on 9 March 1785, reads: 'Paid by order of the Trustees to Benjn. Jackson the keeper of the Charity Boys as a Gratuity for his Care . . . £1 12s. 7d.'; a payment which reduced the balance in hand to £52. The Charity House at Gallowbarrow was occupied at the time and for long afterwards by John Walker, a carpenter, and I do not know precisely where Benjamin Jackson lived, though almost certainly it was somewhere in Hawkshead Town. He had six Charity boys for the whole of the year, and a seventh for part of it. But it would be better to let the disbursements for that year tell their own story, with only such changes as bringing

[1] *Remarks . . . Tour from London to the Lakes* (1792), p. 58.

down to the general level any letters written above the line, using the treasurer's classification of entries as subheadings, instead of leaving them at the side where he put them, and distinguishing in what is now the usual way between the pound sterling and the pound avoirdupois, for both of which he used £. With these changes the disbursements read:

	£	s.	d.
Board			
Ben. Jackson—Board of 6 Boys at £4 15s. pr Boy, from May-Day 1787 to Do. 1788	28.	10.	0.
Do. One Boy 32 Weeks at 1s. 10d.	2.	18.	8.
Linen			
Do. 33 Yards of Linen Cloth	1.	10.	6.
Do. 20 Shirts making 10s. Shirts mending at 6d. pr. Boy 3s. 6d.		13.	6.
Do. 10 Neck Stocks making.		1.	8.
Woollen			
Mr. John Jackson—8 lb Wool 4s. 6d.			
2 St[one] Yarn £1. 9s. 6d. Making 20½ Yards of Cloth 16s. 10d. Car[riage] 6d.	2.	11.	4.
Benj. Jackson—Taylor, Meat & Wages 17 D[ays]	1.	8.	4.
Do. Buttons, Thread, Bees Wax, Candl		8.	9.
Do. Mending Woolen Cloaths at 2s. 6d. pr Boy		17.	6.
Do. 18 lb. Wool dying 5s. Spinning 9s. oyl 8d.		14.	8.
Do. 11 pr Stockings knitting 5s. 6d. 15 pr footing 2s. 6d.		8.	0.
Shoes, Clogs, &c.			
Tho. Stamper—8 pr new Shoes £1. 15s. 2d. Mending Shoes 10s. 8d.	2.	5.	10.
Ed. Satterthwaite—8 pr new Clogs 11s. 9d. Mending Clogs 4s. 7d.		16.	4.
Jos. Keen—Clogs Shod with Iron		10.	5.
Ben. Jackson—blacking Shoes 3s. 6d. Cutting Hair 2s. 4d.		5.	10.

Books, &c.

Mr. Todhunter—6 Common Prayer Books 9s. One Do.			
1s. 7d. Bible 2s. 6d.	13.	1.	
G. Parke—a Slate 10d.		10.	
Mrs. Jane Swainson—8 Q[uire] Paper	8.	0.	
Ben. Jackson to Cl. Sat [terthwaite] for Ink,	1.	6.	
Mr. Varty—4 Boys 8 Q[uarte]rs Writing & Accounts	2.	0.	0.

Medicine

Mr. [Matthew] Hodgson—Medicine	1.	8.

Taxes, &c.

Lord's Rent for the High	1.	4½d.
Mr. Stephenson—4 Bills £24 each Poor Rate	7.	4.
Mr. Coulthred—6d. in the pound to the Highways	1.	4½d.

Expenses

Allowed to be expended at the Meeting.	1.	0.	0.

	48.	16.	6.

Receipts for the year exceeded disbursements by £5. 2s. 4d.

Benjamin Jackson was still 'keeper' of the Charity boys in 1790, in which year there were nine of them, the most ever mentioned in the detailed accounts. He was succeeded in the following year by Mrs. Sarah Jackson, his widow I fancy.[1] She started with seven boys, but very soon the number fell to six and then to five, the boarding allowance for each being raised from £4. 15s. 0d. to £5. 10s. 0d. a year by 1795 at the latest. By 1801, when Mrs. Sarah Garnett was in charge of the boys, and had been for some time, it had become £7. 7s. 0d. a year; and she received £7. 2s. 9d. 'for Making & mending their clothes &c', which is about three times as much as was paid for these services in 1788. As it happens she had the same number of boys, for though she began with five and finished with four there was a jump to seven in 1801 and the following year, the extra money needed being found from somewhere, presumably by reducing the credit balance, which may have meant expending the

---

[1] An entry in the Hawkshead Parish Register for 20 April 1772 indicates the marriage of 'Benjamin Jackson Servant Man and Sarah Midlefell Spinster'.

greater part of John Scales' legacy. Between 1804 and 1820 there were usually four Charity boys, with a fifth when funds permitted. From 1820 to 1825 they were boarded with John Walker at Gallowbarrow in what had once been the Charity House; a fact that has given rise to some misunderstanding as to the length of time it was in use as such.

The cost of having the boys taught at the Grammar School to write and cast accounts was a good deal higher than the £2 entered in the disbursements presented on 26 February 1788, might suggest. The following are examples of the annual payments made by the Trustees to successive Writing Masters during the next fifteen years: to Mr. Bowstead, £4. 15s. 3d. in 1789 for 7 boys; £5. 5s. 3d. in 1790 for 9; £4. 4s. 6d. in 1792 for 7, and £3. 1s. 6d. in 1793 for 6; to Mr. Townson, £4. 8s. 6d. in 1794 for 5; to Mr. Varty, £7. 15s. 3d. in 1796 and £6. 6s. 10d. in 1798, in each case for 5 boys; and to Mr. Lynn £7. 8s. 6d. in 1801, £9. 12s. 0d. in 1802, and £8. 10s. 2½d. in 1803 for 7, 7, and 5, respectively. Most of these totals include refunds of money spent by masters in providing the boys with paper, copybooks, and other things required for their work. But in some years the Trustees made direct purchases of such requisites: thus in 1794 they paid Alexander Sutherland, who had succeeded William Todhunter as bookseller and stationer, 13s. 5½d. for 'Paper, Pens, Ink, &c.', and in the following year 9s. 6½d. for 'Paper, Quills, Ink, &c.'. In the 1790s expenditure on Bibles and Books of Common Prayer was very limited; and there is no mention at all of *Whole Duties of Man* until 1806, when six copies were bought at a total cost of 8s. 0d. As to modulating the Charity boys' voices by teaching them to sing psalms, the first indication in the accounts that anything was done about it is a note made at the annual meeting on 30 March 1803, that '2s. 0d. for 3 Books of Psalmody be added to the balance due to Mr. Brathwaite, Deputy Treasurer for Mr. John Jackson for the year 1802'.

The only information available about the proceedings of the Grammar School Governors in the 1790s relates to the sale by them in 1791, possibly before but more probably after the Rev. William Braithwaite was elected a Governor, of part of the original endowment of the school, and to the ways in which the money received for it was laid out afresh or otherwise expended. The property sold consisted of a number of dilapidated houses at Wakefield in the county of York situated in the streets there named Kirkgate and Northgate. Prior to their sale the houses were let to a Mr. Smallpage for £23. 10s. 0d. per annum; and it was he who purchased them, the price at which they changed hands being £762. 10s. 0d. When paying for the houses, the buyer rejected a claim that nine months' rent, amounting to £17. 12s. 6d., was then due from him, his contention being that, according to custom, he had always paid his rent in advance. There is no evidence that he counter-claimed for three months rent due to him by way of repayment; and certainly he did not get it. On the other hand, the Governors saw to it that the Master of the Grammar School did not suffer, for they paid him £17. 12s. 6d. out of the proceeds of the sale. The 'deeds and other expenses of conveyance' of the property to Mr. Smallpage meant a further deduction from the proceeds of £4. 4s. 0d.

Reinvestment was delayed until 1793, in which year the Governors bought for £548 the customary estate known as Knipe Fold, in the Fieldhead district of the Hawkshead Quarter of the parish. It consisted of a farmhouse and cottage, twenty-two acres of enclosed land, a peat-moss, and right of turbary. The auction duty, and other expenses arising from the purchase, totalled £10. 12s. 4d. Improvements to the holding were put in hand, and during the next year or two £164. 19s. 2d. was spent on repairs, building a barn, and draining the land. The result was a property that could be let at from £30 to £40 a year, and that would cost little to maintain for many years to come. A little still remained of the proceeds of the Wakefield sale, and in 1796 a small slip of land called Sark Sleeve was purchased for £15, the legal costs incurred being £2. 2s. 0d. It adjoined, and was added to, the school tenement, which in late sixteenth-century deeds is described as lying at Hawkshead Church Stile.

There was yet another office to which the Rev. William Braithwaite was elected after he ceased to be a recluse. It was that of a Trustee, together with William Taylor and Thomas Hodgson, both of Briers, of the little school at Far Sawrey built and endowed by William Braithwaite of Fold in 1766. It was in this capacity that Thomas Braithwaite in 1795 left to him the sum of £40 in trust for the benefit of the school at Sawrey, and directed that the interest on it should be applied to that end in such manner as he and his successors thought fit. The testator left a further sum of £25, the interest on it to be used 'in the purchase of books for the poor children attending the said school'. Evidently this, too, was bequeathed to the Rev. William Braithwaite, as the Charity Commissioners reported in 1820 that both sums, secured by promissory notes, and bearing interest at $4\frac{1}{2}\%$ per annum, were then in the hands of Miss Ann Braithwaite of Hawkshead; and she, as his will makes plain, was his sister and sole heiress. The interest on the £40, we learn, 'is regularly paid to Philip Braithwaite, the present school-master'; whilst for many years that on the £25 had been received by William Taylor, a Trustee lately deceased, 'but it appears that he applied part of it only in supplying the children with books, and expended the remainder in the repair of the school'. The Commissioners add that 'the interest will now be paid to the present trustees', Thomas Hodgson, his son Braithwaite Hodgson, and William Fisher, 'and we have reason to hope that the application of it in future will be conformable to the directions of the testator.' The Rev. William Braithwaite left all he possessed to his sister Ann; but she, by her will dated 6 December 1824, bequeathed £100, to be held in the names of the incumbents of Hawkshead and Windermere, 'the interest of which to be paid to the Master of Sawrey School'. She died on 19 May 1826, aged sixty-two, and probate was granted on the following 18 September.

There is little I can add to what has been said already about the Rev. William Braithwaite's other main activity in the 1790s, namely the building of a summer-house on the high, rocky hill above the Ferry Inn overlooking Lake Windermere, and the planting on this hill of upwards of 40,000 young trees and shrubs and a great many acorns. It was not treeless when Thomas West knew it, for in his *Guide to the Lakes*, published in 1778 (the year before his death), he spoke of 'Ancient yews and hollies' growing fantastically among the fallen rocks at its base; of two small oaks serving as a guide to the view-point; of the hill rising 'in an agreeable wildness, variegated with scattered trees and silver-grey rocks'; and of the trees at the summit being of 'singular use in answering the purposes of fore-ground, and of intersecting the lake'.[1] Evidently it was typical of the

[1] See pp. 59–60.

scenery of Claife Heights at its boldest. Why then did William Braithwaite, who had always known it like that, seek to clothe it in trees, or at any rate its steep slopes on the western side of Windermere, and go to so much trouble and expense to achieve that end? The answer would seem to be that, living as he did in the Romantic Age at the Lakes, he himself was a romanticist in regard to landscape scenery, and hence had an urge to 'improve' it so far as his own property was concerned. It looks as if he planted some foreign species, for Jonathan Otley, whose *Concise description of the English Lakes, and adjacent Mountains* first appeared in 1823 and reached a fifth edition in 1834, says in the latter that the path leading up to the summer-house, or Station as he called it, was 'decorated with native and exotic trees and shrubs'.[1] Be that as it may, it is nonetheless true that a century later the finest bit of woodland rising from the western margins of Windermere was that above the Ferry Hotel. 'This beautifully wooded hill', as Baddeley remarked, was 'one of the most glorious sights on the lake at the fall of the leaf'. So William Braithwaite may be forgiven for his attempt at landscape 'improvement' for which the only authority, by the way, is Joseph Budworth.[2]

On William Braithwaite's death, or just before, the Station and the hill on which it stood became the property of John Christian Curwen of Workington Hall, Cumberland, and Belle Isle, Windermere, who a few years earlier had acquired Great Boat; and it is just possible that he had rebuilt, enlarged, or otherwise altered the summer-house before any description of it appeared. Had he done so, however, the fact is almost certain to have been mentioned by one writer or another either during his lifetime or not long after his death in 1828, for he was very well known. Besides, if he had been in any degree responsible for building the Station, Cowper could hardly have failed to hear of it. For these reasons, and despite Wordsworth's use of the phrase, 'first pleasure-house' in his dictated note,[3] there is a good chance, I consider, that the two-storey summer-house described by Jonathan Otley and others was the one built by William

[1] See Otley, p. 4.
[2] And 8th edition of West's *Guide*, see above, p. 259, n. 1.
[3] See p. 258.

Braithwaite in the 1790s.[1] Its upper windows, says Otley, 'being partly of stained glass, give a good representation of the manner in which the landscape would be affected in different seasons'. The building in general, and this feature in particular, were lavishly praised by several of the nineteenth-century guide-book writers and tourists, but a few were critical, and one or two condemned it as being in bad taste, whilst to Cowper it was no more than 'a queer place'. Now it is in decay, and there appears to be no desire to save it.

William Braithwaite's erection of a summer-house on the hill above the Ferry Inn may be taken as further and surer proof of his romanticism. But as a romanticist he seems to have been more restrained than some of his contemporaries, one of whom writes:

Eminences are as naturally fit places for objects intended to attract the distant eye, as they are for enabling the eye to survey distant objects. Hence to decorate them with *columns, obelisks, temples, & c.* has the sanction of natural fitness. And if to this consideration we add that of the inherent beauty of the objects themselves, and remember, that there is nothing sets off the beauties of nature so much as elegant works of art,— justifying motives for these erections can never be wanting to anyone who has a taste for rural beauty, and is willing to accomplish as much of it as is in his power. . . . The practice of it is certainly patriotic. For such elegant ornaments will at least naturally contribute to diffuse a serenity and chear-fulness of mind into every beholder. . . . The most simple of these erections

---

[1] Otley's description is on p. 4 of his book. T.W.T. has not noticed that William Green in his *Guide to the Lakes* of 1819, as had the 1802 edition of West's *Guide*, attributed the summer-house to William Braithwaite: 'The Station-house stands upon a hill above the Ferry. It was built by Mr. Braithwaite, from whom it was purchased by Mr. Curwen. It is a short but pleasant walk to it from the Ferry-house. An aged female, inhabiting a pretty cottage within the inclosure surrounding the Station, will conduct the party by an excellent road to the building: this road is graced on each hand by oak, ash, and birch trees, springing from the sides and out of the fissures of picturesque rocks; to these trees have been added hollies, laurels, and other evergreens, with an abundance of garden and field flowers, all filling the eye with a most pleasing assemblage of nature and art. On this ascent the eye is not allowed to roam beyond the enclosing wall, for this is a local sort of beauty, and can-not come in composition with any of its neighbouring scenes, or with distant mountains.

The Station-house is two stories high: the lower story consists of dining and other rooms, but the upper is a tasteful drawing-room; from this drawing-room there are two fine views of the lake.' (Green, I, p. 228.) And see Additional Notes, Appendix V, for a comment by Wordsworth.

are obelisks, and properly formed summer-houses. . . . This kind of summer-house should either be octagonal, or at least have more than four sides . . . [and if] not placed on very pointed hills, care should be taken to raise them (either by raising the earth on which they stand, or by giving them a high rustic base, &c.) . . . Perhaps a summer-house standing on proper rustic arches (through which the sky might be seen) would . . . in some cases have a good effect.

I have been quoting from an anonymous article entitled 'Further account of Furness Fells; or, observations on placing objects on the eminences, and planting trees in the vallies . . .', which appeared among the addenda in the later editions of West's *Guide*, the citation here given being from the fourth, which was issued in 1789.[1] The writer, whom later editions identify as a Mr. Cockin, begins his pronouncements on tree-planting by declaring that the 'greatest nicety and perfection . . . lies in the use of exotics, and an ingenious mixture of foliage, in order to decorate, for *near inspection*, the marginal views of a lawn, walk, &c.' We need not follow him further.

From about 1791 or 1792 to 1798 William Braithwaite seems to have lived mainly at High Satterhow, but doubtless he stayed from time to time with his sister Ann in Hawkshead; and in an indenture dated 16 May 1799, he is said to be 'of Hawkshead'. It is an agreement between John Christian Curwen on the one part and the Rev. William Braithwaite of Hawkshead, William Taylor of Colthouse, and Anthony Wilson of High Wray ('representing the proprietors and landowners of Claife') on the other, and relates to the purchase by the first named of the Heald, a portion of the common lands called Claife Heights that is situated to the south of and adjacent to his tenement known as 'Sandbeds otherwise Bellegrange'. Evidently he had been set on securing it for some years, as the Claife Enclosure Act of 1794 was stated to apply to all the commons, 'except a certain plot of land called the Heald'.[2] Stretching for some way along the lower, eastern slopes of Claife Heights towards Harrowslack, it served him as a planting site for timber trees, and in time the whole or the greater part of it became Heald Wood. Of the three who

[1] See West, pp. 287–8.
[2] The Heald (along the western side of Windermere) was probably sold to Curwen to meet the costs of the Claife Heights Enclosure; but see p. 131, n. 2.

negotiated its sale to him, William Braithwaite obviously represented the 'proprietors and landowners' of the Low End of Claife, where his Satterhow property lay.

A bare nine months after the agreement was signed he was in his grave, for an entry in the Parish Registers made early in 1800 records that 'The Revd William Braithwaite of Satterhowe, Master of Arts, Vicar of Risely in Bedfordshire, and Vicar of Burton Petwarden in Lincolnshire Dyed at Hawkshead on the 8th Day of Feb^ry, and was Buried in the Church on the 12th. Aged 46'. His was only the second burial in the church after its re-pewing, the first being that of a 'Mr' William Braithwaite in 1797, the fee having been raised to £5. 5s. 0d., and the costs greatly increased by the need to remove and replace fixed seating. In accord with family custom, no memorial to him was placed in the church, there being none at that time to any of the Braithwaites, of Briers, Satterhow, or Harrowslack. The date of his death is not given in either Scott or Venn, but in the latter it is stated that he was Vicar of Riseley, Bedfordshire, from 1787 to 1799, and probably of Burton Husey or Burton Petwardine, Lincolnshire, from and to the same dates, which suggests that he gave up both his livings a short while before he died. The making of his will he left until 24 January 1800, and probate was granted on 19 February, only eleven days after his death. The probate abstract, for a copy of which I am indebted to Mr. Sharpe France of the Lancashire Record Office, merely states that the 'Rev. William Braithwaite of Hawkshead bequeathes the whole of his property to his sister Ann Braithwaite', and puts the value of his 'personal Effects' at 'under £2,000'.

Bartholomew Purcel, itinerant conjuror

Wordsworth has already been quoted as saying that when he was a small boy he delighted in the view from the hill above the Ferry Inn, and that once he led there from Hawkshead an Irish youngster about his own age who was 'a servant to an itinerant conjuror'. Presumably the boy lived with his master, who may have resided at Hawkshead when not on his travels. If he did, or had ever made his home in the parish, he could hardly have been anyone but the Barty Purcel referred to by John Ireland as a Hawkshead 'Conjuror & Magician' who went round 'to fairs & places in a tilt cart same as the Potters'. They, I may add, were a nomadic or semi-nomadic caste, found mainly in Cumberland, Westmorland, and Furness, who had some Gypsy blood in their veins, and a fair sprinkling of words of Romani origin in their cant, and who evidently hawked earthenware at one time, but have not done so for the past hundred years or more. The only other information about Barty Purcel I noted from John Ireland's *Memoir* is that he was 'a good hand at pattering', and that John in his Kendal days, perhaps about 1775 or a little later, lent him £10 when his tilt-cart and most of the things in it were destroyed in a fairground blaze.

The description of Barty as a 'Conjuror & Magician', though open to objection on the ground that it attributes to him powers he did not possess and may not have claimed, is nonetheless welcome for its suggestion that his tricks were not confined to those depending solely on his own dexterity, but included also seemingly miraculous recoveries, reappearances, and transformations of articles, the basis of which was unnoticed substitutions. To facilitate them the conjuror at one time wore an apron with pockets, rather like a game-bag; but later this tell-tale garment was discarded in favour of a table with a cover reaching almost or quite to the ground. It concealed a small assistant, commonly a boy, who contributed to the working of most of the illusions of this type, either by handing to the conjuror the articles he needed as he passed behind the table, or by pushing them up to him through trap-doors in the table-top. In the second half of the eighteenth century this *modus operandi* was general; so Barty Purcel, among others, would require someone small and sharp to assist him when he was performing tricks that were impossible without substitutions. It was then, I fancy, that well-timed pattering would be of the greatest service to him and his fellow conjurors.

In the Hawkshead registers Barty's name is invariably given in the seven entries in which it appears as Bartholomew Purcel: his occupation—and he may have had more than one—is not recorded in any of them; but in the last, which will be cited in a moment, he is stated to have been an Irishman. On 11 September 1744, he married Mary Atkinson, and in the next seven years he and his wife, whose abode is given first as the How in Hawkshead Field and then as Near

Sawrey, had four children baptized at Hawkshead, James (who died in infancy) in 1744, Eleanor in 1746, John in 1748, and Elizabeth in 1751. After that there is no mention of any Purcel in the registers until 1779, when the following baptismal entry occurs: 'Hannah Daughter of John Watson Far Sawrey Shoemaker Son of John Watson a Scotchman by Hannah his Wife The Mothers name Mally D^r of Bartholomew Purcel an Irishman Born Jan ye 28 Baptized Feb ye 21st'. The fact that there were no Purcel registrations at Hawkshead from 1751 to 1779, the period during which Mally must have been both christened and married, forces one to the conclusion that Barty and his wife made their home elsewhere at this time. There is nothing to show that she ever returned; and certainly she was not buried at Hawkshead. Nor was Barty for that matter, but there is documentary evidence that he came back and was living in his old age in the Hawkshead Quarter of the parish. It takes the form of an entry in the Poor Accounts for that Quarter in the year 1793-4 which reads: 'To Bartholomew Pursel . . . 5s. 0d.' Probably it was paid to him in sickness or other disability, for he was never in regular receipt of poor relief. This grant to him should mean that the Hawkshead Quarter was his place of legal settlement, the alternative being that he had lived there long enough to be regarded locally, if not in law, as a person who was entitled to assistance by its Overseer of the Poor if and when he was in need of it. In either case it is beginning to look rather more likely that his home was in or near Hawkshead when Wordsworth was a small boy at school there.

About the time of Barty Purcel's marriage there was a little Irish colony at Sawrey, the men being 'colliers', as charcoal burners or makers of wood charcoal were then called. The Mulveys or Mulbys, who lived at Near Sawrey, were the principal family, and the only one whose name appears in the Hawkshead registers for any length of time. I am mentioning them because there is a possibility that the Irish boy who was a servant to an itinerant conjuror round about 1780 was one of them, or a relation of theirs, for Arthur Brydson had heard, probably from Mrs. Benson Harrison, that he was a Sawrey boy. As he was about the same age as Wordsworth, who was born in 1770, he could have been a grandson of the Michael Mulvey who married Margaret Roach by licence at Hawkshead in

w

1737, and had two sons baptized there, James in 1738 and Daniel in February 1740/41. However, there is no record in the registers of the christening of a Mulvey or Mulby boy in 1770 or near that date. Daniel Mulby, a pauper in his old age, died at Sawrey in 1812, but the registers show that by no means all the family stayed there; so the boy in question, even if he was one of them, may have been born and reared elsewhere. If he was, and not at Sawrey, it is more understandable that Wordsworth took him to view the scene from West's Station. As to his duties, I imagine he served as house-boy when his master was at home, and as conjuror's assistant when he was travelling round to 'fairs & places'.

William Braithwaite's sister Ann, the last of the Braithwaites of Satterhow—the trustees of her will—bequests to relatives—to residents of Hawkshead—to friends in Windermere—the Flemings

The Rev. William was the last of the male Braithwaites of Satterhow, but the estate was still in the possession of his sister Ann when she died unmarried at Hawkshead on 19 May 1826, at the age of sixty-two. She was buried in the churchyard, where a flat stone bearing a simple inscription marks the site of her grave. There is also a memorial to her inside the church, in the form of a mural tablet 'erected by those Friends who are desirous of recording their grateful Remembrance of Her'. There were many, both old and young, whom she had in mind when making her will, which is dated 6 December 1824; and at the risk of being charged with irrelevancy I am going to note and consider her main personal bequests, details of which, and of some lesser ones, I owe again to Mr. Sharpe France. But first I must say something about her choice of trustees, to whom she refers as her friends, and who were the Rev. Thomas Bowman of Hawkshead, John Jackson of Ulverston, 'common brewer', and Lieut. William Hodgson of Colthouse. Thomas Bowman, who was sixty-five when she died, had been Master of the Grammar School since 1786, and her brother William had served with him in the 1790s on the committee responsible for overseeing the work of re-pewing the church and adding a vestry, as a Trustee of the Thomas Sandys Charity, and as one of the Twenty Four. She may have known John Jackson about as long, as her acquaintance with him and its continuance undoubtedly resulted from her early and enduring friendship with Martha Irton, who on 3 January 1787, married William Fell, a relation of his who joined with him in establishing a 'common brewery' in Ulverston. John Jackson, the older of the two partners, was described as a gentleman when he and Agnes Fell, both of Ulverston, were married there in 1776, and William Fell as a merchant when his daughter Martha was christened in 1796. He and his wife lived in Market Street, Ulverston, where they often had relations and friends to stay with them: Martha's brother Samuel Irton of the East India Company died there in 1813. They also entertained their neighbours in town and country both frequently and generously, but without ostentation, which was distasteful to both. I do not know just when William Fell died, but he was no longer living when Ann Braithwaite made her will. Her remaining executor, Lieut. William Hodgson of Colthouse, was a very much younger man than the other two. Born in 1795, he was the seventh child and third son of Matthew Hodgson, surgeon, by his second wife Frances or Fanny Irton, who was ten years older than her sister Martha, and six than Ann Braithwaite.

By her will Ann declared that her trustees were to divide her plate, china, glass, and table-linen between them. She also bequeathed £50 each to the Rev. Thomas Bowman and John Jackson, and £200 to William Hodgson; but he died at the age of thirty-one on 14 September 1826, just four days before probate of her will was granted. To Martha, widow of William Fell of Ulverston, common brewer, she left £100, and 'to her daughters Martha wife of Richard Smith of Urswick, esq. and Elizabeth Fell £50 each', making another £200. And here I will interrupt for a moment to say that Richard Smith's full name was Richard Wordsworth Smith,[1] and that

---

[1] Presumably the son of John Smith (1755–1807), Broughton-in-Furness, and his second wife, Mary (1766–99) who was Wordsworth's cousin, the second daughter of his Uncle Richard Wordsworth of Whitehaven (see *Early Letters of Wordsworth*, ed. Shaver, 1967, p. 121). Shaver describes John Smith as a 'tavern-keeper'. He is presumably the John Smith Junior of Broughton described as a liquor merchant, one among many owed money by William Strickland of Ulverston, gentleman. This is in a document dated 9 April 1800 in the archives of the Public Library, Barrow-in-Furness.

Elizabeth Fell subsequently married Thomas Alcock Beck of Esthwaite Lodge, Hawkshead, author of the sumptuous *Annales Furnesienses: History and Antiquities of Furness Abbey*. Ann's other Ulverston bequest was £50 to Elizabeth, sister of John Jackson.

To relations she left £1,400 in all, the particulars being: to the children of deceased cousin George Braithwaite £400 between them; to his brother Joseph Braithwaite of Edinburgh £300; to their two sisters Mary and Ann £100 each; and to the children of deceased cousin William Hodgson of Wood Gate in Lowick, spademaker, £500 between them. As she had very few relatives, and none really close after the death of her brother William, I am inclined to think that the Braithwaites she named were sons and daughters of the George Braithwaite of Harrowslack who died in 1786 at the age of fifty-three, and whose son George, about whom little is known, did not keep on his father's farm; and further, that her deceased cousin William Hodgson was a brother of the Braithwaite Hodgson, one time at Great Boat, who succeeded the younger George Braithwaite at Harrowslack. Indeed, the evidence I have at hand clearly points to these conclusions, and admits of no others; but it is only fair to say that in neither case does it amount to strict proof.

The bequests that Ann made to residents in the parish of Hawkshead other than her executors fall into two groups. The first comprises £200, together with her clothing, bed, and bed-linen, to her servant Mary Satterthwaite: £130, 'with request that she take care of dog as long as it lives', to Mary Ladyman, servant to her deceased friend Miss Martha Braithwaite; £100 to Mary Rigby of Keen Ground, widow; and £100 to John Kirby, her farmer at Satterhow. The second group, which takes us to the opposite end of the social scale, announces legacies of £100 each to 'John, Ellen and Jane children of Miles Sandys of Graythwaite, esq.' In 1790 he married Elizabeth, daughter of Sir John Dalrymple, Bart., of Oxenford Castle, near Edinburgh; and when in 1792, on the death of his uncle Myles, he inherited the Graythwaite estate, he and his wife came to live at the Hall. They then had two sons, the younger of whom was christened John Dalrymple at Old Hutton, near Kendal, in 1792. Eight more children were to follow, all born at Graythwaite, Ellen, who was their fourth child and first daughter, in 1796, and Jane, the youngest of the family, in 1807. She had a second baptismal name, given in the Hawkshead registers as Robits, and incorrectly by Burke as Roberts. The parents were about Ann's age, Myles Sandys being two years older than she was, and his wife three; and in the 1790s he and the Rev. William Braithwaite were associated as Grammar School Governors, Sandys Charity Trustees, and fellow members of the Twenty Four. But mutual attraction, ripening into friendship despite the difference in social standing, seems to me to have been the main reason for Ann Braithwaite's bequests to a son and two daughters of Myles and Elizabeth Sandys. John succeeded his father at Graythwaite, and in middle age Jane became the second wife of Jedediah Strutt of Belper.

The rest of Ann's major bequests, and two minor ones I may as well mention in passing, tell us something about her friends in the parish of Windermere, and at the same time afford a parallel to her Sandys legacies. They were: £50 to her goddaughter Ann Butcher of Bowness; £100 to the Rev. Fletcher Fleming of Rayrigg, and £100 each to his brothers Thomas and Herbert, 'esquires'; £50 to Isabella Taylor of Belfield near Bowness; and £10 each to Jane and Ann daughters of the Rev. William Barton of Bowness, deceased.[1] That is the order in which Ann set them down, but it will be convenient to begin with Isabella Taylor, who was no longer living at the time of Ann's death, for on a memorial to her at St. Martin's, Bowness, the Parish Church, it is stated that she died at Belfield on 13 February 1826 'in her 77th year'. Second daughter of the Fletcher Fleming who bought Rayrigg in 1735, she became the wife of Peter Taylor of Whitehaven in January 1770,[2] and lived there until his death early in the nineteenth century, when she returned to her native parish, and spent the latter end of her life at Belfield, a large, new house overlooking Bowness Bay. She has been credited with having it built for her; but it would be truer to say, I think, that her husband, having decided to retire to a house in the Lakes, then a

[1] An influential local figure, 43 years Rector of Windermere, one of the three commissioners appointed by Parliament to carry out the Claife Heights Enclosure Act. A memorial in Bowness Church records his death on 3 February 1823, aged 75. His wife died in 1826, Ann in 1847, Jane in 1855.

[2] For Peter Taylor and family, see Additional Notes, Appendix V.

fashionable thing for a wealthy merchant to do, was having it erected during the last year of his life, and that it was nearing completion when he died, so that all she had to do was to see to the finishing of the work, including the laying out of the grounds. Below Bowness, says the Rev. John Hodgson, 'the landscape is enlivened with Mrs Taylor's house at *Bellfield*.' Be that as it may, it seems to have been needlessly big for a widow, even if, as is probable, her unmarried daughter Isabella Agnes, who died in the village of Bowness in 1837 'in her 67th year', was living with her at the time. After her death it was sold. She and Peter Taylor had three sons, all educated at Hawkshead, but at least two lost their lives in the wars, Joseph in 1801, and Fletcher in 1809. About Peter, the youngest, I cannot be sure.

Jane Taylor, a younger sister of Isabella Agnes, became mistress at Rayrigg in 1794 as a result of her marriage in the summer of that year to her first cousin the Rev. John Fleming, Wordsworth's school friend, for he, as we have seen, inherited it as a boy, and adopted the surname Fleming in place of Raincock.[1] He and Jane, who made Rayrigg their home from the start, and evidently became friendly with Ann Braithwaite, had eight sons, of whom Fletcher was the eldest, Thomas the fifth, and Herbert Octavius the youngest, their respective dates of birth being 1795, 1810, and 1818. Fletcher, who was educated at Hawkshead and Sedbergh schools and at St. John's College, Cambridge, succeeded his father at Rayrigg in 1835. He was Rector of Grasmere from 1857 to 1863, and served Rydal Chapel from 1825.[2] Thomas also went to Cambridge, where he became a Fellow of Pembroke College; and he, too, was ordained.[3] Herbert,

[1] See above, p. 208.

[2] The Wordsworths were not entirely uncritical of their curate; Coleridge's daughter, Sara, just married in Keswick, stayed at Rydal Mount on her way to London. Dorothy Wordsworth wrote on 11 September 1829: 'On Sunday the Bride *appeared* at Chapel, and dear Mr. Fleming gave us one of his very *goody* sermons; with so much heartfeeling that it was impossible not to sympathize with him—yet at the end of it you could not say what his object had been.' (*Letters of William and Dorothy Wordsworth: Later Years*, 1939, I, p. 400.)

[3] A glimpse of the Fleming family and of Thomas's situation after his father's death in 1835 comes in a letter of Wordsworth to Wrangham, 2 February 1835, in which Wordsworth makes clear his disapproval of young men being ordained curates 'in places where they had been brought up, or in the midst of their own relatives.' Mrs.

on the other hand, was serving as a Lieutenant in the Marine Light Infantry when he died of cholera at Hurrypur in the East Indies in 1846. All John and Jane Fleming's sons grew to manhood, but both the eldest and the second of their three daughters died in infancy. They were buried in the chancel of Windermere Parish Church, where several of their fore-elders had been interred; and so was John Fleming's youngest brother George Raincock, 'Gentleman', who died at Rayrigg in January 1820.

The Rev. John Fleming's ecclesiastical preferments, the chief of which were to the Prebendal Stall of St. Andrew in Llandaff Cathedral in 1800, and to the Rectory of Bootle, Cumberland, in 1814, did not result in his leaving Rayrigg, at any rate not until after his wife's death on 10 November 1828, 'in her 55th year', But when his distant kinsman, the Rev. Sir Richard le Fleming, Bart., of Rydal, after securing the Grasmere living in 1822, was nominated Rector of Windermere in 1823, John undertook to officiate for him there. So it must have been he, if it was not the Rev. William Barton, who christened Ann Braithwaite's goddaughter, Ann Butcher of Bowness. The child's father is likely to have been the Captain William Wain Butcher who is listed as a Bowness resident by Parson and White in their 1829 Directory; a relative newcomer to the district, I should think, who may or may not have been akin to the John

---

Wordsworth had been promoting, and in the event, successfully, the claims of R. P. Graves to the vacancy at Windermere. Wordsworth writes: 'Mrs. W. judiciously and properly stated in her letter that it was not her desire, and she trusted it was no one's else, to interfere with any claims which in the judgment of the Bi[sho]p the sons of our late friend might have. Had she not made this proviso, I should have regretted she mixed at all in a business of so delicate a nature; but I will not conceal from you that out of these well-intended and right endeavours of hers has arisen much uneasiness to herself—from the circumstance that Mr. Thos. Fleming, who was his Father's Curate at Bootle, is now likely to be without employment. Of him *personally* we have but slight knowledge, but it redounds much to his honour that he had set aside, before his Father's death, the proceeds of his Fellowship to maintain a younger Brother at College, his Father not being able to do it; he himself living upon his stipend as his Father's Curate. This fact was mentioned some little time ago to Mrs. W. by a friend and benefactress of the family. It grieves me to add, that the eldest Son [Fletcher], our Minister,—a most excellent Person and a zealous Pastor,—has taken offence at what we have done in this business, the whole particulars of which were laid openly before him.' (*Letters of William and Dorothy Wordsworth: Later Years*, II, pp. 725–6.) Thomas died in 1867 at Chertsey, Surrey.

Butcher who left Hawkshead School in 1790. This boy's home was at Preesall, Lancashire, on the north side of the Wyre estuary nearly opposite Fleetwood.[1]

The residue of Ann Braithwaite's estate, she willed, was to be divided equally between Thomas Bowman, John Jackson, and William Hodgson, her executors; Fletcher, Thomas, and Herbert Fleming of Rayrigg; and John, Ellen, and Jane Sandys of Graythwaite. Her other monetary bequests, including two more minor ones of £10 each (one of them to buy a mourning ring), and the £100 she left for the benefit of the Sawrey schoolmaster, amounted in all to £3,320. As her personal possessions, some of which were to be distributed, were valued at 'under £1,000', her real estate must have been worth about £2,500. She instructed her executors to sell this, and the residue of her personal property, in order to raise the money needed to pay her several bequests. No particulars of the sale are available, but it seems safe to say that her friend Myles Sandys purchased the Satterhow estate, with the possible exception of the residence sometimes known as High Satterhow, which may have been sold separately. In Parson and White's 1829 Directory John Kirkby is named as the tenant farmer at Satterhow, but no mention is made of anyone living at High Satterhow. Ann Braithwaite's Bowness friendships suggest that she may have lived there after it became hers, but on the scanty evidence available it is more likely that she chose to stay on in the smaller house in Hawkshead Town in which she was living, at first with her mother,[2] when the Wordsworth boys, John Fleming and the Raincocks, Peter Taylor's sons, and Sir John Dalrymple's were among the pupils at Hawkshead School, and where her brother William died in 1800. Judging from the list of subscribers to the S.P.G. collection, seemingly house to house, in 1779, her house was between those then occupied by Isaac Holme, a rather superior joiner with whom Grammar School boys

---

[1] See Alphabetical List, Appendix IV. Possibly the Mr. Butcher, Bowness, who called with Miss Butcher—presumably Ann (see p. 305)—at Rydal Mount in September 1838.

[2] As Miss Nancy Braithwaite she succeeded her mother, Mrs. Agnes Braithwaite (see above, p. 259), in paying Land Tax for the house in 1790. In the Land Tax return, dated 24 June 1790, she paid 2s. 2d. 2 farthings.

are known to have boarded in the 1780s,[1] and John Hodgson, shoe-maker and Parish Clerk. But I cannot identify it, and have no notion who bought it from Ann's executors.[2]

Postscript

AFTER an absence of ten years Wordsworth revisited Hawkshead in the course of a walking tour with Coleridge in the late autumn of 1799. They were joined at Temple Sowerby, Westmorland, by Wordsworth's brother John. Wordsworth mentioned this visit when writing to his sister Dorothy on 8 November, but all he told her about it is contained in the parenthetic clause 'great change amongst the people since we were last there'. I value these few words as evidence that the local inhabitants were uppermost in his mind when he came among them once more, and as proof by implication that they had meant something to him during the years he boarded with Ann Tyson.

---

[1] One of his boarders was Richard Benson: see his letter, Appendix III. The Senhouse accounts show that Holme was paid for a fishing-rod for one of the boys, and the le Fleming accounts that he supplied paint and linseed oil to John Gibson of Rydal (letter of 22 November 1784, Record Office, Kendal).

[2] T.W.T.'s interest in Ann Braithwaite's will makes an abrupt, perhaps uncadenced close to this book: to him, of course, the pleasure was to see some of the Hawkshead schoolboys and their families appearing in an epilogue. The will offers a sense of the old interrelationships carrying on for more than a generation. T.W.T. might have wished to integrate this a little more into his study, had he been able to revise it; but he was not. In his postscript, typically enough, he places the people of Hawkshead in the centre of his concern.

APPENDIX I

(a) Charles Farish

For a discussion of Charles Farish's poem, *The Minstrels of Winandermere* (1811), see Eric Robertson's *Wordsworthshire* (1911), pp. 73–85. Robertson questions whether Farish might have read his poem to Wordsworth during their time as undergraduates, before Wordsworth began *Evening Walk*. Manuscript evidence shows that at least four of the poems sung by the schoolboy minstrels in Farish's loco-descriptive poem were written before he went to Cambridge in 1784. These poems in their early form have a special interest as they were written by one of the more talented of the older schoolboys at the time that Wordsworth, aged between thirteen and fifteen, was committing himself to being a poet. But first, it is worth recollecting the overall structure of *The Minstrels of Winandermere*.

The incident that the poem revolves around is that of a group of nine schoolboys from Hawkshead making an excursion along the road to Kendal, some to Ings Chapel, two miles from Staveley, and others up the valley of Kentmere till they can see Hawes Water and the woods of Lowther. Ings Chapel with its marble floor was rebuilt by Robert Bateman, a native of the place, who made his fortune as a merchant, and who, though rumour has it that he was poisoned, became the local example of the man who rose from poverty to riches; it is indeed to this story that Wordsworth refers in 'Michael' when he recounts it as part of Isabel's thinking when she acquiesces in her husband's decision that Luke should go and seek his fortune in the city. That Farish should envisage his schoolboys going to Kentmere and that William and John Wordsworth in 1799 should bring Coleridge through that valley on their way from Hawes Water in North Westmorland to Hawkshead suggests that Kentmere was well known by Hawkshead boys. Essentially, the poem centres not on the excursion, but on the two crossings of the Ferry at Bowness; on the outward journey, the nine schoolboys and the ferryman, George, each have their own songs, and on their return, three of the boys have songs, the rest of the pieces belonging to strangers also waiting for the Ferry and to the ferryman's daughter, Edith.

The poem is introduced and interconnected where necessary by the narrator, who, as observer rather than participant in the schoolboys' outing, is a rather melancholy presence, not least when he describes the haunting effect of Edith's song on the listeners; here, for a moment, the poem becomes almost impressive, but returns quickly for the conclusion to its more usual pedestrian self, withdrawing its praise of Edith as, presumably, improper, and giving her sound advice on her duties towards her husband and children. As there is little narrative, the narrator becomes a general commentator; he laments how the iron industry's demand for charcoal has stripped the countryside of timber, particularly of oak; he alludes to Rayrigg as the retreat of Wilberforce (Farish's brother, William, the Cambridge Professor of Chemistry, married Hannah, sister of Wilberforce's friend and brother-in-law, James Stephens) indicating, by his reference to 'Tombuctoo's wrongs' now removed, that he wrote this section of the poem after 1807 when the slave trade was abolished. But Farish also, like his uncle, William Gilpin, the writer on the picturesque, mingles a concern for the beauty of landscape with a concern for antiquities. Some of the songs decidedly emphasize this element—the ninth schoolboy's song is called 'Furness Abbey'; the boatman's story, 'The Wild Boar', deals with Farish's ancestor, Richard Gilpin of Kentmere; the stranger from Carlisle sings of the Roman Wall, and the traveller from London celebrates the charity of Rahere, the minstrel of Henry I. This allusive and historically orientated poetry seems to be characteristic of Farish's later manner. There are four schoolboy poems in the *Minstrels*, four out of the seven Hawkshead poems to survive in manuscript; these are more personal and thinner in texture. Even so, with some revision, Farish felt able, in 1811, to give them a place in his *Minstrels*.

The manuscript contains, besides the Hawkshead poems, some conventionally pious verse surviving from 1780 when the author would be some fourteen years old at Carlisle Grammar School. But it is the Hawkshead poems that have an obviously relevant topographical interest in any study of Wordsworth's Hawkshead, and besides, these are the only surviving poems, apart from Wordsworth's very early verses, to have been written, in part at least, at Hawkshead School under the tutelage of William Taylor. The group of seven poems was sent in 1791 by Farish's sister Margaret to their sister Elizabeth, by this time married to her first cousin, the eldest son of William Gilpin. The manuscripts are among the Gilpin papers in the Bodleian Library, Oxford. Margaret wrote on 10 August 1791:

My dear Sister
    I have as you desired copied you out some of the young man's poems. I would like to know what poems amongst these I send you, you have seen—for if you have not seen most of them I should be glad, as they will be new to you.—Charles

knows not that I have sent you any of them.—The ode to Contemplation was occasioned by a present of a seal which I sent him to Hawkshead—the emblem of which was contemplation, & he wrote that poem & sent it me.—The poem upon *shadow wood* is a pretty little thing—the wood was within the distance of a short walk from Hawkshead—but it has now been some years levelled with the ground. Those poems upon the Vacation & upon Spring, are very beautiful—& I rather think you must have seen them.—That to a friend & schoolfellow requires perhaps some explanation—Mr Tyson it seems was very desireous of going to sea, which his Father was much against, however such is the force of inclination that the young Man went from school unknown to his Father, & Charles wrote those verses upon him—w^h by some means, or other, got into the Hands of the Lads Father who was much pleased with them. What I send you are mostly dated & you will find a great many that were written long ago—I shall make no farther remarks upon them—but leave that you to do, &—I know not how far Charles would be pleased with my sending them—but as I said before he knows nothing of it—I consulted my Mother & she gave me leave & thought there was no harm in my sending them to you & so that gave me satisfaction.—

I dare say you do not intend to let them be much seen as I don't think Charles would like that—but I have no business to give advice to you or to impose any rules upon you. So do as y^r discretion directs. I thought it necessary to explain one or two of them that you might understand them better than you otherwise would have done.—yrs most affecty Marg^t Farish.

[The four poems later revised for the *Minstrels*, and the poem on Shadow Wood follow in chronological order. The other two poems are slight: the first, with a winter setting, undated, is a compliment to Matilda; the second, of seven lines, dated 'Hawkshead Jany 1783', is a lament for her death.]

Hawkshead. Oct. 12th 1783.

Ode.—To Contemplation.—

Hail Contemplation! Heavenly Maid!
    Thy gentle influence impart,
And lend—O lend thy pleasing aid,
    To raise, & to enlarge my heart!

Led by thy hand oft let me go
    By babbling Caldew's verdant Side:
Or thine, O Eden winding slow!
    Where the rough steep oerhangs the tide.

Here lost in fancy let me roam,
    When first the orient splendors rise:
When Early from my much-lov'd Home
    The smoke high-curling shades the sky's.

Or in the Solemn hour of Night
　　Along those shores which Esthwaite laves,
When Phoebe sheds her silver light
　　Far glittering o'er the heaving waves:

As pensive here alone I wander
　　Help my Silent Meditation!
Help my Thoughts, in swift meander
　　Rambling thro' the whole Creation!

Lo! I feel the Sacred Motion!
　　Lo! I feel the high controul!
I feel—I feel heaven-bred Devotion
　　Thrilling thro' my raptur'd Soul!

Whilst stars unnumber'd deck the pole,
　　And pour their Lustre o'er the Land:
Whilst suns & worlds around me roll:
　　The Work of an Almighty Hand!

Yet whilst amaz'd these woods I see,
　　And view this universal Frame,
Oft let me—let me think on thee
　　From whom the pleasing present came.

[See the Third Boy's Song, *Minstrels of Winandermere*, pp. 46–8.]

C. Farish　Hawkshd

Shadow Wood

How oft O shadow was I wont to stray
　　Pleased & bewildered midst thy waving Trees,
(Where rapid Purla winds its rocky way)
　　To taste the fragrance of thy cooling breeze.

Oft have I wandered by thy babbling stream
　　And heard the chiding of thy white cascades,
To shun the fervour of the noon day beam,
　　When lowing Oxen seek the wat'ry glade.

And oft when Phoebus wak'd the feather'd groves,
　　I've walk'd unheedful of the falling dew
And Listen'd to the Linnets lay of love
　　Or Raven croaking from the baleful yew;

Oft have I seen the Hare pursu'd in vain
　　By baying Dogs, o'er many a foot of ground,
Return delighted to its seat again
　　And mock the tracing of the mouthing hound.

When on the Cliffs, the far resounding horn,
    From distant rocks re-echoed shrill & clear,
Was on a Zephirs gentle pinions borne;
    And lofty swelling met my raptur'd ear.

Oft have I trod upon the steepy brow,
    And seen the Hare, lay panting on the ground,
Beside the foaming stream, that dashed below,
    Which startling, prick'd its ears at ev'ry sound.

[Farish did not publish this poem. Shadow wood is marked on maps based on the 1848 and 1888 surveys as being about half a mile north-west of Hawkshead.]

C. Farish
Hawkshead.   April 22^d.
1784.

On Spring

When Nature tunes the feather'd choir,
    And gives the warbling groves to Sing
Say, shall the Muse forget the lyre,
    Nor hail the sweet return of Spring?

Lo! now the Angry storms are fled,
    Winter recalls his baffled train:
No tempests vex the mountain's head,
    No billows ride the peaceful main.

The gloomy clouds no longer lower,
    But Phoebus shoots a chearful ray,
And smiling thro' an April shower,
    Calls forth the snow-drop to the day.

Hark! thro' the thicket wild & clear
    The Linnet swells its little throat:
And, pleas'd with the reviving year,
    Fills all the woodlands with its note.

The whistling Peasant drives his wain,
    Or plods behind his weary plow:
And reaps in thought the golden grain,
    Where late he trod the flaky snow.

Where Late the Boy, devoid of care
    On Esthwaites fetter'd bosom stood,
And, bending o'er the sharpen'd share,
    In circles plow'd the Marble flood,

Now swans their downy feathers lave,
    And sail with wings uplifted high:
Or swallows skim the dimpling wave,
    And dip their pinions as they fly.

Hark! Nature speaks to Reason's ear,
    And stamps this lesson on the mind.
(My Soul, 'tis Nature speaks, revere!)
    'In ev'ry sorrow be resign'd.

'What tho' conflicting Tempests frown,
    'And fortunes blasts assail thy head:
'Soon shall those blasts be overblown,
    'And soon the Sun his lustre shed.

'Should sickness shake his locks of care,
    'And round thee hang a wintry gloom:
'Bear it, O Man, with patience bear,
    'For Health, the spring of Joy shall come.'

[See The First Boy's Song, *Minstrels*, pp. 42–4.]

June—1784
C. Farish   Hawkshead

To a Friend & School-fellow.

Tyson Farewell!—but take one parting tear:
One friendly token from a friend sincere!—
When sunburnt Nation's meet your wandring eyes,
When other climes you feel & other sky's
Where direful Slav'ry with her ruffian bands
Waves her black banners o'er the wretch'd land
And drags the Captive Negro from afar:
Plunging his Country in the woes of War:—
When you my friend o'er that sad land shall roam
Far from your weeping friends & pleasing Home,
Ah! think on Hawkshead!—when the Star of day
With scorching fervor points a downward ray,
And faint you seek the shelter of a wood,
Or cool your weary limbs amid the flood—
Ah! then remember on one stormy day
Pleas'd how we row'd, nor wish'd the Storm away,
While Esthwaites waves in wintry fetters bound
Indignant mutter'd deep a boding sound:
Then from the Ice a fragment huge you tore
And steer'd a desperate Voyage from the Shore.
I little knew so soon that shore you'd leave
To plough in larger Bark the Atlantic Wave!

——But stay not long!—soon to the western gale
Unfurl once more thy weather-beaten sail,
Mark with returning keel the willing main:
—Ah! soon return & live those hours again
In converse sweet!—But go!—be vertue thine!
And may she round thy brows a wreath entwine,
A wreath of joy:—may peace thy pillow spread:
May Heaven on thee its choicest blessings shed:
May Guardian Angels all thy steps attend!
——Such is the prayer of Farish for his friend.——

[Survives in The Seventh Boy's Song, entitled 'Esthwaite-Water',
Minstrels, pp. 20–1.]

C. Farish   Hawkshead

On the Vacation

'Go'! is the word: & lo! the impatient Boy
Rushes impetuous from the bending seats:
Hark! in what shouts that speak the general joy!
See! with what transports every Bosom beats!

Not with more joy the weary Trojans spied
The shore deserted & disburthen'd main:
Not with more joy their Gates they open'd wide
And pour'd imprison'd millions on the plain.

But Oh! my Friends, employ'd at School no more,
Let not the Syren tongue of Sloth invite,
For ah! what woes the hapless Trojans bore
For the sad sloth of one disastrous night.

Lo! as I walk where Esthwaites waters wind
And hear once more the dashing breakers roar,
Hark! every echo speaks the vacant mind:
The voice of gladness sings along the Shore.

But ah! I mourn—why do I mourn alone?
From me alone why bursts the lab'ring sigh?
Why from my single tongue proceeds a moan?
Why fall the lonely sorrows from my eye?

The Sun shines clear; Creation round looks gay:
No driving clouds along the welkin scowl:
The quiv'ring Lark exerts her lofty lay
And sings in tuneful discord to my soul.

Yet Nature mourns: & to my Sorrows true
The hollow blasts in murmurs seem to blow:
Hoarse croaks the Raven from the baleful yew:
Slow runs the rill, in wailing accents slow.

x

Must I then leave thee Hawkshead? Must I go?
And go alas! not to return again?—
I saw two winters cloath thy hills in snow:
I saw two summers parch thy wither'd plain:

No! not yet two—when ah the hour draws nigh
The fatal hour that summons me away—
(How quickly sorrows come, & pleasures fly!)
The Joys of Mortals are but for a day!

When o'er the limpid *wave* at early morn
In act to drink impends the dappled Hind,
If but the Hunter sound his Horrid Horn,
She flies, & leaves the untasted brook behind

So Esthwaite from thy hills & pleasing Vale
So from thy joys & pleasures must I fly:
But chiefly thee O Science! I bewail:
What Stores of Science yet untasted lie!

[See The Eighth Boy's Song, *Minstrels*, pp. 21–7.]

Farish has not dated this poem, but clearly he is about to leave Hawkshead for Cambridge and the summer is not yet ended. Farish went up to Cambridge in 1784. This perhaps helps to date Wordsworth's first composition: 'The first verses which I wrote were a task imposed by my own master: the subject, "The Summer Vacation"; and of my own accord I added other verses upon "Return to School"' (*Memoirs of William Wordsworth*, ed. Christopher Wordsworth, 1851, I, p. 10). As it was summer when Farish wrote, it is quite possible that he returned to Hawkshead for the beginning of the Autumn Half about the end of July 1784, even as Wordsworth in 1787 was to spend a period at Hawkshead immediately before going up to Cambridge. The poems on the Summer Vacation—we do not of course have Wordsworth's verses— could have been written at that time. Certainly Farish's poem seems to have been written while he was actually in Hawkshead rather than on vacation, and this could have been either at the start of the Autumn Half or in the June preceding the holiday. It does not seem necessary to assume as recent scholars have done that the first verses Wordsworth wrote were 'a task imposed' by William Taylor for the vacation itself; rather they may well have been a school exercise, probably carried out in the late summer of 1784 since Wordsworth did some extra composition, 'Return to School'.

(b) John Bernard Farish

Wordsworth's note to line 81 of 'Guilt and Sorrow' when it was first published in 1842 reads: 'From a short MS. poem read to me when an undergraduate by my schoolfellow and friend Charles Farish, long since deceased. The verses were by a brother of his, a man of promising genius, who died young.' The brother was John Bernard Farish, born in 1754, educated at Carlisle Grammar School, St. Bees, Peterhouse, Cambridge, and then Magdalene. He did not take his degree until 1778, and apparently died shortly afterwards in Cambridge. Nothing hitherto has been known of the short MS. poem Wordsworth refers to in his note, but it clearly is the composition, 'The Heath', now among the Gilpin Papers. This is an exercise, first in the manner of Spenser, then in that of Shakespeare, and is dated 'July 1770 J. B. Farish' when John Bernard must have been a schoolboy at St. Bees. Wordsworth later himself attempted such an exercise in the same two styles in his description of the woman crossing a heath (see *Wordsworth Poetical Works*, I, pp. 292-5), and one wonders whether he was remembering Farish's ingenuity, even as a few months before he remembered his actual words in 'Guilt and Sorrow'. The texts of Farish's verses are:

The Heath, July 1770   J. B. Farish
A description in imitation of the manner of Spencer.

> And now we travelled over Barrock hill,
> All dismal, desolate, and dreary round,
> While the bleak, whistling winds blow cold & chill
> Often increasing with a murmuring sound.
> No tree, nor smiling green is on ye ground;
> 'Tis barren heath as far as sees the eye,
> And here & there—doth brood a green-grown pond,
> Beside us stood the Murtherer's gibbet high,
> And hovering round it often did a Raven fly.
>
> Eftsoons we heard the ghastly carcase shake
> His iron chains; up-born upon ye blast,
> While with his weight ye rusty chain did creek,
> Oft swinging he did beat the gibbet mast.
> Before our eyes a griesly terror past,—
> We stood, ne durst approachen for dismay;—
> The raven croaked full sore, and himself cast
> One's wing, and fled, for it did him affray:
> The wind did cease, and darksome wox ye face of day.

The ghost did walk yᵉ heath with solemn pace
And slow, while we stood silent & astound;
Dank, dead, and dim aye looked its hallow face;
Its eyne, like tapers dying on the ground,
Looked thro' the shroud that cover'd it all round.
Its place beside the murther's feet it took,
There oped its shroud, and showed a ghastly wound,
Pointing to where was given the fatal stroke,
Like wind it shrieked, & vanished as a curl of smoke!

A description of the same in imitation of the manner of Shakespeare.

And now we travelled over Barrock hill,
A dreary blank, bleak, bare & comfortless;
Upon whose turf the squalling winds do feed,
Leading the mantle of the pool in waves.
The piercing blasts do overcome our nature,
Biting the very bone,—before us stood
The Murtherer's Gibbet, round the which did fly
A Raven, with his level wing broad-stretched
Oft wheeling round, as fearing to approach
The thing so lately man,—which to & fro,
Grinding the rusty chain, swung by the blast
Up-born, and kicked its shrunk feet 'gainst yᵉ post,
'See those shrunk limbs!' exclaimed we, 'that black scull!
Design lived in it once black as itself!
See that fal'n hand!—it did a deed of death!'—
While yet we moralysed, the Raven croaked!
And drew off sheer with the wind. Deep darkness grew
Upon our sight! a shrouded Ghost was stalking
Slow o'er the heath towards us!—We beheld it!
Our souls did die within for very horror!—
Dim was its ghastly visage, like the Moon
Behind a cloud.—It came!—we saw it stalking
Slow o'er the heath towards us. It was near!—
It stood!—We stood!—The wind was silent!—Lo!
It did unfurl its shroud, that parted as two mists!
We saw the wound!—It pointed to the south,
And shrieking sunk upon the hollow wind!
It vanished as a torch blown out!

It is worth recalling Wordsworth's words when his sailor, guilty of an unintended murder, happens upon a gibbet, on which, as was the custom, the body hung in chains:

with scarce distinguishable clang
In the cold wind a sound of iron rang.
He looked and saw on a bare gibbet nigh
In clanking chains a human body hang
A hovering raven oft did round it fly
A grave there was beneath which he could not descry.

(See *Wordsworth Poetical Works*, I, pp. 98 and 336). Wordsworth added these lines to his original poem of 1794 after he went to Racedown in 1795. To his first tale of 'The Female Vagrant', he brought a second bitter story, that of the sailor, a victim of social injustice and an outcast figure who, because of an accidental murder (or manslaughter) has to suffer the final indignity of the gibbet. J. B. Farish's image is clearly a seminal point for this new mood.

APPENDIX II

Hawkshead and the Presbyterian Meeting House

Thom's letter raises teasing problems, as the comments in it do not sit easily on a Quaker interpretation, and yet the location of the Quaker meeting at Colthouse is appropriate. The perfect answer has proved impossible to reach, but the search has uncovered much of interest about the patterns of nonconformity in Hawkshead over a good number of years. Some of the documents for this—some relating to Wordsworth and others not—have been incompletely presented.

J. H. Thom's letter to Stopford Brooke was written on 8 July 1890 on the occasion of the setting up of the Dove Cottage Trust. I give his reminiscence from the letter in full since it is interesting in itself and it allows the reader to assess the carefulness of the account. It is worth saying first that in a long obituary article (by V. D. Davis) of 1895 it is recorded of Thom that 'His memory was remarkably full and accurate in regard to events both recent and long past', and examples are given to emphasize this point (*The Liverpool Unitarian Annual*, 1895, p. 28). The relevant section of Thom's letter is as follows:

I had one opportunity of close intercourse with Wordsworth, the impressions of which are all in harmony with your sketch. We were dining at Lancrigg with that magnificent old lady Mrs. Fletcher & her daughter Lady Richardson, the only other guests being Mr. and Mrs. Wordsworth. After dinner we were left alone for a considerable time. No one could be less formidable, or stately, more easy, simple & kind. The Prose style of Poets happened to be spoken of, which he said was generally admirable, giving Examples, among them Southey, adding with a very kindly smile, 'Perhaps you will say that is not very much in point, as his Poetry is hardly Ever quoted.' Mrs. Fletcher, I suppose, had told him who & what I was—an escapade of my wife's mountain pony having kept them waiting a little for dinner. At a pause of our conversation he said suddenly 'when I was a boy at Hawkshead on a very wet or a very hot Sunday we used to go to the Presbyterian Meeting House, as the nearest, & what I chiefly recollect is that they were always telling God Almighty of the Attributes, rather than seeking spiritual communion with Him for themselves. ['] On my confessing that there was a time when the Worship of English Presbyterians was certainly of that Character, but that I thought he would find it at present to be more that of dear Children, without ceasing to be that of penitent Servants,—he said he was quite willing to believe that it was so,—and with a peculiar Expression of countenance & intonation, 'Ah Well! I go to Church for the sake of the Prayers—the Sermon you know is an Accident.'

When their pony carriage came he took leave, Mrs. Wordsworth remaining for some last words. After a little he returned & said, 'My dear the carriage is waiting' 'Well', she replied, 'do'nt be cross.' When he said playfully in the sweetest tones, of voice, 'Ah, I wish we could; it would be a little ripple upon our lives.'

On speaking to Mrs. Fletcher of his simplicity & graciousness of manner she said, 'Yes—but people are too afraid to give him an opportunity of showing him-self as he is—I asked a lady staying at Grasmere to meet him at dinner, who replied "What dine with Wordsworth! I should as soon think of dining in York Minster!" —There is an impression, or tradition, among the people of the District that he was reserved & unsociable, arising no doubt from being absorbed in thought & composition, according to your preserved saying of his Servant, that his Library was in the House but his study was in the fields.'

On parting with us he very kindly inquired where we were staying. I said 'at Wansfell, ['] the house then of Mr. W. R. Greg, my wife's Uncle. He drew him-self up with the air of a man slightly offended, & said 'I know a Mountain of that Name,'—Evidently resenting a great Liberty taken with the Mountain, to which one of his Sonnets is addressed.

The large element of the prosaic & the didactic in his works has interfered with his reputation,—& chiefly with the unpoetic. Blanco White gave the fiercest answer to this on some one remarking on it—'Yes, he was a great musician who did himself the injustice of printing his Voluntaries'—These are trifling recollec-tions, which yet have given me the feeling of knowing the Man Wordsworth.

John Hamilton Thom (1808–94) probably paid his visit to Lancrigg, in Easedale, Grasmere, in October 1846, for in that month his name appears in the Rydal Mount Visitors Book, and a visit to the poet's home would clearly be appropriate after a meeting at dinner. Thom states that he thought that Mrs. Fletcher had told Wordsworth who and what he was; and she may well have told Wordsworth that Thom was one of the lead-ing Unitarians of his day. He had recently, in 1845, edited a life of Blanco White, that Spanish Roman Catholic priest of Irish descent who, after years as a member of the Church of England, rounded off his career in 1835 by becoming a Unitarian in Liverpool. Further, Thom had been editor of the *Christian Teacher*, which had recently merged with the *Prospective Review*, and he was one of the four editors of this; the others were James Martineau, Charles Wicksteed and J. J. Taylor (whose *Life*, 1872, Thom was responsible for).

Brought up in the north of Ireland, Thom, whose father, a Presbyterian Minister, had died when his son was an infant, attended the Belfast Academical Institution where the 'presbyterianism' was 'non-subscribing', that is, did not compel acceptance of the Westminster Confession of Faith. It was more liberal, unorthodox and Arian than the characteristic English Unitarian rationalism. By the time he came to England in 1829 Thom had also been deeply and lastingly impressed by the American W. E. Channing whom he regarded 'not as the founder of a school, but as the destroyer of all schools, except the school of the spirit'. (From Thom's speech at the Channing Centenary Meeting quoted in the obituary cited above.) From 1831 to 1867 (with a break of three years when Channing's son was minister) Thom had charge of Renshaw Street Chapel, Liverpool. It is helpful to recognize that Thom's Presbyterianism has nothing to do with the Scottish form, or with its off-shoot, the Presbyterian Church of England which, as an organized body, dates from the 1870s. The term 'Presbyterian' in the 1840s, when Thom and Wordsworth were using it, seems to have come back into currency with prolonged litigations such as that beginning in 1830 over the eighteenth-century Lady Hewley's Charity. Many Unitarian congregations were derived from older Presbyterian Meetings and they had come to administer important Presbyterian Funds; their right to do this was challenged by other non-conformist groups. (See H. L. Short's essay in *The English Presbyterians*, by C. G. Bolam, and others, 1968.) The litigation was brought to an end in 1844 by the Dissenting Chapels Act.

Although it is difficult to believe that Thom, with his background, could loosely use the term 'English Presbyterians' as a description of Quakers and similarly, although it seems unlikely that Wordsworth himself, especially in conversation with an eminent Unitarian, should confuse the terms, it must, yet with some hesitation, be concluded that, behind the confused terminology in the conversation, there was intended by Wordsworth a reference to the Quaker Meeting House at Colthouse. There is too the possibility of Thom's recollection being inaccurate; but the detail of the letter as a whole seems convincing, establishing beyond doubt that Wordsworth did go on occasion to a Meeting House, whatever its affiliation. The lack of clear evidence of a Presbyterian Meeting House in Hawkshead has led scholars easily to assume that the Meeting House in question must be Colthouse. It is likely that it was; yet it is wrong to assert that there was no other meeting place for non-conformists in the late eighteenth century (Moorman, *William Wordsworth: Early Years*, p. 85). There were indeed Baptists in the village, and it seems worth while here to bring together some of the evidence from scattered records and present an outline of non-conformity in Hawkshead from somewhat earlier to somewhat later than Wordsworth's time there.

Mrs. Moorman notes that there had been a Presbyterian *meeting* at Hawkshead Tower early in the eighteenth century. From the records it becomes clear that the meeting was Baptist and that there is no place called Hawkshead Tower. Indeed, one of the confusing elements in such records as we have is terminology, where, as markedly in the Thom letter, the word 'Presbyterian' seems not to have a fixed meaning. The source of Mrs. Moorman's 'Presbyterian meeting' must be T. S. James (*Presbyterian Chapels and Charities*, 1867, p. 665) who mentions a Presbyterian Church at 'Tower of Hawkshead'; this was repeated in Benjamin Nightingale's *Lancashire Nonconformity* (1890, p. 255), with the information, again from James, that there was a congregation of eighty-eight, of whom eighteen were county voters, and with a minister named Gardiner, at some point between 1717 and 1729. Dr. Geoffrey F. Nuttall, to whom I am indebted for much of the information in this paragraph, made a significant discovery when he consulted the early eighteenth-century MS. upon which the 'Tower of Hawkshead' is based. I quote from his letter to me, 26 February 1970: 'I examined at Dr. William's Library the Evans MS. which is the source of the statement by Nightingale, following T. S. James. The first word in the entry is certainly "Tower", but it would appear to me likely that Evans misread the name "Torver" in the communication about the Lancashire congregations sent in to William Tong. The word given by James and Nightingale as "of" is, in fact, an ampersand, i.e. the original entry probably read "Torver & Hawkshead". This congregation is on a page on which all the congregations are marked P for Presbyterian, not, as on some pages, A for Anabaptist.' At first sight this might seem a strong argument for the existence of a Presbyterian meeting in Hawkshead even though some of the eighty-eight persons in the congregation were Torver people. But, despite the P for Presbyterian, the Baptist community must be the one referred to; firstly, Torver and Hawkshead are associated together in Baptist annals and seem to have shared Baptist ministers throughout the eighteenth century; secondly, the congregation in the Evans MS. had a named minister, Gardiner, and this implies a fairly established organization which could support a living for a minister.[1] There

---

[1] I have not yet found the name 'Gardiner' among the ministers of Hawkshead Hill Chapel, but so far as it is possible to glean a list of names from Douglas's *History of the Baptist Churches in the North of England* the ministers were as follows: George Braithwaite, 1707–12; Richard Coultherd from Knaresdale in Northumberland, 1722–72; Thomas Harbottle from Cockle Park, near Morpeth, Northumberland, 1777–80; Henry Dawson from Bishop Burton, Yorkshire, where he appears to have been a schoolmaster and local preacher, 1781 until at least 1789. There is a gap in the list, 1712–22 and during some or all of these years Gardiner was probably minister. There

was an endowed 'cause' at Hawkshead Hill meeting house,[1] apparently the gift of George Braithwaite, Baptist Minister, 1707–12, a native of Hawkshead and educated at the Grammar School and at Oxford. Braithwaite between 1707 and 1709 obtained by gift or by purchase land from William Denison, and from this time Hawkshead Hill rather than Torver becomes what Douglas calls 'the principal station for the church' (*History of the Baptist Churches in the North of England*, 1846, p. 100).

The building was registered in the Quarter Session Records for January 1709:

George Braithwaite of Hawkeshead in the sd County Maketh Oath that hee this depon. was requested by William Dennysen of Watersyde neare Hawkeshead aforesd to goe to Lancr and Petition the Court of Qur Sessions Holden for ye County Pal. of Lanc on behalfe of the sd William Dennysen to have a certaine house att Hawkeshead hill belonging to the sd William Dennyson recorded ffor a meeting place ffor an assembly of Protestants dissenting from the Church of England and that the sd William Dennyson att the same time did give his ffree Consent thereunto and desired that the same might bee recorded accordingly and further saith not

George Braithwaite.

Jur. in Cur.
11 Januar Recorded
1708/9.

There is confirmation of the registration in Bishop Gastrell's 'Notitia Cestriensis' (Chetham Society, 1st series, vol. 22, p. 517), where Hawkshead has the marginal note 'Diss. M.P.'[2] In neither of these records is the particular affiliation given; the words 'Protestants' or 'Diss[enters]' are unhelpful and Nightingale has confusingly printed the Quarter Sessions Record as a Quaker document (*Early Stages of the Quaker Movement in Lancashire*, 1921, p. 192). Indeed, without the essential identification of

are two additional points: we know that the Torver meeting had a dispute in 1718 with a Gabriel Fell who refused their call to be minister to them; we do not know whether or not this involved Hawkshead; secondly, in 1783, eleven years after Coultherd's death, the meeting house at Hawkshead Hill is listed in the land tax returns as 'Mr Coultherd meetin hous': in the same year a Mr. Richard Coulthred [*sic*] is listed separately as living in Hawkshead, and is perhaps the minister's son (see Lancashire County Records, Preston)—if so, he was quite a wealthy man, paying some 7s. 5d. in Land Tax, while the Baptist meeting house paid 6d.

[1] The term 'meeting house' seems to be more generally in use in the early history of Hawkshead Hill than the word 'chapel', Swainson Cowper's term in his *Hawkshead*; the association of Dissenters with a 'chapel' came from Methodist usage.

[2] Mr. B. C. Redwood, the Cheshire County Archivist kindly checked this for me against the original.

George Braithwaite as a Baptist minister there is nothing in these records or in the 'P' of the Evans MS. to contradict the general notion that sometime early in the eighteenth century there was a Presbyterian meeting house in Hawkshead. There is no doubt that all this refers to the beginning of Hawkshead Hill Baptist Chapel and it seems likely that 1709 was the date of its foundation, not 1678 as H. Swainson Cowper has it (*Hawkshead*, p. 21); this last date was when the Torver Baptist meeting was founded.

Later in the century Reginald Brathwaite, vicar of Hawkshead, catches sight of the Baptists now in a declining state. In 1789 Brathwaite answered as follows in his return to the Articles of Enquiry in the diocese of Chester, and Mr. B. C. Redwood had extracted the relevant section:

III. Are there in your Parish any Presbyterians, Independents, or Anabaptists, Quakers, or other Sectarists? And how many of each Sect, and of what Rank? Have they one or more Meeting Houses in your Parish, and are they duly licensed? What are the Names of theirTeachers, and are they qualified according to Law? Is their Number lessened or increased of late Years, and by what Means?

There are many Quakers, & Anabaptists in my Parish. The reputed number of Quakers is—32 besides children. The reputed number of Anabaptists—10 besides children. No other Sectarists.
William Rawlinson Esq. of Low Graythwaite is a Gent. of good family & fortune & a Quaker: there are some others of the Sect who are Slate Merchants, & who have acquired handsome fortunes:—they have one Meeting house at Colthouse near Hawkshead. The Anabaptists have one Meeting house: the name of the Teacher is Dawson who is not licensed.

As Henry Dawson had become Baptist minister in 1780, Brathwaite, as vicar and magistrate, had had ample opportunity to object to Dawson's teaching had he so wished. It is perhaps an indication of the tolerant spirit of the times; in the same climate of tolerance Wordsworth could attend the Quaker services occasionally and, apparently, Quaker boys could attend Hawkshead Grammar School. The Baptists were declining when Brathwaite made his report, and by 1833 they had died out as a community, though some five years later Hawkshead Hill was revived by David Kirkbride as a preaching station connected with the new Baptist chapel founded at Coniston. Kirkbride had been sent there to try to reach the scattered mining population of the area (see W. T. Whitley, *Baptists of North-West England*, 1913, p. 190).

Wordsworth has a description of Hawkshead Hill among the unpublished drafts of his *Description of the Scenery of the Lakes*, written between 1807 and 1809. It is a paragraph which characteristically evokes the melancholy of place and its people long dead; it also indicates Wordsworth's sense that earlier times had been far less tolerant than the present, and, quite interestingly, in view of our knowledge of the decline in numbers at Hawkshead Hill, shows that the meeting house was still an important centre over a wide area, especially for baptisms. Wordsworth wrote:

A mile further on we begin to ascend into the Vale of Hawkshead having from the high ground a sight of the upper part of Windermere stretching to the left. In the first cluster of houses we come to named Hawkshead Hill stands a meeting-house by the road side belonging to a congregation of Anabaptists called by the Country people who are not of their own persuasion Whigs. The Building is mean & from the outside has so little to distinguish it as a place of worship that one might think it had been so constructed in an intolerant age for the purpose of avoiding notice. This conventicle is endowed with Lands that produce a respectable income for the Minister. I mention this because this is the only establishment of the kind that I know of in these mountains. Behind runs a streamlet which is occasionally diverted in to a reservoir wherein adults are dipped—some coming from a considerable distance for the purpose. A little detached from the building lies also a small cemetery with only two headstone[s] in the centre—the inscription scarcely to be traced on account of the lichens that have crept over the stone. This obscure burial place is of a character peculiarly melancholy. The ground is humbly fenced & not a tree to dignify or adorn it—But among this little company of graves how much mortal weariness is laid at rest how many anxieties are stilled what fearful apprehensions removed for ever.

[Selected from drafts: MS., Dove Cottage Library.]

Something of a complicating non-conformist element comes to the surface in the middle of the nineteenth century with the foundation of the Union Chapel in the centre of Hawkshead in 1862. This is now thought of as a Methodist establishment, but the chapel's centenary programme printed in 1962, makes it clear that explicit affiliation with the Methodist church dates only from 1922; before that the chapel had been independent, serving a variety of preachers. Mr. Stanley Garnett, a trustee of both Hawkshead Hill Baptist Chapel and the Union Chapel, whose family were involved with the foundation of the latter, remembers that at the beginning of this century a preacher would take services at both chapels on the same day. He also tells me that according to a tradition in his family, prior to the Union Chapel of 1862, a non-conformist group used to meet in a farmhouse near Wray and that people used to come across the lake in boats for the meeting. Another group apparently met in Hawkshead itself, and, to the confusion of Wordsworthians, up the steps in an unheated upper room adjoining Ann Tyson's cottage in Hawkshead (see the centenary programme and a typed notice inside the Methodist, formerly Union, Chapel). I can find no evidence that meetings took place there in Wordsworth's time; and some seventy years is a long period for a meeting to have left so little trace. We have seen that there was no independent Presbyterian tradition in Hawkshead in the eighteenth century; the nonconformists of that time appear to be, as Reginald Brathwaite declared, either Baptists or Quakers, and it is with the Quakers that I must conclude.

The main unit of Quaker administration was the 'monthly meeting', responsible for a group of local meetings for worship. Subordinate to the monthly meeting were the 'preparative meetings', usually associated with each meeting for worship. Thus the whole of Furness formed Swarthmore Monthly Meeting with three meetings for worship—Swarthmore (near Ulverston), Height in Cartmel, and Colthouse. Each of these three had its preparative meeting for local business. Swarthmore Monthly Meeting was held at Rookhow, a meeting house central for all three meetings, and built in 1725 solely for the purpose of holding monthly meetings.

Human weaknesses in the Colthouse community were revealed month by month and the Friends exhorted to 'Diligence', whether the matter was 'Some Shortness in the Attendance of Meetings', first day or weekday, or whether the concern was with the parents' duty of discouraging a child from marriage outside the community, involving as it did marriage before a priest and thus tacit recognition of a 'hireling ministry'. There is, for instance, the report on January 1787 that 'a Young Woman within the Compass of this Meeting has taken the liberty to be Married by a Priest to a Man of another perswaison'. A month later it was reported that 'friends Continued to take an Opportunity with Woman & her parents', and in March it is stated of 'Martha Daughter of Michael Satterthwaite, that it appears She Married Contrary to her parents advise'. Thus, though the daughter would now forfeit her membership, the parents would not. In other matters, too, Friends had to show their testimony; they tried to be staunch in their refusal to pay parish dues. There are many references to 'Sufferings', such as appears in the following memorandum. In 1784: 'Geo: Bayliff & Clemᵗ. Satterthwaite are nam'd to take from friends An Accᵗ. of their Sufferings, And how far they Stand Clear in their Testimony against paying Priest Demands & Church rates so called.' Generally, these sufferings took the form of distraint upon goods, an arbitrary and inexact reprisal for non-payment of tithes.

Great effort was made to conduct the affairs of life as far as possible within the community of Friends and thus—and this is one of many examples—it was reported in August 1785 that one 'Skedrich Smithson [of Preston] offers his son as Wanting a Master of the Trade of a Brush-maker or Callicea Weaver or Some Such like Trade or Handycraft.'[1] When a Friend moved to a different area a certificate was sent after him informing the man's new community of his standing in matters of debt or engagement in marriage. Attempts were made to form a small school at Colthouse. In 1782 a John Wilson from Cumberland was hired at £12 per annum, but this seems to have lasted not more than a year and on 25 September 1785 the Colthouse minutes record: 'Friend of this Meet^g. hath contracted with John Buck Schoolmaster for one year, from the 1st of this Month, to Teach friends Children or Such as hath Attended this Meeting, His Wages to be after the rate of Twenty Pounds a Year.' John Buck was still there in 1789 when he represented the Colthouse Quakers at the Swarthmore Monthly Meetings, though, shortly after he arrived at Hawkshead, he and his wife Mary obviously toyed with the idea of moving to within the compass of the Canterbury meeting; at least, his certificate was to be sent there. The words, 'Such as hath Attended this Meeting', are an indication, but the only indication I have found in the minutes, that non-Quakers attended the Colthouse meeting. But their context implies an habitual, rather than the occasional attendance that Wordsworth apparently recollected, according to Thom in his letter to Stopford Brooke.

Another way in which the Quakers of Colthouse moved towards their Hawkshead neighbours was in their effort to instruct them in their own beliefs. Colthouse was involved in the distribution of the bequest of William Rawlinson, a 'Legacy left for purchasing Books for the use of People of other Persuasions'. The following books were suggested at the Swarthmore meeting of 24 February 1786 for approval by the quarterly meeting at Lancaster: books by William She[r]wen, Hugh Turford, William Penn's *No Cross, No Crown* and *Rise and Progress*, and Robert Barclay's *Catechism*. Purchase and distribution was slow; the matter is

---

[1] It looks as though representatives at the Swarthmore Meeting took down notes from the reports and notices and then, when appropriate, wrote them, often phoneti-cally, into the Colthouse minutes, for when this advertisement appeared a month earlier in the Swarthmore minutes it was better spelt and had slightly more detail: 'Shadrick' and 'calico' and, instead of 'Some Such like Trade or Handycraft', the words 'Flax Dresser'. Two years later, Richard Smithson, son of Shadrick, and presumably a brother of the weaver, offered himself as an apprentice to the trade of shoemaker.

reported in monthly meetings for almost two years, and finally it was decided to give, not lend, the books.

An issue of the times upon which Quakers tried to influence others was the slave trade. In 1784 the Meeting for Sufferings in London recommended that a number of books on the subject of 'our fellow Creatures the Affricans' be distributed to the sundry meetings to be disposed of to 'People not of our religious Persuasion'. Ten copies of 'Anth^y. Benezets Tretices on the Slave Trade' were at Swarthmore Monthly Meeting on 27 May 1785: five went to Swarthmore, three to Colthouse and two to Height.

None of this shows worship at Colthouse. Some meetings for worship at that time were conducted entirely in silence; at others the vocal ministry, arising out of the silence, was offered at length. Could Colthouse have earned the surprising rebuke reported in Thom's letter? Isabel Ross ('Wordsworth and Colthouse') suggests that it might have been one of those communities which needed the advice sent out from London, according to her dating, in 1783: Friends were 'to avoid many words and repetitions, and not to run from supplication into declaration as though the Lord wanted information: and let all be cautious of too often repeating the high and holy name, or his attributes, by a long conclusion.' But the first date of this advice was 1775, and it was addressed not to all Friends, but particularly to ministers and elders. In 1783 a large compendium was published, *Extracts from the Minutes and Advices of the Yearly Meeting of Friends held in London from its First Institution* and in this the advice was republished. Among the Queries in this book for the attention of ministers and elders is the following: 'Are the advices recommended in 1775, read at least once in every year, in your monthly or quarterly meeting? and are they under friends care?' The minutes of Colthouse and Swarthmore indicate that the advices were under the care of Friends; thus, even if spirituality was low, as Isabel Ross suggests, these Quakers were attentive to discipline. For Wordsworth to remember them as 'always telling God Almighty of the Attributes', they must have been conspicuously ignoring the advice sent from the Yearly Meeting. More than that, Wordsworth's reported comment on the 'sermon' fits awkwardly with Quaker practice; and our discomfort is heightened by a recognition (which H. L. Short has suggested to me) that Thom's own comment on the practice of former as against present Presbyterians was a frequent criticism made by Unitarian/Presbyterians against their earlier brethren. All in all there is some likelihood that Thom, after so long a period of time, was imposing something of his own pattern of thought upon the conversation.

In connection with Colthouse, though not with the meeting house, there is another reported conversation with Wordsworth, and this appears to have taken place about a month after the one remembered by J. H. Thom. It is an account by William Bennett written on 11 November 1846 when Wordsworth had had tea with the Bennett family; a short extract of this is published by Isabel Ross ('A Newly found Quaker Friend of Wordsworth: William Bennett, 1804–73' *Journal of the Friends' Historical Society*, 48, 1958, pp. 209–12) who summarizes the three conversations that Bennett apparently had with Wordsworth. I give an extract from the second conversation which is in itself interesting for Wordsworth's comments on poetry, and since it is the one document that establishes without doubt that Wordsworth as a schoolboy, as T.W.T. has rightly claimed, spent the greater proportion of his ten years at Colthouse, but quite clearly was not there for the whole period. In the context of Thom's letter the account has a special interest in that Wordsworth talked to Bennett, a Quaker, about Quakers and about Colthouse and gave no indication that he had ever attended a Quaker meeting there.

The tone of Wordsworth's conversation and criticisms were rather depreciatory upon the whole to others. The appellation of the 'Lake Poets' he utterly scorned. There was nothing whatever in common amongst them, and it arose entirely from the stupidity of the Edinboro' Review; which was at that time managed by a party without any proper qualification. He never cared about any criticisms. His Writings must stand by their own character. It was not likely he should have written any 'nonsense' as some said, with his education, for no man in England had been more regularly educated. 9 years, from 9 to 18 had been spent at Hawkshead, then a celebrated school, during a great part of which time he lodged at Colthouse. He had been before the public more than half a Century & knew his Writings were all pure English at all events; and had all been artistically worked out, having one consistent plan, and [being] parts of one great moral end and purpose. Though so often solicited had never contributed to Reviews and Periodicals and never would.

He rose to leave about 7 o'clock on account of the heavy weight of the nursing at home upon his Wife. The boys and I accompanied him. It was quite dark and his step is feeble. It did, indeed seem a privilege of a high order rich and rare to find myself walking along the still margin of his own Rydal Lake, with the Poet's arm leaning upon mine, in free familiar converse. We talked of the Society of Friends. He inquired if they were increasing or diminishing in number. I could not but reply the latter, which he was sorry to hear; for he generally admired them, and did not wish to see their character and influence lost to Society. They were a fact; and the theory of what they had always held forth, was certainly of an unworldly character. But he thought it behoved the Society to look to the causes of their young people leaving; whether there was something in drawing the cord too tight, and denying some things which were innocent or useful in themselves, and therefore violating nature, which was certain to occasion a re-action. Or as Mrs. Barbauld used to say of Dissentors, that she never knew a family keep their carriage, and remain so for three generations.

[MS. Dove Cottage Library, with the note: 'Copied by M. E. Bennett with verbal alterations', and signed 'W^m. Bennett'.]

Bennett, Isabel Ross tells us (op. cit.) was a friend and neighbour of William Howitt, the Quaker and writer who, in Wordsworth's opinion, wrote too much. Wordsworth had known and occasionally talked with the enthusiastic Howitt since at least 1831; in 1845 Browning caught him turning up at Rydal Mount armed with a notebook for recording the poet's conversation. Howitt was prevented from taking notes but he wrote an essay in his *Homes and Haunts of the Most Eminent English Poets* (1849) in which he somewhat eccentrically suggests that Wordsworth's poetry adds up to a poetical Quakerism,[1] and after elaborating on this he proposes ways in which Wordsworth might have acquired his knowledge: reading, solitude, and friendships, he feels, and then says, 'Wordsworth was not only as deeply read in these books as any of them [Southey, Coleridge, Lamb, Lovell, Lloyd] but is still, to my knowledge, remarkably well acquainted with the history and opinions of Friends.' But, despite the sympathetic discussion with both Bennett, and, presumably, Howitt, Wordsworth seems not to have mentioned attendance at a Quaker meeting house.

[1] Howitt perhaps takes a hint from Charles Lamb's notice of *The Excursion* in the *Quarterly Review*, XII, October 1814, pp. 100–11, in which poem Lamb detects a Quaker element: 'In him [Wordsworth], *faith*, in friendly alliance and conjunction with the religion of his country, appears to have grown up, fostered by meditation and lonely communions with Nature—an internal principle of lofty consciousness, which stamps upon his opinions and sentiments (we were almost going to say) the character of an expanded and generous Quakerism.'

APPENDIX III

(a) A Letter from Hawkshead: 1783

Richard Benson wrote to his Aunt Ann (Miss Postlethwaite) about an unexpected day's holiday. The text of this letter is taken from a notebook of T.W.T. which became available just before going to press. T.W.T. notes: 'This letter was lent to me by Dr. William E. L. Allen, Ivy House, Hawkshead in 1947. He got it soon after he qualified from someone in Ulverston who had found several others at Abbot's Reading in a tin box (locked) turned out as lumber *c.* 1887 or 8.'

At Isaac Holmes
Hawkshead Town
Nov^{br}. 3rd, 1783

Dear Aunt Ann

We had a Holiday last week, but I was not able to come and see you & Grandfather & Uncle Myles as I had intended. I cd. not get a Horse off anybody as they had all been spoken for when I asked. I was mad with myself for not asking sooner about one, but I did not know of the Holiday as soon as some did. There are only three Horses at the Red Lion inn now where I have generally got one. There were 6 or 7 not long since all for hire for riding. It is time there was a new Landlord there, it wants one badly.

Being disappointed of a visit to Abbots Redding I joined in with the Hunt. It was got up by Will Ponsonby & John Shaw (two Cumberland boys), and was the best we have had since Isaac Williamson left. He is the one who had a couple of Hound Dogs of his own when he was at School. Please tell Uncle that two of our boys killed a Foumart[1] not long ago. They tried to get a Reward for it off the Parish Clerk, but he said No, they cd. not have one, it was against the Rules for Grammar School pupils to be paid for destroying Varmin. They got 9^d for it though from a man who wanted the Skin to stuff.

Will Dixon has got to Board with me now at Isaac Holmes, and when his Father was here last month to see about changing him to another Place he gave me 5 sh. which I am spending on a Cake each week for the two of us at a Sh. a time. It is Robt. Hewitson that has left.

I am wanting nothing at present except the pair of strong Shoes I have at Bouth. If Uncle Myles is not coming to Hawkshead Market on Monday could you

---

[1] See above, p. 223. Polecat, of the weasel family: 'larger than the weasel, the ermine, or the ferret, being about one foot five inches long.' (Goldsmith, *Natural History*, 1776, III, p. 363.)

send them by the Carrier, & not wait till Uncle is coming, as I need them as soon as possible, the pair I have here being nearly worn out and hardly worth the cost of mending. Martha will get the other pair for you if you send over I cd. also do with some Apples, & a cream Chees when they are making, but there is no hurry only for the Shoes. I pray you will send them on Monday.

My Duty to Grandfather & Respects to Uncle Myles & loving Regards to you.

From y^r. affectionate nephew

Rich^d.

(b) Eleanor Brathwaite: another Hawkshead Dame

An intimate view of life at Hawkshead comes in a group of letters concerned with the schooling of the sons of William Senhouse, Surveyor-General of Barbados and the Leeward Islands. While at school in England the boys were in the general charge of their grandmother, Mrs. Mary Senhouse of Fisher Street, Carlisle, who sometimes writes about them to her elder son, Humphrey, of Netherall, near Maryport. The boys were James Lowther, born in Barbados 17 February 1773 and died in the West Indies in 1794; William Wood, born in Barbados 22 February 1776 and died in 1800; Samson, born in Barbados 17 February 1777 (date of his death not known). The two elder boys, later joined by Samson, must have gone to Hawkshead about 1783, and left it for St. Bees in the second half of 1786. In Hawkshead they lodged with Eleanor Brathwaite and her daughter, Martha. Eleanor, the wife of Reginald Brathwaite, mercer, had been widowed in 1742, and she died, a few months after the Senhouse boys left, on 2 November 1786, aged 80.

Unless otherwise indicated, the letters printed here are from Eleanor Brathwaite to Mrs. Mary Senhouse, the grandmother of the boys (MSS. in the Records, the Castle, Carlisle).

Mrs. Mary Senhouse to her son, Humphrey.

Dear Son

I am told that M^r. Taylor of Hawkshead is Dead, if it be so, I want your directions about these Dear Boys; upon account of the Snow, I cou'd not send them to School at the time they should have gone; & now, I shall not till I hear from you. The Usher[1] I find is a very indifferent one, Willm. is not the least

---

[1] Joseph Satterthwatte of Colthouse; he was about to be replaced by Thomas Bowman.

improv'd this last half year in his reading. As to James' Latin I don't understand. It is very troublesome and expencive geting them back & forwards; the last time they went from hence; They set forwards in the Fly to Penrith on ye Friday, were to go in the Dilligence the next Day to Kendal, where Horses were to meet them from Hawkshead. They were dissapointed of the Dilligence, stay'd at Penrith till the Monday, & then had Horses to hire to the far End. Now when they came to me, as Willm. had been Confined, I sent Ned & a Chaise for them it cost me three Guineas all but Sixpence   Johanna has been very good in hearing them read, & get Spelling off every Day, but they have now been here so long, that they don't regard her so much. I wish to hear soon—   ...

Jan^ry. 15. [1784]^1   Mary Senhouse

> Hawks^hd. 1st May 1784
> Yours by Mr Fairish came

Safe to hand which I shou'd have acknowledgd sooner but waited for Mr Hogs-hons^2 Bill which I have inclosed along with mine for my dear little men they are very well and Good Boys masster W^m takes Charmingly in hand in regard to writing   he shall write to you next time I write and to his dear papa   we every poste hope to hear from him—when he wrote to me from London he orderd me to send my halfe year account to you   I am sorry I could not get a franck neither meet with a convaince any other way   the $\overset{£}{1} - \overset{s}{11} - \overset{d}{6}$ with what I have to receive from masster Benn will answer the Stationers Bills and y^e Ballance shal give to your Good Gransons—I sepose they do not Break up till June but shal lett you know when we know—   ...

> Hawks^hd June y^e 16 –84
> I have this day rec^d yours and

y^e bill for $\overset{£}{20} - \overset{s}{10}$ very Safe which I shal take Care to give you a proper account of in dew time — As to my dear little gentlemens coming home I cannot learn there will be any Chaise coming. masster Pattisons expects Horses and y^e three Wads-worths are not Certon whether y^e go to Whitehaven or Come to penrith^3 if ye Latter would do well. but ye time grows nigh that we canot know. if you madam Could know from m^r Cookson and he conclude to send a Chaise, twoud be ye moste Elegable, otherways I can get a man and two Horses to bring them to penerith   we can not borow a hors for less than two Shillings a day but if you

---

^1 Endorsed: 15 January 1784. Cited by E. Hughes (*North Country Life in the Eighteenth Century*, II, p. 298) as 1786; William Taylor died in June 1786 but apparently had been ill some two and a half years earlier.

^2 The Hawkshead apothecary-surgeon.

^3 This was the first holiday for Richard, William and John since their father's death. Their uncle, Christopher Cookson of Penrith, paid 5 shillings horse-hire for them on 21 June.

aprove of that way of Coming Can have a Carefull man to Come along with them
—in ye mean while muste rest till you or m^r Cookson write not but I shal provide
Horses if we hear no more . . .

Mrs. Senhouse to her son Humphrey; Carlisle 9 July 1784.

. . . My young Men and Maidens are now all wth. me, so that I have a very round
family; and as I have none but myself to take the direction of it, I can't say but I
feel occationally a great deal of anxiety for so great a Charge, at a period of Life
not so fit for fatigue either of Body or mind as might be—but I hope you will
think it right to take a turn now and then with my Dear Hawkshead Boys, to
inspect and see how they advance in their Studys. They are very good, as so many
boys can be in my small Limits . . .

Hawkshead Oc^t ye 25th 1784
. . . they have been to se Sr Michal Fleeming M^r and Mrs Stanley were there at y^e
same time who I hope will give you a pleasing account of them   they are very
Good Boys . . .

Hawksh^d April ye 25 1785
. . . Madam I have long wishd to through of washing for any of ye Boys and now
am detirmind as my Health is so much impaird and other people have done it for
this year past ye masster Reincocks ye Pattisons and masster Joe Taylor who Lodge
at ye next door al wash out at 1 ginea pr Boy ye year which I hope youl not object
as I shal always take Care to mend there Stockings and Linning as usal   I have wrote
to miss Christian and m^rs. Stanley   m^r Taubman was here and thought it right—. . .

Hawkshead June ye 25 1785
I ought ear now to have thankd you for your obliging letter but indeed my Bad
Health makes me rather indolant as I hope youl pardon my neglect   you seemd to
wish my young gentlemen might have there close made here so I have got them
Each a Coat and weist Cooat of a fine plaine as this town dose not afford Broad
Cloths and to send to Kendall one can not judge from pattrens besides when they
come to constant were a plaine does more service   I shal be happy to hear what I
have done meets your aprobation I got them Each 2 paire of Stockings threed and
worsted as ye wash and wear brighter then all worsted   have as much as will make
them Each another paire and before ye winter shal renew there Stock of Common
ones which youl see are yet in wearing
I hope my dear Boys will arive Safe and give you every satisfaction you wish
for as they are very Good and tractable both they and I are glad to hear masster
Samson returns with them   masster James will tell you we do not know whether y^e
Stanleys return or not   I am happy tis no fault of mine   but a quarel Betwixt y^e

Masster and m^r Christian¹ ye Usher had beat some Boys which m^r C found fault with though not his and m^r Taylor was short in his answers which ye other Could not Brook so took his Soon and masster Taubman away that I rather think ye other muste go be that as it may my atention to your dear Boys shal think my duty which I am sure ye other never wanted but I have no more to say only if ye go 5 out of Eight   without any Notice is a Little Hard   but   freindship like yours dear madam is not to be met with as an acknowledgement of which give me leave to subscribe my selfe   your ever   obliged

Humble servant
Eleanor Brathwaite.

Hawkshead Augst ye 13th 1785
I fear youl ear now, have blaimd me or your dear Boys for not giving you an account of there safe arival here in Good time ye evening ye left you it give me great pleasure to see them return in such high Speritts and above all masster Samson who seemd at home ye moment he Caime here is a charming little Boy and would not return to Carlisle upon any acount after ye first Leson   he tould me there was one Boy put below him since that another and thinks there is a therd that reads worse then he   that when Mr Taylor observis it will be drop'd also, he has often saide his Lessons to m^r Taylor which pleases him much   I hope al ye Blunders at School will subside   but were greatly agrevatted by m^r C and none have left ye School on that account but his son and nephews   I am sorry for m^r Stanley it muste be a hardship as his sons were going on very well in there learning he and m^{rs} Stanley have wrote to me in very obliging terms   and with great regard to ye masster—Since I sitt down James has rec^d a letter from there worthy Father they are alwell and is sending them a great many Good things which I am intended to partake of   this letter was designd to have Come by a mr Wilson who is coming to Ingland but something had prevented him for a little time so it Caime by a London Ship and m^r Senhouse will write again when m^r Wilson Comes to whose Care ye Good things are comitted   youl have heard my young men talke of a miss Foard   She was marryd Last Tusday to Dr Ainsley Second Son² She has

---

¹ John Christian's quarrel was with the Headmaster, William Taylor. The usher was Thomas Bowman. The Taubmans and Stanleys were relatives of Christian. The quarrel could have been as early as May when the Christians were near Hawkshead, at Belle Isle: 'The Family are on the Island and passed here Tuesday even. in very gay stile, most splendid equipage. The horses are all returned again yesterday.' (R. Dore to Sir Michael le Fleming, 5 May 1785. The Records, Kendal.)

² Richard Dore wrote of Agnes Ford to Sir Michael le Fleming on 5 May 1785: 'Lady condemned in "this Circle" for not seeing a little more of the World before she adopts her choice. Ainsley and Son H[enry] rode by Monday to dine wth Mr Jenney and the afternoon brought Waterhead Ladies there to tea. Even. The whole party returned together. Mrs. Raincock askt Mr. H. Ainsley if there was any truth in the report of the Match, and he told there certainly was and hoped she approved his

a large fortune and desirvedly well spoke of by all who know her he I hope will make her a Good Husband I had him near 5 years as a lodger when at this School he will practise as a physician some say at Caimbrige where he aquitt him selfe to his credit my dear Boys is out at play but al beg'd there duty to you and else-where dew and love to there Coszens—we here Mr Mingo[1] will be hear ye 23 instant as ye have yours and Uncle Leave need not troble you with inquierys con-cerning him—I rec^d ye mony and have paid it as you orderd ye Balance shal take Care ye young men shal have, but I shal tyer you dear madam so beg leave to subscribe my Selfe after Assuring you of my Constant Care over your Good Boys

your moste obediant

Humble Servant

E Brathwaite

James wuold be glad to know how ye Coachman is
reading over my scrawl I have wrote an untruth when I say none have left ye School but ye Stanleys but it looks like a party affaire ye 2 Pattysons and 2 Williamsons Come no more

Hawks^{hd} Oct^{br} ye 21st 1785

... I shall get them new Close before ye Ball which will be once in 5 weeks hatts they have and every other thing nessecery we shal take Care not to dress in ye new Coats much this winter as there every day Close are with Care very tolarable I think ye now and then Blaime me for making them Chainge there Close but tis expensive enough to there Good Father ...

Hawkshead march ye 6 1786

I am truly sensable how anxtious you must be to hear from us upon dear W^{ms} account and sorry I can say nothing of his recovery neither of his being much worss only he is reduced so much and ye gathering increasing which til broack Mr Hogshon canot so well form a proper judgment not but that he hopes he may do well in time however he writes this day to Dr Ainsley as it muste be more satisfactery to all his freinds when every proper method is taken he continues to take his physick and do every thing that a Child can do I got him some Calfe foot jelly which he likes his drink is Impeerall[2] now and then a little Sago grewell and Chocalet but that he is tierd of and drinks tea in ye morning his play felows

---

choice. He is for accompanying Mrs Ford to Bristol where they are going as soon as the Children recover from Innoculation.' The children here would be the orphans of George and Catherine Knott.

[1] i.e. Mr. Mingay, the dancing master. See above, pp. 92–4.

[2] Imperial drink or water: made from cream of tartar, flavoured with lemons, and sweetened.

has several times shoot him smal birds which he lykes either rosted or made into a little pye which he says is good indeed—. . .[1]

Mrs. Senhouse to her son, Humphrey.

Dear Son

        I am sorry to send you this second account of my Dear Williams illness, it gives me great Uneasiness. Yet I hope every thing is done for him that could, had he been with me. It is one lucky Circumstance that M^{rs}. Brathwaites house is so thin of Boarders, as he has ever since he began, had a bed & room to himself, and a Servant to lay by him. I am in concern too for my good old friend, who in her poor state of Health must be greatly affected, so that it would be cruel to think of removing the Boys, so soon after such proofs of her attachment and great tenderness over Them, that I am a good deal distress'd how to Act . . .

                Your affectionate Mother
                  Mary Senhouse
Carlisle Mar: 10 1786

                              Hawkshead May 12 1786
. . . I doubt not Mrs Senhouse[2] will have lett you know there being taken from hence gives me concern but as I am sensable there can nothing be Lay to my Charge of Neglect in any Casse   it makes me more easey   for had ye bee [tear in MS.] Children I hope I have done every thing a parent Could have done as to Care both of them and every thing belonging them—go where they will my best wishes will ever attend them   I was favour with a letter from mr Senhouse who tells me y^e are to be fixed at St Bees and to leave me at W^{hs}tide   youl please to give me a line in what manner youl have them Come   I shal get Mr Hogshon Bill against that time and likewise send what is dew to me from there last halfe years end   you desire a charge for what Extraordinarys poor W^m had   three Bottles of [?mourten] for jellys &c bread for poultesess and watch lights ye wine . . .

                              Hawks^{hd} June ye 27 1786
Dear Madam

                N.B.   These bank Notes were for £30
    I beg pardon for neglecting writing to you acording to your request   I received ye Bank Notes very safe and shal send you a proper recept when I have presented them—   the reason I did not write here caim a letter from Barbados last Monday but as ye Election for a School master did not comence till Friday I had a minde to lett my young gentlemen know Mr Bowman is Elected without

---

[1] This letter and another of 1 March 1786 are both printed in full by Edward Hughes (op. cit.) but mis-dated 1788.
[2] Humphrey's wife, the boys' aunt.

one desenting voice[1] I wish he may always meet there aprobation   I hope there is no doubt of his diligance   I am sorry there is so great a mistake concerning ye the Lether maile into which we put there Big Coats   and Corded it upon ye trunk and to prevent people opening it turnd it up side down . . .

---

[1] His appointment, dated 23 June 1786 is signed by 'the major Part of the Govenors': Reg. Brathwaite, John Jackson, John Scales, Geo. Law, John Machell, J. Braithwaite; and approved, as was necessary, by the Bishop of Chester. (Lancashire Records, Preston.)

APPENDIX IV

Hawkshead Grammar School and the New Library

The Teaching Staff

The accepted dates of Headmasters (see H. Swainson Cowper's *Hawkshead*, 1899, p. 550) needs some clarification. The archives of the Archdeaconry of Richmond (Lancashire Records, Preston) show that James Peake was Headmaster of the Grammar School from 1766 to the end of the first half of 1781. Edward Christian wrote on 15 July 1781 to the Bishop of Chester asking for a licence to teach and at the same time enclosing Peake's resignation (dated 26 June 1781). Christian's own resignation as Headmaster is dated 18 July 1782. There are apparently no documents surviving related to William Taylor's appointment from this time until his death in 1786. Thomas Bowman became Headmaster in June 1786; he had already been at the school for two years and five months as Usher, according to a testimonial sent to the Bishop on 17 July 1786. Bowman finally resigned in January 1829.

From the various book lists it is possible to name many of the other masters at the school in and around Wordsworth's time there. There appears to have been a staff of four, possibly five: Headmaster, First Assistant, Second Assistant, Writing Master; it is possible that 'First Assistant' is an alternative term for 'Usher'. The Ushers can be listed as follows: Joseph Shaw, whom Wordsworth praised for teaching him Latin so effectively (see *Memoirs of Wordsworth*, 1851, I, p. 10); he left Hawkshead in 1780. William Satterthwaite of Colthouse was Usher, 1780–2. His brother Joseph followed him, 1783–4. Mrs. Senhouse (see Appendix III (*b*)) found Joseph Satterthwaite an ineffective teacher; Thomas Bowman's appointment, probably as Usher, in mid-term, in February or March 1784, suggests an emergency, but since Joseph was back again as Usher in 1786 he must have been acceptable. John Docker, A.B., of Bampton had the post 1787–8. Charles Farish (see above p. 94) is called 'First Assistant' in 1788 in the advertisement for the Hawkshead Military Academy, and since no Usher is mentioned in that advertisement this might well be an alternative title. From 1789–90 the drunken Thomas Burnthwaite (see Alphabetical List of Donors) was First Assistant. Thomas Newton of Ambleside had the post, 1791–4.

The Rev. Peter Richardson, 1781–2, the Rev. John Jackson, 1786–9, and Thomas Garnett, 1783–9, are all termed 'Assistant', though their precise rank is not clear. William Ellery is listed as a Second Assistant, 1789, and William Pearson, 1790, and we know that Pearson, immediately preceding his appointment as Second Assistant had been himself a schoolboy at Hawkshead (see Alphabetical List of Donors). The Writing Masters were Joseph Varty in the early 1780s, and Rowland Bowstead from perhaps 1788. Varty is called 'Usher' by Budworth in 1797 (see above p. 233 footnote), but this is most probably an imprecise use of the term. It is clear from the Sandys Charity accounts that Bowstead was Writing Master until 1793, Benjamin Townson 1794–5, and Varty, returning to his former post, 1796–9.

In the school, writes Budworth in his Tour of 1792, 'upwards of one hundred boys are at present educated. . . . There are many boarding houses for the boys, and, including washing, the expences do not exceed fourteen pounds a year. The head master has the credit of sending out some most excellent scholars; and was expected home this day, from the perambulations he usually takes during vacation-time.' Wordsworth in an unpublished draft for his *Guide to the Lakes* estimates a similar number of pupils: 'Along the eastern end of the Church runs a stone seat, a place of resort for the old people of the Town for the sickly & those who have leisure to look about them, here sitting in the shade or in the sun they talk over their concerns—a few years back were amused by the gambols & exercises of more than a 100 Schoolboys some playing soberly on the hill top near them while others were intent upon more boisterous diversions in the fields beneath.' (MS. Dove Cottage.)

Bowman appears to have begun well as a schoolmaster. The library is one monument to him. Perhaps Bowman's work for this sprang out of a desire to broaden the syllabus (another aspect of this desire shows in the alliance with Mingay and the projected Military Academy). It is perhaps worth stating that Wordsworth never of course used the books given by boys leaving school; indeed some of the books seem never to have been much used at all. Presumably Bowman exerted some influence with an indication of what he wanted—if only to prevent duplication of copies. But whether he did or not, it is even earlier as a bookman that Bowman has some significance for Wordsworth studies. He saw Wordsworth over a five-year period, 1784–9, and his son, a Governor of Hawkshead Grammar School, recollected for the tercentenary celebration of 1885 things his father had said about Wordsworth and reading:

My father used to say that he believed that he did more for William Wordsworth by lending him books than by his teaching, though Wordsworth, mind you, did well enough under him at both Classics and Mathematics, so I understood. But it was books he wanted, all sorts of books; Tours and Travels, which my father was partial to, and Histories and Biographies, which were also favourites with him; and Poetry—that goes without saying. My father used to get the latest books from Kendal every month, and I remember him telling how he lent Wordsworth Cowper's 'Task' when it first came out, and Burns' 'Poems' . . .

Mr. Wordsworth wrote to me after my father died, and in thanking him I mentioned this. He wrote again—and I have his letter yet—saying that my father also introduced him to Langhorne's poems and Beattie's 'Minstrel' & Percy's 'Reliques', and that it was in books or periodic works my father lent him that he first became acquainted with the poetry of Crabbe & Charlotte Smith & the two Wartons. That's what he says in his letter. When I remember him, my father hardly ever read any poetry, but he must have done once as he had a great many volumes of it in his library. . . .

A story he used to tell about Wm. Wordsworth is that he left him in his study once for what he thought would only be a minute or two, telling him to be looking for another book in place of the one he had brought back. As it happened he was kept half an hour or more by one of the school tenants. When he got back, there was W. poring over a book, so absorbed in it he did not notice my father's return. And 'what do you think it was' my father would say, or 'you'll never guess what it was'. It was Newton's 'Optics', And that was the book Wordsworth was for borrowing next. He was one of the very few boys, who used to read the old books in the School Library, George Sandys' 'Travels in the East' and his Ovid's 'Metamorphosis', Fox's [sic] 'Book of Martyrs' & Evelyn's 'Forest Trees'. There were others, but these I remember. . . . He [Wm. Wordsworth] never once won a prize at school. There were none in those days or for long after. . . . My father continued to lend Wordsworth books when he was at Hawkshead on holiday from Cambridge, that is if he was at home. At that time he was great on tours, and went on one every summer very nearly.[1]

But Bowman after the turn of the century seems to have been less energetic; the urgency with which the Governors in 1808 asked that an Usher be appointed at a salary of £40 per annum to be taken out of the Headmaster's income, and with competence to teach the Classics, has an ominous ring. Even so, Dorothy Wordsworth, writing in 1810 about the Wordsworths' plans, says, 'we *must* be in the neighbourhood of a grammar school' and thinks that near Hawkshead would be suitable (*Letters: Middle Years*, I, 2nd ed., p. 387). In fact, Wordsworth sent his sons to

---

[1] I am grateful to Mrs. Eileen Jay, who has the difficult task of sorting T.W.T.'s papers, for providing this text for me; extracts from the reminiscence were first published in her *Wordsworth at Colthouse*, Kendal, 1970, pp. 28–9.

Charterhouse and Sedbergh, and in 1819 he commented sharply to Lord Lonsdale, 'the school at Hawkshead is quite neglected by the Master' (*Letters: Middle Years*, II, 2nd ed., p. 566). According to the Charity Commissioners' Report of 1820, the Grammar School had then only forty boys, and Bowman himself took no boarders.

Thomas Bowman's Proposals for a New Library at Hawkshead School, June 1789

To the Young Gentlemen, Students at Hawkshead School.

Considering the infinite consequence it is to Youth to have opportunities of access to a variety of useful Books, both as the only means of acquiring the General Knowledge which is absolutely necessary to the Happiness and Respectability of their future years, and as furnishing in the meantime the strongest motive to Industry, and the best preventative of Idleness and consequent Viciousness; I have long wished that the plan of our present Library might be extended; so as to take in all the English Classics, History, Geography, Topography, Chronology, Biography, Travels, Description of Manners, Customs and Ceremonies, Books of Taste, Literature, and Criticism, Natural Philosophy in all its Branches, Ethics, Natural History, Elementary Treatises on popular Sciences, and approved Works on all generally interesting subjects whatever.

And for the Execution of this Design, encouraged by the present Concurrence of many favourable Circumstances, and the great probability I think there is of eventual success if the Attempt is but once made, I now offer you the following Proposals, adequate, I hope, if generally complied with, to the End intended:

I. That the Constitution of the present Book Club remain as it is; the first 5s. subscribed entitling the Subscriber to the use of all the Books now in that Library, and those in future to be purchased with such subscriptions.

II.nd That all the Boys in Greek, and as many in the lower classes as think proper, subscribe 5s. yearly for the establishing another Library, of more respectable books for the exclusive use of such Subscribers.

III.d That each Boy on his leaving the School make a present of such Volume or Volumes to the said Library as he may think proper; to be inscribed with his Name, the Time the Gift was made, &c., to be preserved with particular Care as a Memorial of the Donor, and to be lent out only at the Discretion of the Master to such of the upper Boys, Subscribers to this Library, whose Care he can depend on; subject, however, at the same time, to replace the Book or Books so taken with a new Set, in case they are sullied or otherwise damaged.

IV.th That in order to accommodate any Gentleman of Education in the Neighbourhood who may wish it, he shall, with the approbation of the Master, be permitted the use of the said Library on first presenting it with such Book or set of Books as he shall think proper, not already in the Library, and being an annual Subscriber or Benefactor to it so long as he shall continue to make Use of it.

V.th That to encourage it the more effectually, now in its Infancy, all the Gentlemen that are known to have been educated at the School, be applied to for such Donation of Books, or money to purchase Books, as they may think proper, and suitable to their Character and Circumstances, and the obligation they owe to the School; to be inscribed with their name, &c., to perpetuate the Memory of the place of their Education; many of whom, I am sure, will be happy to contribute liberally to a Plan so much calculated for the Benefit of the rising Generation, and of Youth in General, who may be placed here for Education for Ages to come.

For my own part, whilst I continue to be Master, it is my intention to be an annual Contributor to it,[1] and to labour for its Extention and Interests with a Zeal, equal to my idea of its importance—And when it is generally known (as I wish you all to endeavour to make it) that there is now a large Room in the School, appropriated to the sole purpose of a Library, where all Presents of Books will be gratefully received and carefully registered and labelled, by the Writing Master for the time being, with the Donor's name and place of Residence, the date of the Donation or Bequest, &c., when this, I say, is known, I have no Doubt but that many Gentlemen will rather leave their Books to be deposited where they will be so extensively useful, and remain so long a Monument to their Name, inseparably united with the idea of Generosity and Benevolence, than permit them to be sold, as in the Country they are sure to be, for so trifling a part of their real and intrinsic Value.

Sanguine of the success of the plan, because by the united contributions of so many it may be effected without being burdensome to any, it is my intention to provide a Book Case for the projected Library [during] the approaching Holidays; and hope with your Concurrence and Exertions in its Favor, soon to see it in a flourishing condition, and remain, Gentlemen, anxious for your Happiness and Improvement, Your sincere friend,

T. Bowman.

The Hawkshead Library Records

In alphabetical order of donors, a record follows here of those books that were given by individuals to Hawkshead School Library, 1789–99. It is complete in that it contains all the books still surviving which have inscriptions of the period, volumes now scattered randomly throughout the library. These books then are a principal part of what is still to be seen as the New Library, founded by the Headmaster, Thomas Bowman, in

---

[1] In that same year, 1789, Bowman himself gave the first book to the New Library: *The History of England from the Invasion of Julius Caesar to the Revolution in 1688*, by David Hume, 8 vols., London 1782. In 1790 he gave a run of the *Monthly Review*, 1763–89, and continued this annually until 1796. In 1790 he also presented the Library with the *Annual Register*, 1774–9, and the *New Annual Register*, 1780–8, and continued this annually until 1793.

1789. (There was an earlier and fine library established by Daniel Rawlinson; a MS. index of this is among the Browne MSS. at the Record Office, Kendal, and there is a printed account by Copley Christie, 'Old Church and School Libraries of Lancashire', Chetham Society Publications, 1885, Vol. VII, pp. 143–70.) The list is compiled from the books themselves. The Grammar School had its own record of these books, but this is now not to be found. However, just before going to press a notebook of T.W.T.'s has fortunately become available and in it is his copy of the library records taken from a vellum-bound book, its pages *circa* 13″ × 8″. This book contains at the front Bowman's proposals, and then a list, presumably in the order of presentation, of those books that were given by individual donors. At the end of this vellum-bound record book are four further lists: one of boys at school subscribing to the library as borrowers and paying half a crown each half-year; one of books bought by subscription (some ninety-four titles, not presented here); one of subscribers who were formerly schoolboys; and finally a short list of local gentry who also subscribed.

Alphabetical List of Donors to the Library and the Books they presented

The number before each entry indicates the place of that book in the original chronological presentation list as transcribed by T.W.T. In some cases there is a different number for the donor and for 'his' book, and this means a discrepancy between the old list and the book as it is found on the shelf. Possibly sometimes book-plates came to be stuck into the wrong books. Then comes the title of the book taken from the books themselves. I have added information, in square brackets, based on the British Museum catalogue, and have also indicated if that book or edition is not in the British Museum. Sizes and prices are taken from T.W.T.'s transcript. Next follows what is written on the book-plate in the book; the material in brackets here is added from the presentation list as transcribed by T.W.T. The brief notes on donors draw upon standard reference works —Venn's *Alumni Cantabrigiensis* has been especially useful, though frequently supplemented and corrected—and on gravestones, Parish Registers, family papers, particularly in record offices; in some cases where I have been able to draw upon the private researches of individuals, this source is noted at the end of the entry. The injunction, 'See T.W.T.' means that there is some relevant discussion in T.W.T.'s text which will be found by consulting the index.

AINSLIE, Gilbert and James

(30) *An Inquiry into the Nature and Causes of the Wealth of Nations* by Adam Smith, LL.D. . . . 3 vols., 5th ed., London, MDCCLXXXIX. 8vo, £1. 1s.

The Gift of Gilbert and James Ainslie of Quebec on their leaving the School   1795.

Probably brothers of William Ainslie, see below.

AINSLIE, William

(58) The Gift of William Ainslie of Quebec on his leaving this School   1794. [A loose book-plate; Thomas Pennant's *Survey of London*, 4to, £1 10s. was the book he gave.]

Doubtless a relative of Henry Ainslie (1760–1834), doctor and second son of Dr. James Ainslie of Kendal, formerly of Carlisle, who attended Hawkshead schoolboys in their more serious illnesses. For Henry Ainslie, see T.W.T. and Appendix III (*b*). William Ainslie was a book-subscriber, 1791₂–1794₁.

ARMITSTEAD, Thomas

(6) *The Method of Teaching and Studying the Belles Lettres . . . with Reflections on Taste . . . .* by Mr. Rollin.   Translated from the French.   6th ed., 4 vols., London, MDCCLXIX.   12mo, 12s.

The Gift of Thomas Armitstead of Grassingham on his leaving the School   1789

Grassingham, should be Gressingham, 8 miles north-east of Lancaster. Second son and fifth child of the Rev. Robert A., vicar of Gressingham 1758–, and Ellin. Born 2 March 1770; baptized 1 April 1770. Admitted Trinity College, Cambridge, 8 May 1798; a 'Ten-year' man. Matriculated Easter 1808; B.D. 1808. Rector of St. Martin's, Chester, 1795–1806. Minor canon of Chester, 1803–27. Vicar of Backford, Cheshire, 1803–27. Vicar of Weaverham, 1806–23. Vicar of Cockerham, Lancs., 1823–7. Died 1827.

ATKINSON, John

(64) *Essays on the Microscope; containing . . . A General History of Insects.* . . . . by George Adams, London, MDCCLXXXVII. 4to, £1. 10s.

The Gift of John Atkinson of Dalton   Admitted at Trinity College Cambridge from this school   1793   [Presented 1795.]

A friend of Christopher Wordsworth at school and at Cambridge (see Z. S. Fink, *The Early Wordsworthian Milieu*, 1958, *passim*). Fifth son of Thomas A. of Dalton, steward to the Duke of Montagu in Manors of Plain Furness and Hawkshead, Lancs. Baptized 27 June 1773. Admitted Trinity College, Cambridge, 31 October 1792. Matriculated, Michaelmas 1793. Migrated to Clare. B.A. 1797; M.A. 1800. In orders: at Over Kellet, Lancs.; from 1808 at St. John's Lancaster. See also E. T. Baldwin, 'Extracts from some Furness Correspondence of the Eighteenth Century', *The North Lonsdale Magazine and Furness Miscellany*, 111 (June, August, October 1899), pp. 151–4, 174–6, 199–202.

BALDERSTON, Robert [Richardson] (see PRESTON, George)

Born at Ingleton, Yorkshire. Matriculated at Cambridge, Michaelmas 1789, sizar at St. Catherine's. B.A. 1792. Ordained deacon at York, 22 September 1793. Curate of Granby, Notts., 1793. Ordained priest at Carlisle, 13 March 1794. Died c. 1853. [C. R. Hudleston.]

BIRKETT, Edward [Joseph]   (see RAINCOCK, Fletcher)

Son of Henry B. of Carlisle. Born 5 April 1768; baptized 28 April 1768, St. Mary's, Carlisle. Carlisle Grammar School, 1780–2; Hawkshead from either January or July 1783. Admitted Christ's College, Cambridge, 19 April 1786, aged 19. Matriculated Michaelmas 1786. Lodged in Milton's rooms at Christ's where Wordsworth 'pour'd out libations' (*Prelude*, 1805, III, ll. 294–307). In Carlisle cathedral a floor slab records that E. I. Birkett Esq. died 25 December 1831, aged 63, beloved and respected. *The Carlisle Patriot*, 21 January 1842 reads: 'At her residence Etterby Lodge near Carlisle Mrs. Birkett relict of Edward Birkett Esq. 76'. [C. R. Hudleston.]

BOWSTEAD, Rowland

(2) *A General Description of China: containing the Topography of the Fifteen Provinces which compose This Vast Empire; that of Tartary; the Isles and Other Tributary Countries* . . . Illustrated by a New and Correct Map of China. 2 vols. Translated from the French of the Abbé Grosier, London, MDCCLXXXVIII. [B.M. has 1778.] 8vo, 16s.

Rowland Bowstead   WM [Writing Master]   1789

See T.W.T. Bowstead, who wrote many of these labels, 1789–93, is sparse here.

BRATHWAITE, Gawen

(11) *Lectures on Rhetoric and Belles Lettres*   by Hugh Blair, D.D. and F.R.S. . . . 3 vols., 3rd ed., London, MDCCLXXXVII. 8vo, 18s.

The Gift of Gawen Brathwaite of Belmont on his leaving the School   1789

Born 28 November 1774, son of Reginald Brathwaite, Minister at Hawkshead; christened at Hawkshead Parish Church, 1 December 1774   Despite this inscription, he was a book-subscriber at Hawkshead till end of 1792. After leaving Hawkshead was at Sebergh School. Admitted sizar at St. John's College, Cambridge, July 1791; Matriculated Michaelmas 1792; B.A. 1796; M.A. 1799; B.D. 1807. Fellow 1797–1814. Prebendary of Llandaff, 1802–14. Died 29 October 1814, as a result of an accident to the Ipswich stage coach when passing under the gateway of the Blue Boar Inn, Trinity Street, Cambridge. Monument in the college chapel.

BURNTHWAITE, Thomas

(9) *A Year's Journey through France, and Part of Spain* by Philip Thicknesse, Esq. 2nd ed., 2 vols., London, MDCCLXXVIII. 8vo, 10s.

(8) *A Tour in the United States of America containing an Account of the Present Situation of that Country, with a Description of the Indian Nations.* . . . by J. F. D. Smyth Esq., 2 vols., London, MDCCLXXXIV. 8vo, 10s.

z

The Gift of Thomas Burnthwaite of Queen's College   Oxford   1790

Son of William B. of Ulverston, Lancashire. Matriculated 8 May 1787 at Queen's College, Oxford, aged 20. B.A. 1791. The book presentation list terms him: 'first Assistant. 1789'. An unattractive glimpse of Burnthwaite occurs in a letter of John Atkinson; 29 June 1790: 'Burnthwaite arrived from Oxford yesterday with a Face as red as Scarlet, and his Hand shaking like a man of sixty. He was so drunk last night as to be for fighting every Person he met; and he got a good blacking from a country fellow in very bad Language, which was answered with as shameful.' ('Extracts from some Furness Correspondence of the Eighteenth Century', by E. T. Baldwin, *The North Lonsdale Magazine and Furness Miscellany*, III (June 1899, p. 152).

BUTCHER, John

(23) *A View of Society in Europe in its Progress from Rudeness to Refinement* . . . by Gilbert Stuart LL.D., Edinburgh, MDCCLXXVIII. 4to, 12s.

The Gift of John Butcher of Presal on his leaving the School   1790

See T.W.T. Son of Robert and Jane B. of Preesall, baptized 5 September 1773 in the parish of Stalmire, Lancs.

CALVERT, William

(37) *The Life of Captain James Cooke* by Andrew Kippis, D.D., F.R.S. and S.A., London, MDCCLXXXVIII. 4to, £1. 1s.

There is an autograph on the title-page: 'Will. Scullard'; and on the short title-page the inscription: 'From the Author'.

The Gift of William Calvert of Greystoke   late of this School [Presented] 1792

William Calvert, son of Raisley and Dorothy Calvert, baptized at Threlkeld, 5 July 1770, and elder brother of Raisley from whom Wordsworth received a legacy of £900 and who also was at Hawkshead, a book-subscriber till the end of 1792. Their father, Raisley C., 1706/7–91, was steward to the Duke of Norfolk at Greystoke Castle, near Penrith. William Calvert died January 1829. There are many references to him in Wordsworth papers. After his death Wordsworth wrote to Crabb Robinson, 27 January 1829: 'Within the course of the last fortnight I have heard of the death of two among the most valued of my Schoolfellows—Godfrey Sykes, Sol: of the Stamp Off.—and Mr. Calvert, probably unknown to you by name—' (*Henry Crabb Robinson and the Wordsworth Circle*, ed. Morley, I, p. 199).

CHAMBRE, Alan (see PRESTON, George)

Son and heir of Walter C., a merchant of Lowther Street, Whitehaven, and Elizabeth, daughter of James Fox, of St. Bees. Baptized 1770. Admitted at Cambridge, 6 June 1788. Migrated, aged 18, from Queen's to Peterhouse, 3 November 1788. B.A. 1792; M.A. 1795. He had been admitted Gray's Inn, May 23 1788, as 'nephew of Alan Chambre, a master of the Bench'. Ordained at York, 6 July 1794. Married Mary, daughter of Sir John Banks Russell. Probably the Rev. Alan Chambre, of Whitehaven, who was killed in 1800 by being thrown out of an open carriage near that place. Brother of Thomas, see below.

CHAMBRE, Thomas

(35) *A General History of Ireland from the Earliest Accounts to the Close of the Twelfth Century* . . . by Mr. O'Halloran, 2 vols., London, MDCCLXXVIII. 4to, £1. 1s.

The Gift of Thomas Chambre of Whitehaven. On his leaving the School 1791

Brother of Alan, see above. Baptized, St. Nicholas, Whitehaven, 26 January 1775, seventh child and fourth son of Walter and Elizabeth (thirteen children in all). Book-subscriber 1789.

DALRYMPLE, Thomas

(24) *The History of France from the First Establishment of that Monarchy to the Present Revolution* [by Charles Hereford], 3 vols., London, 1790. 8vo, £1. 1s.

The Gift of James Dalrymple of Oxenford Castle near Edinburgh on his leaving the School 1790

Fifth son of Sir John Dalrymple, 1726–1810, and Elizabeth, Sir John's cousin, only surviving child and heiress of Thomas Hamilton Makgill of Fala and Oxenford. Born *c.* 1774. Midshipman in the Royal Navy. Died of yellow fever on board the *Thetis* frigate, 17 October 1796. See T.W.T. for sister's connection with Hawkshead; and see Douglas's *Scottish Peerage* for this family.

DALRYMPLE, North

(43) *Memoirs of Great Britain and Ireland* . . . A New Edition in Three Volumes . . . by Sir John Dalrymple, London, MDCCXC. Inscribed 'From the Author to the Hawkshead Library'. 8vo, £1. 7s.

The Gift of the Author on his Son North leaving the School [at midsummer] 1792

Sixth son of Sir John and Elizabeth Dalrymple; born 1776. Married (1) at Ulverston, Lancs., 27 May 1817, Margaret, youngest daughter of James Penny of Arrad and Liverpool (who died 22 April 1828) and by her had eight children. (2) 23 March 1831, Martha Willet, and by her had one child. Became 9th Earl of Stair, January 1853.

DALRYMPLE, Robert

(51) *The History of Scotland from the Establishment of the Reformation till the Death of Queen Mary* . . . by Gilbert Stuart, Doctor of Law, 2 vols., 2nd ed., London, MDCCLXXXIV. 8vo, 15s.

The Gift of Robert Dalrymple of Oxenford Castle near Edinburgh on his leaving the School 1795 [presentation list has January 1794]

Seventh son of Sir John and Elizabeth Dalrymple. Born 1780. Admitted pensioner at Pembroke College, Cambridge, 1 July 1797. Matriculated Michaelmas 1797. Scholar. No degree. Served in the Army in the 3rd Guards; ensign, 21 December 1799; lieutenant and captain, 24 March 1803. Accompanied the Guards to the Peninsula, and wrote a narrative of the campaign of 1809 up to the Battle of Talavera, where he was killed, 28 July 1809.

DIXON, Joshua

(46) *A Course of Lectures on Oratory and Criticism* by Joseph Priestley, LL.D., F.R.S., London, MDCCLXXVII. 4to, 14s.

The Gift of Joshua Dixon of Whitehaven on his leaving the School [at midsummer] 1793

Son of Joshua Dixon, M.D. of Whitehaven who died 7 January 1825 aged 80, and Ann D. Baptized, St. Nicholas, Whitehaven, 6 May 1777. Matriculated, Edinburgh University, Michaelmas 1795. Entered Medical Faculty there, 19 November 1796. M.D. (Anglus) 1798. Became himself doctor in Whitehaven, 1806. [F. Robinson.]

EDMONDSON, William

(39) *Travels into the Interior Parts of Africa by the way of the Cape of Good Hope in the years 1780, 81, 82, 83, 84 and 85.* Translated from the French of M. le Vaillant [by E. Helme]. 2 vols., London, MDCCXC. 8vo, 14s.

William Edmondson   of Threlkeld   1792

ELLERY, William

(10) *An Inquiry into the Original State and Formation of the Earth* . . . 2nd ed., by John Whitehurst, F.R.S., London, MDCCLXXXVI. 4to, £1. 2s.

The Gift of the Revd William Ellery   of Hawkshead [second] Assistant in the School 1789

The first master of Sawrey school; 'taken from the plough', he qualified for the priesthood. Curate at Winster, farmed weekdays. Buried 20 January 1799 at Hawkshead. See Cowper's *Hawkshead*, p. 560.

FLEMING, John

(5) *Travels into Poland, Russia, Sweden, and Denmark* . . . by William Coxe, A.M., F.R.S. 4 vols., 3rd ed., London, MDCCLXXXVII. 8vo, £1. 10s.

1789. Hawkshead School Library. The Gift of John Fleming Esqr. of Rayrigg. Educated at this School; Removed to S^t. John's College Cambridge   1785

See T.W.T.

GARDNER, George

(45) *Astronomical and Geographical Essays* . . . by George Adams, 3rd ed., London, 1795. 8vo, 12s.

The Gift of George Gardner of London   Admitted at Trinity Coll. from this School   1795

Born 19 September 1778, son of Daniel G. of London (a successful portrait painter, born in Kendal, 1750–1805, patronized by Reynolds, retired early and worth at his death £10,000) and Nancy Hayward. In 1780 Daniel bought Birthwaite in what is now the centre of the town of Windermere; his wife, the mother of George, is thought to have died early. George matriculated, Trinity College, Cambridge, Michaelmas 1795. LL.B. 1801. Went to Paris with his father after the Peace of Amiens and was there at the resumption of hostilities; escaped through the influence of Le Clement, Talleyrand's private secretary. Tombstone in Bowness Parish Churchyard indicates that he died 20 May 1837, aged 59. His son, George Harrison G., born 1814, baptized April 1815, living at Ellerthwaite 16 September 1856 and presumably he, not his father, is the George G. cited by Venn as alive in 1850. See *Daniel Gardner* by G. C. Williamson, 1921, London, privately printed.

GARNETT, Thomas

(25) *Letters on Egypt, containing a Parallel between the Manners of its ancient and modern Inhabitants . . . extracted from Joinville, and Arabian Authors.* Translated from the French of M. Savary, 2 vols., 2nd ed., London, MDCCLXXXVII. 8vo, £1. 1s.

The Gift of Mr Thomas Garnett of Hawkshead Assistant in the School 1783–1789 [inclusive]

See T.W.T.

GAWTHROP, Thomas (see GREENWOOD, R. H.; and T.W.T.)

GREEN, Andrew

(54) *A History of the late Siege of Gibraltar . . .* by John Drinkwater, 4th ed., London, MDCCXC. 4to, £1. 10s.

The Gift of Andrew Green of Cockermouth Admitted at Trinity College Cambridge from this School 1791

Son of Andrew G., sometime of the 35th Foot, of St. Philip's, Minorca and Julia, only daughter of the Rev. W. T. Addison, Rector of Workington. Born 1774. Admitted as a pensioner at Trinity, 23 June 1793, aged 19. Matriculated 1796; Norissian Prize 1798; LL.B. 1799. Married, 5 October 1815, Esther, daughter of Henry Thompson of Cheltenham, and Bridekirk, Cumberland. Owned woollen mills in Cockermouth. The same Andrew Green who unsuccessfully contested Cockermouth in the radical interest in 1832. His wife died 17 May 1833. He died 21 September 1847. Both are mentioned in the *Wordsworth Letters*. The family became Thompson-Green.

GREENWOOD, R. H.

(14) *The History of Ancient Greece, its Colonies, and Conquests from the Earliest Accounts till the Division of the Macedonian Empire in the East. Including the History of Literature, Philosophy, and the Fine Arts* by John Gillies, LL.D., F.R.S., 2nd ed., 4 vols., London, MDCCLXXXVII. [Edition not in B.M.] 8vo, £1. 10s.

The Gift of R. H. Greenwood of Ingleton William Wordsworth of Cockermouth Thomas Gawthrop of Sedbergh and John Millar of Presal Admitted at Cambridge from this School 1787

R. H. Greenwood, see T.W.T. For Gawthrop and Millar, see separate entries.

(15) *Jerusalem Delivered; An Heroic Poem:* Translated from the Italian of Torquato

Tasso, by John Hoole, 2 vols., 6th ed., London, MDCCLXXXVII. [Edition not in B.M.] 8vo, 15s.

The Gift of the Young Gentlemen   Admitted at Cambridge from this School   1787

HARRISON, Thomas

(17) *Orlando Furioso:* Translated from the Italian of Lodovico Ariosto . . . by John Hoole, 5 vols., 2nd ed., London, MDCCLXXXV. 8vo, £1. 17s. 6d.

The Gift of Thomas Harrison of Kendal   and   John Hutchinson   of Watermillock Admitted at Cambridge   from this School   1789 [Presentation list adds name of Godfrey Sykes.]

Thomas Harrison, son of Thomas H. of Kendal, a Quaker, and an attorney, who acted for the Lowthers, and, after 1768, for Sir Michael le Fleming of Rydal. Born 1771. Venn indicates he was a pupil at Sedbergh School after Hawkshead; certainly he was a pupil of the tutor, John Dawson of that town. Admitted pensioner at Queen's College, Cambridge, 5 March 1789; Matriculated Michaelmas 1790; B.A. (Senior Wrangler and 1st Smith's Prize) 1796; Fellow, 1794. Called to the Bar, 1802; retired 1809. Deputy High Steward of Cambridge University, 1806–24. Admirer of Fox and supporter of Anti-Slave trade movement. Became 2nd husband of his cousin, Lydia, daughter of George Harrison. Lived at Streatham Park, Surrey. Died 21 March 1824.

For John Hutchinson, see separate entry.

HARTLEY, Samuel

(52) *The Antiquities of Furness, or, an account of the Royal Abbey of St. Mary in the vale of Nightshade, near Dalton in Furness* . . . by Thomas West, London, MDCCLXXIV. [According to the presentation list the Speddings gave this book and Hartley *The British Chronologist*. See W. Taylor, below.]

(56) The Gift of Samuel Hartley of Marsh-Grange in Kirby   Admitted at Eman¹. Coll: Cambridge   from this School   1794

Son of John H. of Beck, Millom, Cumberland. Marsh Grange is at the other side of the Duddon estuary, in the parish of Dalton-in-Furness, Lancs.; baptized 11 December 1773; Admitted sizar, Emmanuel College, Cambridge, 21 September 1793; Matriculated Lent 1795; B.A. 1798. Head Master of Carlisle Grammar School, June 1803–November 1819. Vicar of St. Mary's, Carlisle, 1809–19. Head Master of Haydon Bridge Grammar School from 1819. Two sons. Died 9 July 1825, aged 51. [F. Robinson.]

HETHERINGTON, William

(34) *Fingal   an Ancient Epic Poem,   In Six Books   Together with several other Poems,* compiled by Ossian, the Son of Fingal. Translated from the Galic Language, by James Macpherson, London, MDCCLXII. 4to, 12s.

The Gift of William Hetherington of Burton in Lonsdale   On his Leaving the School   1791

HUBBERSTY, Zachary and John Lodge

(68) *The Ecclesiastical History, Antient and Modern, . . .* by John Lawrence Mosheim, D.D. . . . Translated from the Original Latin by Archibald Maclaine, D.D. A New Edition. In Five Volumes. London, MDCCLXXIV. [Edition not in B.M.] 8vo, £1. 15s.

Messrs Zachary and John Lodge Hubbersty   Presented 1797

See T.W.T.

HUDLESTON, Andrew

(67) *A Collection of Theological Tracts, in Six Volumes* by Richard Watson D.D., F.R.S. Lord Bishop of Landaff . . . Cambridge, MDCCLXXXV. 8vo, £2. 2s.

The Gift of Andrew Hudleston of Whitehaven and Skeffington Lutwidge of Holme Nook   Admitted at Cambridge from this School   1797

Andrew Hudleston, baptized 3 January 1779, elder son of Wilfrid, Vicar of White-haven and Elizabeth, daughter of Thomas Airy, M.D., of Egremont. Admitted pensioner 17 September 1795, Trinity College, Cambridge; Matriculated Michaelmas 1797; B.A. 1801; M.A. 1808; D.D. 1822. Permanent curate of St. Nicholas, Whitehaven, 1811–51. Rector of Moresby, 30 September 1821. Rector of Bowness-on-Solway, 14 November 1828–51. Died unmarried at Whitehaven as of Lowther Street, 22 November 1851. [C. R. Hudleston.]

For Lutwidge, see separate entry.

HULL, Thomas

(61) *Poems*, by William Cowper, 2 vols., 5th ed., London, 1793. 8vo, 11s. 6d.

The Gift of Thomas Hull of Poulton   on his leaving the School   1794

Probably connected with Christopher Hull of Marton near Poulton-le-Fylde, Lancs., the allegedly incompetent Headmaster of Sedbergh School, 1782–99.

HUTCHINSON, John (see HARRISON, Thomas)

Born 1769. Admitted pensioner, Corpus Christi, Cambridge, 21 April 1789; Matriculated Michaelmas 1789; B.A. 1793.

James Losh married by him, February 1798 at Aldingham, Furness [Lancs.]. Of Old Church, Watermillock, Ullswater, by 1812. Married Rebecca Davis. Died 12 January 1846, aged 76, at Horrock Wood, Ullswater. Buried at Watermillock. Nephew of John Robinson of Watermillock and referred to by Christopher Wordsworth as 'H', hitherto unidentified, in his 'Outline of a Poem', 1792 (Z. S. Fink, *The Early Wordsworthian Milieu*, p. 105). He is probably not the 'H' to whom the Outline is addressed (ibid., p. 118).

IRELAND, James

(42) *Philosophia Britannica: or a New and Comprehensive System of the Newtonian*

Philosophy, Astronomy, and Geography, In a course of Twelve Lectures ... by B. Martin, 4th ed., 3 vols., London. Printed for John Francis, Charles Rivington, Thomas Carnan, Andrew Strahan. MDCCLXXXVIII. [Edition not in B.M.] 8vo, £1. 1s.

The Gift of James Ireland of Broughton   Admitted at Trinity College Cambridge from this School   1792

Son of Edward I. of Broughton, Lancs. Admitted pensioner (age 20) at Trinity, 11 October 1791. Matriculated 1792; B.A. 1796; M.A. 1799. Ordained deacon, Bristol, 17 December 1796. Rector of Thurstaston, Cheshire, 1808–.

JACK, Thomas (see PRESTON, George)

Son of William and Elizabeth J. of Sowerby Row (9 miles south of Carlisle), Cumberland. Baptized 31 July 1769. Admitted pensioner, April 29, 1788, St. John's College, Cambridge. Matriculated Michaelmas 1788. A pupil of John Dawson of Sedbergh. B.A. (4th Wrangler) 1792; M.A. 1795; B.D. 1804. Fellow, 1804–6. Ordained deacon 11 August 1793. Priest (Ely) 27 October 1793. Curate of Coveney with Manea, Cambs., 1793–1804. Followed Wordsworth's uncle, William Cookson, as Rector of Forncett, Norfolk, 1805–44. Died 14 February 1844. Monument with inscription in Forncett church.

KNOWLES, Thomas

(63) *Analogy of Religion, Natural and Revealed*, by —— Butler [This is taken from T.W.T.'s copy of the list; the book is no longer in the library.]

The Gift of Thomas Knowles of Halton, who left the School A.D. 1789. Presented 1795

LITTLEDALE, Isaac and Henry

(21) *Memoirs of the Protectorate-House of Cromwell* ... by Mark Noble, F.S.A., 2 vols., Birmingham, MDCCXXXLIV [*sic* for 1784: edition not in B.M.]. 8vo, 10s. 6d.

(22) The Gift of Isaac and Henry Littledale of Whitehaven on their leaving the School 1790

[According to the presentation list, this book was the gift of Christopher Wilkinson; and the Littledales' gave 'his' Goldsmith: see Wilkinson.]

Sons of Henry L. of Whitehaven, and afterwards of Eaton House (1741–96), and Sarah, daughter of John Wilkinson of Whitehaven, died 1808. Isaac was born 14 August 1774; died without issue 13 May 1828. Henry was born 10 August 1775; died 10 March 1795, aged 19. See, *Family Records*, A. P. Burke, 1897. In the accounts of Wordsworth's Uncle Richard of Whitehaven is the entry for 12 December 1789: 'Paid Mr. Littledale for Nephew Christr's. Conveyance from Hawkshead . . . 8s. 6d.' This Henry Littledale in May 1794 was awarded £4,000 to be paid him by Lord Lonsdale: his house was destroyed through mining subsidence. Dorothy Wordsworth wrote to her brother Richard from Whitehaven on 28 May 1794: 'Everyone here is rejoiced at the good news of Mr. Littledale's having gained his cause. I wish ours had been pursued with equal vigour.' (*Letters: Early Years*, p. 123.)

LITTLEDALE, Johnson, Anthony, and Edward

(45) *Galic Antiquities: consisting of a History of the Druids, particularly those of Caledonia: a dissertation on the authenticity of the poem of Ossian; and a collection of ancient poems, translated from the Galic of Ullin, Ossian, Orran &c.* by John Smith ... Edinburgh, 1780. 4to, £1. 1s.

The Gift of Johnson and Anthony [and Edward] Littledale of Whitehaven on their leaving the School   1792 [Presentation list adds Edward as 3rd name, and the date 1793: only Edward left in that year.]

Sons of Henry and Sarah Littledale, see above. Johnson, born 10 September 1776; married November 1796 Isabella Bond; had son, Henry. Anthony, later of Liverpool, born 3 October 1777; married 19 June 1809 Mary, elder daughter of Pudsey Dawson of Langcliffe Hall, and Bolton Hall, Yorks., who died 3 November 1855. Anthony died 16 January 1820. Two sons at Hawkshead and St. John's, Cambridge. (Brother Joseph at Hawkshead; Senior Wrangler 1787; Judge 1824–41; edited Skelton.)

LUTWIDGE, Skeffington (see HUDLESTONE, Andrew)

Born 23 May 1779, second son of Henry L. of Holme Rook, near Whitehaven, Cumberland. Baptized at Walton-le-Dale, Lancashire, his mother being Jane, daughter of Rigby Molyneux of Preston. Matriculated at St. John's College, Cambridge, Michaelmas 1797. His elder brother, Charles, had overlapped with Wordsworth at St. John's in 1789. Skeffington left the university almost at once and entered the service of the East India Company. 1797, a cadet in the 11th Regiment of Madras Native Infantry, became Deputy Judge-Advocate Madras Army, and retired as Major to England, 29 March 1816. Married 1811 a daughter of General William Lockhart of Lanarkshire. Of Holm Rook Hall, Cumberland. J.P. and D.L. for Cumberland. Died 3 February 1854 at Weston-super-Mare.

MAUDE, Thomas (see PRESTON, George; and T.W.T.)

MILLAR or MILLER, John (see GREENWOOD, R. H.)

Son of John and Ann Miller of Hackensall, then in the parish of Stalmire, Lancs. Baptized 27 April 1766. Matriculated Cambridge, Michaelmas 1787, sizar at Jesus. B.A. 1791.

MILLERS, George

(55) *A View of Sir Isaac Newton's Philosophy* [by Henry Pemberton], London, 1728. 4to, 12s.

The Gift of George Millers of Kendal   Admitted at Trinity College Cambridge from this School   1794

Son of Thomas M. of Kendal. Admitted sizar at St. John's College, Cambridge, 2 November 1793. Matriculated at St. John's, Michaelmas 1794 (not at Trinity as the Writing Master has it in the book-plate). B.A. 1798; M.A. 1801. Ordained deacon 1798; priest (Ely) 8 June 1800. Curate of Brinkley, Cambs., 1798. Permanent Curate of Chettisham. Minor Canon of Ely, 1800–52. Vicar of Winston, Suffolk, 1803–6.

Vicar of Stanford, Norfolk, 1808–45. Vicar of Runham, Norfolk, 1811–52. Rector of Hardwicke, Cambs., 1825–52. Kept a private boarding school at Ely for many years. Married 9 July 1801, Mary, sister of the Rev. Robert Forby of Fincham. Died 3 January 1852, aged 76. William Selwyn, also a Canon of Ely (died 1875), wrote to Wordsworth on 27 August 1849: 'We are staying with an old and kind friend, Mr. Millers, who was at school at Hawkshead with your brother, and I believe with yourself. He succeeded to this delightful estate in Duddon Vale on the death of his neice 3 years since.' (MS. Dove Cottage Library.) The estate, through marriage, had been George's brother William's, the brilliant contemporary (Senior Wrangler 1789) of Wordsworth at St. John's and possibly at Hawkshead, for in the book-subscribers list, 1793, Bowman notes: 'my pupil for a space'.

MORLAND, Henry and Charles

(19) *A General History of the World from the Creation to the Present Time* . . . by William Guthrie, Esq. and John Gray, Esq., 12 vols., London, MDCCLXIV[-VII]. 8vo, £2. 2s.

The Gift of Henry & Charles Morland of Kendal on their leaving the School   1790

Sons of Thomas Morland, Lamberhurst, Kent, and Ann Matson, Tytup Hall, Dalton-in-Furness, a widow by 1784 and living in Kendal. On 28 August 1817 James Losh wrote in his diary: 'At Kendal I saw my old friend M^{rs}. Morland now feeble and wrinkled with age: 33 years ago I wrote a copy of verses upon her and her 2 daughters.' Losh was then 21. Henry and Charles were at School in Broughton-le-Furness (master, Jeremy Gilpin) 1784–5; Hawkshead from 1786.

1. Henry: Born 9 December 1772. Matriculated, St. John's College, Cambridge, Michaelmas 1790; Scholar 1790; B.A. 1794; M.A. 1797. Ordained deacon (Rochester) 29 September 1794. Curate of Horsmonden, Kent from 1794. Rector of Horsmonden 1809–21. Married 14 June 1810 Harriet Frances, youngest daughter of James Marriott. Died 14 August 1821, aged 49.

2. Charles: Born 1775. Entered Manchester Academy 1790. Apprenticed 15 October 1792 for 4 years to Messrs. Rawlinson and Alberti, Manchester, to be taught the business of cotton manufactury. [Matson papers, Records, Kendal.]

NEWTON, Thomas

(36) *A Journey through Spain in the years 1786 and 1787* . . . *and Remarks . . . on a Part of France* by Joseph Townsend, A.M., 3 vols., 2nd ed., London, MDCCXCII. 8vo, £1.

Mr Thomas Newton   of Ambleside   Assistant in the School   1791–1794

Probably Thomas, son of John Newton of Nook End, Ambleside, baptized 20 December 1770.

PEARSON, William

(20) *Lectures on Select Subjects in Mechanics, Hydrostatics* . . . by James Ferguson, F.R.S. a new edition, London, MDCCLXXIII. [Edition not in B.M.] 4to, 18s.

The Gift of the Revd William Pearson   of Whitbeck   Student & Assistant in the School   Anno 1785   1790

[Called 'second Assistant in this School, 1790' in library presentation list.]

Second son of William P. and Hannah Ponsonby of Whitbeck, Cumberland. Born there 23 April 1767, 'of good old yeoman family'. Admitted sizar at Clare College, Cambridge, 20 June 1793, but doubtful if he resided. Took orders. Perpetual Curate of Killington, Westmorland, 1799–1801. Rector of Perivale, Middlesex, 1810–12. Rector of S. Kilworth, Leics., 1817–47. Owner of a large private school at Temple Grove, East Sheen, Surrey, 1812–21, where he established an observatory. F.R.S., 1819; Hon. LL.D., Glasgow, 1819. A celebrated astronomer. Died 6 September 1847 at Kilworth. Monument there. He is the subject of a note Wordsworth dictated to Miss Fenwick some fifty years after school-days:

His manners when he came to Hawkshead were as uncouth as well could be; but he had good abilities, with skill to turn them to account; and when the Master of the School, to which he was Usher, died, he stept into his place and became Proprietor of the Establishment. He contrived to manage it with such address, and so much to the taste of what is called High Society and the fashionable world, that no school of the kind, even till he retired, was in such high request. Ministers of State, the wealthiest gentry, and nobility of the first rank, vied with each other in bespeaking a place for their sons in the seminary of this fortunate Teacher. In the solitude of Grasmere, while living as a married man in a cottage of £8 per annum rent, I often used to smile at the tales which reached me of the brilliant career of this quondam clown, for such in reality he was in manner and appearance before he was polished a little by attrition with *gentlemen's* sons trained at Hawkshead, rough and rude as many of our Juveniles[1] were. Not 200 yards from the cottage in Grasmere, just mentioned, to which I retired, this gentleman, who many years afterwards purchased a small estate in the neighbourhood, is now erecting a boat-house, with an upper story, to be resorted to as an entertaining-room when he and his associates may feel inclined to take their pastime on the Lake. Every passenger will be disgusted with the sight of this Edifice, not merely as a tasteless thing in itself, but as utterly out of place, and peculiarly fitted, as far as it is observed (and it obtrudes itself on notice at every point of view), to mar the beauty and destroy the pastoral simplicity of the Vale. For my own part and that of my household it is our utter detestation, standing by a shore to which, before the highroad was made to pass that way, we used daily and hourly to repair for seclusion and for the shelter of a grove under which I composed many of my poems, *The Brothers* especially, and for this reason we gave the grove that name.

> That which each man loved
> And prized in his peculiar nook of earth
> Dies with him, or is changed. [*Excursion*, I, 471–3.]

So much for my old school-fellow and his exploits. I will only add that as the foundation has twice failed, from the lake no doubt being intolerant of the intrusion, there is some ground for hoping that this impertinent structure will not stand. (It has been rebuilt in somewhat better taste and much as one wishes it away it is not now so very unsightly. The structure is an emblem of the man,—persever-

---

[1] From the MS. Printed texts read 'families'.

ance has conquered difficulties and given something of form and polish to rudeness [*added in pencil*]).

[*Wordsworth's Poetical Works*, V, pp. 456–7.]

A second, unpublished, pencilled note reads: 'This boat-house badly built, gave way & was rebuilt. It again tumbled, & was a third time reconstructed but in a better fashion than before. It is not now, per se, an ugly building, however obtrusive it may be.' The boat-house still survives, immediately south of the Prince of Wales Hotel; a stone over the door reads: W.P. 1843.' From the two letters that survive from Pearson to Wordsworth, written on 10 August 1812 and 29 March 1813, it is clear that the 'small estate in the neighbourhood' had been in Pearson's hands for some years before 1812. Pearson clearly was prepared to receive an offer from Wordsworth for the 'Estate of Townend in Grassmere together with the meadows I purchased of the late Mr. Briggs'. He indicates that he had bought the meadows from Briggs for £300, and the Estate from Birkett for £700 (and also that he held land 'in Loughrigg, by the side of Rydall Lake'). He was quite agreeable to the notion of selling, but in 1813 Wordsworth took Rydal Mount and Pearson kept his estates. He had a wife and daughter by 1812. Pearson's letters are thoroughly businesslike, and there is little to reveal previous knowledge of the Wordsworth family: merely the comment, 'I understand your brother Richard is living at Lincoln's Inn Fields; probably you will employ him to negociate for you'; and the acknowledgement of a 'polite invitation', presumably to visit at Rydal Mount where the Wordsworths were soon to live. (Dove Cottage Library.)

PEELE, JOHN JAMES

(26) *A General Collection of Voyages and Discoveries made by the Portuguese and the Spaniards during the Fifteenth and Sixteenth Centuries* . . . London, MDCCLXXXIX. [This work not in B.M., but in London Library.] 4to, 12s.

The Gift of John James Peele of Cockermouth   on his leaving the School   1790

POSTLETHWAITE, Thomas

(53) *The Theory of Moral Sentiments* . . . *to which is added a Dissertation on the Origin of Languages* by Adam Smith, LL.D., 7th ed., 2 vols., London, MDCCXCII. [edition not in B.M.] 8vo, 15s.

The Gift of Thomas Postlethwaite of Dalton   Admitted at Trinity College Cambridge   on his leaving the School   1794

Book-subscriber Hawkshead, 1789₂–1794. Admitted pensioner at Trinity, 10 October 1793. Matriculated, Michaelmas 1794. Migrated to Emmanuel, 26 March 1795; B.A. 1798; M.A. 1802. Ordained priest (Peterborough) 15 June 1806; Curate of Teigh, Rutland, 1806.

PRESTON, George

(16) *The History of the Decline and Fall of the Roman Empire* by Edward Gibbon, Esq., 12 vols. A new edition. MDCCLXXXVIII. 8vo, £3. 15s.

The Gift of George Preston of Hawkshead, John Rudd of Cockermouth, Alan Chambre of Whitehaven, Thomas Maude of Kendal, Thomas Jack of [Bank End, Heskett] and Robert Balderston of Ingleton Admitted at Cambridge from this School 1788

George Preston, son of George P. of Ulverston, Lancs. and Isabel, third daughter of Myles Sandys. Admitted Trinity College, Cambridge, 6 July 1787. Matriculated Michaelmas 1788; B.A. 1792; M.A. 1795. Ordained priest (Norwich) 21 February 1796. Curate of Cartmel, Lancs., 1804–33. Vicar (and Patron) of Briston, Norfolk 1803–40. Rector of Lexden, Essex, 1804–40. Died there 29 September 1840. See also Rudd.

For the other donors, see separate entries.

RAINCOCK, Fletcher

(12) *A View of Society and Manners in France, Switzerland, and Germany: with Anecdotes relating to some Eminent Characters* by John Moore, M.D. 2 vols., 2nd ed., London, MDCCLXXIX. 8vo, 12s.

[An autograph on the title page reads: 'Fra⁵. Dawes/Pet: Coll'; a second-hand book?]

(13) *A view of Society and Manners in Italy: with Anecdotes relating to some Eminent Characters* by John Moore, M.D., 2 vols., London, MDCCLXXXI. 8vo, 14s.

[Autograph on title-page reads: 'Fra⁵. Dawes/Pet: Coll/1781'.]

The Gift of Fletcher Raincock of Rayrigg and Edward Birkitt of Carlisle Admitted at Cambridge from this School 1786

Fletcher Raincock, see T.W.T. Venn's entry puzzlingly gives his school as St. Bees, and adds, contrary to T.W.T. that he married (Miss M. Dawson). Fellowships at Cambridge were not always easily come by, even for a second Wrangler; Christopher Wordsworth wrote to his uncle, Christopher Cookson, on 4 October: [1794]: 'Fletcher Raincock has been down at Cambridge, on his being at length elected Fellow of Pembroke. He left us yesterday morning.' (The Records, Kendal.)

For Edward Birkett, see separate entry.

RAINCOCK, William and Christopher

(41) *Travels in Switzerland in a Series of Letters to William Melmoth, Esq., from William Coxe, M.A., F.R.S., F.A.S.*, 3 vols., 1789. 8vo, £1. 7s.

The Gift of William [who left School 1787] and Christopher Raincock [who left School 1790. Presented A.D. 1792.]

Younger brothers of Fletcher Raincock. See T.W.T. John Yates, a boy of 14 or 15, wrote to his mother from Fredericksburg, Virginia, on 29 May 1793: 'Mrs. Taylor was mistaken in saying I did not see Kit Raincock in Norfolk. I heard from him about three weeks ago, and he told me a good deal of Cumberland news that I did not know before. (*Memorials of a Family in England and Virginia*, compiled and edited by A. E. Terrill, 1887, p. 68.) Christopher Raincock was still in U.S.A. in 1799.

RUDD, John (see PRESTON, George)

Son of John R. of Cockermouth. Admitted pensioner at Trinity College, Cambridge, 18 Dec. 1787. Matriculated Michaelmas 1788. B.A. (10th Wrangler) 1792; M.A. 1795. Fellow, 1794. Vicar of Blyth, Notts., 1813–30. Prebendary of Southwell, 1827–34. Rector of Waltham, Lincs., 1830–4. Married 1813 second daughter of the Dean of Bath, Dr. Ferris. Died 8 July 1834; buried at Blyth. His signature with date 1786 occurs in *Juvenal & Persius,* Hanovia MDCIII, p. 553, a book given to Hawkshead School 'at the request of Daniel Rawlinson by Sir Jonas Moore'. Rudd, Preston, and Greenwood have all written their names at the front of the same book. Both Preston and Rudd have signed certain passages of a large folio edition of Cicero which has lost its title page.

SMITH, Cowperthwaite

(60) *The Philosophy of Rhetoric* by George Campbell, D.D. . . . 2 vols., London, MDCCLXXVI. 8vo, 12s. 6d.

The Gift of Cowperthwaite Smith of Burniside on his leaving the School   1794

Admitted sizar at Christ's College, Cambridge, 8 June 1814; a 'Ten-year man.' Matriculated Easter, 1823; B.D. 1824. Ordained deacon (Chester) May 1807. Curate of Goodshaw, Lancs. Headmaster of Lichfield Grammar School, 1813–45. Died 17 August 1845, aged 71, at Lichfield, having presided over the decline of the school.

SPEDDING, Anthony and William

(52) *Anecdotes of the Life of the Right Honourable William Pitt Earl of Chatham*; [compiled by J. Almon.] . . . In Three Volumes, 4th ed., London, 1794. [Edition not in B.M.] 4to, £1. 1s.

[According to the presentation list, the Speddings gave West's *Antiquities.* See Hartley.]

The Gift of Anthony & Wᵐ. Spedding of Armathwaite who left this School   Anthʸ. D. 1792   Wᵐ. 1794

Anthony was the third son of John S. of Armathwaite Hall; born 1775, baptized 14 January 1776. Entered Inner Temple 25 November 1802; attended Dr. Bristowe, a law crammer, at Neasham, London. Married Isabel, daughter of Henry Gibson, surgeon, of Newcastle upon Tyne. William was baptized at Bassenthwaite, 26 October 1777. He died unmarried in 1806. Their brother John (baptized 16 February 1770) was Wordsworth's contemporary at Hawkshead; Matriculated Oriel College, Oxford, 11 March 1788, and took his B.A., 1792. Became a Captain in the Army and married in 1799 Isabel Gibson's older sister, Sarah. Died 1851.

SUNDERLAND, Thomas

(31) *A Journey through the Crimea to Constantinople in a Series of Letters from the Right Honourable Elizabeth Lady Craven to his Serene Highness The Margrave of Brandebourg . . . Written in the year MDCCLXXXVI*, London, MDCCLXXXIX. 4to, 18s.

The Gift of Thomas Sunderland of Ulverstone on his leaving the School [at Xt.mas] 1791

Younger son of Colonel Thomas S. of Littlecroft, Ulverston, Lancs., and Anne, daughter of William Dickson, of Beck Bank. Baptized 7 February 1775. His elder brother, John, after Hawkshead and Rugby, was at Trinity College, Cambridge, and was Wordsworth's exact contemporary at university; 1807-36. J. was vicar of Ulverston. The father was the fine landscape artist (see I. A. Williams, *Early English Water-colours*, 1952).

SYKES, Godfrey

(3) *The History of the Reign of the Emperor Charles V. with a View of the Progress of Society in Europe* . . . by William Robertson, D.D., 4 vols., 6th ed., London, MDCCLXXXVII. [Edition not in B.M.] 8vo, £1. 1s.

The Gift of Godfrey Sykes of Sheffield on his leaving the School 1789

Born 18 January 1772, eldest and only surviving son of Dennis S. of Sheffield, a cutler and merchant, 1748-1819, and Hannah Pashley. At Hawkshead under Taylor and Bowman. Matriculated, Sidney Sussex College, Cambridge, Michaelmas 1789. A pupil of John Dawson of Sedbergh. B.A. 1793, 10th Wrangler; M.A. 1796. Fellow. The Sykes pedigree in Jackson Collection 1245, Sheffield Public Library, calls him 'of Middle Temple, London, Esq., Barr'. at Law & Sol'. to the Board of Stamps & Taxes. Nov. 1814. of Powis Place, London. Died 31 December 1828.' Married 16 September 1808 Sarah Milnes Wheat, daughter of James Wheat of Norwood Hall and Sheffield; she died 1846, aged 73; there were three children. Sykes referred to by Wordsworth as 'our lamented friend' in a letter to John Spedding, who would also know Sykes, as Spedding was at Hawkshead School before going to St. Bees (see above p. 54, footnote); the letter perhaps should be dated later, even by ten years, than the date assigned to it, 1 March [1819], *Wordsworth Letters, Middle Years*, II (1970), pp. 525-6. See also entries for Calvert and Harrison [P. J. Wallis.]

TATE, William

(33) *Eboracum: or the History and Antiquities of the City of York, from the origin to this time, together with an Account of the Ainsty, or, County of the same and a Description and History of the Cathedral Church* . . . 2 vols. York, MDCCLXXXVIII. 8vo, 12s.

The Gift of William Tate of Whitehaven on his leaving the School (at Christmas] 1791

Son of Joseph T. baptized at Holy Trinity, Whitehaven, 24 May 1772.

TAYLOR, Fletcher and Peter

(49) *The History of Spain from the Establishment of the Colony of Gades by the Phoenicians, to the Death of Ferdinand, Surnamed the Sage* by the Author of the History of France [Charles Hereford], 3 vols., London, 1793. 8vo, £1. 1s.

The Gift of Fletcher and Peter Taylor of Whitehaven on their Leaving the School [Midsummer] 1793

Sons of Peter Taylor, 1738–89, and Isabella Fleming (second daughter of Fletcher F. of Rayrigg who died 1826—see T.W.T.). Fletcher was the second son. The family tombstone in Bowness churchyard records of him: '1st Lieutenant of HMS La Virtu who fell a sacrifice to the Yellow Fever on the 5th Day of June 1809 in the 28th Year of his Age and was buried at Port Royal.' Thus Fletcher was only twelve when he left Hawkshead School, his brother, Peter, younger. Peter was said to be 'at the Cape of Good Hope' 22 June 1797 (*Memorials* . . . ed. A. E. Terrill, p. 105). In the Royal Westmorland Militia: his commission is dated 1807; a major, 28 March 1813. In *Militia List*, 1820; not in 1825. He married Margaret Lewthwaite, who died 1835; no children. The oldest brother, Joseph, was also a pupil at Hawkshead in April 1785, and lodged in the same house with his relatives, the Raincocks and the Pattensons (Senhouse Papers); he died, aged 30, 22 March 1801 in Cuba, a Lieutenant of H.M.S. *Cleopatra*. [C. R. Hudleston.]

TAYLOR, William

(56) *The British Chronologist; comprehending every material occurence, ecclesiastical, civil or military, relative to England and Wales from the Invasion of the Romans* . . . 3 vols., 2nd ed., London, MDCCLXXXIX. [Edition not in B.M.] 8vo, 12s.

(62) The Gift of William Taylor of Manchester [from Bryers] on his leaving the School   1795

[According to the presentation list, Taylor gave *Anecdotes* . . . *of Chatham*: see Spedding.]

The son of William T. of Briers (Hawkshead) and Annabelle Hodgson (died 29 April 1781); born 14 February 1779. Taylor the father (see T.W.T.). was a Manchester merchant and moved to Green End, Colthouse, after the death of Mrs. Rigge, 1790. On his death in 1819 he left his property ('under £9,000') to his nephew, Braithwaite Hodgson.

THOMPSON, Henry

(4) *The Principles of Moral and Political Philosophy* by William Paley, M.A., 6th ed. corrected, 2 vols., London, MDCCLXXXVIII. 8vo, 15s.

The Gift of Henry Thompson of Cockermouth   on his leaving the School   1789

THOMPSON, Joseph

(57) *A View of England towards the Close of the Eighteenth Century* by Fred. Aug. Wendeborn, LL.D. Translated from the Original German by the Author himself. 2 vols., London, MDCCXCI. 8vo, 15s.

The Gift of Joseph Thompson of Cockermouth on his leaving the School   1795

A book-subscriber at Hawkshead from 1791₂–1794₁

THOMPSON, William

(27) *Elements of Criticism* [by Henry Home (Lord Kames)], 4th ed. with Additions and Improvements. 2 vols., Edinburgh, MDCCLXIX. 8vo, 10s.

(28) *An Account of the War in India: between the English and the French, on the Coast of Coromandel from the year 1750 to the year 1761* ... by Richard Owen Cambridge, Esq., 2nd ed., London, MDCCLXII. 8vo, 5s.

The Gift of William Thompson of Cockermouth on his leaving the School 1791

THORNTON, William

The School of Arts; or, An Introduction of Useful Knowledge ... A New Edition, by John Imison, London, n.d. [B.M. dates ? 1790.] [No size], 10s. 6d.

The Gift of William Thornton of Dalton on his leaving the School 1792 [presentation list has January 1793].

TOWNLEY, Jonathan

(29) *Travels through Holland Flanders Germany etc. in the years 1768, 1769 and 1770* ... by Joseph Marshall, 2nd ed., 3 vols., London, MDCCLXXIII. 8vo, £1. 4s. [A fourth volume was given: *Travels through France and Spain in 1770 and 1771* by Joseph Marshall, London, MDCCLXXVI.]

Jonathan Townley of Belfield [near Rochdale] Lancashire on his leaving the School [at Christmas] 1791

Admitted pensioner Clare College, Cambridge, 19 October 1792; matriculated Michaelmas 1793; B.A. 1797; M.A. 1801. Permanent Curate of Colton, Lancs., 1824–34, Vicar of Steeple Bumpstead, Essex, 1834–48. Died 17 December 1848. Family connected by marriage to the Gales of Whitehaven.

TYSON, Edward

The Principles of Natural and Politic Law by J. J. Burlamaqui. Translated into English by Mr. Nugent. 3rd ed. Revised and corrected, printed for C. Nourse, 2 vols., London, MDCCLXXXIV. [Edition not in B.M.] 8vo, 12s.

The Gift of Edward Tyson of Eskdale on his leaving the School [Oct^r.] 1793

Presumably son of Nicholas T. of Brantrake, baptized at Eskdale 6 August 1776, and to be distinguished from the Rev. Edward Tyson, 1771–1854, see T.W.T.

VICKARS, Matthew

(48) *The History of the Reign of Philip the Third, King of Spain.* First 4 Books by Robert Watson, and the last 2 by William Thomson, 2nd ed., 2 vols., London, MDCCLXXXVI. 8vo, 14s.

The Gift of Matthew Vickers of Eskdale on his leaving the School [Midsummer] 1793

WHITLOCK, Edward

(59) *A Dissertation on the Rise, Union and Power, The Progressions, Separations, and Corruptions of Poetry and Music* ... Written by Dr. [John] Brown [Vicar of Newcastle upon Tyne], London, MDCCLXIII. 4to, 10s. 6d.

AI

The Gift of Edward Whitlock of Skelton   on his leaving the School   1794

Skelton registers record baptism on 1 July 1773 of Edward, son of William and Rebecca Whitelock of Skelton, yeoman. An Edward Whitelock, schoolmaster of Barton, Westmorland (where Wordsworth's uncle by marriage, Thomas Myers, was headmaster, 1762–98), occurs as bondsman in 1795 to marriage licence of Isabella Whitelock to William Thompson of Skelton. Edward Whitelock was ordained Deacon at York, 2 October 1796; assistant Curate at Rawcliffe; ordained Priest at York, 1 October 1797; Curate at Ousby, 1799; assistant Curate at Hamsterly, 22 November 1802; sub-Curate at St. John's Chapel, Weardale, 1809–10; Permanent Curate there, 27 October 1810–21. Married (1) Ann Dealtry, died 9 June 1806, buried 11 June at Hamsterly; had issue. (2) Phoebe Emerson of St. John's, 31 January 1809; had issue. Died 22 March 1821. Seven children. [C. R. Hudleston.]

WILKINSON, Christopher

(22) *A Survey of Experimental Philosophy* . . . by Oliver Goldsmith, M.B., 2 vols., London, MDCCLXXVI. 8vo, 10s. 6d.

(21) The Gift of Christopher Wilkinson of Naddle in St. John's   on his leaving the School   1790

[Probably not Wilkinson's gift; see Isaac Littledale above.]

Son of John W. and Ann of Shoulthwaite, baptized at Crosthwaite, Keswick, on 22 October 1770.

WILKINSON, Robert

(40) *The History of Rome, from the Foundation of the City by Romulus to the Death of Marcus Antoninus.* In three volumes. by the Author of the History of France [Charles Hereford], London, 1792.

[The Library presentation list has: '*The History of Rome* 5 vol. 8ᵛᵒ. The gift of Robert & William Wilkinson of Stang-End in Irton on their leaving the School 1792', £1 15s.]

The Gift of Robert Wilkinson, Esqʳ.   of Irton   on his leaving the School   1792

Son of Robert W., baptized at Irton, 7 August 1774. Doubtless the father of Robert, born at Ravenglass, Cumberland (4 miles from Irton), also a pupil at Hawkshead, later at Trinity College, Cambridge.

WILKINSON, William

The Decline and Fall of the Roman Empire, by Edward Gibbon. Abridged, 2 vols.

The Gift of William Wilkinson of Irton, on leaving the School in 1791
See Robert Wilkinson.

WILSON, Thomas and John

(42) *The History of the Reign of Philip the Second, King of Spain* by Robert Watson, LL.D., 3 vols., 4th ed., London, MDCCLXXXV. 8vo, £1. 1s.

The Gift of Thomas and John Wilson of Liverpool; On their leaving the School
[Midsummer] 1793

WOOD, Jonathan

(32) *Account of the Russian Discoveries Between Asia and America* . . . by William Coxe,
A.M., London, MDCCLXXX. 4to, 15s.

The Gift of Jonathan Wood of Lorton on his leaving the School [at Xt.mas] 1791
Son of Jonathan W., baptized at Lorton, 4 miles south-east of Cockermouth, 27
December 1773. In the accounts of Wordsworth's uncle, Christopher Cookson (later
Crackenthorpe), as administrator of the estate of Wordsworth's father, is entered for
21 April 1784: 'Jonathan Wood for butcher's meat at various times . . . £3–16–8;
and for 4 May 1784: 'Jonathan Wood for Oats. . . . £2. 2. 0.

WORDSWORTH, Christopher

(38) *An Historical Disquisition concerning the Knowledge which the Ancients had of India*
. . . by William Robertson, D.D., F.R.S. MDCCXCL. 4to, £1. 1s.

The Gift of Christopher Wordsworth of Cockermouth Admitted at Trinity College
Cambridge from this School 1791

See T.W.T. and Wordsworth Papers generally. For Christopher at Hawkshead see
The Early Wordsworthian Milieu, ed. Z. S. Fink.

WORDSWORTH, Robinson

(7) *The History of the Life of Marcus Tullius Cicero* . . . by Conyers Middleton, D.D.,
3 vols., 2nd ed., London, MDCCXLI. 8vo, 13s. 6d.

The Gift of Robinson Wordsworth of Whitehaven on his leaving the School 1789
See T.W.T.

WORDSWORTH, William (see GREENWOOD, R. H.)

YEATS, Edward

The Lusiad; or, the Discovery of India. An Epic Poem. by William Julius Mickle, 2nd
ed., Oxford, MDCCLXXVIII. [Not in presentation list.]

The Gift of Edward Yeats of Beetham Admitted at Trinity College Cambridge
from this School 1798

Son of John of Beetham, Westmorland. Matriculated, Trinity College, Michaelmas
1798. B.A. (4th Wrangler) 1802; M.A. 1805. Fellow, 1804. Ordained deacon (Peterborough) 1806; Priest, 1807.

YOUNG, Thomas

(18) *An Essay concerning Human Understanding in Four Books* by John Locke, 2 vols.,
18th ed., London, MDCCLXXXVIII. [Edition not in B.M.] 8vo, 12s.

The Gift of Thomas Young of Greensike in Cumdivock in the Parish of Dalston
Admitted at Trinity College Cambridge from this School   1790

Son of Thomas Y. of Cumdivock (5½ miles south-west of Carlisle), husbandman, and
Rachel. The Youngs were a family of long-established yeoman farmers at Greensyke.
Baptized at Dalston 29 December 1772. Admitted, sizar, at Trinity, 27 October 1789.
Matriculated Michaelmas 1790; B.A. (12th Wrangler) 1794; M.A. 1797; Fellow,
1795; Assistant tutor, 1801–11; Tutor, 1811–13; Senior Dean, 1806–9. Rector of
East Gilling, Yorks. 1813–35. Married, 1814, Mary S. Blamire. Died 11 November
1835, aged 63. Son, William.

*List of former staff or schoolboys who donated money to the New Library,
1789–98*

Drawn from T.W.T's copy from the library records; he identifies it as
principally in the hand of Thomas Bowman.

[*A after the donor's name indicates that he gave 10s. 6d., B £1. 1s., C £2. 2s.*]

1789

Willm. Penny of Bridgefield in Colton & St. John's College, Cambridge   *A*; Rich^d.
Gilpin, Staveley, Westmorland   *A*; Joseph Taylor of Whitehaven   *A*; John
Dalrymple of Oxenford Castle, near Edinburgh   *B*; David Huddlestone of Langdale;
now at Kendal   *A*; Edm^d Irton, Esqre of Irton, Cumberland   *C*; Thos. Harrison of
Burneside, now in Kendal   *A*; Rev^d. Peter Richardson, Cartmel, Assistant 1781–1782
A; Edwd. Holme of Kendal; now at Manchester   *A*; John Docker, A.B., of Bamp-
ton. Usher 1787–1788   *A*; Geo: Borwick of Borwick Ground, Hawkshead   *A*;
Joseph Littledale, A.B., of Whitehaven; now at Lincoln's Inn   *B*; Sam^el. Gibson of
Roger Ground, Hawkshead; now at Kendal   *A*; Chas: Farish, A.B., of Carlisle &
Queen's Coll: Cambridge   *B*; John Shaw of Bootle, Cumberland   *A*; Willm. Keen
of Dublin (by his grandfather Joseph of Hawkshead)   *A*; John Steel of Cockermouth
A; Michael Rowlandson of Grasmere   *A*; Rich^d. Holden of Thornton in Lonsdale
A; Geo: Hutchinson, A.B., of Egglestone [Co. Durham]   *A*.

1790

Willm. Losh of Woodside near Carlisle   *B*; John Atkinson of Baysbrown in Lang-
dale   *A*; Isaac Swainson of Kendal   *A*; Arthur Benson of Liverpool & Bouth in
Colton   *A*; Rich^d. Benson do. do.   *A*; Rev^d. Willm. Braithwaite, A.M., of
Satterhow, Far Sawrey   *B*; Joseph Steel Esqre. of Cockermouth   *B*; Jonathan
Thexton of Beetham & Kendal   *A*; Rich^d. Hinde of Lancaster   *A*; Willm. Hutton of
Penrith   *A*; Rev^d. Willm. Satterthwaite, A.B., late of Colthouse, Hawkshead.
Usher 1780–1782   *A*; Rev^d. Joseph Satterthwaite, A.B., his brother. Usher 1783–
1784 & 1786   *A*; Thos. Dixon of Bellman Ground, Windermere   *A*; Jas. & Edwd.
Keene of Dublin, each 10s. 6d.   *B*; Thos. Barrow of Kirkby Ireleth   *A*; John Birley
of Kirkham, Lancashire   *B*; Henry Birley his brother   *A*; Willm. Lewthwaite of
Whitehaven; now of Millom   *B*; John Lewthwaite do. do.   *B*; John Rowland-
son of Grasmere   *A*; John Burrow of Crosthwaite, Westmorland   *A*; Robinson
Cartmell do. do.   *A*; Edwd. Starkey of Skelton, Cumberland   *A*.

1791

Rev^d. John Jackson, Church Coniston, late of Hawkshead, Assistant 1786–1789 *A*;
John Sunderland of Ulverston & Trinity College, Cambridge *B*; Isaac Littledale of
Whitehaven *B*; Jas: Pritt of Broughton, for himself *A*; And for Willm. Pritt, his
brother *A*; Moses Nicholson of Lamplugh, Cumberland *A*; Anthony Bigland of
Cartmel Fell *A*; Thos. Thompson of Patterdale; now at Barton *A*; Rich^d. Dickin-
son of Lamplugh (by his brother Mr William Dickinson of Broughton) *A*; Mr.
Willm. Towers of Hill in Hawkshead *A*; Henry Birley of Kirkham, a further sum of
A; Thos. Hartley of Whitehaven *B*; Rich^d. Cartmell of Crosthwaite *A*; Willm.
Burnthwaite of Ulverstone *A*; Rich^d. Harrison of Liverpool *A*; Milham Hartley
of Whitehaven *B*.

1792

Isaac Williamson late of Wythburn & Magdalen Hall, Oxford *A*; Thos. Fell of
Kendal; now at Newcastle *A*; John Littledale of Whitehaven *A*; Rev^d. Willm.
Wilson, A.M., St. John's Coll. Cambridge; formerly of Hawkshead *B*; Fra^s.
Graham of Dalston, Cumberland *A*; Anthony Myers of Whicham *A*; Wilson
Atkinson of Underbarrow, Kendal *A*; Joseph Maude of Kendal, & Warren, his
bro. each 10s 6d *B*; Willm. Machell of Pennybridge *B*; Sam^{el}. Dixon of Far
Sawrey, Hawkshead *A*; Joseph Hodgson of Houghton [deleted] Carlisle *A*; Sam^{el}.
Kilner of Ulverstone *A*; Willm. Birkett of Birkett Houses in Cartmel Fell *B*; John
Wordsworth of Cockermouth (by Xoph^r.) *A*; John Airey of Kentmere *A*; Rev^d.
Edwd. Gorrell of Kendal; now at Whalley *A*; John & Anthony Harrison of Pen-
rith, each 10s. 6d. *B*; Abraham Williamson of Charleston, South Carolina (by
Jacob) *A*; Rowland Cookson of Troutbeck, Windermere; now at Kendal *A*.

1793

George Lewthwaite of Millom & Queen's College, Oxford *B*; Willm. Braithwaite
of Orrest Head, Windermere *A*; John Gaskarth of Legberthwaite *A*; Thos. Littledale of Whitehaven *A*; Raisley Calvert of Greystock *B*; Edwd. Pedder of Preston,
Lancashire *A*; Fred^{rk}. & Willm. Maude of Kendal each 10s. 6d. *B*; Christopher
Lewthwaite of Kendal *A*; Smith Wilson of Kendal *A*. (These Subscriptions were
made at the Dinner to mark Thos. Harrison's success. W^m. Millers, my pupil for a
space, also subscribed 10s. 6d.); Willm. Hodgson of Carlisle *A*.

1794

Rich^d. Peddar of Preston *A*; Roger Woodburn of Ulverstone *A*; John Borwick of
Borwick Ground, Hawkshead *A*; Henry Gaitskell of Egremont *A*; Thomas
Wilson of Kendal *A*.

1795

Rev^d. Willm. Rumney A.B., of Watermillock & Queen's College, Oxford; now at
Alcester *A*; John Barnabas Maude of Kendal & Queen's College, Oxford *A*;
Edwin Maude of Kendal *A*; Willm. Atkinson of Dalton, late of Lancaster *A*;
Rev^d. Peter Strickland, Assistant, 1795–6 (*no sum recorded*).

1796

John & Rich^d. Machell of Pennybridge, each 10s. 6d. *B*; Thos. Rodick of Kendal;
now at Liverpool *A*; John Lowthian of Sebergham & Trinity Coll. Cambridge *A*;

Joseph Cowper of Unthank in Skelton psh.   *A*; Geo: Hoskins of Great Broughton, Cumberland   *B*.

1797

Rich^d. Dixon of Whitehaven & Queen's College, Oxford   *A*; Braithwaite Hodgson of Far Sawrey   *A*; Aaron Nicholson of Lamplugh   *A*; Jas: Pennington of Banrickhead in Colton psh.   *A*; Charles Maude of Kendal   *A*.

1798

Rich^d. Roper of Backbarrow   *A*; Chas. Skelton of Papcastle   *A*; Willm. Skelton, his brother   *A*; John Fisher of Kendal; now at Wakefield   *A*; Edwd. Littledale of Whitehaven, now Liverpool   *B*.

This is the end of the list. Then three names are bracketed together with the words, 'Left this School in 1794–5': Joseph Porter of Eskdale & Magdalen Hall, Oxford; George Gardner of London & Trinity College, Cambridge; Barnabas Maude of Kendal & Queen's College, Oxford. Finally there is the following brief list:

Fred^ck. Story	Army
Chas. Skelton	Navy
John Taubman	Army
Willm. Skelton	Navy
Rowland Wilson	East India Comp^y.
Rich^d. Stanley	Army
Edwd. Armstrong	Army or East India Comp^y.
Willm. Moore	Army

List of boys still at school who subscribed to the New Library (excluding those whose names appear in the book presentation list). The dates indicate the terms in which they paid subscriptions. See section II in Bowman's Proposals.

Philip Jenney 1789₂; Isaac Steele 1789₂; Thomas Rumbold Taylor 1789₂–1790₂; W^m. Atkinson 1789₂–1790₂; Anthony Rosenhagen 1789₂–1792₁; Christopher Wilson 1789₂–1790₂; Thomas Thompson 1790₂; John Shepherd 1790₂; Michael Rowlandson 1791₂; W^m. Stephenson 1791₂; John Church 1791₂; John Jackson 1791₂–1792₁; Rich^d. Towers 1791₂; James Kitching 1792₁; Thos. Southcote 1792₁; W^m. Pennington 1792₁; James Morland 1792₂–1794₁; Robert Leeson 1792₂ (see Z. S. Fink, *The Early Wordsworthian Milieu*); Michael Vickars 1793₁; John Taylor Oldham 1793₁–1797₁; Thomas Picard 1793₁–1794₁; Martial Houlche 1793₂; John Mattinson 1794₁; Henry Lutwidge 1794₁; John Wellock 1794₁; Geo: Raincock 1794₁; William Singleton 1794₂–1795₁; Thos. Parker 1794₂; John Addison 1794₂–1797₂; John Moore 1795₁–1797₂; William Moore 1795₁–1797₂; John Rogue 1795₁–1796₁; Josiah Maynard 1795₂–1796₂; William Mawson 1796₁–1797₁; Robert Birkett 1796₂–1797₂; Jn^n. Cautley 1796₂– 1797₂; Christ^r. Picard 1796₂–1797₂; Willm. Knott 1796₂–1797₂.

List of persons living locally who subscribed to the New Library

Rev^d. Reg^{ld}. Brathwaite, Belmount *C*; Geo: Law Esqre., Brathay *C*; Timothy Parker Esqre., Conistone Waterhead *B*; M^r. John Rigg, Keen Ground *B*; M^r. John Atkinson, surgeon, Hawkshead *A*; Myles Sandys, Esqre., Graythwaite *C*; D^r. Henry Ainslie, Kendal & Grizedale *B*; D^r. Isaac Pennington, St. John's Coll: Cambridge, Professor of Chemistry in the University (by the Rev. Reg^{ld}. Brathwaite) *C*; M^r. Geo: Jackson, Attorney, Hawkshead *A*; M^r. Matt^w. Hodgson, Surgeon, Hawkshead *B*; Rev^d. Thos. Clarke, Satterthwaite *A*.

Additional Notes

Page 48. Gilbert Crackenthorp was elected Master of Kendal Grammar School, 24 February 1740, and thus taught for more than three years before he received his licence—a situation unlikely to arise at Hawkshead where appointments as well as licences had to have the Bishop's approval. Crackenthorp's unexpected appearance in John Wordsworth's accounts raises the possibility that, at some point after his early retirement from Kendal, he assisted at Hawkshead Grammar School.

Page 97. For the uncertainties of travel to and from Hawkshead, see Appendix III *passim*. Obviously families were sometimes able to share costs; the only clear case of this is in the accounts of Uncle Richard Wordsworth, where, on 12 December 1789, the 8s. 6d. noted by T.W.T. is 'paid M^r. Littledale for Newphew Christ$^{r's}$. Conveyance from Hawkshead'. In the preceding January Christopher had gone to Hawkshead by chaise for 10s., and from the price one presumes that again conveyance was shared: there were several boys, besides the Littledales, who travelled from Whitehaven, amongst them, of course, Robinson Wordsworth and young Richard of Branthwaite. It would seem too, from the various accounts, that boys tended to travel by horse in summer, and chaise in winter. When the Senhouse brothers, three of them by 1786, travelled from Hawkshead for the last time in May of that year (they left at Whitsuntide) Mrs. Braithwaite's account reads: 'To 2 horses 9s and the man 3s to Penrith =12s.' The circumstance here is similar to one involving the Wordsworths, where the man would take the youngest boy on his horse, and the other two would ride together; T.W.T.'s sense that 5s. would be insufficient payment seems just in view of the Senhouse price.

It is not safe to assume a regular pattern of the Wordsworth boys spending entire winter holidays at Whitehaven and whole summers at Penrith; the accounts give clues of mobility, and not necessarily involving all four boys at a time. Richard Wordsworth of Branthwaite, eldest son of Uncle Richard of Whitehaven, a solicitor and executor of John Wordsworth's will, has an entry dated 31 July 1790: 'Paid Horsehire & Exp^s. at Keswick on the Road to Hawkshead carrying Rich^d. Willm. John and Christ^r. from Branthwaite to Hawkshead School at sev^l. dif^t. times'— £8. 12s. 0d. Apart from this composite bill, the only detailed payment cousin Richard makes is for a journey from school to Branthwaite, entered 19 December 1786, 'Cash p^d. Chaise hire for the Boys from Hawkshead and Exp^s.'—£1. 16s. 0d.

Page 98. Only Uncle Richard's accounts clearly indicate the 'full purses' with which the boys returned to school; the amounts he gave correspond with their ages. On 11 January 1786, William received 15s., John 10s. 6d., and Christopher 8s.; the following year, on 8 January, William was given a guinea, on 15 January John received 12s. and Christopher 10s. 6d. Similar sums crop up in Uncle Christopher's accounts, the oddest perhaps the summer of 1784 when William received 15s. 6d.

and Richard 10s. 6d. The three Senhouse boys, a little younger than the Wordsworths, were given a straight 2d. per week pocket money, 5s. on leaving home, and 6d. each for the Spring Fair—in 1785 specifically called the 'Easter Munday faire'. In 1784 their 'Cash for the faire' was recorded for 22 May—possibly a late entry for the Easter Fair expenses, or perhaps for a Fair on Ascension Day, or at Whitsuntide. In the autumn of 1784 the Senhouse boys again got 6d. each for a fair; the entry is dated 2 October. For the dates of the Hawkshead Autumn Fair, a confusing matter, see H. S. Cowper, *Hawkshead*, pp. 272–3. For Wordsworth's description of a country fair see *The Prelude* VIII, 1–61, where

> The Children now are rich, the old Man now
> Is generous; so gaiety prevails
> Which all partake of . . .

Page 107. With bills of any size it does seem to have been the case that the guardians would have details of the accounts run up by the boys in Hawkshead, but T.W.T.'s suggestion that the guardians paid tradesmen directly is less convincing. It seems to have been Uncle Christopher's practice to note down amounts due to individual tradesmen or teachers separately from the amount due to Ann Tyson; while Uncle Richard omitted the detail and simply wrote, for example, on 14 January 1786, 'By Cash to my Nephews for Discharging the Bills at Hawkshead and Chaisehire'—£36. It would seem that both guardians sent the cash by the boys, either for Ann Tyson, or later, for the boys themselves to disburse. This is the first such entry in Uncle Richard's accounts and there are similar ones each January until 1792. Earlier, Uncle Christopher had paid the four bills for the Halves, 1783₂–1785₁; thereafter he and Uncle Richard alternated, Christopher Cookson paying for the Halves ending in June, Richard Wordsworth for those ending in December. It is worth reminding ourselves that all the administrators' accounts are fair copies made, apparently in 1804, by which time, of course, both uncles were dead; Richard Wordsworth's seem to have more orderly records behind them, but in Christopher Cookson's there is an imprecise element about some of the dates. Thus £22. 1s. 5d. is entered, the month undated, as a payment to Ann Tyson along with a short list of Hawkshead bills, at the close of the accounts for 1784. This is followed immediately by a similar entry dated January 1785, 'To Cash paid Mrs Tyson . . . £27. 7. 11½', with small amounts paid to 'Mackreth Shoemaker' and George Parke. At a first reading one would suppose that the sum dated January 1785 was paid at that time and would thus refer to the previous Half, 1784₂, making the earlier sum refer to some vacation boarding (as Mark Reed supposes: *Chronology: Early Years*, p. 61); but the suggestion is untenable, for we find that the so-called January payment is clearly for the Spring Half 1785. In Ann Tyson's ledger a receipt is written opposite the details—the candles and coals and board for that Half—: 'Paid £27. 7. 11½ August 4th. 1785'. Mark Reed's dating of the undated £22. 1s. 5d. as 'apparently September' has no basis in the accounts; it is absolutely appropriate for the Autumn Half 1784, and must have been presented in December and paid in January. Some of the importance of all this is that it disposes of the suggestion that the boys spent the first summer after their father's death in Hawkshead; and indeed there is no reason to think that they spent more than a few days of any school holiday there. Nor is there any evidence for the view that Wordsworth, later, in his long vacations, both before and at

Cambridge, 1787–9, ever spent the period of the actual school holidays in Hawkshead.

Page 109. (1) Why Gordon Wordsworth thought Park was an ironmonger is not clear: there is an unnamed ironmonger's bill for 7s. 10d. in 1784₂ in the accounts of Christopher Cookson (and this could have been for skates), and in the same accounts for 1785₁, a full year before Ann's entry of £1. 8s. 6d., a payment is made to 'Geo. Parke' of 14s. 10½d. T.W.T.'s research into the Churchwardens' accounts (p. 203) seems convincing evidence that Park was ironmonger as well as saddler.

Page 109. (2) The shoemaker is not mentioned by name in connection with the £6. 4s. 9d. which, in any event, does not represent a single payment, but is the sum of three amounts covering the three Halves, 1783₂–1784₂; thus expenditure on shoes was not at all excessive for three boys. The three Senhouse boys from October 1785 to April 1786 spent £3. 5s. 8d. with the Hawkshead shoemaker, Thomas Stamper; each boy had two new pairs of shoes at about 4s. 2d. a pair, a pair of half boots at 7s. and new pumps at 4s.; and frequently during this time they had shoes soled, heeled, and 'toe'd'.

Page 110. Shirt making and probably socks were family matters, see above p. 72; but in 1786 and 1787 it is clear from the accounts of Uncle Richard Wordsworth that the boys had suits made in Whitehaven during the Christmas holidays. There are two payments of over £12 'to Mʳ Potter for my Nephews Wᵐ. Jnᵒ. and Christʳ. Cloaths'. In February 1786 an additional £1. 8s. 4½d. is paid 'to Antrobus the Taylor for making 3 Suits of Cloaths'. Such large payments to Potter and smaller ones to Antrobus continue through the accounts, but not in a regular pattern.

Page 114. Irregularities in postal charges could of course be due to the size of a letter as well as to the distance it had to cover. The letters of Eleanor Braithwaite in Hawkshead to Mrs. Senhouse in Carlisle, for example, normally have 3d. written on them, but when they contain the accounts and are 'double' the price is 6d. The complication here is that frequently in these boys' accounts, 1d. only is entered for letters sent both to and from Carlisle, and other places, including Barbados. In these cases it seems likely that for letters going from Hawkshead Mrs. Braithwaite prepaid the postage as far as Kendal, 1d., and that on incoming letters Mrs. Senhouse, for example, had prepaid also as far as Kendal so that Mrs. Braithwaite had to pay only 1d. on them. Altogether, caution is needed; and I have no explanation for the fact that while several letters from Carlisle are priced 4d. in the accounts, one is 5d.

Page 127. In Coleridge's *Notebooks* (ed. K. Coburn, I, entry 510) there is an enigmatic entry for November 1799: 'Sandbeds—Bell grange—Curwen let in.' In that month Coleridge, with William and John Wordsworth, was walking from Kentmere via Troutbeck, Rayrigg, and the Ferry to Hawkshead. His notebook entry suggests that their walk was down the eastern shore of Windermere as far as Belle Grange (formerly Sandbeds); the nearest way to Hawkshead from there would be over Claife Heights and through Colthouse.

Page 129. When and how often Wordsworth met Curwen is not known, but certainly Edward Hughes's assertion that Curwen and the poet never met is unsupported by the letter of Dorothy Wordsworth that he himself cites (*North Country Life in the Eighteenth Century*, 1965, II, pp. 385–6). In this letter Dorothy expresses surprise that Wordsworth never met, *not* John Christian Curwen, the father, but his son, Henry, whose daughter, Isabella, Wordsworth's own son, John, was about to marry. Dorothy's very surprise indicates that Wordsworth had known John Christian.

Page 131. There are uncertainties about who owned the ferry and the Ferry Inn (or Great Boat) before it became Christian's property. Swainson Cowper (*Hawkshead*, pp. 246–9) relies on James Clarke's *Survey of the Lakes* (1787), p. 144: 'The ferry or navigation cross there is a freehold, paying a merk lord's rent, and is the property of Mr Brathwaite of Harrow Slack.' George Braithwaite died on 10 October 1786; confusingly, he had a son, also George; but by 1790 a Braithwaite Hodgson, said by Swainson Cowper to be George Braithwaite's heir, took Harrowslack. I can also add that in the Land Tax Bill for 1783, George Braithwaite 'or Occup^{rs}. of Great Boat' paid one shilling tax. It is worth saying that James Clarke appears to have been preparing the Windermere section of his Survey in October 1784; thus his information, quite properly, is supported by the Land Tax return of 1783, but is out of date before publication (since Christian owned the Ferry from at least 1786). The earliest date, as I shall now show, by which George Braithwaite could have held the Ferry is 1782.

A document (in the Browne MSS., IV, 109, the Record Office, Kendal) of May 1782 shows that the 'Great Boat House Lands and Hereditements with the Appurtenances' belonged to Thomas English, the impoverished erstwhile owner of Belle Isle, who, through his lawyer, Thomas Yeates, was threatening to distrain upon the goods to the value of £78. 1s. 7d. of the then occupier of the Ferry, Thomas Nicholson. English is called 'your Landlord' and Nicholson must have owed some 2½ years' rent. Presumably English sold the Ferry property soon afterwards, either to George Braithwaite, who by 1786 had sold it to Christian, or, and this seems more likely, to Christian, who perhaps leased it first to one of the Braithwaites until early 1786, a few months before the father's death, and then certainly to George Robinson who, as we have seen, was paying rent to Christian from Ladyday 1786. That Braithwaite was paying land tax for the Ferry does not necessarily indicate ownership of the property—in 1789 the tax was being paid by George Robinson, and there is no doubt whatsoever that Christian was then the owner.

Page 139. Unfortunately, there are no actual milestones along this road now and Mr. Langstaff of the Ordnance Survey kindly tells me that no milestones on the Windermere Ferry–Hawkshead road appear on O.S. maps or on their records from their commencement in the 1840s. Scholars agree in thinking that the meeting with the discharged soldier did take place along this road, and T.W.T.'s precise identification of the spot, supported by particulars from *The Prelude*, exactly three miles from Hawkshead, is where a milestone easily could have been in the late eighteenth century. The Claife Heights Enclosure, 1794–9, led to a realignment of parts of that road, and milestones were perhaps removed during the 'improvements'; this particular stone, of course, might quite properly and simply be Wordsworth's invention. It certainly has a symbolic force.

Page 165. C. Roy Hudleston points out to me that the Benson Harrison arms impaling those of the Wordsworths are to be seen in the east window of Ambleside Parish Church. Dorothy Wordsworth (1800–90) was the daughter of Cousin Richard Wordsworth who was, by marriage to Mary Scott, of Branthwaite near Whitehaven. Dorothy Wordsworth, always a favourite at Rydal Mount, was Hartley Coleridge's 'Chucky Doro', and he characterizes her in a letter to his brother, Derwent, of August 1830, as 'the same happy, plump, ever smiling, never excursion-reading creature she ever was—yet a most excellent wife to a man double her own age—but rich—which is everything' (*Letters*, ed. Griggs, p. 116). Dorothy Wordsworth was married 27 September 1823, and the Benson Harrison house, Green Bank, is now the Charlotte Mason College, Ambleside. For the parentage of Benson Harrison, see pp. 216–17.

Page 231. William Taylor is described as 'Yeoman' in a 1799 'list of persons in the Township of Claife in the parish of Hawkshead . . . liable to serve as Jurors'. The list gives the names of seven freeholders, their ages, their 'place of abode' and 'rank in life'. They are: 'W^m. Taylor, 60, Colthouse, Gent.; Jos. Hunter, 37, High Wray, Yeoman; Braithw^{te} Hodgson, 40, Harrow-slack, Yeoman; Thos. Hodgson, 38, Briers, Yeoman; Edwd. Braithwaite, 40, Sawrey, Yeoman; W^m. Fisher, 37, Sawrey, Yeoman; and Wm Towers, 37, Sawrey, Yeoman.' This was 'Taken upon Oath at Belmount . . . Oct 4th. 1799 before me. Reg. Brathwaite.' The Constable also signed. 'Yeoman', in such a document as this, is the term used for the rank just below that of 'Gentleman'; several of these men we know were men of substance.

One notes from this list that John Christian Curwen had yet to acquire Harrowslack.

Page 259. The Rev. William Braithwaite apparently owned the Station area for less than a year before his death in 1800. According to the Commissioners for the Enclosure, the land (marked A5 and A6 on the Commissioners' plans, County Record Office, Preston) came to him when Thomas Hodgson of Briers renounced to him his own customary rights over this common land, in a deed executed 20 April 1799. Budworth's note of 1797–8 shows, of course, that Braithwaite was already planting and landscaping the area before he was officially the owner; Braithwaite and Hodgson were clearly good neighbours. John Christian Curwen acquired the land shortly after Braithwaite's death, and on his own estate plans (Records, The Castle, Carlisle) the Station area is marked '1801', that presumably being the date the property was transferred to him. This same map of John Christian's indicates, interestingly enough, that he had begun planting sections of the land he was to acquire under the complex Claife Heights Enclosure Act by 1798, that is a full year before the completion of the Act.

Page 264. George Law traded in Kingston, Jamaica from 1769 (see G. Chandler, *Four Centuries of Banking*, II, pp. 125–33). In the late autumn of 1784 Wilberforce names him as 'the gentleman who lately bought the Brathay estate' (Law lived in the house later occupied—in 1800—by Charles Lloyd, now known as Old Brathay). George Law was among the Governors of the Grammar School who appointed Thomas Bowman in 1786 (see p. 341, note). His new house, Brathay Hall, was completed by at least 1797, when James Plumptre visited Law there. Coleridge, when walking with William and John Wordsworth through the Lakes in October 1799, viewed his house with dismay, as almost certainly did Wordsworth. Coleridge wrote in his Notebook: 'Mr Law amid the awful Mountains with his 20 cropped Trees, four stumps standing upen[d] upon on the Trunk of each, all looking thus like strange Devils with perpendicular Horns—Head of the Lake of Wynandermere—Mr Law's White palace—a bitch!' (*Notebooks*, ed. Coburn, I, 511.) Law died in 1802.

Page 266. Wordsworth felt the addition of the vestry 'strangely disfigured' the church because its roof 'runs in a line with the lower roof of the Church cutting off the base of the Steeple so that all the lightness which that part of the structure possessed as being in shape distinctly separated from top to bottom of the body of the Church is destroyed.' He objected also to 'the window of this excrescence' as not being uniform with the others. (From a draft MS. of *Guide to the Lakes*, Dove Cottage Library.)

Page 276. 'The Old Cumberland Beggar', composed 1798–1800, was written against the background of the political economists who were 'about that time beginning their war upon mendicity in all its forms, and by implication, if not directly, on alms-giving also' (from the Fenwick note to the poem, Grosart, III, p. 185). Wordsworth hated the 'heartless process' of the new Poor Laws. His Cumberland beggar lived himself in a spare, even noble harmony with nature, and was also subtly beneficial to society, encouraging at once the impulse to give, and the awareness of bonds between man and man. He was an image, Wordsworth writes, 'Observed, and with great benefit to my own heart, when I was a child'; from the poem's title, the beggar was presumably not a Hawkshead figure. In his letter to Fox of 14 January 1801 he argues urgently against the evils of institutionalized charity, 'parents are separated from their children, and children from their parents; the wife no longer prepares with her own hands a meal for her husband, the produce of his labour; there is little doing in his house in which his affections can be interested, and but little left in it which he can love.' He then instances a couple both over eighty who despite illness had been able to manage with neighbourly help, but 'her infirmities encrease. She told my Servant two days ago that she was afraid they must both be boarded out among some other Poor of the parish (they have long been supported by the parish) but she said, it was hard, having kept house together so long, to come to this, and she was sure that "it would burst her heart".' One can see from this and from T.W.T.'s description of how Poor Relief operated in Hawkshead that Wordsworth would certainly prefer the old ways to what he deemed the inhumanity of the new measures.

Dorothy Wordsworth's description of a Grasmere funeral arval at John Dawson's (How Top Farm, some 200 yards from Dove Cottage up the hill on the road to Rydal) confirms T.W.T.'s point (p. 277) that funerals for paupers were not dissimilar to those for statesmen. She wrote on 3 September 1800:

I then went to a funeral at John Dawson's. About 10 men and 4 women. Bread, cheese, and ale. They talked sensibly and chearfully about common things. The dead person, 56 years of age, buried by the parish. The coffin was neatly lettered and painted black, and covered with a decent cloth. They set the corpse down at the door; and, while we stood within the threshold, the men with their hats off sang with decent and solemn countenances a verse of a funeral psalm. The corpse was then borne down the hill, and they sang till they had got past the Town-End. I was affected to tears while we stood in the house, the coffin lying before me. There were no near kindred, no children. When we got out of the dark house the sun was shining, and the prospect looked so divinely beautiful as I never saw it. It seemed more sacred than I had ever seen it, and yet more allied to human life. The green fields, neighbours of the churchyard, were as green as possible; and, with the brightness of the sunshine, looked quite gay. I thought she was going to a quiet spot, and I could not help weeping very much. When we came to the bridge, they began to sing again, and stopped during four lines before they entered the churchyard. The priest met us—he did not look as a man ought to do on such an occasion—I had seen him half-drunk the day before in a pot-house. Before we came with the corpse one of the company observed he wondered what sort of cue our Parson would be in! N.B. It was the day after the Fair.

Page 297. Of some significance, though he does not name the first owner, the Rev. William Braithwaite, are Wordsworth's own more critical comments on the Station and its surroundings. The passage is from Wordsworth's essay in Wilkinson's *Select Views in Cumberland, Westmoreland, and Lancashire* (1810) and was not afterwards reprinted by Wordsworth in his later *Guide to the Lakes*: 'Before the Traveller, whom I have thus far accompanied, enters the Peninsula, at the extremity of which the Ferry House stands, it will be adviseable to ascend to a Pleasure-house belonging to J. C. Curwen, Esq. which he will see upon the side of the rocks on his left hand.— There is a gate, and a person, attending at a little Lodge, or Cot adjoining, who will conduct him. From this point he will look down upon the cluster of Islands in the central part of the Lake, upon Bowness, Rayrigg, and the Mountains of Troutbeck; and will have a prospect of the lower division of this expanse of water to its extremity. The upper part is hidden. The Pleasure house is happily situated, and is well in its kind, but, without intending any harsh reflections on the contriver, from whom it was purchased by its present Proprietor, it may be said that he, who remembers the spot on which this building stands, and the immediate surrounding grounds as they were less than thirty years ago, will sigh for the coming of that day when Art, through every rank of society, shall be taught to have more reverence for Nature. This scene is, in its natural constitution, far too beautiful to require any exotic or obtrusive embellishments, either of planting or architecture.' This 1810 passage suggests that one of the buildings Wordsworth had objected to in 1799 was Braithwaite's Station: '. . . went on to the Ferry—a cold passage—were much disgusted with the New Erections & objects about Windermere—' (*Wordsworth Letters: Early Years*, ed. Shaver, p. 271).

Page 305. Peter Taylor was, as we saw earlier (p. 128), one of Isabella Curwen's trustees. On Isabella's marriage to John Christian in 1782 Taylor relinquished his trusteeship to her husband, and Isabella, to show her 'esteem' presented him with £500. By his marriage to a Fleming of Rayrigg, Peter Taylor was drawn into the Fleming/Raincock family complex; it is perhaps worth re-stating that Peter Taylor and William Raincock married Fleming sisters. Thus, we find Peter Taylor, when he writes to Henry Addison, John Christian Curwen's Penrith lawyer, sending messages to his Raincock in-laws of Penrith. His three sons, like their Raincock cousins, were contemporaries at Hawkshead of Wordsworth and his brothers (see Alpha-betical List, Appendix IV). Peter Taylor died at Whitehaven 10 February 1789. Besides his property, Lucy Close (near Whitehaven), he owned estates (according to his will) in South Carolina with 'Negroes and Utensils thereupon'; all this was to be sold for the benefit of his wife Isabella and their family.

T.W.T.'s speculation that Peter Taylor had built Belfield is not borne out by the Yates family letters (*Memorials of a Family in England and Virginia*, ed. A. E. Terrill, 1887); nor is his notion that the house as originally built was a large one. A letter of March 1794 notes: 'Mrs. Taylor has bought an estate about two miles from Rayrigg, and means to build herself a little box upon it.' In June she is 'building for herself near Bowness' and exactly three years later, we learn, she is 'enjoying the new house she has built, and the beautiful prospects from it, on the banks of Windermere.' On her death, her only surviving son Peter, one of the administrators of her estate, has the address Belfield, Windermere.

It is perhaps worth stating that, on the map of Windermere in Clarke's *Survey of the Lakes* (1787), the owner of Calgarth Estate is given as 'P. Taylor', but I have not been able to identify this Taylor with Peter Taylor of Whitehaven; it appears then to be a coincidence that the Bishop of Llandaff acquired Calgarth just a few months after Peter Taylor died.

Select Bibliography

A.E. (signed), 'The Library at Hawkshead Grammar School, and the Schooldays of Wordsworth', *The Eagle*, XVIII (1894), pp. 383–8

Armitt, M. L., *Rydal* (Kendal, 1916)

Budworth, Joseph, *Windermere: a Poem* (London, 1798)

Budworth, Joseph, *A Fortnight's Ramble to the Lakes*, 3rd edn. (London, 1810)

Chandler, G., *Four Centuries of Banking*, II (London, 1968)

Charity Commissioners, *The Public Charities of the Hundred of Lonsdale North of the Sands*, a report dated January 1820

Christie, Richard Copley, *The Old Church and School Libraries of Lancashire*, pp. 143–70 (Chetham Society, 1885)

Clarke, James, *A Survey of the Lakes of Cumberland, Westmorland and Lancashire* (London, 1787; 2nd edn., 1789)

Coleridge, S. T., *Notebooks*, I (in 2 vols.), ed. Kathleen Coburn (London, 1957)

Cowper, Henry Swainson, *Hawkshead* (London and Derby, 1899)

Cowper, Henry Swainson, ed., *The Oldest Register Book of the Parish of Hawkshead, 1568–1704* (London and Derby, 1897)

Curwen, John F., *Kirkbie Kendall* (Kendal, 1900)

De Selincourt, Oliver, 'Wordsworth's Lodging During His Schooldays at Hawkshead', *Review of English Studies*, XXI (October 1945), pp. 329–30

Farrer, W. and Brownbill, J., eds., *The Victoria History of the County of Lancaster*, VIII, Lonsdale (London, 1914)

Fell, Alfred, *The Early Iron Industry of Furness and District* (Ulverston, 1908; reprinted by Cass, 1968)

Fink, Z. S., *The Early Wordsworthian Milieu* (Oxford, 1958)

Gastrell, Francis, Bishop of Chester, *Notitia Cestriensis*, with notes by F. R. Raine, II, Part III (Chetham Society, 1850)

Gibson, Alexander Craig, 'Hawkshead Parish', *Transactions of the Historic Society of Lancashire and Cheshire*, 1866, pp. 153–74

Hawkshead: *Archbishop Sandys' Endowed School . . . Tercentenary Commemoration* (Kendal, 1885)

Hughes, Edward, *North Country Life in the Eighteenth Century*, II (London, 1965)

Hutchinson, William, *An Excursion to the Lakes in Westmorland and Cumberland in 1773 and 1774* (London, 1776)

Leonard, Kathleen, ed., *A Register of Marriages in the Parish of Hawkshead, Lancashire 1754–1837* (London 1969)

Leonard, Kathleen and G. O. G., eds., *The Second Register Book of the Parish of Hawkshead, 1705–1787* (Hawkshead, 1968)

Local Chronology: Kendal (Kendal and London, 1865)

Lonsdale, Dr. Henry, *Worthies of Cumberland*, 6 vols. (London, 1867–75)

Lonsdale Magazine III, 31 May 1822, pp. 161–2

Moorman, Mary, 'Ann Tyson's Ledger: An Eighteenth-century Account Book', *Transactions of the Cumberland and Westmorland Antiquarian and Archaeological Society*, L, N.S. (1951), pp. 152–63

Moorman, Mary, *William Wordsworth: The Early Years, 1770–1803* (Oxford, 1957)

Nicholson, C., *The Annals of Kendal*, 2nd edn. (London and Kendal, 1861)

Nicholson, F. and Axon, E., *The Older Nonconformity in Kendal* (Kendal, 1915)

Nicholson, Norman, *The Lakers* (London, 1955)

Otley, Jonathan, *The English Lakes* (Keswick, 1823; 5th edn. 1834)

Parson, W. and White, W., *History and Directory of Cumberland and Westmorland* (1829)

Pryme, George, *Autobiographic Recollections* (Cambridge, 1870)

Reed, Mark, *Wordsworth: The Chronology of the Early Years, 1770–1799* (Cambridge, Mass., 1967)

Robertson, Eric, *Wordsworthshire* (London, 1911)

Ross, Isabel, 'Wordsworth and Colthouse near Hawkshead', *Modern Language Review*, L (October 1955), pp. 499–501

Satterthwaite, Elizabeth J., *Records of the Friends' Burial Ground at Colthouse, near Hawkshead* (Ambleside, 1914)

Schneider, Ben Ross, *Wordsworth's Cambridge Education* (Cambridge, 1957)

Scott, Robert Forsyth, ed., *Admissions to the College of St. John the Evangelist in the University of Cambridge*, Part III (Cambridge, 1903)

Taylor, S., 'A Lakeland Young Lady's Letters', *Transactions of the Cumberland and Westmorland Antiquarian and Archaeological Society*, XLIII, N.S. (1943), pp. 96–116

Thompson, T. W., *Hawkshead Church, Chapelry & Parish* (Hawkshead, 1956; and 1959)

Venn, J. A., *Alumni Cantabrigiensis* (Cambridge, 1922–54)

Walker, A[dam], *Remarks made on a Tour from London to the Lakes* (London, 1792)

Wallis, P. J., *Histories of Old Schools: A Revised List for England and Wales* (Newcastle upon Tyne, 1966)

West, Thomas, *Antiquities of Furness* (London, 1774)

West, Thomas, *Guide to the Lakes* (Kendal, 1778; 4th edn., 1789; 8th edn., 1802; 11th edn., 1821)

Wilberforce, R. I. and S., *The Life of William Wilberforce*, by his sons. 5 vols. (London, 1838)

Wilkinson, Joseph [and Wordsworth, William], *Select Views in Cumberland, Westmoreland and Lancashire* (London, 1810)

Wordsworth, Christopher, *Memoirs of William Wordsworth*, 2 vols. (London, 1851)

Wordsworth, Dorothy, *Journals*. (1) Ed. de Selincourt, 2 vols. (London, 1941); (2) ed. H. Darbishire (London, 1958)

Wordsworth, Dorothy, *Recollections of a Tour made in Scotland, A.D. 1803*, ed. J. C. Shairp (Edinburgh, 1874)

Wordsworth, Gordon, 'The Boyhood of Wordsworth', *Cornhill Magazine*, CXXI (1920), pp. 410–20

Wordsworth, William, *Guide to the Lakes*, reprint of 5th edn. (1835), ed. de Selincourt (1926)

Wordsworth, William, *Poetical Works*, ed. William Knight, 11 vols. (Edinburgh, 1882–9)

Wordsworth, William, *Poetical Works*, ed. de Selincourt and Darbishire, 5 vols. (Oxford, 1940–9)

Wordsworth, William, *The Prelude*, ed. de Selincourt, 2nd edn. revised H. Darbishire (Oxford, 1959)

Wordsworth, William, *Prose Works*, ed. A. B. Grosart, 3 vols. (London, 1876)

Wordsworth, William and Dorothy, *Letters: The Early Years, 1787–1805*, ed. de Selincourt, 2nd edn. revised by C. L. Shaver (Oxford, 1967)

Wordsworth, William and Dorothy, *Letters: The Middle Years*, ed. de Selincourt; 2nd edn., vol. I revised by Moorman (Oxford, 1969); vol. II revised by Moorman and Hill (Oxford, 1970)

Wordsworth, William and Dorothy, *Letters: Later Years*, ed. de Selincourt, 3 vols. (Oxford, 1939)

Index

† See Appendix III.
* See Appendix IV (* before a name indicates a boy who appears in the annotated Alphabetical List of those who donated books to the New Library, pp. 348–69; * after a name indicates an appearance elsewhere in Appendix IV, most probably in the lists of subscribers, pp. 369–72).

In the absence of registers this index thus includes a basic name-list of over 200 boys, and most of the masters, at Hawkshead Grammar School in the last quarter of the eighteenth century.[1]

Not all names occurring once only in T.W.T. are entered here; not necessarily all members of a family.

[1] A few schoolboys discussed by T.W.T. do not recur in Appendixes III and IV, and these therefore appear in the Index without a symbol: John Benson, junior; Philip Braithwaite: Kit Gilpin; J. Gunson; John Ireland; Rev. George Park; Ned Tyson; the two Richard Wordsworths, the poet's brother and cousin.

AMBLESIDE

To Whitehaven
thro' Grasmere & Keswick &c &c
5 Miles from Hawkshead

Water

Clapersgate
Roman Station
Water Head

ow Park
Park Ho
Park Ho
River Brathy
Brathy
Bridge
T B

Skelwith
12

Butt
Close
Field Foot Ho

Low Wood

side

Flag Quarry
Low
Wray
11

W
I
N
D
Ecclerigg
10
Troutbeck
Bridge

Blelham
Tarn

Field
Head
High Wray

Out
Bull
Yeat
Atent

Trout Beck

To Penrith

Orwick
Castle
Hall
Rev. Mr. Braithwaite
Sand
Cold
Garth
Crooke

Skinner
Laindthwaite
Middlethwaite
To Penrith

KSHEAD

Walker
Ground &c
Courthouse

Raven

Roger
Ground
Water

Millbeck
Stocks

How

BOWNESS

Feild
Yeat

Mr. Christian Esq.

Earthwaite
Hall

claife

Brathy Fold
Low Houge
Michaels Field

dale

Canter
Houge

Biggin
Brink

E
L
L

Low Canter

edale

Highdale
Park

Sandys
Highdale

Hetholwait

Town
Wood

Hartbarrow

F
E
L
L

Crowthwaite
Hall

Force
Mill
Mr. Rawlinson